A Weary Land

Early American Places is a collaborative project of the University of Georgia Press, New York University Press, Northern Illinois University Press, and the University of Nebraska Press. The series is supported by the Andrew W. Mellon Foundation. For more information, please visit www.earlyamericanplaces.com.

ADVISORY BOARD
Vincent Brown, *Duke University*
Cornelia Hughes Dayton, *University of Connecticut*
Nicole Eustace, *New York University*
Amy S. Greenberg, *Pennsylvania State University*
Ramón A. Gutiérrez, *University of Chicago*
Peter Charles Hoffer, *University of Georgia*
Karen Ordahl Kupperman, *New York University*
Mark M. Smith, *University of South Carolina*
Rosemarie Zagarri, *George Mason University*

A Weary Land

Slavery on the Ground in Arkansas

Kelly Houston Jones

The University of Georgia Press
Athens

Paperback edition, 2022
© 2021 by the University of Georgia Press
Athens, Georgia 30602
www.ugapress.org

All rights reserved

Most University of Georgia Press titles are available from popular e-book vendors.

Printed digitally

The Library of Congress has cataloged the hardcover edition of this book as follows:

NAMES: Jones, Kelly Houston, author.
TITLE: A weary land : slavery on the ground in Arkansas / Kelly Houston Jones.
DESCRIPTION: Athens : The University of Georgia Press, 2021. |
    Includes bibliographical references (pages 247–262) and index.
IDENTIFIERS: LCCN 2020952835 (print) | ISBN 9780820360201 (hardback) |
    ISBN 9780820360195 (epub)
SUBJECTS: LCSH: Slavery—Arkansas—History. | Slaves—Arkansas—
    Social conditions. | African Americans—Arkansas—History. | Arkansas—
    History—19th century. | Arkansas—Social life and customs—19th century.
CLASSIFICATION: LCC E445.A8 J66 2021 (print) |
    DDC 306.3/6209767—dc23
LC record available at https://lccn.loc.gov/2020952835

Paperback ISBN 978-0-8203-6368-4

For Jerry

Contents

	Acknowledgments	xi
	Introduction	1
1	The Morass	11
2	Domains	33
3	Alluvial Empires	74
4	Flesh and Fiber	104
5	The Material of Survival	147
6	Battlegrounds	177
	Conclusion	203
	Notes	211
	Bibliography	247
	Index	263

Acknowledgments

Like many working-class first-generation college students, I began as a business major, seeking training that I could leverage into a high-paying job. When I switched to history, my family became (understandably) nervous about my prospects. Thanks to professors and mentors at the University of Arkansas at Little Rock, like Carl Moneyhon, the late C. Fred Williams, and Kristen Dutcher Mann, for showing me that I made the right choice. During my studies at the University of North Texas, Randolph B. "Mike" Campbell taught me how to roll up my sleeves for deep research in often overlooked sources. He was incredibly patient and generous with his time and I cherish his continuing friendship. Jeannie Whayne broadened my questioning about life on the ground for enslaved people. She understood my vision for this project from the beginning and never wavered in her confidence in me. I also benefited from Patrick Williams's sharp eye and sharper mind. I am grateful for research support provided by the University of Arkansas Department of History, the Mary Hudgins Research Fund, the Diane D. Blair Center of Southern Politics and Society at the University of Arkansas's Fulbright College of Arts and Sciences, and the Southern Historical Collection at the University of North Carolina, Chapel Hill.

More scholars, archivists, and panelists advanced my thinking, research, and writing than can be listed here. In particular, the professionals at the University of Arkansas Library's Special Collections, the Arkansas State Archives, and the University of Arkansas at Little Rock Bowen Law School/Pulaski County Law Library provided invaluable assistance. Like everyone who studies Arkansas, I am also indebted to the experts at the Butler Center for Arkansas Studies, the Shiloh Museum of Ozark History, and the Historic Arkansas Museum. Thanks to Story Matkin-Rawn for generously sharing the story of Reuben Johnson and to Debbie Liles for the source on Worthington's trek to Texas. Special thanks to my anonymous reviewers who provided thorough readings that saved me from missteps, pushed my thinking, and increased the quality of the book. Remaining shortcomings are mine alone.

Thanks to Becky Howard for helping me navigate the National Archives, serving as my go-to Ozark expert, and always being willing to talk out historical problems whether in late-night ramblings or on the road to a conference. Thanks to my support system of colleagues (both at my first job at Austin Peay State University and at Arkansas Tech University), friends, and family. Alana and Carly are two of the best cheerleaders. I may not have achieved a life of luxury but I have found meaning in this work that would not have been possible without all of the folks mentioned above. Since beginning the project, my family has experienced earth-shattering losses that made research and writing seem trivial. I could not have survived any of it, and certainly couldn't have gotten back to work on this book, without Chris Jones, the best partner anyone could ask for.

A Weary Land

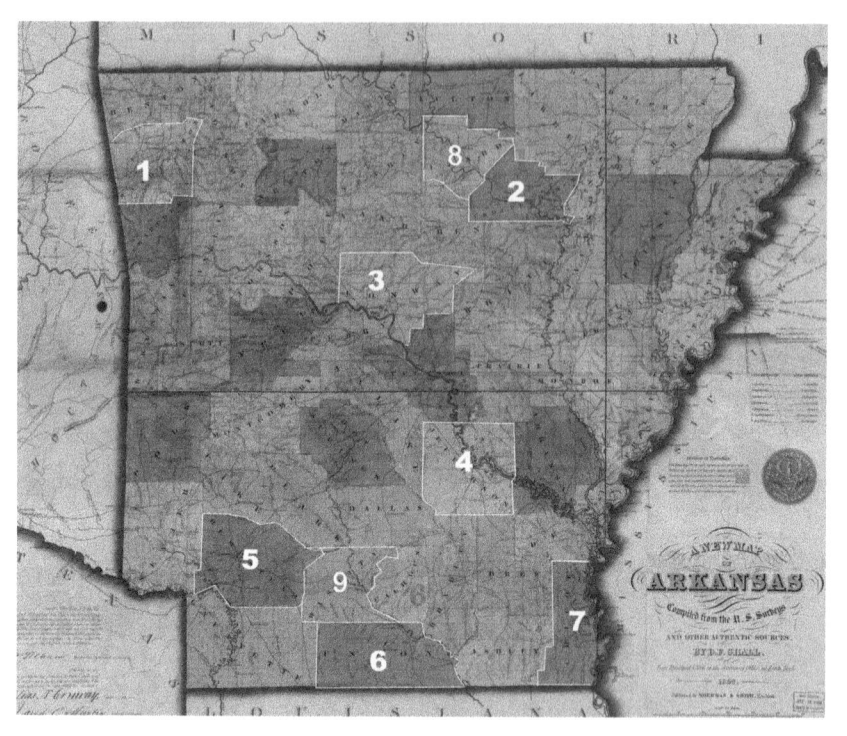

"A New Map of Arkansas," 1852. Counties frequently mentioned in this book: (1) Washington; (2) Independence; (3) Conway; (4) Jefferson; (5) Hempstead; (6) Union; (7) Chicot; (8) Izard; and (9) Ouachita. Library of Congress.

Introduction

Reuben Johnson's life on a plantation south of Little Rock changed forever when he heard a man read from the Bible one Sunday. From that moment, Johnson became determined to be able to do the same. But he was an enslaved black man—chattel, under the laws and conventions of Arkansas and the South—and therefore forbidden from achieving an education. Nevertheless, the determination to learn to read and write engulfed him, and Johnson found ways to teach himself. He listened to recitations of the alphabet outside the white children's schoolhouse, and eventually he managed to secure a book to study on his own. Although his enslaver confiscated the book and whipped him for having it, Johnson raised money for another by gathering walnuts to sell to passing peddlers. This time, a hollow log housed the precious contraband. Johnson snuck into the woods to bring out one page at a time for studying in the quarters. Eventually, however, whites found him out. Again his book was seized, and again he paid for it in lashes. Johnson persevered, however, securing yet another book by enlisting the plantation wagoner to help him sell hay he had been gathering at night. Johnson again relied on a log to conceal his latest prize but now restricted his study to sessions in the woods. Johnson finally realized his dream of literacy after fleeing his enslavers in 1864 to fight for the United States Army against the Confederacy.[1]

Reuben Johnson, like hundreds of thousands of other enslaved people across the South, made calculated use of space to navigate his bondage.

The traffic of the public road delivered passing customers for the nuts he gathered from the forest; Reuben probably concealed himself in the woods that bounded the road's edges until the right person passed. Swaths of tall grass in clearings or, perhaps, abandoned acreage became marketable hay after he combed his neighborhood in the night to cut and gather it. The forest provided the forage he converted to cash for at least one book purchase. The woods also offered the safest place to store each book he acquired. While the "quarters" initially incubated Johnson's study, they proved too dangerous for his subversive pursuit of literacy. He made the woods his classroom.[2] In recent decades, historians have provided a rich re-creation of American life under chattel slavery by emphasizing the context of space and place, crucial factors for understanding the experiences of people like Reuben Johnson in the places they lived. For example, the "charter" generation of Africans in early New Orleans experienced very different work routines and took advantage of different opportunities to resist than people held in bondage in North Carolina during the antebellum years of bondspeople's exportation from that state. Change over time interacted with place and space to create the experience of slavery on the ground. The storytellers of American slavery have begun to better understand how bondspeople comprehended and interacted with their surroundings, developing a sense of place in their search for rootedness.[3]

But the place where Reuben Johnson lived, worked, and resisted—the southern periphery—remains underrepresented on history's bookshelves. Scholars have devoted relatively little attention to places west of the Mississippi River, where, even as late as 1860, slavery was young and the terrain only thinly (yet rapidly) occupied by westward-moving settlers. Token mentions of slavery in Missouri, Arkansas, Texas, and northern Louisiana make their way into general histories, but the field requires more in-depth investigation into the daily lives of enslaved people on the southern fringes. Even renowned historian Walter Johnson's magisterial work on slavery in the Mississippi Valley, *River of Dark Dreams*, casts its gaze almost exclusively on the eastern side of the river when discussing points north of New Orleans.[4] Traditionally, the scholarship on American slavery has focused on the eastern, higher-populated, and longer-settled zones of the South. As that continues to change, Reuben Johnson's home, Arkansas, should gain greater attention.[5] Orville Taylor's *Negro Slavery in Arkansas*, published in 1958, remains the only published statewide study of slavery in the "natural state."[6]

To examine the experiences of Johnson and the 111,000 other men, women, and children enslaved in Arkansas is to explore bonded life in rugged space. Arkansas's ground was remote, sparsely populated, and mostly "undeveloped," by white American standards, even at the start of the Civil War. While most of the "Old" South should be described as rural, the population thinned out dramatically at its western edge. Although he resided only a few miles from the state capital, Reuben Johnson did not live near a very large city, even by southern standards. The larger cities within the South (even when excluding the larger border cities like St. Louis and the old port city of New Orleans) held populations in 1860 that Little Rock (the most urban place in Arkansas, by far) would fail to reach until the next century.[7] Little Rock's 1860 population, at 3,727, paled even in comparison with that of other modest river towns of the Old Southwest. The inhabitants of Little Rock numbered little more than half of the population of Natchez in 1860 and amounted to nearly 1,000 fewer than Vicksburg's that same year.[8] Arkansas's youth as a state, position on the far side of the Mississippi River, lack of any truly urban centers, border with Indian Territory, and exponential growth of slavery in the decade before the Civil War all combine to form a landscape of bondage that cannot be adequately represented in studies that privilege the Southeast.

Particularly unfortunate is the fact that historians' interest in the culture and resistance of enslaved communities has yet only barely touched Arkansas history. Reuben Johnson's struggle in the quarters, woods, and fields of central Arkansas represents exactly the aspect of slavery that is wanting in Taylor's 1958 study, and exactly the kind of stories that slavery scholars have emphasized in recovering enslaved people's agency, especially in the last few decades of bottom-up studies of autonomy. Taylor demonstrated slavery in Arkansas as a powerful and quickly growing force in the state's development—a significant feat at the time—but stopped short of investigating the viewpoint of Arkansans held in its clutches. While black writers like W. E. B. DuBois had long emphasized the black point of view only to be ignored by the white academy, mainstream historians eventually shifted toward emphasizing the vantage point of the enslaved—beginning just as Taylor wrote *Negro Slavery in Arkansas*.[9]

Since then, the keepers of this history have gone on to emphasize bondspeople's resistance to dehumanization, through their culture, families, communities, and religion, despite the brutality of their bondage. In this light, Reuben Johnson's story becomes striking not only because of the brutal whippings he received for attempting to self-educate but also for his persistence, despite the risks, in his quest for literacy.

Scholars not only celebrate lives like Johnson's as evidence of resistance to dehumanization but investigate them for what they show about the ties of kinship, cultural autonomy, acquisition of property, and more. These histories have only become richer over time, developing increasingly sophisticated considerations of gender, space, and property in their exploration of the lives bondspeople maintained apart from whites.[10] Because of this ongoing effort, students of slavery can read about such topics as print culture, clothing, and hairstyles, and even eclectic cultural elements like pet ownership. As the scholarship has evolved, historians have continued to explore the complexities of enslaved people's humanity.[11] New histories of slavery's capitalism have tempered the emphasis on celebrating bondspeople's cultural agency while pivoting attention to enslavers' speculation, standardization of management, and networks of finance that figured into slavery's expansion and profitability. When these histories investigate the ground level, they emphasize the ways in which the economic and political processes increased the commodification, brutality, and privation endured by enslaved people.[12]

Environmental historians have added an important layer as well, revealing the imprint of race on the landscape across which the above-mentioned horrors of capitalistic American slavery expanded. Tracing the intersections of nature and culture, scholars have only scratched the surface of this story in the western South. And while historians have thus far explored the environment's role in shaping the South more deeply for the twentieth century than earlier periods, some of the most significant leaps in the field have related to slavery, particularly in the form of Mart A. Stewart's work on rice cultivation in the Georgia lowcountry. Environmental histories and landscape studies reveal just how close to the land enslaved people lived.[13]

Although the study of American slavery has benefited from these fresh subfields and methods of historical inquiry, the microhistoriography of Arkansas remains underdeveloped. Sixty years after *Negro Slavery in Arkansas*, Reuben Johnson's story still has not been told, and no one has picked up where Taylor left off in Arkansas. The need for a bottom-up study of slavery in Arkansas remains. Some works have expanded from Taylor's original points by further exploring the role of slavery in Arkansas's history but without spending much time looking out from the enslaved vantage point. Most of these studies are structured primarily "top-down" in order to meet their goals, lightly touching on the experiences of bondspeople themselves.[14] This is not to say that no one has been looking to unearth stories like Johnson's, but the works are few and far between and never book length. General histories of the natural state incorporate the perspectives of enslaved people while some smaller-scale studies have targeted specific parts of their lives.[15] By far, the most detailed published investigation of enslaved people's comings and goings in Arkansas history is S. Charles Bolton's National Parks–produced study on runaways, employing newspaper advertisements to analyze escapees' journeys in search of freedom. Bolton followed this study with a broader look at fugitivism in the lower Mississippi Valley overall, which prominently features the engaging stories of Arkansas's freedom seekers.[16] Several microhistories enrich our knowledge of the institution's many faces across Arkansas while providing bits of insight into enslaved people's day-to-day lives, but none of them resolve the need for a broad and in-depth look at the experience of black enslavement on the ground in Arkansas.[17]

A Weary Land answers the call to tell this history, emphasizing the role of the ruggedness of Arkansas's landscape and privileging the tension between whites' designs for Arkansas's acreage and the meaning enslaved people made of their surroundings. Arkansas, and the spaces and places that composed it, should not be understood as simply points on a map but, as philosopher Henri Lefebvre explained, as "social realities" created by power structures and economic processes. If the meaning of spaces and places is created by the practical relationships between people, then the experience of slavery in Arkansas can be illuminated by investigating the actions and interactions that various spaces permitted, suggested, and prohibited. The narrative offered here follows the lead of historians who seek to highlight "boundaries and opportunities" of enslaved life in order to map the oppressive system and the resistance to it. Paying attention to the tension between ideals of power and realities on the ground helps in diagramming the enslaved experience.[18]

Slavery shaped the constructs of Arkansas's political boundaries while pressing a fingerprint into the landscape itself. Slavery and enslaved people defined Arkansas's ground in the lowlands and the upcountry alike. Enslaved black farmers built Arkansas's predominantly agricultural economy, enriching the region's most prominent leaders. Arkansas's natural features attracted an increasingly harsh system of chattel slavery, displacing thousands of people to the margins of the South. When whites forced black men and women into Arkansas as chattel, they transplanted them where most space remained uncultivated—*because* most space remained uncultivated. Their coerced labor created the productive landscape, converting woods and prairies into profitable fields, and innumerable trees into homes, stores, and fuel for endless steamboat traffic. Yet whites' predominantly agricultural empire intended to alienate enslaved people from the land. Captive laborers were supposed to act as tools, not participants. Black men and women sustained the nineteenth-century ideal of creating order out of the "wilderness" called Arkansas, making it productive by those standards but without achieving control or ownership of it. They lived out a contradiction to fundamental nineteenth-century American concepts of landed independence. Because whites designed enslavement to limit bondspeople's movement outside of productive activity, enslaved people's deep knowledge of agriculture and their familiarity with farms and plantations upon which they worked were coerced. Their intimacy with what Mart Stewart terms "uncultivated spaces"—the forests and swamps between and beyond the fields—was often discouraged.

Arkansas's natural landscape may have nurtured the nineteenth century's newer, harsher form of slavery but it also provided enslaved people with means to resist. Like enslaved people elsewhere, captive Arkansans did their best to survive within public white spaces and claim the seams between white domains for their own. They coped with their bondage through their family, society, and culture and with their cunning in enslavers' homes, but also in their use of Arkansas's vast uncultivated spaces like the woods, river bottoms, and canebrakes.[19] Swamps and woods provided cover for runaways, parties, and religious observances, as well as a bounty of food and resources. For Reuben Johnson, this meant nighttime harvest of walnuts to finance a book, a safe place to hide his contraband, and eventually a secluded space to hide and practice. The landscape of resistance did not create unconditional solidarity, however. For example, some fellow enslaved people assisted Reuben Johnson in his quest for literacy, while others betrayed him. All in all, the meaning Arkansas's bondspeople conferred onto the spaces in which they moved translated into a definition of freedom as mastery over space and landscape.

African American Arkansans defined freedom as the ability to control their movement and use of space and the ability to own land and modify it for themselves. As Kimberly Smith explains, slavery created in African Americans a sense of self-mastery that required "the right to make a home and the right to leave it."[20] The system of chattel slavery that took root in Arkansas generated profit by dictating black interaction with agricultural land while denying black belonging and ownership in relation to it, yet slavery did not succeed in alienating bondspeople from

Arkansas's land. Instead, they developed their own concepts of the landscape, mapping their own meaning onto it in terms of neighborhoods made up of dwelling places and productive spaces tied together by their social and material lives. Enslaved people did not experience alienation from agricultural work, rural life, or the natural world around them—these provided important foundations for their placemaking—but resented the *power structure* ordering that interaction in their constant struggle for rootedness. Because slavery coerced intimate engagement with cultivated land, perhaps it *should* have been alienating for enslaved farmers, but as the system crumbled, African American Arkansans identified as farmers, as Arkansans, as country people.

Like many historians, I employ the term "cotton frontier" to describe Arkansas and neighboring places in the years ranging from about 1820 through the Civil War. Historians some time ago ceased to use the term "frontier" to mean anything like Frederick Jackson Turner's westward-marching line of (white) progress and civilization—a usage that downplays and eliminates the existence and actions of native and African-descended people. Scholars instead usually employ "frontier" to mean the meeting place of different cultures in a zone in which the boundaries of polities and cultures are in flux. In this book, "cotton frontier" is used to refer to the western swath of the South's expanding cotton cultivation.[21]

Chapter 1, "The Morass," begins the story with early interactions on the land that would come to be defined as Arkansas. Africans, whites, and Native Americans built a small-scale commercial farming and frontier exchange economy that would give way to staple crop production supported by chattel slavery. Seen as a morass for more than just its impenetrable swamps, early Arkansas represented the lawlessness, land speculation, and "slave-stealing"—real and imagined—that perturbed whites in the Old Southwest. Nevertheless, Arkansas's fertile ground attracted whites who mapped, gridded, and claimed thousands of acres, driving Native Americans out as impediments to cultivation while forcing African Americans into the region as a captive labor force. Slavery provided the foundation to Arkansas's "becoming," first as a territory then as a state.

The following chapter, "Domains," explores the creation and maintenance of the various spaces in which enslaved people were forced to contend—in short, what Reuben Johnson and his compatriots were up against. Spatial theorists explain that spaces focus people's intentions and make claims about status, creating boundaries that are physical and social. Status determined who could cross what boundaries, when, and in what ways. This chapter is intended in part to provide some answer to Kimberly Smith's invitation to explore how these conventions "persisted or were transformed in frontier areas."[22] Whites worked efficiently to transplant slavery into Arkansas by crafting laws and society that hardened over time, forcing enslaved people to create an ordered agricultural domain. Enslaved people also navigated a geography of power within homes, as well as on farms and plantations, crafting their own sense of dominion. The interstices between farms as well as the forests and prairies beyond them facilitated that process.

Chapter 3, "Alluvial Empires," offers a bird's-eye view, touching down at various points to highlight the experience on the ground. Arkansas's landscape is diverse, ranging from rugged upcountry with isolated fertile valleys to flat, rich delta expanses. And yet like its waterways, slavery cut through it all. Identifying the population centers and regions that anchored varying experiences of slavery in and around Arkansas, from eastern steamboat stops to western posts, "Alluvial Empires" argues for the primacy of rivers.[23] In the east, the Mississippi River drove much of Arkansas's plantation development. Arkansas's upcountry slaveholding regions converged geographically and historically with those of Missouri, tangled by the White River, while the southwestern Red River Valley housed its own plantation region connected to eastern Texas and northern Louisiana. The Arkansas River sliced through the heart of the state, nurturing a belt of intensive cultivation that stretched from Indian Territory to the Mighty Mississippi.

Arrival on the fringes of the South meant hard labor for black men and women forced to do the work of transforming the forests and prairies into productive fields of cotton and corn. Bondspeople who had previously worked on farms needing little improvement or who had experience only with tobacco or rice in the east faced adjustment to the novel demands of the cotton frontier. Chapter 4, "Flesh and Fiber," explores enslaved Arkansans' deep knowledge of Arkansas's ground via coerced agricultural labor, walking readers through the rhythms in various geographies encompassed by Arkansas's borders. Captive farmers navigated place and space across time, among different crop cultures, in animal husbandry, and on farms of various sizes. Their work defined Arkansas's ground as well as their own status. Enslaved people tended corn and livestock before cotton, and those tasks remained a central part of their agricultural work for the life of the institution in Arkansas. Enslaved farmers worked their family and community life into the seasons of work as best they could, overlaying family milestones on top of the agricultural rhythm.

Bondspeople survived the daily drudgery in part by acquiring and creating goods and objects to supplement their diets and material lives. Chapter 5, "The Material of Survival," describes enslaved families' lives through their housing, food, medical care, and relationships linked by trade, sharing, and the creation of resources. Enslaved people like Reuben Johnson engaged in activity that included illicit trade and harvesting nature's bounty. The quarters harbored the fruits of these efforts. This "slaves' economy," as historians have termed it, proved difficult to sustain in the more isolated zones and/or on strictly managed plantations of the cotton frontier, making it all the more precious. Bondspeople's day-to-day experiences accumulated to build their sense of identity, place, and rootedness.

Finally, Chapter 6, "Battlegrounds," explains how the understandings of home, land, and borders affected the black experience of the Civil War and emancipation, exploring the ways in which Arkansas's ground, both public and private, woods and fields alike, took on new meaning with the coming of the war. The chapter moves topically rather than in a linear process because, as Amy Murrell Taylor explains, "wartime emancipation was a profoundly localized process." While some enslaved people inched closer to freedom, those in other places—even a short distance away—experienced setbacks. Enslaved people's "journey" to freedom should be understood as a circuitous one.[24] Rather than offering a complete treatment of the process of emancipation in Arkansas, which is still sorely needed, "Battlegrounds" focuses primarily on the experiences of people held at some level of bondage through the war and how the conflict tweaked and transformed the landscape of that oppression. Slavers sought to preserve slavery while bondspeople, aware of the war's implications, navigated the conflict with a wide range of strategies influenced by their location. They assisted either side, both, or neither in order to remain near loved ones or to simply survive, aware that the war was changing their lives forever. Bondspeople's use of rivers and woods to flee whites had the potential to bring bigger gains than ever, but for many, their occupation of brush and cane became coerced as whites invaded these spaces to hide their slave property. At the same time, many enslaved Arkansans found themselves able to claim public spaces like never before and others negotiated unprecedented power struggles in their enslavers' households and fields. The war enlivened and enabled African American Arkansans' desire to claim spaces heretofore off-limits and modify the landscape for their own benefit.

A Weary Land will not be the last word in the effort to understand slavery in Arkansas, but it brings enslaved people's lives there more prominently into the academic conversation, provides researchers, teachers, students, genealogists, and the public with the stories of people like Reuben Johnson, and stokes further scholarship and conversation on the topic of bondage in the natural state. With every passing anniversary of Arkansas's most notorious outrages—the 1919 Elaine Massacre and the 1957 Central High Crisis—the legacy of slavery and racial oppression in Arkansas is recalled anew. *A Weary Land* adds to the resources available to those seeking to grasp the long history of the black struggle in Arkansas. Perhaps it will also instill in readers some awe for enslaved Arkansans' resilience—when men and women, such as Eva Strayhorn's family, sang "Oh Jesus is a rock in a weary land, a weary land, a weary land . . . a shelter in the time of storm," they revealed a breathtakingly hopeful spirit to be laboring on ground so desolate of freedom.[25]

1 /   The Morass

The first black men and women to find themselves in the Quapaw-French community known as Arkansas Post slogged up the Mississippi River from French New Orleans and floated down it from the American Northwest Territory in the eighteenth century. They inhabited a northern periphery of the Atlantic core of New Orleans, a zone that would transform into the western fringe of the expanding "second slavery." In the early nineteenth century, all of Arkansas was associated with the disease and disorder of the "great swamp" that covered much of its eastern region. Most white Americans on the east side of the river regarded it as an iniquitous wasteland best avoided due to its thick swampy landscape, remoteness, and reputation for lawlessness. For years this "morass," to use Joshua Rothman's word, harbored slavery's escapees. But whites systematically removed native groups, claimed acreage for cotton, corn, and livestock, and drew the borders that protected a haven for chattel slavery. Edward Casey posits that political territories like Arkansas should not be understood as a static state of being but rather "closer to an action or event." The creation of Arkansas Territory and Arkansas the state indeed represented a happening, a process in which the more "order" white Americans brought to the landscape as they "tamed" it for agricultural production, the more restricted black life there became. Enslaved people took advantage of the morass to undermine mastery while whites succeeded in claiming its ground for a newer, harsher form of chattel slavery.[1]

Situated at the intersection between the Mississippi and Arkansas Rivers, the earliest enslaved Africans in the area numbered only a handful and inhabited the small, remote commercial and diplomatic hub of the Arkansas Post, a borderland crossroads where French, Africans, Osage, and Quapaw traded, worked, and contested power. The first flags at the post went up in 1686, when Henri de Tonty, an Italian exploring on behalf of the French, distributed land grants to French settlers in a Quapaw town, Osotouy. Commandants relocated the post three times over the years due to flooding, and it remained sparsely settled by French soldiers, hunters, and farmers. Enslaved Africans' forced importation to the area was initiated in 1717 by Scottish entrepreneur John Law when he geared up his Compagnie d'Occident, a doomed speculative scheme to support settlement of land granted by the French crown. Two years later, the deal forced more than six hundred Africans to Louisiana as chattel, although very few found themselves driven as far north as Arkansas with Law's settlers in 1721. It is likely that those who did originated in Senegambia, like two-thirds of the Africans unloaded from slave ships in New Orleans between 1726 and 1731.[2] The black population of Arkansas remained small for many years. A French inspector of the post mentioned only six enslaved people in 1723. The next year, when the Law endeavor folded, whites moved most if not all of them, along with many indentured servants, to plantations south of what is now Arkansas, and closer to New Orleans. By 1749, enslaved men and women made up fourteen of the forty-five permanent inhabitants of the post. Half of those were held by Quebec native Charles Linctot. This handful of enslaved farmers probably cultivated "widowed" acreage—old fields abandoned as more Quapaw succumbed to European disease.[3]

In 1787, the meaning of the continental landscape shifted to make Arkansas's ground more attractive for prospective slaveholding settlers when the young United States government passed the Northwest Ordinance, which officially organized the Northwest Territory north of the Ohio River and prohibited slavery there. A few French families forced enslaved people down the Mississippi River to Arkansas onto soil where they could remain masters. In 1791, two widows—recorded only by their surnames: Menard, a merchant, and Derriseau, a farmer—held the most bondspeople at the post. Of the probable "refugees of the Northwest Ordinance," the largest slaveholder in 1793, Joseph Bogy, held eleven people. Even with these newcomers, only forty households occupied the entire site of Arkansas Post, meaning that enslaved men and women there probably came to know each other well.[4]

Few sources illuminate what their world would have looked like in these years, but the farm seasons, trade patterns, and realities of necessity on the French-Quapaw frontier created structures more real to bondspeople's daily lives than any codification from distant seats of power. Numbering about forty, they lived and worked among a permanent population of around two hundred, laboring alongside hired men at agricultural tasks, as well as loading and unloading the goods and supplies that sustained the post. They neighbored soldiers and German and French families who traded in skins, furs, oil, and supplies for coureurs des bois. They also became acquainted with traveling hunters and traders, about one hundred of whom filtered in and out of the post. African Arkansans also neighbored the Quapaw, who had established strong diplomatic and economic ties with the French. The rules of enslaved Arkansans' existence under the French flag technically fell under the Code Noir, a set of laws implemented in 1724 to regulate slavery in French Louisiana. Officially, the code prohibited manumission without the approval of French authorities, provided for the instruction of bondspeople in the Catholic faith, disallowed the sale of young children from their mothers, recognized enslaved couples' marriages, and criminalized marriage or concubinage between whites and blacks or mulattoes.[5] It is difficult, however, to determine how energetically French officials enforced this code in Arkansas, either to punish enslaved people or to implement those few protections for enslaved families. Laws against intimate connections, for example, proved difficult to enforce, and scholars have identified a type of "sexual diplomacy" evident in the cohabitation of African women with French men as well as between African men and Quapaw women in French Louisiana. Relationships between individuals and groups held most consequence. Ultimately, like everyone else at the post, African Arkansans had to contend with the official structure and authority issued from the various commandants who came and went over the years. For example, during the interlude when the Spanish controlled the post, black workers and farmers simply went about their business while Spanish, rather than French, soldiers manned the stockade, but they would have keenly felt the subsequent troubled political landscape that resulted in Osage attacks.[6]

In these years, whites' claims of Spanish land grants set in motion the increased relocation of enslaved people to Arkansas and, in turn, the transformation of Arkansas's ground by those bondspeople at the demand of whites. Claimants had to clear, drain, and improve the sections of land during an initial probatory occupation in order to secure permanent rights to it. Essentially, colonization was the proposition that the land was unused or misused as is and needed to be civilized. To claim the land, grantees had to properly inhabit it. Claimants with access to enslaved labor leveraged bondspeople's presence on the land and their work, transforming it to execute settler colonialism; the improvements enslaved people made to such farmsteads supported white claims to it.

Speculation and Spanish grants conferred after Louisiana had been passed back to the French but prior to the United States' purchase confused the system. A commission by the U.S. government later investigated claims, honoring those by farmers who proved they had occupied and improved their lot as promised. When the descendants of claimant Elisha Winter fought for the right to a large swath of Arkansas in the nineteenth century, they put forward an account and argument that revealed how white colonists understood rightful settlement of the land. In 1797, after making friends with colonial officials in New Orleans, Elisha Winter received a sizable grant near Arkansas Post and planned to join the forty to fifty families already in the vicinity. When Winter arrived, he proudly marked the southeast corner of his grant with an enormous hewn stone that he had hauled all the way from Kentucky, placing it "with a good deal of public ceremony." Having claimed native land with the blessing of the Spanish crown, Winter relied on enslaved workers and hired servants, whom he had driven to Arkansas along with livestock, to execute his vision. Slave and free likely worked side by side clearing brush, erecting fences, and raising buildings. They cleared acreage for wheat, flax, hemp, and even some cotton. Those who labored at Winter's demand also cared for stock like sheep (according to Winter's heirs, the first at the post). Their work transforming the land was intended to make real the claims that otherwise existed only on paper.[7] Winter's designs on Arkansas's ground provide early, if small-scale, evidence of what Mart Stewart has argued about plantation districts elsewhere—that slaveholders needed to control bondspeople in order to control the environment. As Stewart put it, "The domination of nature and the domination of one group of humans by another evolved mutually. The slaves . . . became instruments of environmental manipulation. The environment . . . then became an instrument to control the slaves." While not yet widespread and involving only small numbers of people, the dialectic that would long shape Arkansas was already in motion.[8]

In 1803, Arkansas's ground, as part of French Louisiana, came into American hands, partially due to the fierce freedom fighting launched by African-descended people elsewhere in the French colonies—St.

Domingue. (At least a few of the slaveholders who fled eventually came to Arkansas.) The Haitian Revolution—for French whites, an annoying and unforeseen ripple of the French Revolution—proved devastating for France's finances. Exasperated at the difficulty in controlling American colonies, exhausted from fighting to suppress the slave revolt and war for independence in St. Domingue, cash-strapped, and preparing for war with England, the French sold the eight hundred thousand square miles of Louisiana to the United States at a bargain. This transaction changed the meaning of Arkansas's landscape even though the physical terrain had not been altered by the deal. The Louisiana Purchase, which signified Jefferson's agrarian ideal for the republic, redefined Arkansas as a fertile western fringe of the American South. Fewer than one thousand enslaved people inhabited Arkansas at the time of the purchase, but African Americans would now settle Arkansas in greater numbers as the chattel of incoming white settlers.[9]

Until 1805, Arkansas made up a portion of the District of Louisiana, within the Territory of Louisiana. When the state of Louisiana entered the union, Arkansas constituted the southern portion of Missouri Territory. The enslaved population steadily increased in these years (to 1,613 by 1820), but bondspeople as a percentage of the total population decreased due to the influx of small farmers. At the turn of the nineteenth century, then, Europeans, Africans, and Americans thinly inhabited the hills, valleys, prairie, and swampland of Arkansas—many in bondage and all increasingly encroaching upon the homelands and hunting grounds of indigenous Arkansans. Before intensive cotton and corn cultivation took hold, African Arkansans mostly experienced a frontier exchange economy. Some sense of their trials in the years following the Louisiana Purchase can be pieced together through surviving legal records from the period. Their lives were marked by movement in relation to their exploitation and resistance. Although "King Cotton" had not yet begun his rule, the labor of enslaved people and their liquidity as assets proved immensely profitable to white Arkansas settlers who farmed, hunted, traded in skins and furs, and set up stores to provision newcomers and those passing through the territory.[10]

Because their very persons represented commodities, where enslaved people were located was central to claims of ownership over them. Their value meant that African Arkansans lived in constant danger of being "stolen" or spirited away. Whites fought each other in court over disputed ownership of black men and women in Arkansas; they often slung accusations that other whites had "enticed" fugitives away.[11] In 1813, an enslaved woman named Jenny, thirty-five years old, appears in the record, but there is very little detail. While George Hook claimed ownership of her, Jenny labored, either for loan or for hire, on Perly Wallis's farm on the Little Bayou Meto, near Arkansas Post. Jenny's relocation to that place profited both parties, but it also created uncertainty when she did not remain. Wallis, an early attorney at the post, accused two men, William Morrison and Robert Clary, of stealing Jenny "out of the house and out of the yard" in 1813; it is unclear whether she went willingly. Jenny seems to have been caught up in a long-running feud between the men. Back in 1811, Wallis had accused Morrison of stealing corn and oxen and threatening to shoot him. The record shows Wallis prosecuted another suit involving Jenny and another white man, heard in St. Louis in 1824, but the outcome is not clear. Valued by whites at $350, Jenny represented an investment to be jealously guarded by Wallis and coveted by his enemies; she was haplessly caught in the middle of a personal and economic struggle. On the other hand, perhaps the record should be read as the story of a black woman, supposed to be chattel, coming and going of her own volition often enough to frustrate white men's attempts to claim mastery over her.[12] Because bodies like Jenny's represented valuable assets, sometimes whites captured them to secure the compliance of litigants or suspects. Sam, for example, purchased by Sylvanus Phillips (after whom Phillips County, Arkansas, would be named) at a public auction, spent a year in the custody of a county sheriff as surety that Phillips would appear to answer a suit.[13]

Slavery is not simply a part of Arkansas's history but a fundamental principle guiding Arkansas's organization as a territory and then a state—a shaping force in Casey's "event" of becoming a place. Southern whites envisioned Arkansas's land as a haven for slavery from the beginning and, in 1819, succeeded in claiming it as such. Having made up the lower section of Missouri Territory, Arkansas required reorganization when the northern chunk of Missouri sought statehood. Missouri's bid to enter the union with no restrictions on slavery agitated the question of slavery's fate in the Trans-Mississippi. Representative James Tallmadge of New York proposed an amendment to the Missouri statehood bill that held two provisions: prohibiting the further importation of bondspeople into Missouri and freeing those already there at the age of twenty-five. The Tallmadge amendment would have slowly eliminated slavery in Missouri; it kicked off a firestorm of debate as southerners in Congress fought to defend slavery's expansion. As Robert Pierce Forbes explains, "An unanticipated amendment to a routine bill had turned into nothing less than a referendum on the meaning of America." Arkansas's future was also decided in this watershed moment. Representative John W. Taylor of New York had energetically defended his colleague's amendment to the Missouri bill and proposed the same two restrictions on slavery in an amendment to the bill creating Arkansas Territory. By preventing additional slave importation and emancipating enslaved people when they reached age twenty-five, the Taylor amendment would have extinguished slavery in Arkansas, setting the future state on an entirely different trajectory. Like the Tallmadge amendment, Taylor's amendment eventually perished. No one in Congress proposed any further restrictions on slavery in Arkansas, and the territorial organization became official in 1819. Whites had succeeded in legally claiming Arkansas's land for slavery, unleashing the ground-level agricultural expansion that would fully realize that claim.[14]

Both the new state of Missouri and the new territory of Arkansas attracted slaveholding newcomers in the following years, but their histories diverged. Ten thousand enslaved people already inhabited Missouri by 1820, and those who came after mostly lived as the chattel of whites looking to replicate the smallholding agriculture they knew in the upper South. Few planters migrated there, discouraged by Missouri's proximity to free territory and its relatively inferior potential for cotton. For example, Missouri's 180-day growing season compared unfavorably to that of the upper third of Arkansas, which lasted from 200 to 220 days. The lower two-thirds of Arkansas, marked off by a nearly straight east-west line, experienced a growing season of 220 to 240 days. Migration to Missouri peaked in 1835, and although both states ended up with similarly sized enslaved populations in 1860 (about 115,000 in Missouri, 111,000 in Arkansas), Missouri's total population of more than one million amounted to more than double Arkansas's that year.[15]

Whites and their black captives traveled slowly and uncomfortably into Arkansas, trekking over crude paths and floating the small flatboats and keelboats that crept up the Arkansas, Ouachita, White, and Red Rivers.[16] Enough settlers made these journeys that the total population of Arkansas more than doubled in the decade after the territory was established (from 14,273 in 1820 to 30,388 in 1830).[17] At 30,388 in 1830, Arkansas's total population amounted to less than a quarter of that of each of the surrounding states, including Missouri. The earliest population centers of Arkansas Territory dotted the banks of the Arkansas River and the hills of northwest Arkansas where the land was less prone to flooding and disease-causing mosquito infestation. Bonded communities were initially concentrated on the more easily drained cotton ground of southwest Arkansas, along the Red River, just across from New Spain (after 1821, Mexico). But enslaved Arkansans did not border freedom in that direction. While the government of newly independent Mexico officially restricted slavery, the use of extended indentures and Texas's exemption from Mexico's general emancipation order combined to keep the institution alive and vibrant to the southwest. Enslaved farmers grew cotton, corn, peas, beans, and potatoes, and while landowners focused most of their efforts on subsistence, they became increasingly concerned with marketing their yields.[18]

The timing of Arkansas Territory's creation was not coincidental. It occurred just as the newest and most profitable phase of American slavery arose. Leaders had opened Arkansas for the infiltration of what some historians have termed the "second slavery." This second phase of American bondage, made possible in part by the cotton gin and new methods of investment and management, represented a more intense capitalistic version of chattel slavery, growing at an exponential rate and reinvigorating the internal slave trade. The second slavery focused overwhelmingly on producing huge quantities of one crop: cotton. The new system's calling card was its rapid transformation of the economies of areas that had been before only peripheral. It had already touched Mississippi, parts of Missouri, and western Alabama. Arkansas Territory's creation without restrictions on slavery invited whites to pour into Arkansas with their captives and carve out the freshest parts of this growing cotton kingdom. This process had already transformed much of the social and physical landscape further down the Mississippi River. By 1820, the young state of Mississippi was already home to 42,176 whites and 32,814 bondspeople. Soil depletion and erosion from years of cultivation would affect the Natchez region by the time the crop took a firm hold in Arkansas in the 1830s. A widespread economic depression that began in 1819 slowed the second slavery's development in Arkansas (and slowed the transformation of other places like Mississippi) but did not stop it. Corn, cattle, and subsistence farming remained Arkansas's most common agricultural activities for a time while the trade in skins retained its "princely power." This in-between period—when black Arkansans lived out the last years of the frontier exchange economy and the beginning of a harsher cotton regime—is exemplified by R. C. Byrd's 1829 advertisement announcing to his debtors the options of settling up via seed cotton, pelts, beef hides, bear skins, bear oil, beaver furs, or otter furs. The enslaved population of Arkansas spiked from 1,617 (11% of the total) in 1820 to 4,576 (15% of the total) in 1830—sparse in comparison to its neighbors. The second slavery began as a trickle but would come to dominate Arkansas's economy and society.[19]

White Americans fed the second slavery with Indian removals. As cotton production became more profitable, particularly along the Mississippi, Arkansas, and Red Rivers, whites implemented a series of expulsions designed to claim Arkansas's landscape for staple crops. They pushed out native people, whom they viewed as dangerous and inhibiting progress, making way for the importation of enslaved people to convert the land to moneymaking fields of cotton and corn. Populations of Cherokees, Choctaws, Delawares, and Shawnees already resided in Arkansas by the time of the Louisiana Purchase, forced there by land-hungry whites back east. The 1804 legislation to separate Upper Louisiana (of which Arkansas was part) from the Territory of New Orleans had designated Arkansas's land as available for the resettlement of southeastern Native Americans. In 1818, the Quapaw ceded twenty-eight million acres below the Arkansas River to make room for Indian groups being removed *to* Arkansas.[20] White Tennesseans had pushed Cherokees into Arkansas in previous years and pressed them into the Arkansas River Valley, including areas that the Osage had hunted since the eighteenth century and the ancestral home of the Quapaw. The Quapaw appealed to white Americans to stave off encroachment by whites and other Indian groups. The Quapaw's "settled" agricultural activity fit with the economic approach whites believed to be "civilized"; indeed Quapaw commercial corn farming sustained their neighbors. The Cherokee made the best of their circumstances in Arkansas, which, economically, meant bringing enslaved African Americans with them. White observers appreciated elite Cherokees' use of enslaved people, who were forced to work livestock and cultivate large farms. Indeed, whites coveted these captive workers and some tried to seize them for themselves. By 1813, clashes between the Cherokee and Osage in Arkansas reached deadly new heights, and within three years, the Osages were beaten badly enough that they ceded most of their land along the Arkansas River. Because whites viewed them as relatively "civilized," the Cherokee successfully wrangled for the former Osage ground.[21]

Yet when the government of Arkansas achieved territorial status, whites used their voice in the national government to make it clear that they did not want any more Indians coming to Arkansas, "civilized" or not, reacting with fury to an 1820 treaty granting a huge tract of land between the Arkansas and Red Rivers to the Choctaw. Not only did whites seek to prevent additional removals to Arkansas, they clamored for the extraction of native groups currently on Arkansas ground. White settlers believed their government existed to make desirable agricultural land available to them. White farmers and land speculators intensely coveted the Quapaw's sizable strip of fertile land along the Arkansas River—250 miles of potentially prime cotton acreage—and successfully stripped the Quapaw of any Arkansas ground by 1824. Meanwhile, the Cherokee held out hope that their society represented a level of "civilization" that would exempt them from further removal.[22]

But whites persisted in Indian Removal, quite literally shaping Arkansas. The western border became defined by the 1828 treaty removing the Western Cherokee of Arkansas to the west of a line running north-south from Fort Smith. (A treaty in 1825 had already initiated removal of the Choctaw west of that line.) As soon as the Western Cherokee were expelled from northwest Arkansas, white families like the Beans, Pyeatts, and Marrs hustled to settle the zone, becoming profitable slaveholders over the following decades. The Indian Removal Act of 1830 concluded the process of clearing Native Americans under tribal governments from the southeast United States and through Arkansas to Indian Territory. Native groups like the eastern Cherokee, Seminole, Creek, and Chickasaw passed through Arkansas in waves through the 1830s. White businesses and infrastructure benefited from federal funds granted to those in Arkansas seeking to facilitate journeys across the state. Slaveholding merchant Maurice Wright got his start in Cane Hill, Washington County, bordering Indian Territory in the 1830s, in a partnership with his brother selling pork to newly arriving Cherokees. Indian removals and the second slavery cannot be disentangled. As Sven Beckert put it, whites needed the ground of the Old Southwest to become "legally empty."[23] They forced Native Americans and their tribal governments *off* Arkansas's ground and hurried displaced groups *through* it in order to force captive African Americans *onto* it. One "citizen" writing to the *Gazette* spoke for most whites in expressing a vision of an Arkansas no longer a morass populated by buffalo and "savages" but rather an agrarian paradise where "the earth is made to perform the offices for which she was intended by the God of nature."[24]

Plenty of mechanisms existed to transfer Arkansas's fertile ground into the control of whites looking to facilitate the "intended offices" of an empire for slavery. Whites claimed ground via preemption claims, military bounty land grants, and New Madrid claims—grants of public lands for those whose acreage had been ruined by the massive earthquake of 1811–12. In addition, whites engaged in a flurry of land speculation prompted in part by government "donations" of land to offset the loss to whites displaced by the creation of a Cherokee reservation immediately northwest of Arkansas's new territorial line. Land speculators scrambled to buy up such claims or to inhabit and lightly improve lands to claim ownership via preemption then sell the acreage at a profit. Land speculation led to the relocation of Arkansas's territorial capital upriver from Arkansas Post to Little Rock—enriching some of Arkansas's most famous and well-connected enslavers. Sometimes these land dealers infringed on one another's designs and feuded publicly, even from afar. William H. Gaines of Kentucky sent his brother with a small group of enslaved people to work land in Arkansas in order to secure preemption. Enslaved people found themselves caught up in this land grab not only as laborers to be placed upon fresh acreage but also as currency. Arkansas's ground could just as easily be paid for with black bodies as with cash or, as J. S. Conway specified, with "young negroes."[25]

Settlers constructed and sustained the seats of power and trade in territorial Arkansas with the labor and value of African Americans as chattel. Enslaved people proved crucial in the establishment of the earliest trading posts in the territory not only by their labor but also by their value as assets. John Miller and Frenchman William Drope, for example, set up a partnership for a venture in Davidsonville, the most important trading post of northeast Arkansas Territory, on the Black River. Miller and Drope relied on the labor of an enslaved "boy," not named in the record (who may very well have been a grown man). Drope, who already owned a store, agreed to pay Miller to run it, buy skins and furs, and transport goods. Drope promised to provide the "negro boy" to "beat and preserve Such peltries and furs as might be purchased" from traders at the post. Drope allowed Miller to employ the bondsman for his own personal use as he bought, processed, and transported goods. The enslaved man would have found Davidsonville, established in 1815 and the seat of Lawrence County, to be relatively deserted between court dates and land sales. Downriver from Pocahontas, Davidsonville was home to at least a few hundred, maybe as many as two thousand, people, drawn to the area by War of 1812 bounty lands and New Madrid claims. The man forced to work for Drope and Miller lived and worked in this early Arkansas hub where people met to exchange land claims, pelts, and wampum beads in taverns and in the post office. Davidsonville's business did not prove harmonious for Drope and Miller, however, who dissolved their partnership after a few years; what happened to the enslaved man is unknown, but he likely remained with Drope. The venture benefited Miller enough that he took a "draft" from John Crittenden in 1824 to purchase nearly $4,000 worth of men and women in New Orleans. Either Miller planned to begin his own slaveholding farm or he intended to sell the bondspeople.[26]

Indeed, many Arkansas enslavers got their start running early Arkansas trading posts, later to invest their gains in the second slavery. Arkansas's first stores served as incubators for her later planters. In 1824, Ephraim Merrick partnered with John Johnson to buy a stock of goods in New Orleans, brought them north via the Mississippi and Ouachita Rivers to Camden, and then went on to Washington, in southwest Arkansas, to open a store. By the early statehood period, Merrick had converted his profits into a growing cotton plantation enslaving twenty-eight men and women.[27] Outside investors also shaped this growth. As wealthy men engaged in speculation from other parts of the South they aided the development of the southern periphery into a slaver's paradise. For example, James Sutherland Deas of Mobile, Alabama, and his business partner, Thomas Broom Lee of New Orleans, traded in land and human chattel in southwest Arkansas from the territorial days through the Civil War. Purchasing a New Madrid claim from Jane Bradley and additional acreage from Davidson and Eliza Bradley from 1834 to 1836, Deas used an agent to set up a plantation in Arkansas seemingly without ever leaving the gulf.[28]

Slaveholding and enslaved migrants to Arkansas Territory experienced what Conevery Bolton Valencius called a "frustrating search for order in self and surroundings."[29] As whites' pursuits become increasingly profitable, enslaved Arkansans became more strictly bounded by a code of laws meant to ensure that the institution transplanted to the frontier remained regimented and profitable. Creating order out of Arkansas's landscape and coercing profit from its earth meant controlling the movement and opportunities of enslaved people. The legal code, although intended to secure Arkansas for slaveholders' interests, revealed contested ground. Gone was the recognition of enslaved marriages and the ban on separating small children from their mothers that the old Code Noir had provided. Yet the territorial code provided mechanisms for enslavers who sought to liberate their captives and for bondspeople seeking freedom under the law. Enslaved people held the right to petition courts for their freedom, and whites were empowered to manumit them in wills. Some laws restricted free blacks, whom whites watched closely for signs of "burdening" society or influencing their bonded compatriots. Counties reserved the right to hire out freedpeople who failed to pay their taxes until they recouped the unpaid balance. The code included no restrictions concerning where free blacks could live or travel. The territorial statutes allowed for the execution of whites who knowingly placed a free black person into slavery through theft or sale. Arkansas Territory's courts prohibited blacks and mulattoes from serving as witnesses against whites.[30]

As the forced migration of African Americans increased the territory's enslaved population, white policymakers passed laws to create and protect the caste system and its profits. In large part, this meant limiting black movement in ways that modeled the policies of older slave states. Bondspeople needed a pass to leave their enslaver's residence, and those caught "strolling" by the patrols faced whipping on sight. Later territorial statutes reflected the fear that rippled across the white South after Nat Turner's rebellion in Virginia in 1831. Like other white southerners, Arkansans reacted by closely monitoring enslaved people's gatherings—groups could not gather for longer than four hours at a time and whites vowed to disband and punish gatherings they deemed suspicious or riotous. Bondspeople caught inciting insurrection were to be punished with death. Fines awaited whites connected with unlawful gatherings of enslaved people and those who dared to illegally trade with them. Revealing of the fear that at least temporarily swept the region, the law declared that a bondsperson could face the death penalty as punishment for administering medicine unless it was proven (by whites) to have been administered without ill will. At the same time, the law reflected whites' trust of bondspeople out of necessity and convenience. As most slaveholdings were small in size, most slaveholders did not anticipate insurrection and many preferred their bonded laborers to be able to protect themselves and hunt on Arkansas's rugged ground. The law provided that bondspeople (and free blacks) could keep and use guns with permission from their enslavers. When convicted of crimes, enslaved people's punishment generally came in the form of "well laid on" whippings for men and women alike.[31]

Taken together, Arkansas's territorial law reveals contradictions in slaveholding whites' concerns. In allowing enslaved people to use guns, for example, whites recognized the practicality and benefit of gun-wielding bondspeople who could protect themselves and hunt (the latter of which is discussed more fully in later chapters) in a zone they considered wild and undeveloped. Restrictions on black gatherings, however, reflect whites' uneasiness with an increasing enslaved population on the heels of the Nat Turner Revolt. Bondspeople felt more scrutinous eyes upon them in groups than they did individually.

Enslaved people's movements in the morass forced whites to react and undermined white mastery on the territorial cotton frontier. Territorial statutes include the editorial warning that "many times slaves run away and lie hid and lurking in swamps woods and other obscure places, killing hogs and committing other injuries to the inhabitants of this district." Arkansas remained covered with such "obscure places" from which fugitives could benefit.[32] Toby took advantage of them. Born in St. Domingue during the Haitian Revolution, he was sold by Jean Baptiste Labatant and Celestin Chiapella (perhaps refugees from that conflict) along with eight other bondspeople to Marie Celeste Lanusse and Paul Lanusse in New Orleans in April 1823. Records describe him as "Mulato—about 5 feet high," with a broken front tooth. Within three years, Toby appeared in Conway County, Arkansas, on the plantation of William Flanakin. He had fled New Orleans in the spring of 1825, soon after Paul Lanusse died. Lanusse's widow claimed Toby was "stolen," but it is not clear whether he had been captured by Flanakin or went with him willingly as a preferable alternative to widow Lanusse. Left with the financial ruin of her husband's failed business ventures, Marie Lanusse fought to recover Toby, who, she claimed, was worth $700. Lanusse won her suit, but it is not clear from the record whether her victory forced Toby to return to Louisiana or if Flanakin simply paid her Toby's value.[33]

Accusations of slave-stealing in the morass flew as whites vied for power, profit, and influence. Andrew Latting, a landowner and politician of southeast Arkansas, made enemies in the territory and developed a reputation among some as a murderer and a thief, charges often made in connection to his comings and goings with enslaved Arkansans. A feud between Latting and Chicot County rival Benjamin Miles came to light when Miles circulated a flyer featuring charges against Latting's character. Although the text of the handbill has not survived, "slave-stealing" seems to have been the main theme.[34] Sometime in the summer of 1816, an enslaved man, who is never named in the records, came into the company of Andrew Latting under circumstances that area whites found suspicious. The man's enslaver had been a Mr. Morehouse, until he died, whereupon the man became the legal property of General Hughes of Ouachita (south-central Arkansas). Suddenly the bondsman was gone. Unable to conceive of the black man as having his own designs, General Hughes blamed Andrew Latting for "enticing" the man away while he had visited the area, claiming Latting had hidden in the swamp for several days, meeting with the man and "treating him with whiskey." Indeed, neighbors spotted the man with Latting after his return from Ouachita. Hughes sent his overseer, Frederick Foy, to retrieve the absconded man. If he had gone with Latting uncoerced, the unnamed man put his trust in a sketchy character who embodied the trickery and murkiness associated with the morass. In testimony connected to the resulting legal dispute, Latting's alleged sins piled up. While serving as justice of the peace, Latting had already damaged his reputation when he allegedly abused his position for economic gain, charges that made it to the governor's desk in "a scandal to the Territory." Latting's neighbor Henry Robinson claimed that Latting had tried to enlist him to help recapture Hughes's bondsman from Foy, the overseer, and declared his plans to kill Foy. Another of Latting's neighbors, Abram DeHart, likewise considered Latting a scoundrel, claiming that he had poisoned DeHart's father. Others pointed to bad deals in which Latting reneged on his part and swindled them. Nicholas Merriwhether declared that he wouldn't allow Latting into his home. Henry Robinson summed up Latting's general reputation among his enemies, declaring he would "Take every advantage he can just or unjus" in search of "property or revenge." Detaining and trafficking black men and women was one way Latting's enemies claimed he "took advantage" in territorial Arkansas.[35]

According to one of the many stories that his enemies levied to prove Latting's true character as a thief, he unlawfully held possession of a man (unnamed in the record) purportedly owned by a Mr. Ruth of Natchez. The enslaved man, who had probably been hired to Latting, moved about freely. A neighbor claimed the bondsman joined him on a days-long hunting trip, during which the bondsman rode one of Latting's horses. Back in Natchez, Ruth arranged to sell the man, but as the date of the sale drew near, he disappeared. Latting claimed that the man had run away from him. Latting's enemies, however, believed that the missing man actually lay concealed "in the cane by a hole of water" near Latting's house, and in cooperation with him, to avoid the sale. Neighbor DeHart claimed to have encountered the hidden man, and upon confrontation the man disclosed that "Latting had put him there."[36]

It seems that this bondsman from Natchez was not the only enslaved person to cooperate with Latting's designs. In another instance, a man and a woman (who are unnamed in the record) from Mr. Nichols's place had been hanging around Latting's farm. According to neighbors, the fugitive couple hid during the day and came to the house at night for provisions, sleeping in a hut with the wood choppers. It is difficult to determine from the surviving record whether they were fugitives from Nichols, temporarily enjoying Latting's protection, or hired bondspeople who cooperated with Latting to avoid returning "home." The details are murky, but according to those looking to corroborate the charges Benjamin Miles levied against him, Latting planned to take the two downriver and either sell them or hire them out, declaring offhand that it would be no one's business if he made a few hundred dollars off of them. The man and woman looked to have found themselves pinned between Latting's scheme and the hands of Nichols's overseer, named Freeman, who eventually arrived to recapture them. While Freeman overtook the woman, the man slipped from his clutches, escaping with his gun. Latting's angry neighbors claimed that this man found his way back to Latting, "lurking" and "skulking" around the area, sometimes on Latting's horse, but Latting denied having anything to do with him.[37] Unfortunately, the eventual fate of the enslaved people in these cases is obscured. The disputes clearly immediately related to the respective parties' personal and political concerns, but both sagas proclaim the ways in which Arkansas's rugged physical and social landscape made enslaved people's whereabouts crucial to both whites' profits and the order of their society. That ruggedness also facilitated opportunities for enslaved people, whose unauthorized movements frayed whites' mastery of land and labor.[38]

Because their bodies held such high cash value, enslaved men and women found themselves caught up in all manner of deals and disputes, sometimes as the subject of the feud and other times simply as valuable leverage. An enslaved man named Murray found himself detained by the superior court of Arkansas Territory in February 1827 in Pulaski County. He was held in slavery by Alexander W. Mitchell of Little Rock. When Wright Daniel sued Mitchell, claiming that he had not been paid for work he performed using his own team, wagon, and bondspeople from his "Big Rock" farm in present-day North Little Rock, the sheriff took Murray, along with four mules and one horse, as security to ensure that Mitchell would appear in court to answer the suit. Murray likely remained in the custody of the sheriff until the case was dismissed in April 1828, upon Daniel's death.[39]

The whereabouts of enslaved people figured prominently in disputes between white men relating to their economic ventures in the territory, disrupting business partnerships, dividing property holders, and prompting men to close ranks with their factions. George Bentley went into business with William Montgomery, David Miller, and Robert Crittenden in 1822. The partners planned to establish a store. They gave

Bentley the use of a boat and someone to pilot it at the mouth of the White River. For his part, Bentley's obligation included transportation of goods, merchandise, and some bondspeople to Cadron on the Arkansas River. His cargo included about fifteen tons of goods belonging to the venture and several enslaved people, along with about thirty tons of his own belongings and, finally, his own family with their bondspeople. However, Bentley dragged his feet, lingering for sixty days without departing. His partners (represented by Chester Ashley, a slaveholding attorney who would become a prominent politician) successfully sued, claiming Bentley's delay in delivering the labor and goods cost them $2,000, an incredible sum at the time.[40] A few years later, Bentley went head-to-head with Ashley again when Oppolis (also known as Opp) escaped from him. Bentley blamed William Woodruff, an ally of Ashley's. Bentley claimed that Woodruff, best known as the founder and longtime editor of the *Arkansas Gazette*, but who was just as much a slaver and land speculator, had intercepted Opp (valued at $700) and held him for his own benefit despite knowing where Opp rightfully belonged. Woodruff and his friend Chester Ashley had sent Opp for hire to the Elliott family, who lived six miles south of Little Rock. When Bentley sued, the pair claimed the whole affair as a lawful mistake.[41] Black men like Opp (as well as black women) only enriched white settlers of territorial Arkansas when forced into place at the right time at the right task. Whites who failed to fulfill those obligations suffered sharp repercussions while blacks who fled their enslavers within Arkansas undermined whites' ability to both profit from and control the landscape.

Adding to whites' apprehensions, the morass attracted slavery's fugitives from other parts of the Old Southwest. In the 1820s, the *Gazette* complained of runaways "lurking" around Little Rock, hiding in the "thickets" during the day, sneaking into town at night to steal provisions, and craftily avoiding the posses sent to subdue them. Arkansas's ground proved a magnet for escapees from the cotton South's more settled areas. In just one example, Jack ran away from James K. Polk's plantation in Sommerville, Tennessee, and headed for the morass on November 28, 1833. He had broken into a store five miles from Polk's plantation, stealing flour, sugar, tobacco, and whiskey. In retaliation, the overseer, Ephraim Beanland, laid two hundred lashes on Jack's back, intermittently salting his flesh. When Jack fled, the future president enlisted his network of relatives and friends in Tennessee and Mississippi to help, leading to Jack's apprehension in Helena a few weeks later. After his recapture, Jack beat the overseer on the head with a stick and in turn received three stab wounds from Beanland, who ultimately chained him up. Unsurprisingly, Jack escaped again, this time heading for the notorious outlaws' lair in Arkansas called Shawnee Village. Knowing the morass's reputation as well as anyone in west Tennessee, Beanland wrote pessimistically to Polk, "I tell you the fact I donte thin[k]e that you will ever git him" from that "den of thieves." Jack didn't go alone. This time Phil, a twenty-two-year-old enslaved blacksmith and shoemaker from a neighboring plantation, accompanied him. After this second recapture, Jack's reputation in the Tennessee neighborhood became such that Polk's overseer advised him to sell Jack because the neighbors feared him and his influence on other bondspeople to flee west.[42]

It would be a mistake to assume that most of territorial Arkansas's fugitives were men. In 1834, Margery and Clarissa fled from the clutches of A. H. Sevier (future senator, and leader of Arkansas's Democratic political machine called "the Family"), each with a young child in tow. In 1831, authorities in St. Francis County apprehended Bill and Haney, man and wife, along with Ben and Hetty, man and wife, and Hetty's sister Nancy, all ranging in age from nineteen to thirty-five years old. The group fled from Julius Bettis at Bayou Fiddle about thirty-five miles north of Grand Gulf, Mississippi. Another man had accompanied them, but he split off from the group about forty-five miles below Arkansas Post. The men and women carried a rifle, a shotgun, and ten dollars that they took with them from Bettis's place, along with some clothing, another shotgun, a bag of shot, and two axes purloined along the way.[43]

These were exactly the kinds of excursions on the part of African Americans that contributed to eastern Arkansas's reputation as the "morass" and undermined white mastery on the cotton frontier. Newspaper editors on the east side of the Mississippi referred to Arkansas's ground as "infest[ed]," where thieves and outcasts became "impregnable in their marshy skulking places, as to make their detection almost impossible" when they retreated to the "almost impervious canebrakes." "Slave-stealing" vagabonds like the notorious "land pirate" John Murrell thrived. Enslaved people who considered making a run for it to the woods and swamps of Arkansas proved to be "unsteady asset[s]" for slaveholders, and Murrell had a knack for finding them. Murrell and his ring ran a Mississippi River operation that included robbing flatboats that ran aground in eastern Arkansas, fraud, and counterfeit activities, often using runaways from slavery in Arkansas for their own gains—acting in league with them for a time only to sell them as chattel later. This last might have been the model Andrew Latting used in southeast

Arkansas in the 1810s. Because whites found it difficult to conceive of black people as initiating and executing their own designs, they were eager to believe in conspiracies, making bogeymen out of Murrell and other whites with base reputations. This tension came to a head at the end of Arkansas's territorial period. Murrell's famous trial in 1835, on the heels of Nat Turner's 1831 revolt, represented somewhat of a turning point for slavery and mastery on the cotton frontier. Increasingly paranoid whites began to suspect that in addition to the "slave-stealers," horse thieves, and gamblers disordering Arkansas's landscape, perhaps even abolitionists lurked there and in other parts of the Old Southwest. If operations like Murrell's went unchecked, the cotton frontier could never be safe for slavery. Black appropriation of the swamps and cane of the morass complicated white designs for territorial Arkansas, showing them what would happen if they failed to make order out of the wilderness.[44]

As in the creation of Arkansas Territory, Arkansas the state came into existence as an event that secured slavery. By the early 1830s, as the population of Arkansas neared the 40,000 needed for statehood admission, politicians touted their ability and willingness to bring Arkansas out of her territorial status as soon as possible. Arkansas's leaders anticipated a struggle. No slave state had attempted to enter the union since Missouri, and the balance of twelve slave states to twelve free states secured a measure of harmony in the Senate.[45] Among Arkansas's territorial leaders, perhaps its delegate to Congress, Ambrose Sevier, pushed hardest for statehood. He was born in Tennessee to prominent political connections, that state's first governor. Sevier was a member of "the Family," a political faction of territorial Arkansas held together by family ties of blood and marriage, and protected that faction's interests in pressing for statehood. Arkansas's status as a state rather than a territory would better enable the Family to support Richard M. Johnson, the brother of Sevier's father-in-law (Benjamin Johnson), in his upcoming bid for the presidency. The Family's political interests merged with its interest in ensuring the security of slavery. Sevier argued that as soon as Arkansas had the appropriate population and a treasury free of dangerous debt, it should apply. When Michigan applied for consideration in 1834, Sevier pressed more urgently.[46] If Congress admitted Michigan, the balance between free and slave states in the Senate would be upset. Florida was preparing to apply for admission as a slave state, and if it succeeded, Arkansas would have to wait indefinitely for a "sister state," as the next probable free state, Wisconsin, remained far from ready. Arkansas needed to apply for statehood quickly with Michigan in order to be considered in the near future. Prostatehood Arkansans initiated the process of electing a constitutional convention so that the new state's constitution would be ready to submit with the bill rather than coming later. Some opposed this initiative, declaring it illegal, but the states of Vermont, Kentucky, and Maine had all entered the union in the same fashion.[47]

The politics of slavery created division among white Arkansans in the statehood process. More whites agreed on Arkansas's right to begin writing a constitution than on how the writers should be chosen. Prominent white Ozarkers, who knew that slaveholders from plantation districts with higher enslaved populations would dominate state politics otherwise, desired representation in the convention to be based on free white population alone. This push did not mean that slavery's existence on the hillsides was less significant or that it did not profit slaveholders. It instead reflected the simple calculus that counting enslaved people toward apportionment would give large slaveholding parts of Arkansas a greater voice in the creation of Arkansas's constitution, which would surely set up the same system for Arkansas's statehouse, much as the U.S. Constitution's Three-Fifths Compromise imbalanced the U.S. Congress in favor of slaveholding states. Prominent southern whites, in turn, demanded that the enslaved population count toward apportionment.[48] After all, they argued, the inclusion of the enslaved population in Arkansas's overall count helped make statehood possible in the first place. In the end, politicians created a formula in which delegates to the convention were chosen fairly evenly across the state, but controversy continued as the constitutional committees debated the issue of legislative representation in the future state of Arkansas. Ultimately, the state general assembly's representation relied on the white population alone.[49]

White Arkansans designed their state constitution to tame the morass. As it defined Arkansas as a place and a society, the fresh founding document protected and promoted mastery. Only a few provisions of the constitution dealt with slavery, but they were foundational and in line with the provisions of other slaveholding states. The general assembly claimed the authority to prevent the entrance of bondspeople into the state who had committed crimes in other states or the entrance of enslaved people "for the purpose of speculation, or as an article of trade or merchandise." These measures intended to prevent "bad slaves" from entering Arkansas and keep unscrupulous speculators at bay. Policymakers did not object to the trafficking of African American people on principle but sought control over what *kind* of people came into the state. The constitution forbade the emancipation of bondspeople without the consent of the slaveholder and directed that enslaved people be treated "humanely." In addition, the constitution guaranteed the right of enslaved people to an impartial jury and state-appointed counsel. The constitution also protected the right to human property by newcomers but did not ban free blacks from the state. Defining Arkansas's social and racial landscape, the state's founders altered their original phrase "That all men are born equally free and independent and have certain inherent and indefeasible rights" to "That all free men, when they form a social compact are equal, and have certain inherent and indefeasible rights." People imprisoned as chattel could not enter social compacts and did not have inherent rights. Civilizing Arkansas's swamps and forests meant reinforcing its labor regime and racial order.[50]

As the bill to admit Arkansas with this constitution was reviewed in Washington, some proposed amendments that would have limited slavery there were defeated, including a proposal by Representative (and former president) John Quincy Adams that the state's power to limit emancipation be stricken from its constitution. On June 15, 1836, President Andrew Jackson signed the bill admitting Arkansas into the union. Soon after, many Americans felt the pinch of the Panic of 1837, which hit Arkansas particularly hard due to the doomed speculative scheme known as the Real Estate Bank. Although the debacle surely slowed yeoman immigration and added to Arkansas's chaotic reputation, the planter class managed to cushion the blow of the economic downturn.[51]

Meanwhile, the institution of slavery solidified to the southwest, surrounding enslaved Arkansans with ground hostile to freedom. The province of Texas had fought for independence from Mexico—in great part to allow the spread of American slavery there to continue unchecked—in a backlash to Mexican regulations against American immigration. The resulting Lone Star Republic moved quickly to protect slavery and wrote into its constitution a prohibition on any law that might prevent immigrants from importing bondspeople. In 1845, Arkansas's neighbor entered the union as a quickly growing cotton empire and a destination for many Arkansas bondspeople who were forced to resettle with westward-moving whites. By 1850, enslaved people in Texas numbered more than 58,000, about 10,000 more than inhabited Arkansas, a population that grew to over 180,000 in Texas by 1860, much greater than Arkansas's 111,000 at that count.[52]

Ultimately, black life in the morass proved dangerous, despite its ample cover for runaways. Exploited, degraded, and sick from the displacement to what nineteenth-century Americans viewed as the edge of their mapped civilization, African Arkansans struggled to survive the social and natural landscape. The record provides only brief glimpses of their travails. A "decrepit old Negro man" suffered insults and a beating in northeast Arkansas by Lawrence County lawyer Seaborn Sneed when he had dared enter the room where Sneed "was shuffling his books." Among others, three enslaved people, held by Ferobee, Rightor, and Irwin, died of cholera in Helena on the Mississippi River in the summer of 1833. On a trip back from New Orleans with John Pyeatt and John B. Mosby, a bondsman of Pulaski County, central Arkansas, suffered severe frostbite after being forced to walk ninety miles across the wet and partially frozen southern prairie. Ben, enslaved by Antoine Barraque, a Frenchman and founder of New Gascony, lost his life during the height of Osage rage against whites and other native groups in Arkansas; he was one of seven men killed in a hunting party made up of whites and Quapaws that was ambushed in western Arkansas Territory.[53] Many more experienced dramas and suffered degradations that will never be known. Yet black Arkansans continued to frustrate their enslavers, including the most prominent founders of Arkansas's white society, who worked harder and harder to convert Arkansas's ground from the morass into an empire of the second slavery.[54] Enslaved people's mobility and their claims of Arkansas's vast uncultivated zones showed whites what would happen if they did not enforce their sense of order on the social and natural landscape.

Arkansas as a place was also an event, a happening, an action undertaken by its inhabitants who competed to shape its boundaries and landscape, both social and natural. Whites drew physical, social, and legal lines to create meaning out of the swath of the Trans-Mississippi that came to encompass several geographies. Whether they imagined Arkansas's ground as prime for corn, cotton, or mercantile endeavors, whites' use of enslaved labor provided an economic foundation. Like its becoming as a territory, Arkansas's formation as a state was predicated on the use of enslaved people to civilize and improve the landscape, a process dependent on the ability to control their movements and alienate them from the land. Captive laborers served as tools of settlement, evidence of civilization, and currency to facilitate exchange. The process was neither linear nor wholly successful. As Valencius's work demonstrates, nineteenth-century migrants, both captive and free, thought of western lands in terms of "newness." This newness, this becoming, must have filled the thoughts of the inhabitants who created Arkansas, as they asked: What happened? What will happen? What is this place? What will it be? Their conflicting answers to those questions required ongoing "fabrication and reinforcement." It is to these actions that the next chapter turns.[55]

2 /   Domains

Parmelia may or may not have wanted to go, but she had little choice. She said her goodbyes to Kentucky and headed to central Arkansas (Conway County) in 1840 at the behest of the Menifee family to wait on and "nurse" her enslaver's female relative there. Nimrod Menifee, to whom she must now answer, practiced medicine but, like so many other slaveholders, originally built his wealth on land speculation. The Menifee family enjoyed economic comfort because in previous years the doctor had bought up land along the Arkansas River and sold it in lots to create the town of Lewisburg (near present-day Morrilton). As the patriarch of that branch of the family, Menifee held responsibility for Parmelia, although she did not permanently reside with him and he never legally claimed ownership of her. Parmelia often fell ill, so she was periodically sent to his place for treatment. Parmelia endured the disorientation of the forced move from the border South to the cotton frontier as chattel, but she also navigated a shift from the "domain" of one enslaver's household to another's. On another level Parmelia lived subject to her "mistress's" judgment of her frailty and the doctor's sense of dominion over her person and her health. Parmelia seems to have lived and worked in a mostly domestic realm, a decidedly gendered one, and because so little record is left of her life, we can only imagine the ways in which she understood her new home and worked to carve out some breathing room.[1]

The day-to-day domains that enslaved Arkansans like Parmelia navigated were linked to their captors' efforts to subdue, order, and commodify Arkansas's ground. Boundaries connected to concepts of public, private, domestic, productive, cultivated, uncultivated, free, slave, white, and black defined points on this landscape, but their practical interactions created tensions between these ideals and realities on the ground. The "rules" were dictated by customs and laws that did not simply exist but had to be created and maintained. Bondspeople staked claims by making meaning of the spaces and places at the sites of their captivity and in their wider neighborhoods, working to master space in order to master self. In some instances black Arkansans shared whites' concepts of places but in most they diverged, most significantly by staking claims away from the fields.[2]

White deed holders, surveyors, speculators, and legislators carved up Arkansas's ground between the Mississippi River and Indian Territory in order to tame the landscape that most other Americans still saw as a morass. In making the case that parts of the South until the 1840s still had not fully shifted from what he called "wild" to "domestic" food, geographer Samuel Bowers Hilliard explained, "Parts of Georgia, central Alabama, Tennessee, most of Mississippi, and virtually all of Arkansas were considered wilderness and were avoided by all but the most adventurous travelers." The thick forests and swamps, perceived dead end created by the presence of Indian Territory to the west, and recent debt crisis kept Arkansas's ground from becoming as populated as its Trans-Mississippi neighbors in the antebellum period, which in turn meant that the landscape remained relatively uncultivated. Whites filed land deeds and grants with county courthouses to secure and organize the acreage enslaved people worked, but they also made claims as they presided over bondspeople's physical construction of the contexts of mastery and servitude—raising "big houses," felling trees, draining swamps, and laying out fences. Arkansans lived out Lefebvre's contention that people's ideas of a place are informed by production and consumption, while their production and consumption are in turn informed by place. For whites, the landscape they created represented a picturesque achievement in society, as well as in their business and personal lives. When overseer John Pelham proclaimed his desire to continue to work on Rice Ballard's Chicot County plantation, he declared he wanted to stay and continue to develop the riverside site, "for it is a beauty."[3]

Landowners received some assistance in gaining potential farmland via federal policy facilitating the sale and drainage of eastern Arkansas's extensive swamps. The federal Swamp Land Acts of 1849 and 1850 turned over publicly owned swampland to states to stimulate their agricultural development. The U.S. government granted the state of Arkansas more than eight million acres of public swampland. Arkansas, Florida, and Louisiana received much more swampland reclamation acreage than other states, more than thirty-seven million acres together. The program assisted enterprising agriculturalists like planter, politician, and later Civil War general Gideon Pillow. The state sold the land granted by the federal government and used the proceeds to issue scrip to pay landowners to drain it and improve levees.[4] Landowners profited while shrinking zones long held to be unhealthy and disorderly.

As slaveholders populated the new ground, enslaved people endured a seismic forced migration from the upper South. Ira Berlin termed this upheaval the "second Middle Passage" in order to invoke the horror and disorientation felt by millions of Africans in earlier generations forced from their native shores to the Americas. As generations of tobacco cultivation exhausted eastern soil, places like Virginia and Maryland became exporters of enslaved people to fresh ground for cotton—western regions of Tennessee and Mississippi, southern Missouri, east Texas, and Arkansas. As the artificial ecosystem created in the eastern South failed, planters and smaller-scale farmers set out to create a new one.[5] Between 1820, the first census since Arkansas became a stand-alone territory, and 1860, the last census taken while American slavery still existed, probably around 900,000 black men and women made this move from the seaboard South to newer cotton states. Between 1810 and 1860, more than 80,000 enslaved people were forced into Arkansas. By 1860, enslaved Arkansans numbered more than 111,000 (an increase of 136% in ten years), amounting to one-quarter of the state's population, held by more than 11,000 enslavers.[6] When white slaveholders, often young men financially backed by their families and connections in the more populated eastern South, sought Arkansas's fresh fertile ground enslaved people suffered. This migration often happened in multiple steps. James Trulock, of a wealthy South Carolina family, forced forty men and women from southwestern Georgia to Jefferson County, Arkansas. Dave, a blacksmith, was forced to make the move when a wealthy family expanded their reach across the South. A planter's son picked Dave out from among his father's holdings in Georgia, taking him with others to Mississippi and then Arkansas before settling in Louisiana.[7]

The slave trade engineered more than half of this forced migration, and maybe as much as 70 percent of it. New Orleans supplied countless men and women to power Arkansas's farms and plantations, including Rora and Susan, who made the journey up to Henry Shugart's farm from New Orleans in 1839, followed by Nat, Martha, and Charity the next spring.[8]

But while New Orleans and Memphis were the two main large-scale slave-trading points for Arkansas, Mississippi River towns like Vicksburg figured in as well, and private slave sales took place all over. Indeed, all enslavers must be recognized as slave traders, by virtue of dealing in humans as property, whether they operated commercially or not. James Hines Trulock's cousin Uriah Trulock traded slaves from Virginia and South Carolina to Arkansas. After moving to Arkansas, James purchased Peter from him in February 1846, eighteen-year-old Charles (bought in Chester, South Carolina), and Maria and her children Martha, Jim, Sam, and Nancy (bought in King George County, Virginia) sometime between 1848 and 1854. Such deals drove the development of antebellum America by allowing for the rapid expansion of the South and providing the labor force to pump out raw material needed by textile factories in the North and in Great Britain.[9] Therefore, when Molly Finley's father was sold in Kentucky to traders who then sold him in Tennessee to Baker Jones, who brought him to Arkansas, he moved in service of a global market.[10] The trade in Arkansas may not have been as visible as in more populated parts of the South. But, for example, partners Templeman and Richardson, with connections to New Orleans, kept a "negro yard" (reportedly plagued with whooping cough) in Pine Bluff. Other traders offered men, women, and children for sale in Camden. Years later, Solomon Lambert recoiled at the memory of a Camden slave-trading yard bounded by high fences, calling it "the worst thing I ever seen or heard tell of in my life."[11] Wealthy absentee planter Rice C. Ballard got his start in the slave trade with partners that included Franklin and Armfield and went on to create Ballard, Franklin, and Company, leveraging the profits from those ventures to establish a multistate plantation empire supported by the labor of bondspeople in Mississippi and Louisiana and the seventy-eight people he forced to Arkansas. Other entrepreneurs like Ballard merged the trading and employment of people as property.[12]

Black men and women experienced displacement as whites fled from debts and other obligations, like estate settlements, often as the result of a combination of several factors, including gifting, flash sales by those needing quick cash, and dispersal when dead planters' heirs fought over their estates.[13] White women should be understood not only as complicit but as active agents in the uprooting of enslaved families to the cotton frontier. Court records show them as calculating as men in their financial dealings with slave property, especially when widowed.[14] In 1826, Thomas Humphreys willed Cynthia and her unborn children to his daughter Susan Mills in Kentucky. Four years later, Cynthia was forced to move with Susan and her husband, Ambrose Mills, to southeastern Arkansas. Whatever sentimental feelings Susan might have had toward Cynthia faded three years later when Ambrose died. Cynthia and her eleven-year-old child sold for $500; what became of them is unknown.[15]

Whatever the immediate causes for black men's and women's forced move to and through Arkansas—white migration, the domestic trade, individual sale, escape from or satisfaction of creditors, or family property disputes—overland journeys from the seaboard South to the Trans-Mississippi cotton frontier created monumental landmarks in their memories. The migration's "uneven violence," as Valencius termed it, created a gulf between their new and previous lives. Cora Scroggins remembered: "My mother spoke of her one long journey on the steamboat and stagecoach. That was when she was brought to Arkansas. It made a memorable picture in her mind." For men, women, and children who suffered this displacement, the journey marked the beginning of a process of finding meaning and rootedness in their new surroundings with little to connect them to the lives they previously knew.[16] A lucky few could grasp threads tying them to the communities and neighborhoods they left behind. Jenny, forced to southwest Arkansas with the Allen family of North Carolina, enjoyed bits of news about her family and friends via whites' letters to "Aunt Jenny," as they called her, long after arriving at the cotton frontier. Although it is not clear whether Jenny could read or whether someone read the notes to her and recorded her replies, Jenny no doubt passed the news on to the other enslaved people who had come to Arkansas with the Allens. Most displaced bondspeople did not have the chance to send missives back and forth (or visit, which the letters suggest Jenny may have eventually done), but many did experience the forced migration in groups with others they knew, whether family, friends, or acquaintances. When enslaved people made these moves with people they knew, they carried a portion of their sense of place and rootedness with them in the people and relationships that survived the transition. And they could begin again together.[17]

Most who endured the relocation experienced massive disruption. Like Jenny, Harve Osborne came to Arkansas from North Carolina, but his story contrasts sharply with Jenny's. He was born in 1825 on the Osborne farm near Asheville, North Carolina, only a short time and distance from Jenny. Morgan Osborne, seeking opportunities to profit from cotton cultivation in the west, drove Harve and others to Arkansas in 1850. After more than a month of travel, Morgan Osborne settled on a large tract of land along the White River about ten miles from Batesville, in northeast Arkansas. Upon arrival, Osborne hired Harve out for a year to another plantation, perhaps while he prepared to begin the new operation or because he needed some cash to get started. Harve had become temporarily separated from the few people he may have known from his home back east and never saw his parents again.[18] Such abrupt disconnections were the norm, and stories of family separations abound in ex-slave interviews. T. W. Cotton's mother left behind a son in Virginia whom she never saw again after the move to Arkansas, while Molly Hudgen's mother suffered permanent separation from her family in North Carolina.[19] Moriah was married to a man named John before the Bullocks moved her, their children, and several other men and women from North Carolina to Dallas County, Arkansas. John, enslaved by a different family, had to say goodbye to his wife and daughters, Polly and Jenny. Moriah probably already knew Billy, another captive of the Bullocks, who had also left behind a spouse and endured the additional agony of separation from his own children. Moriah and Billy each intimately understood the other's pain and, finding solace in each other, married. They patched together a new sense of home on the cotton frontier.[20]

Most bondspeople forced out to Arkansas created agricultural operations from scratch. When Emmeline Waddell described being forced out to Arkansas in 1851—at about twenty-five years old—she recounted ferrying across the Mississippi River and trekking through the "bad and boggy woods" to present-day Lonoke County. Women prepared hoe-cakes, fried deer meat, and made coffee for supper, then slept in the wagons while the men "kept watch for wildlife." It was during this initial setup of slaveholding farms that the material lives of slavers and enslaved differed least. Practicality trumped performance of wealth and status in the temporary setup, and slaveholders later looked to upgrade to designs that better reflected their visions for their dominion. Until then, black and white alike endured a "spartan like pioneer experience."[21] Some scholars have referred to the dynamic created by this pioneer situation as a "sawbuck equality" as slaveholder and enslaved lived closely, laboring at the same work and doing without the same comforts. This thinning of the barriers between them did not eliminate bondspeople's status in servitude; it merely put each side in closer proximity to the other's experience.[22]

The first thing enslaved people were made to do was clear out space in Arkansas's woods and cane. "The country was kind of wild in those days," Ellen Briggs Thompson described it. Even Little Rock settlers remembered burning fires to scare away predators. Molly Finley's father had to clear land around the Arkansas River for the Jones family, who owned a home in Tennessee and looked to expand into Arkansas. He worked with other bondspeople in "huddles" presided over by armed overseers who protected the plantation outpost from "panther, bears, and wildcats." Enslaved pioneers prepared the land for cultivation at the same time that they prepared the farm for habitation. James Gill described how enslaved men and women arrived in Phillips County from Alabama in late January and set right to work building the Gill farm, where cane gave way to cotton: "the hands was put right to work clearin' land and buildin' cabins.... they just slashed the cane and deadened the timber and when cotton plantin' time come the cane was layin' there on the ground crisp dry and they set fire to it and burned it off clean and then planted the crops." Elsewhere in the same county, enslaved people and their white enslavers, the Wilborns, slept in tents until their log homes were ready.[23] Eight miles from Arkadelphia in south Arkansas, enslaved people built the Bullock plantation bit by bit. They began with the construction of a weaving room, which served as whites' quarters while bondspeople's cabins and the main house were being built. In the Ozarks in the valley between Rhea's Mill and Prairie Grove, William and Eliza Wilson lived in a crude log cabin while the years-long work of a more elaborate home progressed. The eleven bondspeople they held resided in two nearby cabins.[24]

Enslaved people cleared the way for and built the structures of power that would order their everyday lives. The household, "a spatial unit defined by property," organized family life and agricultural production in the nineteenth century. The foundation of the unit was land, which gave proprietors rights to the labor of their dependents on farms of all sizes.[25] The arrangements of farms and plantations reflected slavers' sense of order, reinforcing difference between those who were made to serve and those being served. Arkansans' homesteads were made up of sets of unspoken signifiers. The use of objects and space reinforced the habits and interactions that bolstered slavery's regime on the ground. This use was more about difference and status than separation. When possible, slaveholdings' physical organization kept the unpleasant sights, smells, and grit of bondspeople's *work* away from slaveholders but not necessarily their persons—constant service required close proximity. The typical layout of a larger slaveholding farm placed the white residence close to but distinct from enslaved people's cabins with easy access to fields. Small and large holdings alike defined status in this way. As Stephanie McCurry put it, "Power and authority clearly had spatial grounding."

Bondspeople had to not only negotiate that grounding but physically construct it.[26]

Establishing the household and agricultural units engaged enslaved people in removing trees and profitably processing that wood either for sale or for construction materials in order to, as Erin Mauldin phrased it, "gradually simplify ecosystems." This work dominated enslaved people's working hours in these days but continued to be a major aspect of their labor on operations of all sizes due to shifting cultivation. After bondspeople brought down larger trees, they heaped them into piles. In the process of "rolling logs," they used chains to drag the timber into piles where it could be burned. This work could be dangerous: Jim Marsh split his big toe, "the whole length of it," at that task in January 1849.[27] The practice of "deadening" timber provided a labor-saving but slower method for the removal of larger trees. Workers girdled the trees by making a deep cut around the circumference, causing them to slowly die. First, the limbs began to drop off, providing firewood. After a few years, a tree would die and fall over without leaving a stump in the ground. Enslaved farmers planted the first crop in a new field around these large, slowly dying trees.[28] Henry Morton Stanley described the system of clearing pine from Major Ingraham's plantation in Saline County, where he watched men "chopping up timber into portable or rollable logs, some were 'toting' logs to the blazing piles, others rolled them hand over hand to the fires, and each gang chanted heartily as it toiled." What Stanley interpreted as slaves' enjoyment of invigorating exercise actually represented the degree to which enslaved woodsmen had fine-tuned the process at hand, working in rhythm as a unit. Demanding group tasks required cooperation and the ability to overcome not only tired limbs but mental exhaustion as well.[29]

As slaveholding agricultural operations took shape, their forms mapped race and status on the landscape. Many formerly enslaved people recalled long "lanes" leading up to the farms and plantations where their families were held. These drives were one of the ways that slaveholders sought to lay out the domains of their status in the antebellum period in what Kimberly Smith has termed a "processional landscape."[30] Slaveholdings with proprietors present were anchored by a "big house"—the center of white family life and mastery, crafted with the better materials available and placed on healthier, higher elevation. If the slaveholding held more than a few bondspeople, they were housed separately in modest cabins in view of the "big house." On large plantations, whites' abodes would be surrounded by rows or organized clusters of cabins housing enslaved people. The quarters that radiated from the main part of a plantation were also part of the performance of planters' wealth. Overseer John Pelham declared that the new quarters planned for R. C. Ballard's Mississippi River–fronted Wagram plantation would be "handsome. Not excelled by any on the river." Pelham described the planned domain of the plantation (which Ballard intended to give his daughter) in Chicot County, southeast Arkansas: "I send you my plan of arranging the quarters which I think you will like as every house can be seen from the back gallery and I think they look well. The plantation cookhouse is convenient."[31] R. C. Smith described the Smith farm on which he labored in northwest Arkansas. While the natural landscape differed greatly between the two sites, the same essential themes existed on both Smith's Ozark farm and the Mississippi River plantation:

> Our family didn't live in no quarters but we lived in one open room of the big house. The house was built in the shape of an "L." A big white house, three rooms across the front and three in the "L." We lived in the back one of the "L." The kitchen was away from the house but was joined to it by a plank walk. All around the house was big trees. . . . They made heavy shade . . . they was a row of cedars from the gate to the house. The house was built in a rocky place and up above the house pappy built a stone wall and we had a garden on the level place along side of the wall. We called it the high place. There was enough level ground for a nice size garden. We also had a peach and apple orchard.[32]

Formerly enslaved people recalled variations of the same basic setup. The Ford family lived in a big white house right on the main road to Arkansas City, while those they enslaved, including Sarah Winston's family, lived in cabins across the field. For many, the "big house" did not figure into their politics of space in the same way, however, if their enslavers were absentee owners as at Wagram. Katie Rowe lived in log quarters close to Bois d'Arc Creek in southwest Arkansas, on the edge of the Little River bottom. An overseer lived there while the owner of the operation resided in a house in town with more enslaved people.[33] At the Bullock plantation in Dallas County, the cabins for enslaved people sat 600 to 800 feet from the main house, with gardens adjoining each cabin. Rose, who cared for the children during the day, had a home to herself set off from the other quarters. At Wagram, enslaved families made do with a rougher setup, sheltered in shacks (without gardens) that they slowly replaced with sturdier structures as the plantation took shape.[34]

After the contours of a slaveholding homestead or plantation took on greater definition, the yard—the open space around the "big house" and stretching between that symbol of slavers' power and the slave quarters—became a type of small domain for enslaved people held there. Many required tasks took place in that space as men and women stacked wood, fed poultry and stock, tended fires, boiled clothes, and processed carcasses. As many enslaved people passed through on their various business, a "communal spirit" and sense of ownership could arise in that space. This was especially true for black children, who often played in the yard, enjoying the few and soon to fade carefree moments that their restricted lives under slavery would allow. If enslaved people were allowed to cultivate gardens, those would be close to their quarters for easy tending. The greater space of a larger slaveholding farm was dotted with various outbuildings, such as a smokehouse (a symbol of whites' control over food stores), a gin house, a corn crib, barns, tool sheds, or even a weaving house. Symbols of subjugation also pervaded the space within a plantation complex, such as an overseer's bell house, stocks, or a jail to confine defiant bondspeople. Slaveholders interred their captives' bodies at the edges of farms and plantations in crude plots, many of which will never be identified, often with little or no ceremony.[35]

Kitchens were the most ubiquitous structures on slaveholding farms besides slave cabins—even more than "big houses" because while not all enslavers lived on-site, all enslaved people (and overseers) had to eat. Kitchens, where black women sweltered over hot fires, wrestled with heavy iron pots, and toiled at some of the messiest and thankless tasks, were almost universally separated from whites' homes, at least by a hall or breezeway. In R. C. Smith's recollection, a plank walk stretched between house and kitchen—to keep the feet that were constantly coming in and out of the kitchen from touching the ground and soiling the floor of the main house. While kitchens, distinct outbuildings sometimes with their own attached porch, often sat apart from whites' daily domestic existence, the food preparation required there was intimate, closely tying enslaved cooks to their enslavers. This physical separation helped prevent a potential kitchen fire from threatening the slaveholders' residence. But beyond concerns of property damage and whites' safety, the designated separation of the kitchen space and its workers created social distance and hierarchy ordering how enslaved people and their enslavers interacted. Cooks often slept there. Even when loosely attached to the house by a walkway, the separated kitchen symbolized the distance between those being served and those serving—no matter how many times a white "mistress" entered that building. The farther the kitchen sat from the "big house," however, the more frequently enslaved cooks might be able to enjoy deep breaths away from white supervision. Archaeological excavation in Washington, southwest Arkansas, revealed a slaveholder's kitchen separated into two parts divided by a chimney, a design traditionally found in both European and African architecture. In one side of the building a bondswoman prepared food for the white family and her fellow bondspeople, while the other half served as both storage and her quarters.[36] Molly Finley remembered white preachers teaching enslaved believers that if "you obey your master, if you don't steal, if you tell no stories" then they could look forward to the everlasting reward of toiling in the "kitchen of heaven." Slaveholders' certainty of their domestic dominions reached even to the hereafter.[37]

The work of those who labored within their enslaver's home—usually a log cabin or modest frame dwelling—maintained the space and material that sustained white slaveholding households on the southern periphery. Although their work was not to clear the forests and build plantation homes, domestics constructed much of what white mastery meant. For whites who lived on-site, clean floors, hot fires, full tables, pampered guests, and all of the finishing touches and pretty details that occupied domestic workers' waking hours propped up whites' sense of mastery—be it over grand cotton estates or corn and cattle operations—even if they were usually looking out from isolated log houses carved out of the Arkansas backwoods. Not only that, as Thavolia Glymph writes, whites intended black women's work in slaveholding homes to support a particular model of civilization via domesticity. Ironically, although black women helped construct the order upon which this civilization depended, as black women they represented to whites the antithesis of civilization. This process was heavily gendered because it was usually white women who ruled the homes in which black women worked. The experience in Arkansas was no exception to Elizabeth Fox-Genovese's succinct explanation of this domain: "The privileged roles and identities of slaveholding women depended upon the oppression of slave women, and the slave women knew it."[38] Eliza and Betsey were two of those women. In 1847, southwest Arkansas small slaveholder Simon Sanders's first wife, Zenobia, died. For seven years, Betsey (who had been given to Zenobia when she married), who was probably in her forties at the time, and Eliza, around twenty years old, would have managed the domestic affairs of the household in the town of Washington, caring for Sanders's three daughters until he remarried. Eliza had to start again in another household in 1853 when Sanders gave her to his daughter Sarah when she married.[39]

Countless girls grew up shadowing their mothers and grandmothers at this work, many of whom inherited the burden when they came of age. Senia Rassberry and her sister both spent their days in the Hall house along the Arkansas River in Jefferson County, following their mother's lead and assisting her as she was made to serve Jack Hall's family. Eva Strayhorn experienced a similar childhood upriver, helping her mother cook on the Newton place in Clarksville, Johnson County. Although her mother's forced fieldwork robbed Ellen Briggs Thompson of enough quality time with her, Thompson spent her childhood in the "big house" with her grandmother, who cooked, made clothing, and performed other domestic chores for the Mitchell family of Hempstead County. Although the children and grandchildren of enslaved domestic workers may have been underfoot, the fact that they were able to spend time with and look out for those youngsters as they went about their work was significant. However, enslaved domestic workers endured the expectation to put the needs of the white family before their own.[40] At the Bullocks' Sylvan Home plantation in Dallas County, Moriah cooked (assisted by her daughter Polly), Aunt Clay weaved, Emily and Leah worked as maids, and Lisa was assigned as nurse to Harriet, one of the white children. Although Anthony Kaye has demonstrated that domestic service was often "a family trust," in which bondswomen passed down their domestic skills and responsibilities to their children and nieces, many recently established plantations of Arkansas had not been settled long enough to create the "Gordian knot" of generational family domestic labor relationships that Kaye found in some places around Natchez. Men, usually elderly, performed domestic work, too. "Uncle Tony" Wadd worked small jobs around the house in Arkansas County, while Edmund's tasks kept him in and around the Brown home at Camden.[41]

Domestic servitude involved difficult work under close watch because of its setting in white spaces and because of the visibility of the "products" of that labor. Housework encompassed cooking, sewing, weaving, cleaning, washing clothes, keeping fires, caring for the white children, and more. Some slavers expected one or two women to do it all. Laura Shelton's mother and grandmother both worked in the house, her mother performing chores like churning and caring for children, while her grandmother prepared the food for everyone on the plantation. It would be wrong to imagine domestic work as a strictly indoor affair. The tasks of enslaved domestic workers sent them running back and forth to the "barn, orchard, milk house, and things like that" and including laboring over outside fires.[42]

Domestic work was intimate work; domestic workers' duties brought them especially close to whites' lives and bodies but miles away from their status as white proprietors. Harriet Daniel, the planter's daughter at Sylvan Home, recalled that "we children had never been required to wash our own faces"; slave women and girls were assigned to do it for them.[43] Whites considered these bondspeople responsible for their physical comfort both at home and in their travels. Rob in Chicot County was entrusted with protecting the white mistress Miriam Hilliard when her husband was out of town overnight. She slept with a knife under her pillow and set Rob outside her bedroom door as "sentinel."[44]

Bondspeople who had been performing domestic work for the same white family for a long time were carriers of that white family's culture and lore, whether they liked it or not. Moriah the cook was the one who related much of what Harriet Daniel knew about her own deceased mother.[45] Because their job sites were almost constantly under the noses of masters and mistresses, domestics could come under punishment often, or even lose their place. Annie Page remembered the cruel attack she endured as a girl at the hands of her enslaver, William Jimmerson, when she fell asleep fanning him and his wife, Lucy, as they napped. "I guess I must a nodded and let the fan drop down in his face," she recalled. "He jumped up and pressed his thumbs on my eyes till they was all bloodshot and when he let loose I fell to the floor." When Richard, the personal bodyservant of John P. Walworth, fell out of favor in March 1849 he was sent to the fields, to be replaced by Charles. It is not known what Richard did to incur Walworth's wrath, nor whether he and Charles actually preferred house or field.[46]

Not only did domestic workers become intimately acquainted with whites' bodies and business; their work in the household placed them squarely in the middle of white domestic politics. While enslaved people who spent their time in the fields periodically tested new overseers, those in the house spent their lives navigating the demands and quirks of a growing white family until they were sold or gifted to another one. As slavers imagined a particular domestic realm, they expected enslaved people to create and maintain it. Women working at Sylvan Home waited anxiously to see who their new "mistress" would be when the widowed Bullock, whose temper flared more often after his wife died, decided to shop around for a new wife—"on the carpet," as the bondswomen whispered to each other. He brought in a girl the same age as one of his daughters and expected the house servants to make sure "everything was done to please" them. Keeping up a party atmosphere for the young girls involved a lot work, and sometimes with little notice, meaning that "All day there was a great stir of baking and cleaning going on in the house."[47] Domestics at the Hilliard place came under increased pressure after Miriam Hilliard returned from a trip to New Orleans where she enjoyed opulent dinners and observed the beautiful homes of family and friends. Domestic workers paid the price for her desire to compete with her sister-in-law when the visit was reciprocated. We can imagine how Hilliard projected her insecurities on her captive workforce when she confided in her diary, "I am on the rack all the time for fear my 'table d hote' will not be prepared and served to please her." When the visitors from New Orleans finally arrived, Hilliard resolved to "put best foot foremost." Hilliard's obsession reveals the heavy lifting that domestic spaces worked by black women did in creating the ideal of domesticity and civilization to which white planter households aspired. She badgered the bondswomen into cooking as luscious a feast as could be mustered on the Arkansas frontier and demanded they spruce up the entire house after she found it wanting. Hilliard wrote, "Three servants scrubbing & dusting all day—and after all, nothing a whit nicer looking." Rob relieved some of the pressure on the women working in Hilliard's house; he saved the day, as far as Miriam Hilliard was concerned, and ingratiated himself to his enslavers when he brought in a "tremendous" turtle and half a dozen "magnificent" trout for the meal. The guests were treated to turtle soup and a fish dinner that "went off admirably" in Miriam Hilliard's eyes. Those working in and around the Hilliard house—like countless others held in cotton frontier households—paid in sweat for their enslaver's quest to impress visitors with her domestic domain.[48]

Indeed, although the domestic landscape had its disadvantages, enslaved people who spent the majority of their time in and near the "big house" encountered unique opportunities to play whites off each other to their own advantage within that realm. In a dramatic and well-documented turn of events in the 1840s, a woman named Mary maneuvered herself into a position of power within the Chicot County household of her enslaver, William Rose, by exploiting the weaknesses and insecurities of his northern-born wife, Nancy. Mary had been running William Rose's domestic affairs on a small plantation with a captive workforce of around twenty bondspeople ever since he moved there in 1839. Nancy arrived in 1841, and Mary picked up on the scorn William quickly developed for his new wife, who suffered frequent headaches and often napped. Mary routinely ignored the newcomer's commands, confident that William would not enforce them. Mary's insubordination developed into blatant contempt for the interloper, as she intimidated and provoked Nancy. Nancy eventually filed for divorce, an extreme course of action for the time, claiming that the hostility in the household made it impossible for her to uphold her duties as a planter's wife. Her testimony claims that William clearly preferred Mary's attentions (waiting on him, removing his boots, fetching his tea) and that William and Mary embarrassed Nancy in front of her guests with their open contempt for her. Indeed, a neighbor claimed that she had seen bruises on Nancy's arms left by Mary's grip. Nancy also claimed that William encouraged *all* of the bondspeople to disobey her, making life at the plantation unbearable and her role as the white female authority in the household impossible. Mary had instilled such fear in Nancy that she sometimes refused to eat Mary's cooking, afraid that she would be poisoned. Although the nature of William and Mary's relationship is not fully clear—Nancy never accused him of engaging in sexual activity with Mary—it is clear that Mary, even as an enslaved black woman, gained more respect and autonomy from William Rose in the household than did his wife. William viewed his Yankee wife as out of place and unfit for the domestic task of "plantation mistress," even referring to her as a "lazy trifling white woman." Mary cultivated an opposite image, successfully defending a measure of power within the Rose home.[49]

Although Arkansans, like other nineteenth-century Americans, understood the home as a space in which women held certain influence, domestic power was not the only command white women had over enslaved people's destinies. As Stephanie Jones-Rogers has detailed, women dealt in human chattel, too. In divorce they might receive alimony in the form of enslaved people. White women sometimes demanded the amount of their dower in cash extracted from their dead husband's estate—money that might have to come from the sale of enslaved people. When Dave and Sarah of Phillips County were sold, widow Elizabeth Bostick was entitled to one-third of their value as her dower. In the 1820s in South Carolina, a bondswoman named Rose was gifted to a young white woman by her family when she married. After the family moved to Arkansas, the bride became widowed and had Rose hidden out of state so as not to lose her property when the estate's assets (which included Rose) would be sold to pay her deceased husband's debts. White women were savvy to the laws and stakes when it came to owning people as property and they protected their interests in them with as much energy as men. Their reach, then, was not limited to the "big house" or kitchens or restricted to association with men's ownership of bondspeople.[50]

The "big house" represented enslavers' power over blacks' time and bodies. It was a place to perform both mastery and white supremacy. On a whim, slaveholders might demand that their captive labor force get dressed up and file into the house for presentation to guests or to witness the white family's big events, like weddings or funerals. When a guest underwent a religious experience at the Bullock plantation in the middle of the night, whites called up enslaved men and women from their repose in their own cabins into the big house to sing and pray. After the white family was satisfied, they were allowed to go back to bed. Katie Arbery remembered how Paul McCall used to summon the enslaved children to him when he wanted to see them dance for his entertainment. McCall got out his fiddle and called, "'You little devils, come up here and dance,' and have us marchin."[51] When it struck his fancy, Dan Wilborn grabbed his fiddle and marched down to the slave cabins on his farm in Phillips County and demanded that bondspeople drop what they were doing and dance for his amusement, sometimes for hours. While some of the people held there might have enjoyed a festive evening, albeit a condescending one, the point is that their enslaver required it of them. It is easy for us to imagine the exasperation of men and women who sought nothing more than a quiet evening with their families away from the prying eyes and ears of whites girding for humiliation when they saw old man Wilborn marching down from the "big house" with his fiddle.[52]

When they gathered, whites enjoyed making enslaved people—whom they stereotyped as superstitious—the butt of their jokes. After bringing in the entirety of the slave community of the Hogan and Stroud families to witness a marriage in the big log house, whites' sense of festivity included a prank awaiting enslaved people when they returned to their dirt-floored cabins. A few of the men had placed carved pumpkins lit with burning pine knots inside to terrify the startled bondspeople. Even though these kinds of pranks might have elicited some laughs out of enslaved people, they knew that the "fun" was designed to be one-sided and could not be reciprocated.[53] Although the white residence was the epicenter of slaveholders' power, there was nothing preventing such exhibitions of domestic dominion from reaching beyond the "big house" and into the quarters.

Some slaveholders claimed their dominion over enslaved people via sexual exploitation. While not all enslavers raped bondspeople, as Calvin Schermerhorn put it, "slavery took place on a landscape of sexual violence. . . . sexual assault established mastery." While both genders were violated, we know more about sexual violence aimed at bondswomen. Close proximity made those who did domestic work more vulnerable, but no bondspeople's cabins were safe. As Amy Murrell Taylor put it, "Rape was thus a spatial problem—made possible by the proximity of space made all the more horrific by the violation of space." Their attachment to and concern for a place was not enough to make their homes safe.[54] Their status as chattel made it impossible for people held in slavery to truly consent to sexual relationships with those who held them in slavery. Elisha Worthington, the wealthiest planter in Arkansas, is probably the best-known slaveholder who fathered children with an enslaved woman. Worthington had two children, Martha and James Mason, with a woman named Cynthia. Worthington's marriage to Mary Chinn of Kentucky lasted only six months before she left him and annulled the marriage based on claims that he was an adulterer. Worthington sent James to school at Oberlin, then Paris. In 1860, James returned to Chicot County, followed by Martha in 1861, where they remained through the Civil War.[55] When interviewed by WPA writers, Augustus Robinson said his enslaver in Calhoun County was also his father (which led to his exile at the hands of the slaveholder's wife). Joseph Samuel Badgett's father was the father of his mother's enslaver. And Minnie Johnson Stewart said her mother Mahala McElroy's father was also her enslaver, Wiley McElroy.[56]

Beyond the homes and outbuildings lay the fields that demanded most enslaved Arkansans' time. Here enslaved people reorganized nature to alter the landscape for production. The South as a whole changed as a result of this labor, but the landscape of Arkansas underwent especially dramatic transformation. For example, Mississippians had added a million and a half improved acres between the census enumerations of 1850 and 1860. While the people of Arkansas cleared fewer in that time, the increase amounted to a *doubling* of the state's improved farmland in ten years. As lightning-fast as bondspeople planted Arkansas's ground, its landscape remained much less developed than that of neighboring states.[57] For example, while Arkansas and Mississippi were home to a comparable number of farms in 1860 (33,190 in Arkansas and 37,007 in Mississippi), much less of Arkansas's acreage had been improved. Arkansas showed fewer than two million improved acres, in contrast to more than five million in Mississippi. Further, Arkansas's improved acreage in farmland amounted to only about 6 percent of the state's land that year, while around 16 percent of Mississippi's land was improved in farms at the same time.[58]

Although the spaces and routines of production are covered more thoroughly in Chapter 4, "Flesh and Fiber," some essential points about that realm should be presented here. The growing cultivated zones of slaveholding farms were the main sites of production, the "factory floor," on small farms and plantations alike. Enslavers closely monitored what happened in that lucrative domain, whether they presided from plantation galleries or worked alongside a few captive laborers. Planter Sterling Cockrill had specific tips for upholding order and ensuring productivity: "The first place for an overseer is to let the women alone, and not be too intimate with the women and to manage niggers is to go among the niggers and to treat them well at the start and to get them on the right side of you, and then commence tightening up the strings. Be punctual with them and never talk to them only about their business. Don't allow them to run about nights. Make it as a rule to *lick* him *shure*—it is Twenty Five licks with a cow hide, keep all other niggers off."[59]

Slavers enforced order in the fields with the whip. Violence and threats of violence maintained the boundaries. While slaps, cuffs, and kicks could take place anywhere, whites enacted systematic whippings outside because of the bloody mess they created. An overseer pulled Minnie Johnson Stewart's mother to the ground by her hair and beat her until blood ran out of her nose when she was only thirteen years old. Because whites drove slave labor with violence, it is no surprise that enslaved people's resistance often took a violent form. Men and women alike threatened bodily harm to enslavers and their hired managers. Whites knew on what dangerous ground they trod by using the lash. One overseer explained that he was reluctant to whip because it "might be attended to with evil consequences."[60] According to one family story, a "riding boss" prepared to whip Mandy Buford's pregnant sister on the ground by digging a hole to lay her facedown for the lashing. Buford prevented the attack by threatening to chop him up with her hoe. Enslaved people did not stop at threats, though, and slew masters and overseers from time to time. In 1849, a St. Francis County bondswoman snuck up behind her master, James Calvert, and beat him to death with a mallet "that had been used for beating hominy." Outbursts like Mandy Buford's set limits on how far some whites were willing to go to extract labor, while deaths like Calvert's struck fear in the hearts of whites that statutes and ordinances could never completely extinguish.[61]

Gender created domains. The most physically demanding field work was first designated to men, not because black women's bodies were seen as delicate but because black men's bodies were believed to be even stronger and inherently designed for such work in hot weather. Bondspeople completed tasks and received training according to gendered divisions of labor, but slaveholders and their managers did not shrink from using any and all labor available when needed, such as harvest season. Steven Hahn describes divisions of labor as "far less pronounced" on smaller farms, which includes most of Arkansas's slaveholdings, but sources show that the boundaries could be fairly fluid on larger operations, too.[62] Although they did have a limited sense of black womanhood in terms of their reproductive potential and lesser physical strength, whites did not consider black women's bodies and mental constitutions to have the same sort of frailty that they ascribed to white women. Women's grit despite heavy demands on their physical labor is a clear source of pride in stories of slavery documented by the WPA in the 1930s. Lucindy Allison declared that her "Ma was sure 'nough [a] field hand" and that her Aunt Mandy kept pace with the men in the field, speculating that Mandy may have been under extra pressure to exert herself in the field because she never bore children. All three of Adrianna Kerns's aunts worked in the fields and "could handle a plow and roll logs as well as any man." Sallie Crane's words speak for themselves: "I had to do anything that came up—thrashing wheat, sawing logs with a wristband on, lifting logs, splitting rails. Women in them days wasn't tender like they is now. They would call on you to work like men and you better work too."[63]

While whites usually ordered bondspeople's work by gender, skills separated their tasks as well, creating a measure of hierarchy. At the Shugart farm, Tom's carpentry work included roofing, building repairs, and other projects like constructing a sled for hauling water. Ginnis, on that same farm, created a coal kiln as one of his projects.[64] Some bondspeople with knowledge, training, or experience in specific tasks, like blacksmithing or weaving, received and capitalized on the trust and privileges bestowed by whites who valued their talents. Here, gender decided who had the opportunity to learn certain skills. Shops for metal or woodworking were men's domains. Enslaved women were prevented from acquiring these skills and thus blocked from their potential advantages. For example, enslaved men with those skills were more likely to encounter chances to leave the farm. Bondspeople with especially sought-after abilities and knowledge, however, endured closer attention from enslavers and their managers. For example, R. C. Ballard expected overseers to send detailed reports of the work done by the carpenters he deployed to Chicot County.[65] While skilled bondspeople had specific duties related to their expertise, this did not necessarily tie them completely to their forges and workbenches to the exclusion of the fields. Rarely was an enslaved person on a farm fully exempt from the rhythm demanded by the crop. Skilled bondspeople produced the most wealth when at their craft, but whites wanted all hands to the crop, especially if unexpected weather or some other crisis occurred; possessing skills did not quite mean "an emancipation from the fields."[66]

The life and work of the domestic domain and the cultivated spaces cannot be disentangled. Women on large operations juggled field and house work. When John Brown's daughter married, he planned to wait until the crop was finished before sending Martha and her child, Sally, to wait on her. Until then, he moved Nancy from the field to help in the Brown home.[67] Women often spent the colder months between crops spinning thread or making cloth. When the time was right, whites sent them back into the fields to make room for the new crop.[68] In preparation for a semiannual distribution of clothing, overseers might set women to sewing in the spring while others plowed. One overseer explained: "The sewing is far behind. Sarah has made three garments per day ever since I came up. I find she will need help and my womens work is up so I shall start Caroline to help sew tomorrow and I think it likely I had better start two others. I am in the habit of giving out summer clothes 1st Sunday of April and winter clothes 1st Sunday Oct. or Novr. I can now spare three or four women very well to help."[69] At Wagram the responsibility of sewing lay primarily with Sarah, but other women helped her again for a few weeks in April in order to get the winter clothes ready before the field work resumed. The overseer explained, "When the crop gets ready for work there will be no time to help her and attend to other work."[70]

To escape from the oppressive domains of house and field, enslaved people staked their own claims, consistently seeking refuge in Arkansas's abundant woods, canebrakes, and swamps, if only temporarily. Indeed, for enslavers and bondspeople alike, the phrase "in the woods" was synonymous with runaways, who more often laid out for a limited time rather than undertaking long-distance flight. The woods, brush, and swamps around farms and plantations were the closest and easiest hiding places for those who absconded. On a Chicot County plantation, Franklin exasperated a "mistress" who noted that he was "in the woods" one summer. Charlie McClendon's father laid out "in the woods" of Jefferson County for at least a month on one occasion. Another man on the same place, Miles Johnson, "just stayed in the woods," stealing away so often that his enslaver eventually decided to sell him off.[71] Enslaved people as property were so valuable, and whites' certainty of someone retaking them so solid, that slaveholders routinely bought and sold enslaved people while they were in the woods. John Allen sold Bennet, who was at large, to Robert Bates for $550 in 1833. E. A. More put a notification in the paper declaring that he had sold a man named Frank, currently "in the woods," and would no longer be offering a reward for him.[72] Bill ran away from Shugart's plantation so often that Shugart called him "Old Runaway Bill." When a man named George fled Matthew Leeper's place near Fayetteville, Leeper appealed to friends and neighbors like David Walker to help when no one else would, exclaiming, "good wishes with nothing else is of but little use to a man when his Negro is in the bushes.... The scoundrel George being aware of my necessities has taken advantage of them.... Of my intended movements I say nothing publicly with a hope that George will think I have left the country." By cautioning discretion Leeper acknowledged enslaved people's extensive communication networks.[73]

A major aspect that made Arkansas's vast forested zones appealing to escapees and truants was the fact that pursuers could not follow very quickly on horseback—a symbol of whites' enforcement. In swamps, of which eastern Arkansas hosted many, that mode of transportation was impossible. In wet or brushy zones it was also easier for runaways to hear the approach of posses and their dogs. Walter Johnson has described the runaways' woods as an "aural" landscape where escapees enjoyed an auditory advantage.[74]

Enslaved people brought food and provisions to their friends in the woods. In Dallas County, June and Damon ran away together into the canebrake across the Ouachita River from the Bullock plantation and hid in a small cave they had dug into the earth. They foraged for food but also relied on what their friends brought out to their hiding place. In fact, to catch the two runaways, Bullock's men simply followed the trail left in the cane by other enslaved people from Bullock's place who had been provisioning them. (Later, June ran away alone and drowned trying to cross the river. Decades later, Harriet Bailey Bullock Daniel included June's fate in a disturbing poem she composed about the bondspeople on the plantation: "June was the smithy and ever gave trouble, 'til he swam in the river and sank with a bubble.")[75]

Peter Brown recalled a significant story of his parents' short-term escape to the woods in Phillips County. When the Hunts forced his pregnant mother to submit to grueling physical labor, his father "stole her out" to the canebrake to spare her health and protect their unborn baby. According to Brown's account, when a panther stalked his parents in the night, his father killed it with a bowie knife. Afterward, his mother gave birth in the canebrake. The Browns made a deal with their enslaver, who desired the father's labor back in the fields as soon as possible and who appreciated the reproduction of his human property. Thenceforward, as long as Brown's father promised to "stay out of the woods," his mother (now recognized as a "good breeder") would no longer have to work in the fields. Whether the details of the remarkable story are true or exaggerated by a proud son, Brown's story suggests the power of the bargaining chip that bondspeople wielded when they fled into the surrounding forests. We may also interpret the tale as supporting Kimberly Smith's argument that because alienation from power over landscape lay at the heart of their bondage, enslaved people linked mastery of land and nature to mastery of self. In Brown's story, his parents achieved some small measure of both.[76]

Most who ran away stayed in the woods only a short time, but a few made longer journeys, striking out for permanent freedom. Three men who ran away from slavery in Desha County arrived at the home of Dr. C. W. Deane, near Fayetteville, some three hundred miles away, in 1859 on their way out of slave country. Bob had been sold by Deane to someone in Memphis then sold again to Desha County. Authorities suspected him of being the culprit in a recently reported murder of a white man in south Arkansas who had attempted to arrest a runaway slave. Cameron had been held by George Graddy of Desha. The third man, whose name is unknown, had been claimed by J. P. Johnson of Desha. After arriving at Deane's—Bob's former neighborhood—they "made their appearances at the kitchens of J. W. Washbourne and Judge Davis, asking for ammunition, etc." Heading to the kitchens would have meant stopping in at information posts and centers of provision. According to the newspaper report, the men claimed they were going to "make a rise" and head to Kansas, which had been embroiled in a bloody fight over the future of slavery there. The men from Desha County had "stationed themselves in a very dense thicket" a mile from Fayetteville along the road to Mount Comfort. A white posse gathered round and flushed them out of their base. When the fugitives refused to surrender, whites opened fire, killing Bob and wounding the other two, who were taken to jail.[77] In another example, Nelson Hackett famously fled Arkansas for Canada in 1841. Held as butler and valet to Alfred Wallace in Washington County, Hackett escaped on Wallace's horse while on a trip with him to central Arkansas, successfully reaching Sandwich, Ontario. Hackett's flight roused abolitionists and created an international incident over the extradition of escapees from slavery before he was ultimately recaptured and pressed back into slavery. Because bondspeople had already experienced the long passage to the edge of the South, their geographic knowledge and travel experience may have emboldened those living in and around Arkansas to flee long distances.[78]

More often enslaved people coped with their day-to-day challenges in safer ways, and their time away from the sites of production did not always indicate fundamental subversion. Uncultivated zones offered some distance from whites' gaze as bondspeople's everyday activities took them there. Springs and creeks, for example, were sites for relative leisure. Nelson Taylor Densen said, "My first clear memory is playing as a child on the banks of the river near whar I lived in Arkansas." Molly Finley remembered how water brought black men and women together near the Jones place in Arkansas County: "We lived around Hanniberry Creek. It was a pretty lake of water.... We fished and waded and washed."[79] Interaction with those zones just outside the bounds of the fields in the immediate vicinity of the farm, more so than with the deep woods and swamps, was more likely to involve whites. Enslaved people could not expect that their daytime movements in these areas would occur without the company of white adults or children. And because their time was not their own, activities in the natural landscape surrounding farms and fields during the day came with responsibilities to whites. Law Lewis, for example, taught his enslaver's sons to hunt and swim. The Cornwall children routinely accompanied enslaved teens and children to the creek near the farm. In one instance the two white boys joined Jimmy and Ranza on an excursion to the creek "for amusement" to "bathe and swim." The younger of the two white children, a small boy less than four years old, fell in and was rescued by Ranza, who thereafter kept the child playing with him in the shallow area.[80]

However, Arkansas's forested and swampy zones away from farms and fields did not offer an unqualified haven. Sometimes the uncultivated landscape provided the backdrop for brutality. When Woodruff Norseworthy took an enslaved man off into the woods of Jefferson County to punish him for stealing a visitor's shirt, young Horatio Williams followed. He told an interviewer "he took that nigger down in the bottom and I crawled through the brush and watched. They tied his feet together over the limb and let his head hang down and beat him till the blood run down on the roots of that tree."[81]

As they navigated white domains and the forests and swamps that surrounded them, enslaved people constructed a sense of place and neighborhood. The geography of their community reached beyond the confines of the farm, creating a network that included adjoining farms or plantations as well as the creeks and hollers. Often the most unguarded activities took place in the latter. Anthony Taylor described the patchwork of ordered and "wild" space owned by the Bullocks: "Most of the farm was fur pine country land. There would be thirty or forty acres over here of cultivation and then thirty or forty acres over there of woods and so on." Bondspeople created meaning out of both types of spaces via sanctioned and secret movement. Planters perceived enslaved people's movement in the forests and cane without their permission as chaos, while for enslaved people it created order and meaning. The knowledge that bondspeople like Taylor gathered about the swaths of cultivated and wooded zones around them combined to form a sense of neighborhood.[82]

In Jefferson County, enslaved people held by the Cockrills and Armstrongs lived in a neighborhood dominated by the complex of adjoining plantations knit together by enslavers who were cousins and enslaved who intermarried. Also in Jefferson County, bondspeople held by the Sullivans and Rectors comingled and became as related by kinship as the two white families.[83] The populations of Arkansas's plantation zones offered more chances to socialize, while smaller holdings offered fewer fellow bondspeople to befriend. For example, the populated black social life in the neighborhood that James Milo Alexander described in Phillips County near Helena was built by a concentration of bondspeople that did not exist in many other parts of Arkansas. Alexander had many relatives at the neighboring Joseph Deputy plantation whom he visited two or three times a week. Years later he recalled the ability of bondspeople at the Deputy place to hold a barbecue that included visitors from the enslaved populations of two other plantations.[84] Steven Hahn explains how ties of friendship and family weaved together over generations in the older areas of the South: "On large plantations with deep generational roots, kinship could eventually have linked an individual slave to more than three-quarters of those resident." But on more recently settled portions of the southern periphery, like Arkansas, bondspeople's social lives on farms of all sizes lacked those "deep generational roots" and they created their sense of neighborhood from a much more recent patchwork of alliances, connections, and kinship.[85]

A central part of the domain that enslaved people created for themselves was their religious community. Some of this world was visible to and sanctioned by whites. In black church services, Ellen Briggs Thompson commented, "whites didn't care what they had. They would help prepare for it." She added that enslaved people in her neighborhood might also get passes to attend church meetings nearby in Center Point and Arkadelphia, where they would listen to black preachers. Bondspeople held on Abraham Stover's place north of Van Buren might have been more typical. Whites did not bar them from singing and praying on the place, and if they wanted to hear an additional sermon, they simply walked to the white church on Sundays to listen outside. Others recalled using the same building as white worshippers after they finished their service. Molly Finley described alternating black and white church services in Arkansas County, adding that sometimes black preachers could come to the place and preach to the enslaved faithful. Some bondspeople routinely attended white churches, while others only did so occasionally.[86]

Religious practice with whites in white spaces, however, marked inequality. For example, men and women held by Arkadelphia preacher and lawyer Strotter Adams were *required* to attend church with him on Sundays. Even for those who may have indeed wanted to attend, the demand that they do so added just one more layer to whites' imposition on their lives and movement. Inside the church building, whites used space to ensure that religious observances reinforced mastery. Sweetie Ivery Wagoner's mother had to go to the white church every Sunday with the white "mistress," wife of Newt Tittsworth, and was made to sit "back over on one side of the seat rows."[87] Enslaved people and whites attended services together at the Presbyterian Church in Arkadelphia, but bondspeople listened from the back of the sanctuary in elevated seating. (A partition in the middle of the pews also separated white men and women. It is not clear whether black men and women were similarly separated.) Thus, worship with whites in churches or farmyards could not hold the meaning for enslaved people that their own meetings away from whites did.[88]

A yearly religious meeting in Manchester, south Arkansas, centered on African Americans but was overseen by whites. White preacher Andrew Hunter held this popular two-week revival designed for both free and enslaved black Arkansans in a church building normally used for interracial Sunday services. Though Hunter requested the presence of whites, perhaps to ease any misgivings or suspicions, his targeted souls were black. While free and enslaved African American Arkansans filed into the building, whites took their places as chaperones and spectators in the back pews or listened through open windows while seated outside in their carriages. The white observers took on a condescending attitude, as Harriet Bailey Bullock Daniel remembered: "I fear the white people who sat at the windows enjoyed the talk and actions of the colored people more than they did the preaching." The white preacher instructed churchgoers, but at least one black preacher from a neighboring plantation, named Lany Strong, addressed them, too. The services included energetic "shouting" and emotional prayers from the "mourners bench," including those offered up by Billy, respected by all as an "exhorter." Men and women whose worship became very boisterous received a reprimand from the preacher, who admonished one woman caught up in an emotional description of heaven's glory. According to Daniel's account, he scolded, "You stop jumping up there like a chicken with its head cut off!"[89] Pate Newton's neighborhood in the Arkansas River Valley also held yearly religious meetings for bondspeople.[90]

Traveling openly to church meetings placed enslaved people on public paths rather than hidden back ways to secret meetings. Affronted by their boldness, some whites tried to monitor and limit the mobility that came with bondspeople's gathering for religious services. A group of enslaved men and women returning from a religious meeting—which may have been the one in Manchester—encountered a belligerent patrol and incurred lasting physical injury. The white men beat them so severely that their enslaver sued for the loss of their labor during their recovery from the attack. The members of the patrol seemed to be particularly incensed that the group had been stopping along the way to socialize, "strolling about, from one house to another," on their way home.[91] When the legal battle escalated to the Arkansas Supreme Court, the justices reminded the court of "an implied license for them [bondspeople] to attend religious meetings, when conducted in an orderly manner, on Sunday."[92] In the pews and on the roads, then, enslaved believers faced reminders that although they might be neither slave nor free but "one in Christ Jesus," whites would fight the autonomy that communities of faith offered.[93]

No wonder the appeal, then, of hidden, secretly held religious meetups out of sight of whites, where enslaved people could practice in a less careful, guarded manner. The brush and cane at the edges of farms and plantations provided perfect cover. Bondspeople who were not allowed by whites to worship, who could not worship in the style they preferred, or who simply sought to hide their relationship with the sacred used the woods and brush to house spiritual activity away from whites' gaze. O. W. Green's family secretly met to hear preaching and to "shout"—participate in charismatic worship—in the woods with other bondspeople even though they risked severe punishment if discovered. If the "old masta" of the Mobley place in Bradley County, where Green's family lived, "found you shoutin' he burnt your hand," he recalled. Green's grandmother had suffered this excruciating punishment several times. Far from chaotic "wilderness" to those who made use of them, the woods became sanctified sites where black men and women could worship freely out of sight and earshot of whites.[94] In this activity, enslaved people sought a "reconsecration of their own spaces." George Newton's mother, a house worker at the Newton plantation, recalled intimate practices of faith necessitated by white attempts to control religious activity: "Colored folks could fiddle and dance all they pleased, but weren't allowed to sing and pray. She say sometimes they go out and turn the wash pot bottom upwards so the echo go under the pot an' the white folks couldn't hear the songs. I've heared mother tell that a hundred times."[95] Carrying a pot to the edge of the farm or plantation and positioning it so as to stifle the sounds of prayer or song helped alleviate the pressures whites placed on black faith. Bondspeople who were forbidden from possessing Bibles or who wanted to protect the content of their prayers for freedom covertly continued their practice. Enslaved worshippers held strong beliefs about Christian salvation that might clash with whites'. The Bullock family, for example, allowed their captive Christians to be "sprinkled" in baptism but forbade immersion. Bullock's daughter later recalled, "Some of them secretly lamented this. Aunt Rose said folks could not go to heaven unless they went under water." While Daniel did not report any bondspeople breaking this ban, it makes sense that the fiercest believers in immersion would have. Daniel did write that "when the war was over and our slaves were set free, all of them went down to the river and were immersed."[96]

The map of enslaved people's neighborhoods and community activity did not completely exclude all whites. Cautious friendships emerged between some bondspeople and nonslaveholding whites in their neighborhood.[97] The desire to relieve the work routine with a bit of music and booze could find them in common cause. While "much of the convivial drinking between slaves and poor whites took place in the predominantly masculine realm of southern grog shops," such places were harder to find on the southern margins. Drinking and gambling involving bondspeople and poor whites in Arkansas were probably more often enjoyed in private gatherings, and these activities were most safely conducted outside public spaces.[98] Bondspeople might socialize with a mixed group on the outskirts of towns and farms, as did a Desha County man, unnamed in the record, who camped with a group of white men and Native Americans one night. The white men prevailed upon him to play a fiddle at a gathering with a group of Indians who were passing through. The whites wanted to "have a frolic with the Indian women." But the native men became offended by the conduct of the white men and "drove them off," while the bondsman remained. He slept in a tent with an Indian man, but the two got into a fight sometime in the night, during which he killed the native man.[99] Such outcomes confirmed to enslavers the evils of interracial get-togethers. Laws against whites' activity in "harbor[ing] or entertain[ing]" bondspeople sought to limit that kind of interaction. In fact, crime involving whites and enslaved people is what generated many of the available records on enslaved-white socialization. For example, prosecutions of rape against two enslaved men, Frank and Dennis, along with a white man named Jeduthan Day confirm socialization between enslaved black men and white men (the three men were together whether or not they committed the crime) and confirmed for whites their fears of the "evil" accompanying such ties. In short, the safest spaces for whites and blacks to socialize or trade lay outside public view.[100]

But for the slaveholding class, including yeoman farmers, white labor had its uses, especially if the work required might endanger valuable enslaved bodies. Thus, white hired hands often shared spaces in work with enslaved people on Arkansas's farms and plantations. This was a more common and intimate arrangement on smaller operations, a group to which most of Arkansas's slaveholding farms belonged. White laborers came and went often on the Cornwalls' farm in Independence County. But faced with the prospect of hiring free labor for brick work at Wagram plantation, overseer John Pelham expressed concern that the men might stir up trouble.[101] White outsiders came onto farms to do temporary skilled jobs like stonework and carpentry. A thirty-five-year-old man enslaved at John F. Graham's farm in Clark County was the only bondsman on the place and lived there with four young white men working as "day laborers." Whites and enslaved laborers toiling in the fields together might avoid each other or strike up friendships. Charles Green Dortch and Adrianna Kerns were the grandchildren of a white man, Wilson Rainey, who worked on the Dortch plantation in Dallas County. He may have taken advantage of their grandmother, as he was described by their mother as "the meanest man in Dallas County."[102] More rarely, a larger white workforce entered the neighborhood. In February 1859, thirty Irish workers came into the Chicot County plantation community to drain part of Grand Lake to free up more cotton acreage. It is not known how much interaction they may have had with enslaved people in the area, but it would not have been surprising for them to cross paths, especially if some bondspeople assisted in that work.[103]

When whites assigned enslaved labor to public construction, they pulled enslaved people all over the state out of the fields and into more public places with whites other than their enslavers. County courts appointed overseers of roads who had the power to require the labor of free and enslaved men between sixteen and forty-five years of age.[104] This work included constructing bridges like the one that bondspeople held by John Brown spent several days building over Tulip Creek in late July and early August 1853.[105] Like other manual labor, this work did not necessarily exclude women, even if the county did not explicitly require the work of bondswomen. Lucindy Allison told a WPA interviewer that her mother helped "grade a hill" and build a road connecting towns in antebellum Arkansas.[106] The state required landowners along the Mississippi River or other rivers subject to overflow to maintain levees "against the ordinary wear of crawfish holes, cattle paths, and washing by river." County courts used levee taxes to support their construction and maintenance. When floods threatened, the levee commissioner had the power to require slaveholders in some places to provide hands for levee repair, on penalty of a fine of five dollars per day per hand refused.[107]

But to traverse the public roads that connected their neighborhoods, enslaved people needed written permission from enslavers or their proxies. Their appearance in public spaces was mostly intended to take place in the service of their enslavers, not of their own volition, and represented whites' desires and power and personhood by proxy, not their own. Sometimes they traveled down these dirt paths on foot or horseback as part of assigned tasks, such as picking up mail, purchasing goods in town on behalf of slaveholders, or running other errands. Men and women also secured written passes to attend social events by and for enslaved people, like dances. Not everyone enjoyed the same permissions from their enslavers, however. Some bondspeople simply never got to go anywhere for socialization, and men and women held in slavery in the mountainous less populated parts of Arkansas could only have dreamed of the size of the gatherings that those imprisoned in plantation districts cherished.[108] Those looking to attend nearby festivities could use the roads and public spaces to travel when their gatherings were permitted by whites but had to slip through the woods and brush for underground get-togethers; enslaved people's social lives existed as a mix of underground and visible, private and public. Many men and women accepted the risk in order to have as much fun together as possible. Mary

Ann Brooks, a self-styled "mighty dancer," declared that she danced all night long at times under slavery when she could; the rare run-ins with patrollers were worth it. Enslaved people looking to dance and sing in group celebration had to navigate their surroundings in order to decide what could be done in the open and what gatherings were best kept to the brush and woods in secret.[109]

Enslaved people also occupied the roads and woods between farms to visit sweethearts and spouses. Abroad marriages—unions between couples who lived on different farms—were common in areas with lower enslaved populations. John Holt's parents in Washington County were one such couple. Maintaining abroad relationships required devotion. Adrianna Kerns grew up hearing her mother tell the story of a man who would walk three to four miles to deliver food to his malnourished wife on another farm. Such unions created familial threads connecting plantations and farms into family plots as real to them as any deed of acreage filed by white landholders in the courthouse.[110] These threads in turn created a social foundation for their sense of rootedness.

For some, however, abroad marriages proved difficult to maintain. Eliza Bogan and Silas Small struggled to keep their relationship going on two different plantations. Silas suffered whippings from his enslaver and both had been caught by patrols before. Both plantation owners eventually allowed them to marry, marking the occasion with a "little tea party." Manuel frustrated his "mistress," Matilda Fulton, by insisting on visiting his wife often and for long periods of time. He was held by the Fultons just outside of Little Rock but split his time between their place and E. Ames's in town. By 1843, Ames either moved away or sold Manuel's love, leaving him heartbroken. Matilda, however, felt relief, writing, "I hope he will stay at home as he has no wife."[111] After a time, John W. of the Bozeman plantation eventually stopped visiting his wife, Rose, across the Ouachita River at the Bullock plantation and married someone on the place where he lived, leaving her grieving "like a widow" for years.[112] A benefit of abroad marriages was that enslaved people could avoid witnessing much of whites' domination over their spouses. However, this probably did not lead as many people to avoid marrying on their own places as John Blassingame asserted because couples' highest priority was to spend as much time together as possible.[113]

Enslaved Arkansans gained intimate knowledge of their neighborhoods, both the public and forested areas. Mart, held by the Bozeman family, would have learned the woods, streams, and blackland prairie surrounding his neighborhood south of Arkadelphia when he moved about in his work, but he also picked up such intelligence when he covered ground with whites on special errands. Mart sometimes accompanied white men in the area when they took long hikes for pleasure or to scope out potential real estate purchases. For example, one spring he joined the plantation's overseer, Henry Bozeman, and a neighbor, D. F. Ross, "a-surveying" down the Terre Noir Creek. Because he knew his way around, Mart may even have served as a guide. Nearby, some bondspeople held at the Bullock plantation periodically made the five-mile trip from Sylvan to Cassamassa for the mail, giving them time out and about in the countryside. The knowledge gained from these excursions armed bondspeople with valuable intelligence that they could use for themselves and pass on to others.[114]

A major utility of this activity was to spread information. The power of news, gossip, and warnings worked against the framework of mastery that whites created to rule slavery's frontier. The network did not destroy the institution but made it more bearable for those held in it. News, gossip, or messages of love and support could enhance black sociability or simply provide entertainment, while intelligence on the whereabouts of whites, their habits and idiosyncrasies, or general political news could ease the burdens of bondage. Even small bits of information helped enslaved people navigate their daily struggles with white individuals and families while informing their overall political consciousness. Thus, people held in slavery made sure to sweep the countryside for information through subtle listening and discreet sharing.[115] What one person picked up while setting out dinner could land on another's ears as they headed out to bring in the cows. Quick hushed whispers while working might do the trick, but to get information spread farther, enslaved people had to tap into the larger network outside whites' homes and fields. John Bates described the spread of news in Pulaski County: "nearly everybody knew what was goin on, news traveled purty fast, if the slaves couldn't get it to each other by gitten a pass, they would slip out after dark and go in to another plantation from the back way to get it scattered." For bondspeople, the "back way" through the trees and brush, away from roads and open spaces, served as the most efficient way to "scatter" intelligence.[116]

The information networks and pathways bondspeople strung between them added to their sense of place. While parties and gatherings brought people together and strengthened already existing connections, enslaved neighbors gained social capital within their own circles with news. Some bondspeople enjoyed special positions to get information and pass it along to friends and family. Skills and leadership in labor allowed some, such as drivers, to be especially well informed about what was going on in the master's house and in the surrounding neighborhood. Bondspeople with skills had the opportunity to travel throughout the neighborhood and could find out the most and pass it along to others. Because they were trained in jobs such as carriage drivers and blacksmiths, men had more access to news abroad than did women, while women working as maids and cooks enjoyed greater opportunities to overhear useful information at home.[117] In a disconnect that mirrored other cultural groups or disparities in power in other times and places, when enslaved people looked around, they viewed a different landscape than did whites, with different sets of significant points interconnected by their pipelines of information of both the social and subversive kind. Whites never gained full access to this map.[118]

Enslaved people's neighborhoods did not necessarily create solidarity or a monolithic community. Like everyone else, bondspeople were discerning in forging relationships. Some did not get along while others simply did not know each other very well. The existence of these loose connections matters because they remind us that not all enslaved people in a given neighborhood had to be worked meaningfully into each other's social circles for those circles to have significance. In his seventies, Aaron Williams testified of Simon Frazier and his family, "I knew him a little down in Bradley Co. where he lived about 6 miles from me. . . . I don't know any thing about his having a woman down in Bradley Co." In another interview, Williams said, "I just knew him when I saw him for 4 or 5 years before the war."[119] Adolph McGee's enslaver was related to Simon Frazier's, but Adolph and Simon did not meet each other until they both arrived in Pine Bluff and enlisted in the Union army.[120] Similarly, Wright Allen, who grew up three miles away from Frazier and recalled that "we had been raised together," did not know all the bondspeople held there.[121]

Some relationships in which parties knew each other quite well did not mean they got along all the time, or ever. As Jeff Forret's research has demonstrated, as in all human societies, sometimes the most intimate relationships were the most volatile. For example, a man held in slavery in Union County may have killed his wife with an ax in 1853. Personal disputes and angry outbursts frayed bondspeople's relationships and created enemies. Nat, of the Chicot County Hilliard plantation, was "attacked by four negroes" who did not seem to be from the same place, becoming "badly hurt." Nat survived but the injuries inflicted on him were serious. Miriam Hilliard noted that "the outer part of the skull is broken, but the inner plate is uninjured."[122] Things got even uglier at Wagram. It seems that George Mills was killed by fellow bondsmen. The overseer overheard married couple Cole and Marinda arguing about the incident, including Marinda's threats to expose what happened. The overseer then beat the rest of the information out of Cole. According to him, George Washington, Dick, and Miles killed George Mills and may have hidden his body on the plantation.[123]

As enslaved people created their own sense of meaning and power in place, sometimes they created tensions with whites other than their enslavers in their neighborhoods. These clashes were dangerous because they could threaten white supremacy. Enslaved people sometimes held disdain for whites in their communities and commonly measured them by their wealth, labeling them "poor white trash" or "quality." Community dynamics and the maintenance of white supremacy sometimes placed enslaved people and poor whites at odds.[124] This was true for neighbors in Lafayette County in southwestern Arkansas. Either the houses of Caroline Brown and William Madison Sims sat quite close, or the Browns occupied a home owned by Sims or on his property. Either way, the Brown children aggravated the neighboring enslaved people in 1854. Sarah, held by Sims, faced charges of "beat[ing], wound[ing], and ill treat[ing]" Mortica (or Mordecai) Brown, Caroline Brown's son. It seems that the little boy threw objects at Sarah, who grew angry and allegedly retaliated by throwing pieces of wood at the six-year-old, before picking the child up and slamming him onto the ground near a shop between the houses.[125]

Brown also pressed charges against a bondsman named Bone, who was similarly annoyed by her children. When William Sims and other white men left the premises, Bone chased the Brown children, cursing them and threatening to "whip them to death," according to Caroline. She claimed that when she asked what he was doing, Bone told her to "Go to hell, God damn you!" and declared that he was on "my master's own land" and that "I don't care for you, none of your children, nor nobody else." According to the story, Bone continued to stalk around the house, brandishing a stick and cursing until Mr. Brown came home, at which time Bone returned to Sims's house. These stories may have been inflated by Caroline, but both Sarah and Bone clearly resented their white neighbors, and it is telling that they both felt confident enough to challenge Brown and her children.[126] Bone's insistence that he could act as he pleased on "my master's own land" reflected a sense of dominion.

In a more obvious example, Wagoola, a man enslaved by Sarah Ridge of Benton County in northwest Arkansas, was accused of using his gun to shoot a neighbor's mare that had been trampling the fence.[127] Wagoola's frustration with the horse had been brewing and was known to neighbors, as shown in testimony of the incident: "A few days before the mare was shot, a witness heard Wagoola tell the plaintiff, that if he did not keep her [the mare] away from the defendant's plantation, he, Wagoola, would kill her."[128] Wagoola held a proprietary attitude toward the land he worked and lived on to the extent that he openly challenged a white neighbor.

While some fissures in the society of enslaved people's neighborhoods were of their own making, the disruption created by never-ending slave sales was not. Arrival to the Trans-Mississippi South did not signal the end of Arkansas bondspeople's displacement. They lived in constant fear that their connections would be sundered and their neighborhoods shredded by sales. Being held in chattel slavery meant that enslaved people were to have no "place" other than where slaveholders wanted them to be; the very meaning of chattel is "movable property." Thus the slave trade remained a perpetual threat to enslaved people's sense of rootedness because they amounted to easily transferable and easily liquidated assets. Even migration with white family groups rather than commercial traders did nothing to guarantee permanence in place. Enslavers routinely sold off men and women if they needed ready cash. William Brown recalled how, as a child, his mother explained to him the sight of enslaved people being driven as traders' wares from Cross County south to Louisiana. Katie Rowe described terrible scenes of separation seared into her memory: "I seen children sold off and the mammy not sold, and sometimes the mammy sold and a little baby kept on the place and give to another woman to raise. Them white folks didn't care nothing 'bout how the slaves grieved when they tore up a family."[129] A group of men and women held by John Humphries of Searcy, in White County, endured upheaval when the "old man" and his sons sold a group of them in New Orleans and brought a new group back in 1844. Nancy Snell Griffith's investigation of Independence County financial transactions involving slave property turned up several instances of enslaved people being mortgaged to distant firms. Had their enslavers not paid the debts, some of the men and women listed in Griffith's catalogue would have been claimed by firms as far away as Memphis and New Orleans.[130]

Whites shuffled these groups of bondspeople around as they uprooted their operations and started anew in another area or began endeavors other than farming. An investigation of the movement of slaveholders out of one southwest Arkansas County—Hempstead—serves to demonstrate how enslaved people were forced to move within Arkansas and beyond. If birthplaces listed on the U.S. Census are any indication, Bolin C. Phillips's family originated in Virginia, but he moved to Alabama, then Mississippi, and finally on to Hempstead County, Arkansas, holding at least one person in slavery there by 1847. Moving again, Phillips held more captives in Sevier County by 1850, relocating to another township within that county by 1860.[131] Robert T. Cook, a small slaveholder in Hempstead County in 1847, had moved to Clark County and increased his captive labor force to eleven by 1850. Somewhere along the way, those who had already been moved had to endure the upheaval of sale again, because by 1860 Cook lived in Arkadelphia, owned no bondspeople, and worked as a merchant.[132]

Some slaveholders moved longer distances within the state, displacing black men and women in the process. C. F. M. Robinson, born in Virginia, began his time in Arkansas in Pulaski County in 1838. He had moved to Hempstead County by 1847, holding seven bondspeople by 1850. By 1860, Robinson had moved with them to Pulaski County. As indicated by the ages in the census, however, these were not the same seven people. While some deaths may have occurred, Robinson most likely took part in a combination of buying and selling as he relocated around the state.[133] Enslaved families became scattered across the region when slavers reevaluated their prospects. George Tarwater, born in Virginia, settled in Hempstead County with at least four slaves by 1847 (a woman and children) but moved to Camden by 1850, where he kept a tavern. By 1860, however, Tarwater had moved to Memphis and was working as a salesman in the seventh ward. By then, only one nineteen-year-old enslaved man lived with Tarwater. His age lined up with that of one of the children listed as owned by Tarwater ten years before, but there is no way to be certain if he was indeed the same person. If so, the young man would have experienced quite a bit of Arkansas by the end of his teens. The woman and other children must have been sold by Tarwater somewhere along the way. As whites like Tarwater changed course, the fate of enslaved people's relationships remained precarious.[134] Slaveholders' "implacement"—the creation of meaning and rootedness in a place—came at the expense of enslaved people's rootedness and was made possible by enslaved people's *dis*placement.

As enslaved people worked to create their own meaningful neighborhoods, at the end of the day, the entire social and legal code supported slaveholders' domination, and the more profitable slavery became in Arkansas, the more rigidly whites protected that dominion. As time passed, legal scaffolding for the institution hardened the barriers that hedged enslaved people's opportunities for autonomy. Laws used by whites to combat slaves' tendency to flee their bondage or gather without whites' permission reveal the increasing sense that all whites could and should assist in policing slavery's terrain. The code intended to protect property and white lives and to order the interaction between enslaved and enslavers as well as between enslaved people and other whites. It was most elaborate at the county level. A constable and his deputies in Arkansas's townships were meant to search out and put down any "riots, routs, affrays, fightings, and unlawful assemblies." Even coroners stood ready to "quell and suppress" unruly or subversive gatherings.[135] In 1854, after a man named Austin split the skull of a white man seeking to recapture him, Arkansas's highest court declared that *any* white person held the right to subdue a slave in rebellion.[136]

While the law of the land enlisted any and all white Arkansans to take the necessary action to enforce mastery, enslaved people were sometimes policed by specially appointed neighborhood patrols. In this system, space was discipline. Where enslaved people were in relation to where their enslavers wanted them to be provided the impetus for the patrols, and the distance a man could travel on horseback in the course of a night influenced the circuits of patrols. When patrollers or others caught escapees, the first question they asked, "Who do you belong to?" was also to ask "Where do you belong?" in what Johnson termed the "geography of ownership."[137] Arkansas's statutes created a loose structure for the patrol system, acknowledging that the landscape of bondage varied widely within the state. Counties and the townships within them were the units of enforcement. As slavery grew in Independence County, a corn county of the White River, the patrol system became more robust over time. In April 1830, officials instructed patrols to make their rounds for no more than ten hours a month, except when something unusually suspicious occurred. In 1841, the local government altered the system to allow patrol for "as many hours in each night as the common council shall direct."[138] Generally, through the 1840s state law empowered justices of the peace to appoint a few patrols of up to five members, who served four-month terms, each headed by a captain. Patrol members received compensation at the discretion of the county court and did not have to respond to calls for works on county roads. This local patrol was activated whenever "three householders" of the township thought it necessary. Patrollers combed their township's ground on horseback, hunting enslaved people who had fled or gathered without permission. The law defined the patrols' purview as "any place in their township where they have reason to believe that negroes will assemble unlawfully," although it is reasonable to assume that their rounds would have bled into neighboring townships from time to time. In 1853, Arkansas law increased recommended patrol activity to at least once every two weeks, although it is difficult to know to what extent officials complied with that provision.[139]

In Arkansas the most significant policing of enslaved people remained ad hoc in the form of posses that mustered whenever an incident occurred or a rumor of one led to worry. In an 1854 ruling, the Arkansas Supreme Court described slave patrols as a dormant network of white community members who stood at the ready to act to protect slavery's domain: "The patrol system is a police regulation . . . a slumbering power, ready to be aroused and called into action, whenever there is an apparent necessity for it. The presumption is, that the people of each township are able to quell all ordinary disturbances occurring in it, by or among their slaves, and this can be better and more appropriately done by those who are neighbors and friends . . . than by strangers, whose interference has not been invited."[140] The enforcement by "neighbors and friends" sometimes led to the lynching of enslaved people, a phenomenon little discussed among historians. Whites perpetrated at least ten known such lynchings in Arkansas, which were usually related to the murder of enslavers or their managers and almost always carried out by people *other* than the slaveholding family. The lynching of enslaved people should be understood as collateral damage for slaveholders. White neighbors were fully committed to the white supremacy that undergirded slavery to the point of destroying a slaver's property. As the cotton economy matured and the enslaved population increased, white leaders of towns like Helena and Little Rock implemented measures from time to time to increase their vigilance in response to perceived threats of slave rebellion. For example, following the hysteria created by a series of unexplained fires in North Texas in 1860, the Little Rock city government hired investigators to look into possible insurrection.[141]

Slaveholders and their accomplices became increasingly more cautious, tightening slavery's regime over time. They watched out not only for enslaved people in concerted "rebellion" but also runaways. In the 1840s Arkansas law required the sale of captured runaways to the highest bidder when they lingered unclaimed in a county jail for two months.[142] In subsequent years, the code evolved such that such men and women could be detained for as long as six months, and might even end up at the state penitentiary. Arkansas law eventually stipulated that any white person could legally apprehend anyone suspected as a runaway, which came to be defined as any enslaved person found twenty miles from "home" without a pass. The toughening of the regime in Arkansas mirrored the increasing hysteria across the South. The prime feature of the new, tougher, federal Fugitive Slave Law of 1850 was its built-in favor of slaveholders and slave catchers, including a financial incentive for northern commissioners to rule against black men and women who claimed they were wrongly detained. White Arkansans inspired a slave-catching culture on the southern periphery when they enacted a law in 1855 that entitled the captor to a $25 bounty from the enslaver for depositing a runaway with a jailer.[143]

Not only did the code make it easy for any white person to supplement his income with the capture of Arkansas's escapees from slavery, it reduced slave catchers' risks. While the laws of Arkansas Territory had prescribed a death sentence for anyone found guilty of kidnapping a free person and placing him or her into slavery, after 1838, the sentence was reduced to prison time of up to twenty-one years. White Arkansans, like other southerners, grew increasingly paranoid that abolitionists had infiltrated their state, passing a law that declared that any free person who, in print or with their speech, claimed "that owners have not right of property in their slaves" faced up to a year in prison and a fine of no less than $500. Authorities outlawed writing, printing, or circulating any material that could encourage rebellion. Additionally, whites could face prison time for "enticing" bondspeople to run away.[144]

As white lawmakers put increasing effort into shoring up the boundaries of slavery in Arkansas, they cast an ever more critical eye on certain members of black neighborhoods: free blacks. Formerly enslaved and free people of color in Arkansas who never managed (or wanted) to "pass," or cross the racial boundary into white society, lived on increasingly hostile ground. Conevery Valencius explains that "the tight binding of race and region explains some aspects of the singular hostility directed at free blacks." The mobility of the frontier caused whites to develop anxiety about continuity in racial identity, worrying that their work and life on the frontier landscape might threaten their perceived whiteness. Thus, the presence of free African Americans in the neighborhood who exhibited the dark skin of the bottom rung of society but did not reside there flouted the rules of race and status. White Arkansans' growing uneasiness with the presence of free blacks led them to limit their numbers and restrict their activity. Although during the territorial period free people of color could receive permission from whites to carry firearms, antebellum law barred it. In 1843, Arkansas prohibited free blacks from moving into the state. In addition, free people of color living in Arkansas, whether newcomers or long-time residents, were required to bring documentation to county officials for registration and put up a $500 security bond to their county court. Clearly black Arkansans did not universally obey this measure, because the state reissued the call two years later. Whites' hostility toward the presence of free blacks in Arkansas culminated in the 1859 law requiring them to leave the state altogether or be sold into slavery, a measure that other slaveholding states had considered but not implemented. Of the estimated 700 free people of color in Arkansas, all but 144 left. It seems that none of the remaining were auctioned off as slaves as the law stipulated, perhaps because they had built social capital in their communities and secured white patrons.[145]

Over time the process to legally achieve freedom grew more difficult. Emancipation via a will (or other document with a signature and seal) required two witnesses and filing with the county. Black men and women then received "free papers" from the county clerk. Black Arkansans who attained freedom this way sometimes enjoyed additional provisions for their long-term economic independence. For example, upon his death, John L. Taylor of Washington County freed at least ten bondspeople, including children, and provided them with some money. In the same county, John Wilson filed a will in 1836 that would free Simon and Silvey and set them up with stock and tools to start their new free lives. The will also provided that the couple could stay on the Wilson land for the next crop year after his death and farm it to establish themselves.[146] Enslaved people sometimes took matters into their own hands, enjoying the legal right to sue for freedom, but their success rested on their ability to gain the support of whites. Their suits for freedom often connected to deceased enslavers' wills or verbal promises of freedom. Men and women who brought these suits were assigned counsel (in the fashion of suits brought by paupers). And although Arkansas law stated that bondspeople bringing such suits should not be "subject to any severity" by their enslavers or other whites in retaliation, it is difficult to believe that it never happened.[147]

Sometimes bondspeople sued when the executors of deceased slavers' estates refused to uphold wills that provided for manumission.[148]

Enslaved people's hopes then resided in the very system that defined their bodies as property, and those efforts were not always successful. When whites made promises of freedom, enslaved people—particularly mothers with children—fought in white courts to see that they were kept. Dean, who won his freedom from his Crawford County captor in the late 1840s, was one of many people in Arkansas who succeeded.[149] In 1846–47, a persistent mother named Aramynta fought none other than William E. Woodruff to free herself and her children in Pulaski County when her enslaver, Cynthia Robinson, died. Aramynta had initially enjoyed success, basing her claim on Robinson's promises and the fact that the deceased's debts were already paid by her other assets, but suffered defeat in the higher courts.[150] In southwest Arkansas, Bob, who was born in Virginia and forced to Arkansas as a child, unsuccessfully pressed to make good on his enslavers' promises to free him. The Brown family pledged that Bob would be freed but sold him to another man, who died without carrying out the Browns' original promise. After Bob was sold again, this time to pay off the dead man's debts, he petitioned the Sevier Circuit Court for his freedom. Initially successful, Bob must have ached with disappointment when the Arkansas Supreme Court ruled in 1857 that such promises held no weight. Arkansas's courts viewed manumission as a benevolent action on the part of slaveholders, not as a binding contract or arrangement between enslaver and enslaved. In order for the legal scaffolding to successfully protect slavery's domain, captors could not be legally bound to declarations or promises made to human chattel.[151]

Black Arkansans kept pressing claims even though lawmakers and justices continued to choke off the path from slavery to freedom. After Bob's unsuccessful suit, the state supreme court declared that "the authority given to emancipate by a prescribed method was a prohibition to emancipate any other way" when a Pulaski County woman named Harriet headed the attempt to free herself and several others. According to a will filed in 1838, Harriet and other captives of Gilbert Barden should have been freed upon the death of his wife, Caroline Barden. That same will granted Harriet and her children, Mary Ann and David, a twenty-nine-acre tract of land. Caroline Barden, who died in 1851, had provided in her own will that Harriet and Isaac and Harriet's children, Mary Ann, David Scott, Martha Jane, Lucinda, and Isaac Henry, should also be set free when each turned twenty-one years old. In the meantime, the will provided, they were to be hired out with half of that income going to the Methodist Episcopal Church in Little Rock. But when Harriet and others petitioned the courts for freedom, whites denied them on the grounds that Barden had never had final ownership of the family and was essentially holding them in trust until they were to pass from her to "those beneficially interested." As Kelly Kennington's investigation of freedom suits proved, enslaved people who mounted legal claims to their freedom, even when unsuccessful, exhibited knowledge of law and custom, engaged with legal culture, and harnessed the power of personal relationships.[152]

After being hauled to the southern frontier and forced to carve farms and plantations out of what white and black alike perceived as wilderness, enslaved Arkansans did their best to navigate the domains set out in law and convention by whites. Whites designed slavery's regime to alienate enslaved people from the landscape, treating them "as strangers in a strange land." Slaveholders used bondspeople's labor to created order out of the natural landscape and construct a built domain of domestic and productive spaces meant to maximize bondspeople's output. Whites successfully inscribed a hierarchy onto Arkansas's landscape. Maintained by violence, it created meaning for whites as designed, and proclaimed their sense of race, gender, and status. In their resistance and in ordinary life, however, enslaved people achieved their own sense of dominion and belonging. Culture and power made the acreage on which enslaved people were held into more than simply locations; they were neighborhoods. Because places and landscapes are experienced physically, bondspeople's kinetic creation of their ties, such as traveling between farms or walking in a group to a church meeting, helped create their sense of home and neighborhood. Enslaved people staked their claims to Arkansas's woods and brush. Tracing their interactions with those zones, such as their secret prayers and songs, confirms Edward Casey's contention that humans almost never experience only the natural world or exclusively their cultural creation but an intermingling of the two. Enslaved people's use of Arkansas's vast uncultivated space ranged from the subversive to the routine. One consistency, though, was their frequency in those zones. In fact, when Parmelia's enslaver, Nimrod Menifee, was hacked to death by his white neighbor in the woods of Conway County, the only witness was an enslaved youth who happened to be passing through.[153]

3 / Alluvial Empires

From the valleys of the Ozark and Ouachita Mountains to the Mississippi Valley, rivers formed Arkansas's landscape of bondage by creating the fertile environment as well as providing the connections between places. Like all nineteenth-century people, enslaved and enslavers used waterways not only as their reference points but as the major feature that characterized a place. Using watersheds as the basis for organizing society had long been a practice by Native Americans and colonial newcomers. While French colonists were more likely to base claims on "hydrologic territories," the English often relied on latitudinal lines. The boundaries of what came to be Arkansas relied on both. The state lines drawn by white policymakers encircled varied experiences fashioned by geographic, economic, and political realities. Whites used Arkansas's well-watered ground to build a primarily agricultural economy relying on enslaved labor, while bondspeople understood their river world to mean something very different. While categorizing Arkansas's enslaved communities as either "upcountry" or "lowcountry" based on topography has had general utility for understanding the different experiences overall, a closer look reveals the centrality of river valleys and river bottoms in providing shades of difference. The "dictates of slavery," as Donald McNeilly put it, permeated all of Arkansas, not just the plantation zones.[1]

A bird's-eye view of the landscape of slavery in Arkansas reveals two major topographic divisions in sharpest relief—upcountry and lowcountry—but scholars have generalized too much about what they mean, leaning too heavily on contrasting the two in order to understand the state's social and economic development. It is true that these two general types of Arkansas ground, "upcountry"/"upland" and "lowcountry"/"lowland," have influenced Arkansas's development from initial European and African settlement to the present day. Orville Taylor wrote that "an imaginary line bisecting Arkansas from northeast to southwest marks the approximate division between the highlands and the lowlands, the former lying north and west of the line." He pointed out that some of the highland counties had some similar traits to those of the lowlands, lying along rivers, but as incoming settlers carved additional counties out of the mountains, more "true" highland zones developed.[2] McNeilly's *Old South Frontier* embraces the two-halves paradigm and invokes Ira Berlin's argument for two types of American slavery—"societies with slaves" and "slave societies." In short, slave societies were those in which the economy depended upon the use of enslaved labor, while societies *with* slaves incorporated slave labor but not to the extent that it became fundamental to the social and economic fabric there. McNeilly characterizes the southeastern half of Arkansas as a slave society, while considering the northwestern half to be made up of societies with slaves. He explains: "Antebellum Arkansas was of both worlds. The two geographic regions nurtured the development of two societies. The highlands of the northwest became a world of small self-sufficient farms, many of which had a slave or two. The lowlands . . . developed into one dominated by cotton plantations and the dictates of slavery."[3] While this categorization is useful in understanding the white experience because it offers a top-down view of the economy of slavery in Arkansas, centering the lives of enslaved people reveals a completely different landscape. A closer look blurs the distinction between these two categories when it comes to the lives of enslaved people in Arkansas. When we examine four counties—Hempstead, Conway, Pope, and Independence—we sample the experiences of bonded communities of people who lived and worked on ground that did not fit neatly into either the "society with slaves" or "slave society" category.

The landscape of bondage in the Red River Valley defies easy categorization. In 1830, toward the end of Arkansas's territorial period, more enslaved people resided in Hempstead County in the southwest corner of the state than in any other region (partly because the bounds of the original county were so vast). And although Arkansas's enslaved communities came to be concentrated in the southeast in the Mississippi Valley in the long run, the southwest continued to be a major center of Arkansas's enslaved population through the antebellum years.[4] Most sites of bondage there were smaller operations than plantations, but the number of those large operations climbed steadily in the southwest after statehood, especially during the 1850s. By 1860, 58 percent of bondspeople held in Hempstead County lived on plantations, meaning that while most whites experienced the institution on the smaller scale, those held in bondage were more likely to experience it on plantations.[5] Most of these plantations, however, were of moderate size. Some grew quite large by the close of the antebellum years, the largest with 205 captive laborers.[6] Hempstead County's cotton production levels seem anemic compared to those of Arkansas's most important cotton county—Chicot County—but Hempstead County's cotton production increased by a staggering 548 percent between the harvests of 1849 and 1859—more than double the rate of that of Chicot. All told, Hempstead County was an important lowland river county with widespread slavery (447 holdings in 1860) and a high enslaved population, and produced 3 to 5 percent of the state's cotton, but as Orville Taylor stated, Hempstead did not fit into the "true lowland group" because the scale of plantation slavery did not match that of the southeast. Yet more than half of enslaved people there resided on plantations. They spent their lives growing cotton and corn, with more emphasis on the latter than in Chicot County. Enslaved people's communities in southwest Arkansas never grew as large as those that developed among the more concentrated groups of bondspeople of the southeast, but they were not nearly so scattered as they were in hillier parts of Arkansas.[7] Hempstead County cannot be neatly defined as a slave society, or a society with slaves—it was its own.

As with Hempstead County, forcing Conway County into the usual dichotomy risks obscuring the true conditions of life on the ground for bondspeople. Only 802 enslaved people lived there in 1860, while whites numbered 5,895. Bondspeople made up only 12 percent of Conway County's residents; for the state as a whole about 25 percent of residents were bondspeople. Although this seems to indicate that the region as a whole should be viewed as a "society with slaves," the story of enslaved life at the ground level proves more complicated. Welborn Township, in the southern part of the county along the Arkansas River, was a black majority township—home to 502 enslaved people and 360 whites in 1860. Bondspeople made up 58 percent of the population of the township. Just over half of the enslaved people residing in the county (51%) lived and worked in Welborn. Well over half of the cotton produced in the county, 61 percent in 1860, was grown by enslaved people in Welborn.[8] Most holdings were small; only seven of the county's 110 slaveholding farms could be classified as plantations. But enslaved people living along the river in Conway County held some important aspects of their experience in common with bondspeople in the cotton expanses of the Arkansas Delta that hillside yeoman farmers did not: a black majority community engaging in riverside cultivation of cotton. Spreading the county's slavery data across all townships misses the intensification of slavery at the southern edge along the river, where enslaved people outnumbered whites and where they grew more than half of the county's cotton.[9]

Panning northwest to Conway County's neighbor, Pope, reveals a place where the majority of whites lived a typical upcountry Arkansas experience, yet the majority of enslaved people, concentrated in two townships, did not. Gary Battershell's research into that area revealed that in the upcountry, contrary to what many assume about the foothills of the Ozarks, slavery crucially influenced daily life, politics, and government. Many more whites beyond those few who held bondspeople benefited economically from enslaved black labor. While these findings have been a crucial part of moving the historiography of Arkansas slavery forward, Battershell chose Pope and Johnson Counties as representative of *upcountry* slavery. A closer look, however, shows Pope as less than the quintessential representative of how historians have defined slavery in the "upcountry" due to the concentrated nature of the enslaved population.[10] Although located farther into the Ozarks' foothills than Conway County, Pope County was home to even more enslaved people than Conway County in 1860 (972), hosted double the number of slaveholdings (209), and produced even more cotton than Conway County, by about 500 bales (3,723 bales total). Similarly, the center of Pope County slavery sat not in its highlands but in the valley along the Arkansas River. Pope County's southern townships look similar to Conway County's. Galley (or Galla) Rock—as the major southern township was known in 1860—and Illinois Township together held 500 of the county's 972 total bondspeople in 1860. More than half of the county's enslaved population resided along the river. Only three of the farms where bondspeople lived were large enough to be called plantations, according to the conventional definition (agricultural operations holding twenty or more enslaved people). Twenty-four percent of the population of Galley Rock was held in slavery, in line with the statewide proportion; this percentage was even lower in Illinois Township.[11] As with Conway, Pope County's enslaved population was concentrated enough in one place that it fails to fit the picture of smallholdings spread across the hillsides. Yet it did not host intensive plantation agriculture. Battershell helps us reckon with this landscape when he brings the Arkansas River to his readers' attention, explaining that "the availability of rich bottomland did render these counties somewhat more disposed to large-scale farming than other parts of the Arkansas upcountry. Yet in their ways of life, county residents more closely resembled Arkansans residing" in the upcountry. The day-to-day routines of *enslaved* people on the ground, however, must have been affected more acutely by these differences. With more than half of them living on relatively larger operations on the river, their experience would have been less like what we think of as "upcountry" or "mountain" slavery, but it would have also differed from that in the concentrated Mississippi River communities of southeastern Arkansas.[12]

Finally, as in Hempstead, Conway, and Pope, the terrain on which black men and women lived and worked in Independence County serves as a caution against oversimplifying bonded life in Arkansas. Independence County's location on a map, at the meeting of the Black and White Rivers in northern Arkansas, might suggest that it housed the "upcountry" version of slavery of Arkansas. However, like Pope and Conway Counties, Independence County hosted a strip of more intensified slavery. Of the county's 1,337 bondspeople, almost 67 percent (891) resided along rivers.[13] By measures outlined in Carl Moneyhon's description of antebellum Arkansas in *The Impact of the Civil War and Reconstruction on Arkansas*, Independence County had more similarities with Union County, a plantation zone in south Arkansas, than with its neighbor in northern Arkansas, Van Buren County. For example, although there were only thirteen plantation-sized holdings out of Independence County's 246 total holdings in 1860, the average size of the plantation force was 26.9 captives—significantly lower than that of Union County of southern Arkansas (at 32.7) but drastically different from that of Van Buren County, where no enslaved people resided on plantation-sized operations. To view the measures from another angle, 20.5 percent of enslaved people in Independence County resided on plantations, compared to 33 percent in Union County, and 0 in Van Buren County.[14] Here again, the economic landscape blurs distinctions between what happened in the hills versus the lowcountry.

Rather than splitting enslaved people's communities using a diagonal line from southwest to northeast, this chapter maps their lives by features central to Arkansas's development: the river systems. The examples of communities in Hempstead, Conway, Pope, and Independence Counties require scholars to rethink how we map enslaved people's stories. They lived out a spectrum of experiences not limited to *either* remote scattered hillside smallholdings *or* expansive lowland cotton operations. Enslaved people did not exist on one side or the other of a "dual society consisting of highland farm districts and lowland plantation districts." Their landscape in Arkansas was fashioned by intersecting political, economic, and natural features that could vary widely and thus can defy easy categorization.[15] Certainly rivers and their valleys exist in the upcountry all over the South, and to place them more centrally in our analysis than elevation is not to replace the consideration of either lowlands or mountains but to recognize that Arkansas's waterways concentrated slavery. Rivers fed the economy that drove the growth of slavery and created ribbons of denser communities of enslaved people that often traced south and east across the state, penetrating the highlands and lowlands alike. Waterways teemed with steamboats that carried the fruits of bondspeople's labor while offering the means for their escape. Larger channels like the Mississippi, Arkansas, and Ouachita cultivated an African American "river world." Smaller rivers and creeks cut into Arkansas's hills, creating rich bottomlands that supported slave agriculture on smallholdings. From the earliest days of white and black settlement of Arkansas, rivers supported the development of towns where enslaved people worked in homes, hotels, and stores. Moneyhon and geographer Gerald T. Hanson identify six main river systems in Arkansas: the Mississippi, Arkansas, White, St. Francis, Ouachita, and Red. Whites rooted the enslavement of African-descended people along all of them. We might take a cue from historian Nan Woodruff and call them "alluvial empires."[16]

It was from the Mississippi River that slavery first took hold in Arkansas, anchoring cotton plantation agriculture in fertile eastern soil. Rivers watering the Mississippi from the west stretched that economy and society, along with the experience of enslavement that came with it, westward into the interior of the state. Cotton production sites of eastern Arkansas rooted in the rich alluvial soil plugged into the highway of information, supplies, and people provided by the Mississippi River. Initially, whites' dreams for the area were slowed by the problems of drainage, the task of clearing trees and vegetation for crops, and the ever-present threat of disease. They crowded enslaved populations along the river frontage of southern counties like Chicot and Phillips, creating enslaved communities that outnumbered that of the entire state capital in 1860. Overseers and patrols lorded over enslaved neighborhoods with more frequency and consistency there and whites scared more easily when rumors of insurrection swirled. Because they often outnumbered their oppressors, enslaved people's suspected subversive activities generated white paranoia from time to time. However, enslavers and their white neighbors usually remained surprisingly complacent. They became uneasy during certain periods—often having to do with rumors of abolitionist infiltration during national elections—and they would grow especially fearful with the onset of the Civil War.[17]

In this region black men and women worked under a rigid routine of large-scale cotton production, usually referred to as Arkansas's plantation districts. Some historians have recently revisited the term "plantation." In *The Half Has Never Been Told*, Edward E. Baptist instead uses the term "labor camp," which has been employed by other historians since. A major utility of "labor camp" is that the term emphasizes the production focus of cotton operations without the romantic "moonlight and magnolias" imagery that the term "plantation" might conjure up. Yet the use of "labor camp" is limited because large cotton farms were also usually performative white domestic spaces in addition to factories designed to consistently churn out bales of cotton, a reality that the term "labor camp" may obscure. It may be helpful to continue to use "plantation" to indicate larger operations that also served as planter residences and "labor camp" for those in earlier stages of construction and those not designed to host slaveholders' lifestyles.[18]

While slavery proved brutal in all its manifestations, the Mississippi River regions represented Arkansas's most intensified "second slavery" regime. In these regions of Arkansas, enslaved people were more likely to work for the larger operations—those of elite whites rather than yeoman farmers. Moneyhon has shown how the "elite" class of white Arkansans held more than 85 percent of the enslaved labor force and 78 percent of the land in Chicot County in 1860. In Phillips County that same year, 72 percent of enslaved people worked for those Moneyhon classifies as "elite," who owned 52 percent of the county's acreage. While the percentage of Chicot County land worked as plantation-sized operations held steady at about 70 percent through the 1850s, in Phillips County that took time to develop—growing from 20 to 47 percent from 1850 to 1860. On the ground, enslaved communities were most concentrated in this part of Arkansas. Indeed about 80 percent of all people residing in Chicot County were enslaved between 1850 and 1860. The average population of bondspeople held on plantation-sized operations in that county numbered 48 in 1850 and 81 in 1860. In Phillips County, where more than half of the residents lived in bondage by 1860, the average size of the enslaved population on operations there increased from 33 to 41 during the same time frame. The denser population created a critical mass that offered more choice in playmates, friends, and romantic partners. The neighborhoods of adjoining operations incubated as rich a social life as could survive under the weight of brutal oppression.[19] Yet lovers, friends, and families suffered together under the heavy regime with a "factory in the field" character. James Speed, a white Kentuckian who had previously witnessed slavery only on smaller holdings of the upper South, commented on Arkansas's developing cotton regime, exclaiming, "I will say that I had no conception of slavery until I went to Arkansas.... I was horrified by what I saw there."[20]

It is on absentee-owned operations where slavery in Arkansas must have been its harshest. The profitability of cotton, land, and bondspeople proved so great that Arkansas's side of the Mississippi River drew the investment of many whites who chose to add it to their portfolios from afar, like R. C. Ballard. While it is difficult to generate an accurate count of all absentee holdings, 900 is a conservative estimate of the number of enslaved people held by absentee proprietors in Chicot County in 1860, out of the 7,512 enslaved people who lived there (about 12%). Truly "labor camps," as the sites held no domestic importance for enslavers, these operations served not only *primarily* as sites of production but *solely* as sites of production. Planters who liked to think of themselves as paternalists or sought to perform benevolence in front of guests or family were nowhere to be found, reducing whatever tiny sliver of benefit bondspeople might have received from on-site owners who sought to be thought of as "good masters." Enslaved people instead daily contended with overseers who wanted to be able to make promising reports on the crop and secure the next year's contract. These men came and went often, as described in the next chapter, at times due to sabotage at the hands of the bondspeople they were supposed to manage.[21]

Paradoxically, although the Big Muddy supported a particular cotton economy and black experience in its valley, the Mississippi River also served as both a political boundary and a natural divider to white slavers and investors who tended to focus their efforts on the eastern bank. This division resulted in a significant lag in agricultural development and population growth on Arkansas's side, affecting the lives of enslaved people held there. The difference was stark even in areas directly across the river from each other. Farmland in Mississippi and Tennessee counties along the east side of the river boasted almost five times more acreage in improved farmland—ground that had been cleared, fenced, and otherwise altered to support a farm—than Arkansas's along the west bank. Enslaved communities were also much smaller. The slave population was 78 percent lower in Arkansas counties along the Mississippi as compared to those on the east side in 1850—a massive difference in the concentration of black men and women. That population was at least 63 percent lower than that of the east side in 1860. (Arkansas's total enslaved population amounted to about one-sixth of Mississippi's in 1850, and one-fourth in 1860.) However, the populations of bondspeople living in Arkansas's riverside counties rose faster than those of their counterparts along the eastern bank, by 150 percent between the 1850 and 1860 census enumerations, while those communities in Mississippi experienced only a 34 percent increase during the same time period. Thus, while the convergence of political and natural boundaries in the Mississippi River slowed the growth of the cotton empire on Arkansas's side of the valley, the boom of the 1850s created rapid change there. As newcomers were forced out to the west side of the river to work the fresh cotton ground, they would have noticed a striking difference upon making their crossing.[22]

As lightly populated as Arkansas's side of the river was compared to that of Tennessee and Mississippi, enslaved people in the few relatively urban spaces there, like the river town of Helena, still sometimes found opportunities that most of their compatriots in rural spaces could not hope to enjoy. Although James M. Alexander lived under the bondage of the Alexander family, he "hired his own time and went and came at will" in Helena, running a barber shop (for a time located on Ohio Street) for several years. James Alexander's enslaver, Mark Alexander, plied his trade as an attorney on both sides of the river. Business and family connected the white Alexander and Deputy families with the black Alexanders and Deputys in and around Helena. While there is little known about James Alexander's younger years, by the time he reached his thirties, he had built up a solid clientele in Helena, training his son in the trade by the late 1850s. In addition to the usual haircuts, his services included dying women's hair as well as men's. Alexander also sold perfume and hair products. By 1857, he had expanded his business to open a bath house in Helena, where he treated patrons with rainwater baths or showers from 5:00 a.m. to 11:00 p.m. every day except Sunday. Alexander placed advertisements for his business in the local newspaper. Most of his ads were indistinguishable from the type of text that whites placed, and were usually signed "J. M. Alexander" at the bottom. Yet, a hint of deference appears in one ad's use of the diminutive of his first name at the top: "Jim would beg leave to inform his old customers generally, that he is as polite and accommodating as ever." Certainly, Alexander endured indignities particular to his circumstances the way all enslaved people did. His experience represents a best-case scenario for bondspeople and did not reflect that of the mass of people held in the area. The black Alexanders benefited from the particular opportunities created by the traffic of the relatively more populated river port towns. Towns like Helena linked the surrounding agricultural operations. Slaveholders like Casteel, who kept eight bondspeople at his home in Helena and held twenty-two at his small plantation outside of town, moved between those zones.[23]

However much they may have offered some enslaved people, these hubs also served as carceral points for the capture and detainment of escapees who sought to use the Mississippi River as a highway of deliverance. County sheriffs based in river towns like Helena imprisoned runaway men and women, advertised their capture in search of their enslavers, and, if no reconnection to the previous sites of their bondage could be made, auctioned their bodies to local whites on behalf of the county. While county officials all over Arkansas were responsible for holding and re-placing people who escaped their bonds, points like Helena kept busy as posts of runaway activity along the river. Riverside jailers engaged in a constant game of cat-and-mouse, capturing and dutifully posting detailed advertisements for runaways, scratching their heads when they were bested in instances like the getaway of three men who sawed through the iron door hinge of Helena jail's in 1853.[24] In rural and urban spaces along the Mississippi, most bondspeople lived an incredibly harsh existence as the cotton kingdom in Arkansas underwent the growing pains of its "excruciating becoming," as historian Walter Johnson described it.

If the Mississippi River made the dark dreams of enslavers come true, the Arkansas promised a similarly sinister dominion. Formed from the snowpacks of the mountains of the far west, the waters of the Arkansas River served as the main artery of slavery within the state, running 505 miles. The Arkansas River Valley created a west-east plantation belt that united the state's commerce and agriculture, drawing southeastward to the major artery of the Mississippi. From Fort Smith to Arkansas Post, the Arkansas River worked as heartbeat and highway of agricultural life in the center of the state, linking Indian Territory, the capital city, and the banks of the Mississippi. In 1860, 20 percent of the state's farmland lay within the twelve counties along the Arkansas River. Enslaved families in the Arkansas River Valley cultivated the strip of rich bottomland terrace soils that stretched across the state, dotted by settlements like Van

Buren, Lewisburg, and Cadron. The western valley's sandy loam hills stretched up to the Boston Mountains and in the other direction, to the south and east, gave way to wider expanses of alluvial soil. Bondspeople of Arkansas and Prairie Counties cultivated the eastern prairie earth north of the Arkansas River, where a compact clay subsoil lay underneath the rich silt-loam surface.[25]

Roughly midway between the state's western and eastern boundaries, on the banks of the Arkansas, a dense black community resided in the state's most urban area, the river city of Little Rock. Hardly a true city, Little Rock never reached a population of even 4,000 before the Civil War. While most southern cities were not very large, Little Rock was thinly settled even in comparison to nearby cities, like Vicksburg, which grew to 8,000 people by 1860; only 846 bondspeople resided in Little Rock by that time. Fifty-six percent were women, a significantly greater proportion than for the state as a whole (49.4%), which probably reflects the urban domestic labor market for black women.[26] Over time, slaveholders increasingly converted the acreage outside of town into plantation units. Six percent of Pulaski County's farms could be classified as plantation-sized in 1850, which grew to 13 percent in 1860 (from only 5 such operations to 26). Plantation labor forces there averaged twenty-four souls in 1850, which rose to forty-one by the 1860 count. Some Little Rock slavers, like the prominent Trapnall family, held bondspeople in the city to support their lifestyle in addition to captive labors on Arkansas Delta plantations.[27]

Like Helena, the river town of Little Rock represented a place where black men and women lived in a more concentrated community, with opportunities for mobility and material gain that more scattered zones lacked. In fact, enslaved Arkansans felt whites' attempts to rein in these freedoms as early as the territorial period. In 1826, for example, city ordinances looked to tamp down the gaming and drinking that brought black and white Little Rock residents together, prohibiting whites from playing games or cards or gambling with enslaved or free black people. According to the regulation, enslaved people caught breaking this measure were to receive five lashes on the bare back. In addition, enslaved people were forbidden from moving about at night without permission. If caught carousing at night they could expect to receive ten lashes by city officials. As early as 1830, enslaved Little Rock residents moved about with enough freedom that whites found it necessary to prohibit enslaved people from engaging in trade with whites, hiring out their own time, or going at large. If caught, bondspeople might be put to work maintaining the streets.[28] Little Rock also passed early ordinances preventing free blacks from "entertaining" bondspeople in the city. In fact, white Little Rock leaders so feared the interaction of free and enslaved black Arkansans that free blacks were not supposed to even allow enslaved people to enter their houses without permission from their enslaver or overseer. According to that ordinance, if free blacks were caught breaking this rule and could not pay the fine, the constable was empowered to deal out twenty "well laid on" lashes onto their backs.[29]

Little Rock whites strengthened their grip over time. Whites not only fretted about enslaved people's economic activity in Little Rock; they exhibited concern over groups of bondspeople gathering for subversive purposes. Such regulations reflected a concern directly tied to the Nat Turner Revolt that occurred in Virginia five years before Arkansas's statehood. Ordinances outlawed all enslaved people's gatherings in the daytime aside from public worship without the permission of slavers or their managers. Enslaved people could not gather after dark "on any pretext whatever." Black faith came under closer scrutiny as well. Reflecting whites' focus on the religious nature of Nat Turner's subversion, a Little Rock ordinance forbade preachers from using "any seditious or inflammatory language" or attempting "to excite hatred or contempt in said slaves for their masters or owners," punishable by a fine or prison time.[30]

The new limits on bondspeople's lives arose in part out of the realities of "urban" slavery. By 1841, an economy that integrated enslaved people's hiring out their own time clearly had taken hold in Little Rock. Whites who viewed this as problematic reasoned that otherwise "good" slaves would be ruined by "worthless wandering rascals" who traveled as they pleased, hiring out their own time in the city. White enslavers who allowed and encouraged that activity violated state law and city ordinance. Slavers and bondspeople alike saw the benefit of this economy, however; the ban against slave hiring was not enforced in Little Rock.[31] Whites pushed back against their market activities in 1856 when Little Rock passed an ordinance prohibiting bondspeople from keeping separate households from their enslavers; in addition, the penalties whites could incur for allowing bondspeople to hire themselves out increased as time passed.[32] Whites who distrusted the hiring system preferred arrangements portrayed in P. L. Anthony's newspaper ad in 1849 looking to hire two men and two women from their enslaver for a farm near the city. The slave-hiring economy was one of the central engines of slavery in relatively urban spaces, but many whites worried about how much control enslaved people managed to obtain in that system.[33]

There was narrow space in town for some enslaved people with connections to make good. James Jackson seized opportunity when he cultivated a reputation as an industrious black man among Little Rock whites who both directly participated and looked the other way as he made money for himself and his family. Jackson spent mornings sweeping Little Rock stores, sending his enslaver a portion of his earnings. In fact, Jackson hired out his own time in Little Rock for twenty-five years, leveraging the proceeds to launch a "confectionery establishment," "as fine a one as there was" in the town. His employers included James E. Gibson, a clerk at J. J. McAlmont's drug store. Jackson's material success was a family affair. His wife and children kept the shop while he did the sweeping and other work around town. Jackson managed to provide for his family and eventually purchase some livestock. His family relied on his reputation in the community to secure chances for material gain, and produced and consumed those gains as a household, increasing their security and status. This strategy served Jackson and his family well in later years during the war.[34]

Black nights in Little Rock were a slaver's nightmare. A bell rang at 9:00 p.m., supposedly signaling that all bondspeople should be in their homes rather than out and about. Clearly not everyone obeyed—both within the city limits and around its edges. In 1842, the *Arkansas Gazette* printed a story about horses going missing, clearly stolen. Because one of the animals made its way back—exhibiting signs of having been ridden hard—and the other was found wandering, whites surmised that the culprits were more interested in *using* the horses than keeping them. The *Gazette* speculated, "It is possible that they may have been taken by servants to ride to some of their nocturnal gatherings or frolics," warning whites not to allow bondspeople to wander "after the ringing of the 9 o'clock bell." The editor went on to suggest that the constable should be more enthusiastically pursuing bondspeople who strolled after that time without passes.[35] Whites worked to suppress the socializing that chipped away at the rigidity of the slave regime. The day after Christmas 1856, a group of enslaved people in Pulaski County, possibly overstretching their holiday time "off," spent some time with a white man named George Cadle, who was later charged by authorities with harboring slaves without permission.[36]

Despite attempts to limit its sale, alcohol lubricated nighttime gatherings, which often became rowdy and could even turn deadly.[37] Drinking and carousing in Little Rock led to disaster in 1854 when an enslaved man killed another in a drunken fight.[38] The case of Joseph, held by the

Fultons just outside of town, reveals that less drastic forms of disorder related to bondspeople's social drinking still plagued area slaveholders. Joseph seems to have obtained as much alcohol as he cared to drink at the Anthony House hotel, perhaps from friends working there. On one occasion he drove Matilda Fulton and her children out for a Sunday ride but got too drunk (probably with friends) to pick them up and drive them back home. Joseph became so drunk so often that the family stopped relying on him as a driver. To appease his enslavers, Joseph claimed to have "joined the temperance" for a time, at least. He later ran away and may never have returned.[39]

While domestic work, urban gardening, and labor in hotels and restaurants were the most visible types of work enslaved people were engaged in in Little Rock, some in the vicinity of this river town worked in more industrial capacities, although it is difficult to achieve a good estimate. By 1850, William Woodruff, for example, held ten bondspeople in Little Rock, co-owning a sawmill nearby with a man named Campbell, which employed seven "hands." It is possible that some of them were enslaved people. By 1860 Woodruff seems to have sold his interest in the sawmill and held fourteen bondspeople. In 1850, D. H. Bingham owned a sawmill in Little Rock where he "employed" ten men but only spent twelve dollars per month on labor. At the same time, Bingham held six men in slavery between the ages of eighteen and fifty; these men labored in the sawmill.[40]

The critical mass of black families in Little Rock supported a relatively rich community life. William and Caroline Andrews, held by the Ashley family, ran the Wesley Chapel (now on Philander Smith College's campus), a church for bondspeople in Little Rock established in 1853 near present-day Eighth and Broadway. Services included Sunday school, which might have been a front for teaching fellow bondspeople to read and write. While whites oversaw the church, it existed for enslaved people, and enslaved people sustained it.[41] And although the bondspeople who attended the Wesley Chapel probably exercised caution in the content of their services, it was their own. Some enslaved people must have attended the black Baptist church of Little Rock as well.[42]

Little Rock offered no haven for black men and women, however, and escape into the forests of Arkansas remained a popular strategy for bondspeople in more populated zones. As much as town life might offer bondspeople in relation to rural zones, the woods provided them a place for recreation or simply for time away from whites' demands. Frank, owned by David Fulton, who lived just outside Little Rock, was sent into the woods one day to gather firewood for the night but instead stayed out all day. Frank "sank into the armes of morpheus where he remained until 4 o'clock p.m.," leaving the house freezing and without firewood. In later years Frank, like so many others, finally ran away for good, and was sold while "in the woods." The buyer took on the responsibility of capturing him.[43] The wild spaces surrounding Little Rock during the territorial period hosted a base camp for runaway slaves, who snuck into town at night to steal provisions, and may have supported marooned slaves into the late 1850s.[44]

Wild spaces, however, could be invaded by surprisingly dense slaveholdings, especially when aided by river access. About a hundred miles upriver from Little Rock, in the lower region of the Ozarks, the Titsworth family of Kentucky established a plantation complex in what was otherwise a predominantly small-slaveholding zone. Enslaved men, women, and children experienced an extraordinarily large slave community for this area of Arkansas's northwestern quadrant, leaving a footprint on the area's memory of the landscape. Local tradition holds that a Titsworth patriarch and his sons arrived in the bottoms in the 1810s. By 1850, two of the sons, John Titsworth and Spear Titsworth, had established plantations south of the river near Short Mountain in present-day Logan County. John Titsworth was the wealthiest of the brothers. Fifty-eight enslaved people lived and labored on his place in 1850, probably overseen by his younger brother Daniel. (A free black man named Levi resided with the family and worked as a laborer, but he had left by 1860.) Spear Titsworth held twenty-three men, women, and children that year. By 1860, John had expanded his holdings, including $50,000 in real estate, to ninety-two enslaved people who lived in fifteen houses. (The overseer may have been Daniel Craig from Ohio.) By that census year, the thirty people held by Spear Titsworth lived in uncertainty of their futures because Spear had died and his estate was going through probate. In the meantime, they labored for John.

White family members passed down stories that romanticized the Titsworth plantations as an "eden" for bondspeople. Local lore held that after the crops were laid by either John or Spear Titsworth, he rewarded his enslaved laborers by taking them to a hillside spring near Mount Magazine to picnic and camp. Somewhere beneath the sentimental, whitewashed story of the Titsworth brothers' benevolence may be a true glimpse of enslaved people's bit of respite in the picturesque natural surroundings (for which this area of Arkansas is still known). A local history journal claims that the springs came to be known as "Titsworth Springs" because of this yearly visit.[45]

Following the Arkansas upriver to the state's western boundary leads to a contested edge of whites' empire in Arkansas. As discussed in Chapter 1, the piecemeal creation in the first half of the nineteenth century of what came to be known as "Indian Territory" from ground that used to make up Arkansas Territory's western half was a foundational process for the second slavery. If whites viewed Arkansas's eastern swamps as "evil, dangerous places," they considered the prairie of Indian Territory to the west as an uncivilized den of unwelcome occupants too wild to be worthy of the valuable land and resources afforded them. In 1841, as a group of two hundred Seminoles traveled from Florida through Arkansas to Indian Territory, the *Arkansas Gazette* declared them "sworn enemies of the white man" because of the two wars they had waged with the United States. The editor promised that Arkansans would keep a wary eye on the sixty "fierce warriors" said to be among the group, declaring that the "frontiersmen of Arkansas" would wipe them out if attacked. Because their presence represented disorder, white Arkansans in general did not trust the varied native nations who settled to their west beyond the benefits of trade. For their part, enslaved people who fled west of Arkansas's border could not trust that the territory offered a safe escape. The Cherokee, Creek, Seminole, Choctaw, and Chickasaw all held black men and women in slavery, and native people had been part of the African American slave trade. Escaping slavery through Indian Territory to Mexico, although not unheard of, was a dangerous proposition.[46]

An old trading post dating to the 1810s, and federal military installation to monitor native populations, Fort Smith, on the border between Arkansas and Indian Territory, became a significant point of Arkansas slavery by the 1840s. Jeremiah (Jerry) R. Kannady came west to the fort from Pennsylvania in the 1830s. He set up shop as a sutler provisioning the ready market of U.S. soldiers for several years before setting up a blacksmith shop, a wagon shop, and then a gristmill and sawmill. By 1850, Kannady and wife, Sophia, held an enslaved woman and her child in their household. Within ten years the Kannadys added a sixteen-year-old boy and twenty-one-year-old man to labor in his very prosperous manufacturing operation. In 1850, the enslaved Kannadys lived in the growing city in a one-story log house with a dog trot, but two cabins for enslaved people appeared by 1860. Their enslaved neighbors labored for Fort Smith's attorneys and shopkeepers. Thomas Wilson's early economic success in the region played out similarly. Arriving at Fort Gibson, in Indian Territory, from Kentucky, Wilson came back east a bit to Fort Smith in 1832, as a sutler for U.S. soldiers. Like Kannady, Wilson leveraged his work in connection to U.S. military posts to enter the slaveholding class. Ten bondspeople supported his household and farm in 1850, and although that number dropped to seven by 1860, more of them were adult men.[47]

Close by and north of the Arkansas River, the younger town of Van Buren was built by land speculators and slavers. John Drennen got his start with partner David Thompson speculating thousands of acres of Arkansas land. They bought up unused 1812 military bounty land grants and resold them at a profit. The partners increased interest in the site that would become Van Buren and lined their pockets by chopping lumber to sell to passing steamers on the Arkansas River. In 1836 Drennen put $11,000 of his earnings into the purchase of land that became Van Buren, selling it off into lots. He built his home on a hill overlooking the river and the town, farming the slope. Drennen converted his profitable ventures into black Arkansans as chattel, whose labor supported his farm and lifestyle. The enterprise of the "father of Van Buren" reached from northwest Arkansas to the delta. Drennen bought land early in Chicot County, holding at least twenty-five enslaved people there on a plantation he called Dearfield (later Drennen Dale).[48] When Drennen died in 1855, his thirteen captive workers in Van Buren came under the control of his daughter Caroline and her husband, Charles Scott, a prosperous merchant from Maryland. Sixteen enslaved people supported the Scotts' lifestyle in town and sustained Drennen's minor heirs.[49]

The Arkansas River provided easy access to Indian Territory. Whites in western Arkansas coveted the black (free and enslaved) Indian populations, launching raids on black families in Indian Territory and against those who were traveling through Arkansas to Indian Territory. Black men and women sought protection from this terrorization at the U.S. Army post at Fort Gibson. Some even suggested that perhaps land within Arkansas for free black Seminoles would provide more security than living out in the territory where black bodies were hunted. In one example, the children of a woman named Juana were taken and sold in Fort Smith by a man named Cyrus Hardridge and never heard from again. Sometimes these raiders operated in league with Seminole men or other native people. For example, a Cherokee woman led one of the trafficking rings. The Fugitive Slave Law of 1850, which implicated all Americans, even in "free" states, in the recapture of enslaved people who had fled from their captors, emboldened whites of western Arkansas. The ground of Indian Territory seemed increasingly secure for slavery on the whole as far as whites were concerned, and the neighboring black populations looked ripe for the picking. The Seminoles were already bleeding out some of their enslaved population as runaways to Mexico, whites reasoned, so why shouldn't white Arkansans try to get what (who) they could?[50]

In one of the more well-known incidents, a group of African-descended Seminoles held by Mah-kah-tist-chee (or Molly) lived in a state of quasi-freedom. Adhering to their understanding of the traditional Seminole practice of slavery, the men and women refused to serve Molly as a separate household. As long as she lived with one of their families she could rely on their labor, but they refused to support her separately. Further, the men and women refused to work fields separately for Molly's benefit. The bondspeople held to the traditional customs: either Molly would live and work with them as a unit, or she could expect no benefit from their labor at all. Thus, Molly lived with them and rotated her residence between the families. Perhaps observing that harsher chattel slavery grew ever more profitable to the east in Arkansas, Molly became frustrated and determined to squeeze some monetary gain from her slave ownership.[51]

In April 1853, Molly struck a bargain with a "half-blood" Creek man named Daniel Boone Aspberry. Aspberry could have legal title to as many of the men and women nominally owned by Molly that he could catch, as long as he submitted $100 to her for each one he sold. The enslaved men and women were co-owned by Molly's sister, Mah-pah-yist-chee, but her death freed Molly up to proceed with the deal with no competing interests. Molly, elderly herself, died before Aspberry had successfully captured any of her bondspeople, but he proceeded on his hunt, bill of sale in hand. Aware of Molly's agreement before her death, of its potentially devastating consequences, and that no money had actually changed hands, the community of enslaved families who had been with Molly refused to recognize Aspberry as their new master. According to Seminole law, because Molly had died without an heir, the Seminole leadership had a claim to the bondspeople. For their part, the dead woman's captives sent word that they would not go with Aspberry willingly but would resist him with their lives. The fact that the group's would-be captor was Creek no doubt encouraged other Seminoles to support them in their position that Aspberry had no claim and would do well to stay away. The Creek council, for its part, supported Aspberry and sent thirty men to assist him. Aspberry also enlisted the help of whites, to whom he promised a cut if they helped him capture the families. The slave community at Molly's place made good on their vow to resist; one young man was killed trying to help his mother escape. In the ensuing raid Aspberry and his posse captured at least twenty of the bondspeople, some of whom were sold to white men in Arkansas. Although there were complications in satisfying all of Aspberry's "investors" after the raid succeeded—including giving a cut to a clerk in the regional office of Indian affairs—Aspberry cashed in handsomely from his raid on the black Seminoles. Whites funneled more and more African Americans eastward into Arkansas as the practice increasingly enriched those who raided black Indian households.[52]

Soon the western border became even more dangerous for free and enslaved black families. On March 6, 1854, President Pierce approved a ruling by Attorney General Caleb Cushing that the Fugitive Slave Law of 1850 applied to Indian Territory. U.S. citizens were justified, the ruling held, in heading not only north but now into Indian Territory to retake suspected runaways. As a result, whites from western Arkansas stormed Indian Territory with even greater boldness, capturing African Indians as supposed fugitives and dragging them into Arkansas for sale as chattel. In the summer of 1856, a cadre of white citizens from Van Buren gathered to make claims on black bodies among the Seminole. A cottage industry of slave speculation and trafficking by Creeks and western Arkansas whites emerged. In fact, whites in and around Indian Territory continued to press Arkansas politicians to support their claims to black Seminoles.[53]

The regime continued to harden within the state's lines. While the swamps and canebrakes of the eastern region of the state usually claimed whites' paranoid attentions, as in other population centers along Arkansas's rivers, western Arkansas's enslaved population came under greater scrutiny as the 1850s gave way to the Civil War. For example, enslaved people's access to commodities in trade or theft became a greater source of contention. In 1859 an enslaved man named Willis endured punishment for larceny. He first received a "private whipping" but then, as a public warning to other bondspeople, authorities secured him by his hands and neck to a pillory in Van Buren's square. In September the next year, Van Buren whites organized a county police force, deploying 117 officers, to target horse-stealers and abolitionists. They vowed to enforce a 9:00 p.m. curfew for enslaved people, whom they warned not to go at large after the bell rang each night. Crawford County whites kept a closer eye on bondspeople's handling of cash and liquor. They cracked down on a bondsman named John working in a grocery store, or "dram shop," owned by William Powell, a white merchant from the North.[54] Authorities pressed charges against the seller when Charles, described as mulatto and held by wealthy slaveholder Thomas Aldridge of adjacent Franklin

County, bought two gallons of whiskey from a Crawford County man. Like eastern Arkansas, western Arkansas had long held a reputation for lawlessness, and whites grew increasingly determined to prevent disorder from threatening mastery.[55]

To the north of the Arkansas River, bondspeople had inhabited the region of the White River—flowing north out of the Ozarks' Boston Mountains before doubling back to flow southward through eastern Arkansas—since the early days of white settlement. Near the river's source, they farmed corn and winter wheat in thin, rocky limestone and sandstone soils (enriched by the organic material provided by deciduous hardwoods), with greater yields in the deeper soil of the slender bottomlands of the White's branches. The upper White and its forks drew slaveholders, whose bondspeople worked a variety of tasks. John E. Williams, for example, came to the White River Valley near the Missouri state line a few years prior to Arkansas's statehood, setting up a post trading primarily in horses but also in bondspeople. In 1847 he leveraged those profits to purchase two tracts of land. Mostly residing in single holdings, bondspeople in this region farmed the flat fertile land along the streams and branches that drained the landscape. Although mostly agricultural, their skills and tasks ranged widely, as smaller numbers meant a greater range of responsibilities, while their social lives suffered the limitations of the sparse population.[56]

Several enslaved people on a creek near the White River provided significant labor in building northwest Arkansas from Van Winkle's Mill. New York–born Peter Van Winkle began amassing land in Washington, Benton, and Carroll Counties in the 1840s. By around 1850 Van Winkle had established a complex on the north fork of Little Clifty Creek in War Eagle Township. His development came to encompass a spring, the creek, gardens supported and enclosed by stone terracing, and Van Winkle's home. According to archaeologists, enslaved people probably inhabited a site southwest of Van Winkle's home, across the creek. Bondspeople living there walked by his house to reach the sites of their work, be it the mill or blacksmith shop. By 1860, thirteen enslaved people lived and worked at Van Winkle's complex, including five adult men and two adult women, a number that grew to at least eighteen by 1861, making it an unusually concentrated enslaved community for the region. Men and women held at Van Winkle's lived and worked among free, probably white, laborers. One of the enslaved mill workers, Aaron Anderson Van Winkle, was born in Alabama and served Van Winkle at domestic tasks in addition to his work at the mill. Van Winkle's operation was easily accessed by good roads he had constructed, allowing him to sell and send lumber to Fayetteville, Shiloh (now Springdale), Huntsville, and Bentonville.[57] Even at the relatively crowded Van Winkle place, bonded life in the Ozarks was lonely; enslaved people at the mill lived near few other bondspeople. They may have been familiar with the ten men, women, and children held by Freewill Baptist preacher T. W. Blackburn and wife, Catherine, in the same township.[58]

To the west several of the larger slaveholding farms of Washington County dotted the plateau of Cane Hill. At Tandy Kidd's large operation, sixteen enslaved people cultivated corn fields, tended hogs and cattle, and labored in the Kidd sawmill. Beyond the main house and their two cabins, bondspeople enjoyed access to springs and a thicket. Tandy Kidd had come to the Ozarks from Virginia, amassing 250 acres, 150 of which were under cultivation by 1860. These Ozark enterprises sometimes stretched into other regions, as in the case of the Kidds' Cane Hill neighbor Mark Bean, who ran a "cotton factory" (possibly a textile mill) in Washington County that was fueled by cotton from his Arkansas River Valley holdings. Fayetteville, though not a traditional river outpost, nonetheless arose straddling the watersheds of two major tributaries of the Arkansas: the Illinois River to the west, and the White to the east. Due to the meandering flow of both, Fayetteville's placement offered the most efficient land route to travel directly from the fertile Springfield Plateau drained by those two rivers tracing to the Arkansas River Valley itself. Fayetteville was also the economic center of the region, as well as a slave town. Fully one-third of Fayetteville's inhabitants were enslaved in 1860, well over the statewide average. Enslaved people worked the flour mills, blacksmith shops, hotels, and more.[59] Like other relatively urban areas of Arkansas, Fayetteville offered some opportunities for enslaved people to leverage skills for their own economic benefit. Tobe, an enslaved cobbler held by Thomas Andrew Henson, farmed and repaired shoes in Fayetteville, enjoying some of the proceeds as long as he dispatched a portion to Henson. Some slaveholding farmers, like David Walker, an attorney from Kentucky and the area's richest slaveholder, kept a home in Fayetteville supported by nine enslaved people and a large farm outside of town where twenty-three bondspeople labored by 1860.[60]

Although the concentration of Arkansas's enslaved population thinned out in the Ozarks, the region's white population committed fiercely to the white supremacist structure used to justify and protect it. In 1840, a "committee of citizens" lynched Caroline (described as a "slave-girl"; her age is unknown) after forcing her to confess that she had murdered one of her enslavers. Caroline's daily labor routine began with housework then transitioned to field work with her enslaver, Andrew A. Crawford. One morning, as they started walking to the fields located about a half mile from the house, Caroline mentioned to Crawford that a suspicious man had been at the house earlier that morning, perhaps posing a danger to Crawford's wife. Crawford returned later to find his bloodied and dead wife surrounded by a pile of wood; it looked as though someone was preparing to set fire to the body. When the frantic neighbors failed to find the man Caroline spoke of, they turned their suspicions on her. The account of these events, published more than forty years later, claimed whites observed blood on Caroline's dress and that she confessed to the deed. Whites hanged the young woman, using a pole suspended between two dogwood trees, as she pleaded for water.[61]

Another series of violent events unfolded a few miles outside of Fayetteville in 1856. Two enslaved men slew James Boone with the help of a neighboring bondsman. It is unclear what sparked the attack beyond the usual burdens of bondage, but whatever the trigger, it inspired the men to devise a plan for a nighttime strike. They created noise to draw their victim, Boone, into the darkness of the yard. When he appeared, they leaped from the shadows and beat the wealthy doctor to death. According to the newspaper reporting, all three of the men confessed, but it should be remembered that whites likely violently coerced those confessions from the men. Slain slavers' family members usually avoided lynching because it went against their economic interests. But Boone's sons led an angry mob to take the two men who had killed Boone from the jail in Fayetteville and hang them. The posse, however, did not touch the third man, who underwent a trial and execution. The brutality of slavery's regime haunted the Ozarks no less than it did the delta.[62]

White Ozarkers did not tolerate outright threats to white supremacy or slavery. Minister Anthony Bewley, who had led at least one Methodist Episcopal conference in Fayetteville in previous years, drew hostility from northwest Arkansas whites who discovered he was an abolitionist. In July 1860, when fears of "Black Republicanism" ran high, Bewley stopped in Benton County, Arkansas, on his way from Texas to Missouri. A mob overtook Bewley, questioned him about his views on slavery, and threatened to hang him. The crowd fizzled out as Bewley traveled north but warned him that he could expect to be let alone only if he continued on to Illinois or Indiana. If Bewley intended to head to Kansas—which had been embroiled in bloodshed over the issue of slavery—they would come after him. Bewley must not have traveled far enough fast enough because he found himself in the clutches of a Fayetteville vigilance committee by September. He wrote from Fayetteville on September 5, "At night I am chained fast to some person." A posse took Bewley to Fort Worth, where he was eventually hanged under circumstances that are not altogether clear from the available sources. The Fayetteville *Arkansian* proclaimed his guilt.[63]

From the Fayetteville area, the White River turned north into Missouri, plunging south back into Arkansas at Marion County, before reaching into the alluvial plains, where it fed intensive corn and cotton cultivation. The enslaved people who built the cabin and wealth of a prominent early Arkansan, Jacob Wolf, not only had a view of the confluence of the White and North Fork Rivers but were positioned to observe one of Arkansas's early economic and political hubs, located in Izard County (now Baxter). Jacob Wolf probably brought enslaved people with him upon his arrival in north-central Arkansas, holding 76 acres there by 1829. Ten years later, at least four enslaved people lived on the site and Wolf had expanded to more than 250 acres. By 1850, the enslaved people at Wolf's place numbered at least twelve, doubling by 1860, and residing in three cabins. The Wolf place served as a trading post, crossroads, and political center. Wolf, who was active in early Arkansas politics, represented Izard County in the Territorial Assembly and opened his home as an official space where many people came and went, exchanging political ideas, settling appointments, and delivering speeches. Enslaved people would have witnessed the 1850 meeting Wolf chaired for "southern rights" and heard Wolf advocate that Arkansas participate in the famous Nashville Convention to argue for their "sacred rights" to slave labor. Access to this kind of information helped enslaved people fashion their own concepts of formal politics (including their own understandings of the stakes of the sectional crisis) well before freedom and enfranchisement.[64]

Wolf's defense of slavery received support because of its value to the area's economy. In 1839, bondspeople made up 28 percent of Izard County's taxable wealth and nearly 40 percent in 1843. Ten years later, the proportion had shrunk to 29 percent, still a goodly portion of individuals' assets. Members of the Wolf slaves' community grew corn and cotton, mostly on smaller operations. The average number of enslaved people per household was 5.9 (while the statewide average was nearly 8). In 1860 Izard County (which was slightly larger then), 91 of the 449 enslaved people (20 percent) lived on plantation-sized holdings. A few enslaved people probably worked in sawmills processing the bounty of Arkansas's forests. In 1839, Peter Adams held at least one bondsperson and a sawmill. In 1843, William Creswell held at least two enslaved people and also ran a sawmill. One of Jacob Wolf's relatives worked five enslaved people, who may have labored in his sawmill, in 1853.[65]

To the south and east a port town on the White River, Batesville, in Independence County, linked the rocky hills and alluvial plains. This point, marking the transition to what is known as the Lower White, served as a hub for trading corn, cotton, and men and women as chattel. Bondspeople farming near the confluence of the Black and White Rivers, including an area called Oil Trough, cultivated the zone where the deeper loessal hills and forested coastal plain met the thin Ozark soils. Like the Arkansas, the White stitched the uplands and lowlands together. Slavers there, like Morgan Magness, leveraged profits to expand their operations. The bondspeople held by Magness increased from twenty-three in 1840 to fifty-eight by 1860.[66]

The liquidity and security of slave property facilitated the growth of the economy of Independence County and the rest of Arkansas's corn country. The system of slave mortgages, which Bonnie Martin calls slavery's "hidden engine," allowed small and large slaveholders alike to squeeze the most economic benefit possible from human property and linked nonslaveholders to that economy.[67] Nancy Snell Griffith's exhaustive work in the local records of Independence County reveals this hidden engine at work. For example, in 1853 Freeman and Caroline were mortgaged by Elisha and Taylor Baxter to J. C. and Andrew Gainer for $5,469.74; the mortgage was settled in 1855. The wealth of documents from Independence County provides a powerful example of how whites' reliance on bondspeople as security for debt imperiled enslaved people's implacement. Rachel was mortgaged by Andrew Lyle three separate times in 1861 alone. Jim and Jane were mortgaged twice within a year for debts held by H. F. Fairchild. Over the course of twenty years, Eliza and her children were mortgaged and sold several times to secure the finances of white men and transactions between men and women in Independence County. Some of this activity came from enslavers who benefited from even partial interest in enslaved people's bodies, an arrangement that often resulted from the settlement of deceased slaveholders' estates among their heirs. In August 1856, Archibald and Ann Burns sold their one-half interest in Julia Ann (who was nineteen years old) and her six-month-old baby, Laurilla, to William Petilla for $400. Robert and Ann Lidwell sold their one-seventh interest in Callumbus (who was twenty-two years old) to Charles Moore for $100. Even partial ownership of an enslaved person proved a boon for white Arkansas families' finances.[68]

Dealing in enslaved people cannot be disentangled from the rest of Independence County's commerce. For example, Israel H. Adler partnered with and lived among the family of a wealthy French merchant, Hirsch, basing his slave-trading activity out of Hirsch's general store in Batesville; they invested in some bondspeople together. Townshend Dickinson had a partnership with Henry Neill in Neill's tannery. Dickinson's end of the arrangement included supplying an enslaved person's labor. Bondspeople were also used to secure debt to the Bank of Batesville, the Bank of the State of Arkansas, Burr and Co., and other enterprises.[69]

J. H. Cornwall's reminiscences about his family's farm at Jamestown, six miles southeast of Batesville, on Greenbrier Creek (a branch of the White) provide some insight into the lives of a few enslaved people in northeast Arkansas: Ranza (short for Lorenzo), Jimmy, and Eliza (or Liza). They had been held by Joseph Hardin of Davidsonville. In 1828, Hardin's daughter Nancy married Josephus Cornwall, a Presbyterian minister. Within a few years Nancy inherited Ranza and Eliza from a group of enslaved people that originally included nine. Because her sister Margaret was so young at the time of inheritance, Nancy controlled her part of it (which might have included Jimmy) along with the Greenbrier Creek land, some lots in Batesville, and some cash. The family moved to the Jamestown acreage, which was "overgrown with forest." The Cornwalls and their enslaved farmers carved out a fifty-acre place upon which they cultivated corn, wheat, an orchard, and a garden. The Cornwalls lived in two hewed log houses attached to each other, while a "comfortable but less costly" cabin to the east housed enslaved people, including Ranza, by now a young man, and Jimmy, who was in his teens. Cornwall described the bondspeople's morning routine: "Ranza goes to the barn to bed the horses and mules. Jimmy goes to make the kitchen fire" before helping with the milking. After a breakfast that Eliza prepared, Nancy set out her work for the day while "the colored boys start to the cornfields to plow and hoe," which the Cornwalls' son took part in when not at school. On and around the Cornwall place, black and white residents enjoyed access to "walnuts, hickory nuts, chestnuts. . . . grapes, persimmons, black and red haws, papaw, and other wild fruits" and shared their surroundings with "deer, bear, wolf, squirrel, turkey, rabbit, raccoon, and opossum, not to name others." It is not known what became of Ranza, Jimmy, and Eliza when the Cornwall family left for Oregon in April 1846.[70]

To the east, Mary-Ann Milam made the best of her material circumstances on a farm on the Cache River—which empties into the White—at a crossroads linking Pocahontas and Powhattan. The only enslaved family on the premises, Mary-Ann and her children, including her daughter Betty (who would tell her family's story to a WPA interviewer in Missouri in the 1930s), stayed in a small low-ceilinged cabin. John and Nancy Nutt, their enslavers, resided in a double-pen home with a large porch facing west. Mary-Ann and Betty were not technically owned by the Nutts, however; by law Lewis Hanover (alternatively spelled Hanaver or Hanauer) called himself their master. Hanover was born in Germany and slowly built up a small fortune in the Pocahontas area. He established a mercantile business that dealt in human wares in addition to provisions. By 1855, L. Hanover & Co. owned twenty-five town lots and two taxable bondspeople (defined as those over the age of five and under sixty-five, in most tax years) worth $1,200, while the county taxed Lewis Hanover the individual for forty acres and ten town lots worth $4,000 and one taxable bondsperson worth $600 in the same time period.

Hanover got his start in business with his nonslaveholding brothers. By 1860, the eleven people who were held as Hanover's chattel grew corn (not cotton) and worked stock and hogs on a large valuable farm. Mary-Ann Milam was probably the twenty-three-year-old enslaved woman (along with a small girl and boy) the census listed as enslaved by John and Nancy Nutt in the neighboring county. Mary-Ann Milam's many industrious talents included making moccasins, spinning thread, and weaving. She hunted frequently and, according to her daughter's account, traded skins with passing peddlers. While that part of Mary-Ann's activity remembered by her daughter in the twentieth century may have taken place after slavery ended, it would be unrealistic to assume that Mary-Ann's skills at hunting and processing skins and knowing their value for trade were suddenly acquired after the war. She clearly learned early how to convert her surroundings into material gain. Her family lived in isolation from other black Arkansans, however. The community of enslaved people along the Cache was a small and scattered one.[71]

Mary-Ann's lover and the father of her children was a white man named John Milam. Born in Alabama, Milam had come to Randolph County by 1840, where he resided for at least some time during his twenties with a young bondsman. Before he became involved with Mary-Ann, Milam married and had five children with a woman from Tennessee named Mary. In 1850, the white Milams were small slaveholders in Lincoln County, Tennessee, but had moved (back) to Arkansas by late 1859 or early 1860 where they kept a very small farm. According to his daughter's recollection, however, Milam made his money from a very large still. Although it is not clear when and how Mary-Ann and John Milam met, the fact that she took his name and the manner in which her daughter remembered the relationship indicate a lasting connection. "He had a wife and five children at home," Mary-Ann's daughter Betty explained decades later, "but my mammy said he liked her and she liked him."[72]

Like the lower White, the Ouachita and Saline Rivers fed both small farms and plantation agriculture. In southern Arkansas, the Ouachita and Saline worked their way out of and through the Ouachita Mountains and tied those summits to the gulf coastal plain. Bondspeople, like the small groups clustered in the tributary of Caddo Cove, farmed the fertile soil along the system's streams. The Ouachita and Saline Rivers slowed drastically as they flowed southward, watering the rich valley cotton fields worked by enslaved farmers in south Arkansas. The fertile bottomlands were sandwiched by the acidic yellow-red sandy silt and pine of the rolling forested coastal plain. Cotton increased in importance as the rivers slowed on their way southeast. Bondspeople, like those on John Brown's farm, lived on large holdings and produced thousands of bales of cotton in the Ouachita River valley. The rivers were fed by branches like the meandering Bayou Bartholomew—the longest bayou in the world—before flowing through northern Louisiana and pouring into the Mississippi.[73]

Abby Guy of south Arkansas succeeded in crossing the line from enslaved black woman to free white while living in the watershed of Bayou Bartholomew, benefiting from the anonymity offered by the sparse settlement of the cotton frontier. Born in Alabama to a "mulatto" woman named Polly, Abby came to Arkansas in the 1830s with slavers William Daniel and his brother. Abby's light skin and straight hair, as well as her presence in an area where few people knew her previously as a bondswoman, contributed to her ability to live separately from the Daniels. It is not clear how Abby got away from the Daniels, but by 1844 residents of the area knew Abby and her children (Elizabeth Daniel, Mary Daniel, John Guy, and Malissa Arnold) simply as another Ashley County white farming family. Although the two never legally married, Abby took the last name of a white man named Guy, with whom she lived and had children; she also inherited some land from him when he died. As a free white woman, Guy productively ran her farm, sometimes hiring white men to haul cotton or move fences, turning enough profit to send her oldest daughter to school. Guy and her children socialized and attended church as white people within the white community. In the 1850 census,

Guy is listed as living in Union County as a "mulatto" woman named "Abba" with four children (also recorded as mulatto) to whom she had given the surname Guy (though the older two were born in Alabama), including an eight-month-old baby. Guy's occupation is recorded as "spinstress" and her older daughter as "Belle of Hamburg Dance," which might have something to do with the nearby town of Hamburg.[74]

When Guy made the decision in the mid-1850s to move her family to Louisiana, however, William Daniel began claiming them as chattel. Abby eventually managed to prove her whiteness in court in a society where blackness and slavery were synonymous. During the proceedings, Guy and her children endured humiliating examinations of their physical features for any trace of "negro blood," including their feet. That Abby Guy's mother was a bondswoman would normally have been enough to establish her status as chattel. Indeed, Daniel's attorneys brought in witnesses who had known Guy and Daniel in Alabama and could testify to her previous status. But Guy's life as a free white woman for years, combined with her strikingly "white" features, became more important to a court that stated its reluctance to place such a clearly white person into slavery. Although Guy eventually prevailed, she and her children were forced to work as slaves for several years during the multiple appeal proceedings. Knowing her rights, she sued for reparations for that lost time.[75] Kelly Kennington's study of St. Louis freedom suits identifies mobility as a common theme in legal claims to freedom. Claims like Guy's remained uncommon in Arkansas's history of freedom suits, but for Abby Guy mobility did play a role. Her move to the cotton frontier was not a voluntary one—quite the opposite—but relocation to the cotton frontier created some anonymity that helped her get away.[76]

Part of what made Guy's suit successful was the fact that she had managed to live outside of slavery for so long, owing to the ruggedness of south Arkansas's thinly settled but quickly transforming social and natural landscape. Similar to the east-west Mississippi divide but not nearly as stark, southern Arkansas remained less populated and developed than northern Louisiana. Although a river did not create a border between Arkansas and Louisiana, southern Arkansas counties had only 62 percent of the improved acreage that northern Louisiana had and were home to a little more than half as many bondspeople (25,514 in southern Arkansas versus 47,408 in northern Louisiana). It may be that Arkansas's reputation as a morass and its political troubles in its early years created a real boundary for those choosing to settle the cotton frontier.[77]

To the west, in Hempstead County and its environs, the Red River hosted an early center of slave agriculture linking Arkansas, east Texas, and northern Louisiana. A major obstacle in this region, both physically and economically, was the Red River "raft"—a huge floating mass of logs and debris that impeded river traffic—which had to be intermittently cleared from the 1830s on. Bondspeople there worked a range of soil types. Sandy silty soil made acidic by pine forests met fertile bottomland and blackland prairie, where a rich dark upper layer covered the clay subsoil. Slavers borrowed, traded, and cashed in at the towns of Columbus, Fulton, and Washington, in a region that was such an insulated bastion of mastery that it would come to host the state's Confederate government when Little Rock fell to federals in the fall of 1863. The Red supported a stretch of enslaved communities that reached from southwestern Arkansas into northern Louisiana and carried slave-grown cotton down to Shreveport. Bondspeople cultivated corn and cotton (privileging the latter), much of it along the bottoms of the Bois d'Arc Creek, in a growing plantation economy that did not support holdings quite as large as those found along the Mississippi.[78]

The economy of the town of Washington, Arkansas, held on to the trappings of a frontier exchange outpost into the antebellum period. Enslaved people worked in stores and shops—which advertised their interest in accepting skins and hides as payment for goods—and toiled at the usual domestic work. Two enslaved people, a sixty-five-year-old man and a twenty-four-year-old woman, worked for Benjamin Britton in his store (which sold, among other wares, cloth for "negro clothes"), while Ephraim Merrick's store relied upon captive labor as well. Washington exhibited many of the same relatively urban concerns as those among Arkansas whites in Little Rock. They relied on enslaved labor to assist in maintaining the roads that facilitated commerce. Proprietors of taverns were closely watched for their role in bondspeople's carousing. If enslaved people were caught contributing to disorder in town, the constable could whip offenders "any number of lashes" on sight (as long as it was no more than twenty at once). In fact, the town constable also served as captain of Washington's slave patrol. City ordinance instructed patrollers to visit *every* enslaved person's house, as well as anywhere they suspected unlawful assemblages. If caught "strolling" without a "written permit" bondspeople could expect to receive lashes at the hands of the constable or his deputies. The regulation that whites should not gather "in the night time, in suspicious places, and under suspicious circumstances, drinking or gambling" with enslaved people seems to suggest that those types of gatherings were in fact routine. Whites caught engaging in this forbidden activity were to be "taken" by the patrol to the alderman and "dealt with." Patrolling this southwest post on the Red River could be rewarding: the constable paid his appointed patrollers as much as two dollars a month (but he could only appoint two) and the constable himself could justify taking four dollars per month for his trouble in serving as the patrol's captain.[79]

Whether the Red near Washington or the White at Batesville, the rivers that sliced through Arkansas's ground created varied landscapes of bondage for captive Arkansans, who made their place on terrain that could not always be easily categorized as lowcountry *or* upcountry, bottoms *or* hills. Hubs like Fayetteville, Little Rock, and Helena anchored varied mini-cores of the development of Arkansas's slave society. Arkansas's rivers and watersheds facilitated the economy of slavery, whether relating to corn, cotton, or commerce. Enslaved people understood this map. In exploring the stories of the enslaved experience from the bottom up, we should not understand riverside farming as divorced from the relatively urban experiences of enslavement that took place at Arkansas's posts nor distance the experience from its upcountry and hillside iterations. In fact, the waterways of Arkansas should be understood as ribbons of agricultural life that stitched Arkansas's upcountry and lowlands, linking them in a network in which all pieces fit together to create the greater "terrain of struggle" for bondspeople there.

4 / Flesh and Fiber

Enslaved farmers endured a coerced intimacy with Arkansas's land. They experienced crop cultures "from the ground up," but the deep knowledge they cultivated as they tended corn and cotton was not their own. While bondspeople's conversion of the landscape from woods and swamps to improved farm acreage created a commodity out of the ground, the system under which they labored was designed to alienate them from it. The day-to-day and year-to-year rhythms of their agricultural labor "actualized whites' ownership" of it, not theirs. Chattel slavery kept black Arkansans at arm's length from the typical nineteenth-century frontier convention of associating cultivation of the ground with morality and civility. To bring the land to its full productive potential was supposed to entitle farmers to a sense of status and accomplishment. Instead, enslaved people's labor conferred righteousness and status on their enslavers.[1] Slaveholders made sure that productivity occupied enslaved men's and women's days, weeks, and years on the ground. As Henri Lefebvre writes, a society's creation of space as a social relationship is "inherent to property relationships (especially the ownership of the earth, land)," as well as to "the forces of production (which impose a form on that earth or land)." The rhythms of enslaved people's relationship to Arkansas's land deepened their agricultural knowledge and fashioned their community of farmers, all the while fulfilling captors' ownership of that ground and reinforcing the racialized regime that worked it.[2]

Enslaved Arkansas farmers' lives were held hostage by their forced husbandry. The rhythm of life and the crop cycles tangled in a cadence that defined the passage of enslaved people's time and their concept of the places upon which they were held. The fields were often the sites of important stages of life: birth, childhood, milestones of adulthood, and death. Black Arkansans simultaneously cultivated crops and families, contending with the environment and whites' demands. While different kinds of work punctuated enslaved people's routines according to the season, bondspeople also etched landmarks into their families' histories and sometimes created disruptions in the crop routine. As the crop years and enslaved people's lives unfolded, so did the expansion of farm acreage. Farms of all sizes across the South relied on the availability of additional land for the practice of shifting cultivation. This system brought white farmers to antebellum Arkansas in the first place, and its ongoing application established dynamic boundaries of farmed and uncultivated space upon which enslaved people in Arkansas lived and labored.[3]

Cotton would become king, but first, and for longest, corn and cattle ruled, particularly in the 1840s. By 1840, only a handful of years after Arkansas was granted statehood—and about ten years before the bigger cotton booms of the Old Southwest—Arkansas farmers produced five million bushels of corn. While this haul paled in comparison to neighboring Missouri's seventeen million bushels, only one-fourth as many people resided in Arkansas, whose farmers produced more corn per person than Missouri—about fifty bushels per capita. Corn farmers benefited from the crop as a food source, but they also sold it commercially to white settlers and to the federal government. As whites' wealth in enslaved people and land grew (by around 25% from 1840 to 1845), the connection between corn and slavery only became stronger. Enslaved people understood this all too well. For example, Bannister's enslaver, Humphries, of south-central Arkansas, forced him north to Independence County as security for the payment of a load of corn in the 1840s. Bannister stayed at that farm, owned by Morgan Magness, for six months.[4] Hog production also intensified, amounting to four swine per capita in 1840—significantly more than in other southern states besides Tennessee and Kentucky—with slightly higher concentrations in the uplands. Hillside farmers emphasized cattle, too, in those years. Overall, by 1840, more cattle per person lived in Arkansas than in Missouri, Tennessee, Mississippi, or Louisiana. Sixty-five percent of owners of what Charles Bolton designated "very large" herds *also* held enslaved people. Those bondspeople often worked corn and cotton in addition to caring for cattle. As will be discussed later in the chapter, stock raising remained a central part of enslaved farmers' labor in Arkansas through the antebellum period.⁵

After the mid-1840s, the price of cotton rose (although not without its occasional dips), intensifying whites' determination to draw out profits from enslaved people working it, whether on small or large operations. To maximize their investment, whites refocused enslaved labor. On plantations, even non-cotton work remained "chiefly inputs into the production of the cotton cash crop" because in the long run most tasks figured into the eventual success of the harvest. Slavers overseeing cotton cultivation came to prefer gang labor over the task system when it came to crop work. The task system linked enslaved people's agricultural labor to the concept of space because many tasks were based on the number of rows or portion of land worked. Tasking depended on whites' ranking of enslaved farmers' strength and stamina. After completing their task, enslaved people might be permitted to spend their time on other activities like tending their own gardens. In the gang system, bonded farmers worked in groups. If the labor force was very large their work might be supervised by a driver from among their ranks. Gang labor segregated work more strictly by gender and made child-rearing more of a shared duty. Whites had used the task system in the older eastern fields of the South to instill a sense of responsibility for a particular portion of the field, often assigning the same bondspeople to particular sections. The gang system, however, did not lend itself to that kind of incentive and expanding cotton acreage on any size operation turned greater profit from a more regimented routine. Enslaved people who moved to the second slavery's cotton frontier from tobacco or wheat farms in the east knew that a harsher regime awaited them, even if they had never laid eyes on a cotton plant before.⁶

More than the harsh routine grated on their minds and bodies. The forced migration to Arkansas's ground created a physical experience of disorientation and displacement that was often accompanied by illness. So devastating to the health of enslaved populations was the move to the western cotton South that their slavers readily acknowledged that a period of "seasoning" had to take place before newcomers could handle the new crop, environment, and regime. The suffering became so ubiquitous in Arkansas that people widely referred to it as "Arkansas chills" and "swamp fever."⁷ The men and women held by the Trulocks felt this keenly when they were forced to move from Georgia to Jefferson County, Arkansas. Bodies and spirits suffered. They had experienced a religious revival while in Georgia and created their own habit of holding weekly services for themselves. The group had been so sick and overworked since moving to Arkansas, however, that they did not have the strength to continue their religious meetings. In March 1846, though, after a great deal of the plantation had been cleared and the whites' house finished, the health and spirits of the bondspeople had been sufficiently renewed that they again took up their church services, gathering to hear preaching at the plantation's chapel every other Sunday.[8] Newcomers regularly arrived to Arkansas's cotton fields, reeling from the transition.

Planters and small slaveholders alike extracted enough labor in this system to expand cotton harvests through the antebellum period. The fiber's production in Arkansas exploded between the harvests of 1849 and 1859, more dramatically in some counties than others. The state as a whole produced 367,393 bales in the 1859 harvest. Corn production increased as well, culminating in 17,823,588 bushels in the state's last harvest counted by the census before the Civil War.[9] While most of Arkansas's cotton bales and the state's largest enslaved populations resided in the plantation regions, smaller farms working a few bondspeople were the most geographically widespread form of enslaved agriculture. Choosing from the less prime farmland, small slaveholders targeted well-watered acreage with fewer hardwoods that might slow their progress and made the best of Arkansas's sandier soils.[10]

Bondspeople brought knowledge, not just muscle, to their work, learning and teaching the methods of cash crop production. By virtue of their routine, bonded farmers developed a deep knowledge of cultivated land. Some from the Bozeman plantation even attended a meeting of the Clark County Agricultural Society in 1857. Others tested planting devices in 1859 at Wagram. Enslaved farmers on smaller operations were more likely to gain agricultural knowledge and experience alongside their enslavers, working the fields and doing other tasks together. Whether or not that proximity translated into a lighter work routine or greater autonomy was determined on a case-by-case basis. Bonded farmers laboring for and alongside Simpson Dabney found that upon freedom he offered them stock and land, suggesting that, for some, the arrangement did lighten the burden overall. The knowledge and efforts of black and white farmers created great wealth in Arkansas, raising the cash value of the state's farms from $15,265,245 in 1850 to $91,649,773 in 1860.[11]

Whether held on an expansive multifield plantation or a small farmstead, enslaved farmers launched the new growing season by removing the useless remains of the crop they just finished harvesting. Their white

Table 1. Cotton Production (bales) of Seven Arkansas Counties and State Totals, 1850, 1860

County	1850	1860
Chicot	8,450	40,948
Union	6,270	17,261
Hempstead	2,503	16,318
Independence	274	2,120
Conway	499	3,181
Washington	1	15
Jefferson	4,273	28,586
State Total	65,344	367,393

Sources: DeBow, *Seventh Census of the United States*, 556; Kennedy, *Agriculture of the United States in 1860*, 7.

Table 2. Corn Production (bushels) of Seven Arkansas Counties and State Totals, 1850, 1860

County	1850	1860
Chicot	222,595	329,941
Union	341,406	452,553
Hempstead	278,818	563,093
Independence	388,395	604,470
Conway	164,192	265,119
Washington	557,757	663,510
Jefferson	191,829	490,765
State Total	8,893,939	17,823,588

Sources: DeBow, *Seventh Census of the United States*, 555; Kennedy, *Agriculture of the United States in 1860*, 7.

Table 3. Improved Acreage of Seven Arkansas Counties and State Totals, 1850, 1860

County	1850	1860
Chicot	29,886	66,423
Union	56,841	101,424
Hempstead	32,618	65,548
Independence	23,602	51,769
Conway	11,885	21,747
Washington	38,847	59,379
Jefferson	22,245	65,387
State Total	781,530	1,983,313

Sources: DeBow, *Seventh Census of the United States*, 554; Kennedy, *Agriculture of the United States in 1860*, vii, 6.

Table 4. Enslaved Population of Seven Arkansas Counties and State Totals, 1850, 1860

County	1850	1860
Chicot	3,984	7,512
Union	4,767	6,331
Hempstead	2,460	5,398
Independence	828	1,337
Conway	240	802
Washington	1,199	1,493
Jefferson	2,621	7,146
State Total	47,100	111,115

Sources: U.S. Bureau of the Census, Seventh Census of the United States, 1850, Slave Population; Eighth Census of the United States, 1860, Slave Population.

drivers expected them to eventually incorporate every suitable acre into production, so this phase of the crop year on operations with room to expand included the task of clearing additional acreage for cotton.[12] Shifting cultivation was so important for expanding cotton farms that sometimes bonded farmers began clearing new acreage before the entire previous crop had been completely ginned and shipped. When a larger labor force undertook this process, "trash gangs" of women and children followed the wake of wood-cutting men to pick up brush and debris. Women pulled up and piled cane, vines, and briars with useless wood onto burn piles while men chopped trees. By January 6, 1859, bondspeople at Wagram had cleared sixty acres of new ground, piled all the brush, and within a month had it all fenced. The arrival of four boxes of axes from a steamer signaled more chopping and clearing ahead.[13]

But these chores are not what occupied the minds of bonded farmers beyond the relief that might have come with the end of the bottleneck of picking season. As enslaved men and women pulled or plowed under the old crop and cleared new ground for cultivation, their minds lingered on their own families' seasons and milestones. Jacqueline Jones shows how for women in particular, the energy required for the work they were made to do competed with the energy they needed for their family and community. In 1859, for example, the beginning of the crop cycle at Wagram coincided with an addition to the black community there when Lucille gave birth to a baby on January 1.[14]

By the time enslaved farmers prepared for the next crop, Arkansas's weather had become quite cold all over the state. While slaver John Brown complained in 1853 of catching cold "standing out in the new ground all day when the hands were rolling logs and getting my feet cold," those over whom he presided must have suffered much worse.[15] Lou Fergusson never forgot having to work in the sleet, while Molly Finley recalled that her mother's coattail would freeze while she worked. Sometimes whites understood that it was not in their interest to endanger bondspeople's health in this way, especially overseers who did not want to be accused of neglect. For example, the men and women at Wagram paused their work when the sleet and snow became too heavy in January 1857. Enslaved people suffered from sore throats, colds, chills, and fever working out in such weather. Nearly twenty enslaved people came down with influenza at Walworth's Chicot County plantation at the same time in the winter of 1849.[16]

Cooler temperatures were trumped by even icier tensions, though, on operations large enough to employ an overseer, because their contracts normally began in January. The significance and uncertainty of "newness" that Valencius demonstrates as affecting all who settled the frontier never ended for enslaved people held on operations large enough to employ an overseer because each January held the potential for drastic change. The experience of the same physical place could change radically under a new overseer, who might set a different pace or reorder labor gangs. Enslaved people had to regain their bearings every year. Testing new overseers for weakness and discovering their quirks, benevolent or cruel, was a yearly ritual. Solomon Lambert remembered the beginning of the new year: "That was a busy day. That was the day to set in workin' overseers and ridin' bosses set in on New Year day."[17] While the bondspeople at Bullock's place endured the same brutal manager for years, frequent overseer turnover was more common. For example, five overseers worked at Wagram in three years. Lucretia Alexander remembered several overseers coming and going: "The first overseer I remembered was Kurt Johnson. The next was named Mack McKenzie. The next one was named Pink Womack. And the next was named Tom Phipps."[18]

Unsurprisingly, people held in bondage worked less diligently when not closely supervised by whites threatening them with physical coercion, much to the annoyance of those trying to drive them. Whites interpreted this to mean that African Americans were inherently lazy and it validated their sense that black agriculture was not inherently productive and therefore not worthy of compensation—it required whites' coercion. When John Brown hired an overseer after nine years without one, he wrote, "I feel greatly relieved at the idea of getting a lazy trifling set of negroes off my hands."[19] Some bondspeople's resistance to overseers became notorious. In Hempstead County, one of R. A. Brunson's neighbors claimed that an overseer would be justified in asking for more than the usual pay rate on that place because the bondspeople there were known for their recalcitrance.[20] Despite the tension, overseers—because they moved often—relied on the people they drove for much of their information about the place they managed, especially at absentee-owned plantations like Wagram and Francis Terry Leak's place. When Richard Nicholson noted the mule count shortly after starting at Wagram in 1857, he included that nine were lame, adding, "Said to be the ones bought with the place."[21] Bondspeople's lies, half-truths, or exaggeration could work to the disadvantage of overseers, especially on operations where the proprietor was frequently away. H. L. Berry promised not to put too much stock in what his wards told him, declaring to his employer, "as to listening to negroes I never do I hope you don't think so I never consult them eny way you air all the one I want infermation from." When slaveholders or overseers went out of town for business or for personal reasons, other whites supervised, perhaps providing enslaved people some breathing room and a chance to ease their pace.[22]

Enslaved people took some control over the crop routine, made up part of the power structure that ruled the work, and claimed some dominion over the fields themselves when whites relied on them as drivers or foremen. Most of Arkansas's slaveholding farms were too small to employ an overseer and enslavers could not keep an eye on everything at once. They had no choice but to trust enslaved people with some autonomy in the farm operations. More formally, however, slavers on large operations often placed enslaved men as drivers to officially monitor the work. While these stations could come with material privileges and ingratiate them to whites, men in this role also endured closer scrutiny and at least some tension with other bondspeople. Emma Moore described her grandfather as a "whipping boss," suggesting that he not only supervised work but enforced it. Louis Lucas remembered a black foreman named Jesse who presided over the work of the six or seven bondspeople on a farm on Bayou Bartholomew. Solomon oversaw his compatriots' labor on Bill Newton's farm in Johnson County.[23]

Sometimes slavers distributed positions in the leadership of work across families. At Sylvan Home, Moriah and Billy served as the cook and foreman. Moriah's sister Rachel was married to the leader of the hoe hands, "Uncle Fed."[24] For enslaved people like Moriah, Billy, and Rachel, the work they were forced to do intertwined with their family stories and sense of rootedness in place in the face of constant uncertainty. However, serving as driver placed black men in a position of relative power that sometimes generated animosity from their compatriots. Charles Green Dortch reflected on his father's role as driver: "There wasn't any unfriendliness of the other slaves toward my father. . . . I don't think he ever had any trouble with the slaves any more than he had with the white folks."[25] This comment, meant to assure the interviewer that Dortch's position did *not* stir up rivalries, seems to indicate that those kinds of tensions *were* a real possibility for bondspeople with skills or a privileged position. Enslaved drivers were experienced farmers who knew the land and the crops, and claimed some authority over the day-to-day management of the farm. James (Jim) Pine of Phillips County presided as the foreman of seventy-five fellow bondspeople on the Deputy plantation for ten years. Pine had been taken to Arkansas from South Carolina when he was twelve years old. He said of the white overseer, "He used to take my word for everything."[26]

Slaveholding widow Amanda Trulock of Jefferson County took Reuben's word for everything for years. Although held as chattel, Reuben assumed the role of overseer/driver/manager at the Trulock plantation no later than March 1846, but probably earlier. When Trulock's husband died, Reuben took charge and made the plantation more profitable than it had ever been, dragging the operation out of debt. He worked hard, fretted constantly over the progress of the crop, and felt a sense of competition with white neighbors who managed adjoining and nearby plantations. Reuben held a great deal of power in the decision making—Amanda Trulock routinely used "we" when discussing the deliberation of important decisions, like building a gin. Reuben also enlisted his son, Orrin, in the overseeing effort. Reuben's position was not only at the head of labor supervision but worked into the whites' patriarchal power structure as he and his son sent letters to Amanda Trulock's father and brother in Connecticut, explaining how business was going and justifying his choices on the farm. Reuben's experience contrasted with that of almost all other enslaved farmers because Amanda Trulock's arrangement with him, far from seeking to alienate him from acreage, was designed to establish a sense of responsibility for it. Trulock's unusual approach owed in part to her origins. Raised in Connecticut, she had no experience with slavery before marrying a planter. When her husband died, the responsibility of the plantation fell to her. It is impossible to know for sure whether the men and women working under Reuben and Orrin resented them, or to what extent other bondspeople may have benefited from their special status, but it is clear that father and son made running the Trulock place—and running it profitably—a family undertaking. Reuben's and Orrin's ability to read and write shows that they were enjoying some benefits of their unusual relationship with Trulock.[27]

But enslaved people's annual test of wills centered around white overseers—who came and went more often than slave drivers—so their resolve needed to be assessed as soon as they arrived in January. Enslaved farmers took advantage of the high turnover and began pressing new overseers immediately. Martha Jones began giving trouble during the transfer between overseers at Wagram in 1857. She sized up the new manager's resolve to keep her pace of work, as Pelham wrote, "Sent her out and she tried to stop the same day but failed and has done very well since."[28] Annoyed at having to adjust to five different overseers within three years, the men violently resisted H. C. Buckner at the beginning of his tenure at Wagram in January 1860. By January 4, three had fled: "one Left Monday & the other two left to night in a skift. Miles left Monday morning about sun up I went to Corect him & he struck me with his ax & would of killed me if I had not of goton out of his way I tride to shoot him But my pistole would not shoot. I think they have gon to vicsburgh."²⁹ Miles and the other men returned in a few days. The group remained recalcitrant, though, and Buckner guessed right when he wrote that three "[ap]pear to Be vry much Dissatisfide"—George Kentuck, Jerry Johnson, and Henry Jackson—looking "like the Devil was in them." Only chains would restrain Dick Hill and George Kentuck.³⁰

Upriver and ten years earlier in January 1849, Levi, threatened with whipping by a new overseer at one of Walworth's plantations, pled his case to the second overseer, Horace Ford, who interceded for him. Levi avoided a whipping and the newcomer either quit or was fired the next day. Pedro tested the replacement by feigning sick and was whipped for it. This last overseer quit after little more than a month on the job, "because he could not manage just as he was a mind to." While waiting for yet another replacement, Horace Ford fretted, Levi and Pedro likely enjoyed some peace, and the other enslaved people brooded over the prospect of having to adjust yet again. Ford recorded the tension: "This evening all hands a little cross things go bad no overseer but Levi & myself."³¹ Ford's note suggests that Levi took part in managing the work of other enslaved people on Walworth's holdings, an arrangement that we can only wonder whether Levi preferred or resented. Bondspeople's new-year testing of overseers with fresh contracts was so acute that in mid-January of H. L. Berry's first year managing at Wagram, he proudly recorded, "I have got one weeks work out of them with out running eny of[f]."³²

Enslaved people who were hired out to work according to contracts negotiated between white Arkansans dreaded January for other reasons. The practice of hiring enslaved people facilitated the economy of all parts of Arkansas, and it was almost always arranged on a yearly basis. New contracts often spelled the disruption of neighborhoods. Sometimes hiring took the form of short-lived arrangements limited to particular tasks, such as bondspeople from one farm hauling a neighbor's corn. Annual hires usually occurred as part of deceased slaveholders' estate settlements. For example, in 1851, George and Tom, as estate assets, were hired out in Phillips County while their compatriot Tom was sold for $330. That same year Ed and Jack were hired together for the year for $40. Hiring provided a crucial source of income for widowed white women and their children. It also extended the horror enslaved people felt when a slaveholder died. Not only did the yearly contract hold the potential to threaten their sense of rootedness, it did not eliminate the fear of eventual sale when widows decided it was time to liquidate their inheritance.[33]

The common practice of hiring bondspeople brought many more whites into the fold of Arkansans who could benefit from slavery than is readily apparent from census and tax data. Whites who hired enslaved people profited from the system of slavery and harnessed a bit of the status mastery offered without having to make a large investment. Wealthy white Arkansans frequently sought to pay slavers for the services of enslaved women to cook and perform other domestic labor in their homes. For their part, enslaved people discovered on a case-by-case basis whether the temporary arrangement proved better or worse than the captivity they experienced with the whites who held title to them. When contracted to another slaveholding farm, they became acquainted with new bondspeople, providing potential new friends, lovers, or enemies. Jonathan Martin has described how hiring upended the "conventional polarity" of slavery and mastery by placing enslaved people in an arrangement in which they might potentially play two "masters" off of each other as they wrangled for even incrementally better treatment or conditions. We are provided a glimpse of this dynamic in the case of two men hired out by E. L. Diamond of Phillips County to fellow small slaveholder J. C. Berry; the two ran away and back to Diamond declaring they had been mistreated by their temporary employer.[34]

By and large enslaved people, understanding the violence that so often resulted from pushing back, bore any January surprises and settled into a work routine, breaking the land with plows in February or March. Whether they pushed through the rocky soil of the hills or the dark rich earth of the gulf coastal plain, their work behind the mule and plow required skill and strength. Plowing took up a lot of the time and labor on a farm of any size. By the time cotton boomed in Arkansas, the practice of terracing cotton rows had become routine. Terracing reduced erosion but also required the extra work of ditching. Plow gangs tore across new and old ground with efficiency—eleven bondspeople at Wagram had plowed about 670 acres by February 5, 1857.[35] On smaller farms, whites joined the effort. Plow hands worked over the cotton rows in the early spring, then again in the early summer.[36] Rain slowed the effort because ground plowed while too wet had to be plowed again—something that experienced field hands understood, but they normally had little control over the crop's schedule or whites' wishful thinking.[37]

Plowing represented a crucial task in enslaved farmers' crop year, but this task also made its mark on their families, partially defining gender in enslaved communities. As far as whites who ran the production were concerned, the ability to plow separated children from adults. Childhood as understood today was not afforded to black children held in slavery. As soon as enslaved children were physically able, whites assigned them chores. Children kept fires, carried wood, ran errands, swept, carried water, fed chickens, milked cows, and gathered brush, trash, and rocks from the yard.[38] Decades after slavery ended, Katie Rowe lamented, "Lots of li'l children just like my grandchildren, toting hoes bigger than they is, and their poor little black hands and legs bleeding where they got scratched by the brambledy weeds, and where they got whuppings 'cause they didn't get out all the work the overseer set out for 'em."[39]

Whatever limited sense of childhood slavery did offer was painfully brief, and a teenaged boy's "graduation" from relatively light chores to the more strenuous task of plowing was just one way in which enslaved children were forced to make the "quantum leap from childhood into the world of work," as Wilma King phrased it.[40] Boys whom whites deemed old enough to help work in the fields stopped wearing long shirts and began wearing pants.[41] This transition could grant them access to some adult enjoyments like tobacco and whiskey. Overseer John Pelham described the move from boy to plow hand under the supervision of an experienced bondsman, who also seemed to serve as a sort of driver: "By making Henry attend to the plows instead of plowing I can spare more time about the building. In fact I have had to make him change from plow to plow for several days as I have several awkward new hands at the plow and I had to be at the levee. . . . I made little John Wesley take it and he now plows very well. There are two more little boys I wish to learn, that I may have as many men out as possible."[42] Teaching black boys to plow meant they were no longer children, in whites' reckoning, but they would never be men. Shifting enslaved children to adult labor recognized maleness and adulthood but not manhood. The transition exposed young bondsmen to greater scrutiny and transformed their bodies into a much more valuable commodity, to whites' profit and bondspeople's horror.[43]

Enslaved women plowed countless of Arkansas's acres, too. While this fact might seem contradictory considering the masculine association with plowing, it is important to remember that whites did not acknowledge black women as possessing womanhood. Whites understood and appreciated that they were female, and were often very concerned about their fertility, for example, but they did not ascribe feminine qualities to black women as they did to white women. Whites saw black women as strong, masculine producers without feminine frailty. They preferred putting men to tasks such as plowing first because they assumed that men were physically stronger, but that did not translate into a belief in the delicacy of black women's constitutions, nor did it create an unwillingness to assign women to heavy toil. As Jacqueline Jones explains, an ever-present part of the labor philosophy was the fact that whites considered certain work men's work that women *could* do and certain work women's work that men would *never* do. Thus black women's toil under slavery upheld multiple hierarchies at once. In short, the main priority for slaveholders and overseers was to ensure that any adult could be saddled with the tasks needed to turn a profit.[44]

Many of the women who plowed and performed other crop work only did so intermittently, juggling field and domestic tasks at the whims of their captors. At Wagram, for example, Caroline came in from the fields to help clean the main house and arrange things for a day or two in late February but was sent back out as soon as possible to be used in the plowing effort. The overseer explained that he would "not hinder her or anyone else unless absolutely necessary," in short, explaining that on a frontier plantation—even one of around eighty bondspeople—no time could be wasted in preparing the cash crop.[45]

If plowing marked the arrival of spring, so did heavy rains and rising rivers. The control of water supported life and work, essential for growing crops, watering livestock, and sustaining workers. To slake their thirst through the workday, enslaved men and women drank from barrels in the fields. They washed the sweat and dirt from their bodies and clothes in springs and creeks.[46] But as crucial as water was for farming and sustenance, heavy springtime rain could create a nuisance and even danger for Arkansas's imprisoned labor force. Spring storms blew over trees and crops and created standing water. Stagnant pools fostered mosquito-borne illnesses like yellow fever and malaria.[47]

Freshets often not only disrupted crop work but necessitated emergency land maintenance like ditching to prevent destructive water flow across fields. When hard rains fell, roads could become impassable, and movement around the farm or plantation itself became difficult.[48] If a major feature of the workings of the plantation was to position bondspeople and stock in the right places for the right tasks at the right time, then spring floods interrupted the basic routine in a way that frustrated whites and created additional and more dangerous work for captive farmers. After one spring's heavy rains, two mothers at Wagram had to be ferried across flooded portions of the place from time to time to nurse their babies (to the annoyance of the overseer, who then moved them to other work closer to the house). Bondspeople had to guide stock like oxen through flooded areas to where they were needed as well.[49] They turned plows to avoid standing water and sinks, knowing that they would have to return to add rows when the water receded.[50]

In instances where water threatened the crop, whites were more likely to work alongside bondspeople to salvage it, even on larger farms and plantations. Due to the unusually wet spring of 1853, white and black alike worked to get the crop back on track on John Brown's plantation. He complained: "In a press with the crops all the time. We are vastly behind and the land is so incessantly wet that we work to great disadvantage. I arise early and go constantly all day except an hour at dinner, to eat and take a nap of about 20 or 30 minutes." We can imagine that Brown's captive labor force probably had a similar day, then, but without the nap.[51] Water damaged fifty acres of the Wagram cotton crop in 1859, forcing bondspeople to replant when the Mississippi's overflow receded.[52]

On riverside operations in particular, flooding threatened farm improvement projects, adding to the work of those forced to build a farm while producing a crop. In anticipation of spring floods at Wagram, the overseer forced enslaved people to move the front fence (which was 50 feet from the bank of the Mississippi River) and main house (which was only 150 feet from the river) away from the ever-caving bank. The cable kept breaking in their first attempts, but after an expert arrived from Vicksburg to direct the effort, six enslaved men helped him move the house 400 yards. The frustration of those efforts proved more than enslaved carpenter George Turner was willing to put up with. He ran away only to be recaptured the same night.[53]

Indeed, enslaved people along the Mississippi River constantly fought its movement, maintaining ditches and levees because the river could rise several inches in a day, dissolving banks and threatening acres of cotton. In 1858, men and women in the Arkansas Delta fought flooding so strong that it changed the course of the Mississippi.[54] When overseer John Pelham declared that "levee making and fighting water is an old business to me," he could have spoken for bondspeople up and down the lower Mississippi Valley who battled the Father of Waters every spring. Men and women at Wagram leveed the entire riverfront edge of the place, sometimes working until 10:00 at night. In earlier years, this work represented a hurried temporary fix that bondspeople knew they would have to return to later.[55] In March 1859, overseer H. L. Berry reported that bondspeople had been working on the levee for the previous three days when they should have been planting. He asked the landowner to send some whiskey for the hands "as I have to work in mud and water." Women at Wagram proved crucial to the effort of saving the levee there. While the rest of the women cleared patches of new ground, "eight of the stoutest women" filled in low spots of the levee after men finished constructing it. This toil resulted in sore throats, colds, and fevers.[56]

Even more ubiquitous than their management of water was enslaved farmers' extraction and processing of wood, which busied bondspeople all over the state on farms of all sizes. They removed trees to clear the way for initial crops but continued to do so to add additional acreage for cultivation and to supply the farm or plantation with wood for heat and fuel as well as income. Removing trees made up an essential part of enslaved people's transformation of Arkansas's uncultivated spaces into production for market agriculture. In doing so, they converted spaces that might have harbored private time or resistance into sites of repetitive coerced labor. The success of most of Arkansas's agricultural slaveholdings, no matter their size, depended on the transformation of forests into fields. As Max Edelson wrote, "Planters' landscape always centered on trees and their evocative capacity to bring into view what was otherwise hidden." Enslaved people's labor in expanding acreage made real what slaveholders imagined of Arkansas's ground. As an added perk, the abundance of timber provided whites with additional income; sometimes the first crop or two had to be supplemented with the sale of wood. Enslaved people often extracted and processed timber in winter, when crops did not demand attention. The first trees processed for sale were those closest to waterways because they were easiest to load. Commercial woodcutting was a frequent part of many bondsmen's lives in other contexts as well. Because processing Arkansas's rich wood resources was always an important part of the economy, a few slaveholders purchased bondsmen just for that work. For example, E. F. G. Jacket, a "wood chopper," held two men in slavery and employed four free young white men as laborers.[57]

Much of enslaved people's day-to-day wood work entailed keeping up the modified landscape via building and repairing fences. At the Bozeman farm in 1857, nine men made quick work of fence preparation, splitting 1,100 rails in one day.[58] Although the winter months offered the most convenient time, slaveholders did not set any particular time of year for such improvements; bondspeople integrated it into the crop routine. For example, in 1839, men and women built fences on Henry

Shugart's place during plowing and planting season. Bondspeople on John Brown's southern Arkansas plantation performed that task in July 1852. And at Bozeman's plantation in Clark County, enslaved farmers worked at rails and fencing for an entire February.[59] Constructing and maintaining fences and other structures was the second largest use of enslaved workers' time outdoors besides working crops. This work at the edge of fields and pastures, or deeper into densely forested zones, gave black men some time out of whites' sight. For example, two men, recently purchased by small slaveholder Thomas Edwards of Lafayette County, took their chance at revenge while chopping wood in 1851. They killed Edwards with their axes as he approached their work site along the river and then dumped his body into the muddy water.[60]

No matter what other work needed to be accomplished, though, cotton remained the primary focus of most enslaved Arkansans' labor, and in late spring it was time to get the seed in the ground. Planting the crop that would dog them all year and eventually enrich their enslavers began at the end of March or in April. In a process placing those with the quickest and most precise movements in the lead, the first person opened the ground, keeping a close eye on space between plantings. Another came behind, dropping a few cotton seeds into the hole, while the last covered it with a foot or a hoe. Enslaved people might test new practices, as whites experimented with farming methods and equipment, such as devices to open the soil and deposit the cotton seed more efficiently.[61] Spring planting efforts were divided between the cash crop and food crops, however, and some farmers preferred to get their corn in the ground first.[62]

In fact, while cotton drove Arkansas's agricultural economy, corn fed it. Corn fueled people and stock and always offered reliable income alongside cotton. Thirteen bushels of corn fed one person per year, while four bushels fed a hog for a year.[63] In wide swaths of Arkansas, enslaved farmers worked corn more than cotton. The hillsides and prairies exhibited higher corn-to-cotton ratios than did the river valleys. For example, by 1860, Washington, Hot Spring, and Lawrence Counties produced more than 100 bushels of corn per bale of cotton, while Chicot, Desha, and Jefferson produced less than 25 bushels per cotton bale. Corn remained important everywhere, though. Enslaved farmers at Lycurgus Johnson's Chicot County plantation produced 3,000 bushels of corn in 1850 and more than 10,000 in 1860.[64]

Cultivating both crops at the same time, along with any supplemental food crops, made for a busy spring for Arkansas's bonded farmers.[65] At Wagram, they planted "pepper grass," mustard, collard, and okra.[66] Men and women at Lycurgus Johnson's plantation grew corn, peas, beans, sweet potatoes, and Irish potatoes and even kept bees for honey.[67] Bondspeople at Bozeman's grew oats, wheat, potatoes, peas, watermelons, apples, and peaches.[68] While Arkansans cultivated both types of potatoes across the state, sweet potato crops were more common in the southern half and white potatoes more common in the northwest half. On Ozark hillsides, enslaved people built up earth supported by rock walls to create level spaces suitable for growing vegetables. Bondspeople who were allowed to keep their own family garden plots also had to find time in the spring to get those plants in the ground in addition to the cash crop.[69]

Tender green cotton plants began to push through the soil and make their appearance in April and required care for the next few months. In mid-spring, bondspeople discovered where they would have to replant due to late frosts or flooding. Agricultural reforms in cotton cultivation picked up momentum by the time cotton boomed in Arkansas, contributing to an earlier planting schedule, thus increasing the likelihood that enslaved people would have to replant.[70] The maturing cotton plants required scraping and tending to keep out grass and to thin the plants, creating a distance of about twelve inches between them. Enslaved people carefully chopped and scraped while plow hands worked in succession to pile soil toward the plants, keeping the roots warm and maintaining ditches that provided drainage between the rows. Grass had to be kept out of the corn, too.[71] Enslaved adults bent down between two rows, reaching right and left, working them both as they went along.[72] In May 1839, Henry Shugart proudly recorded in his plantation journal that twenty-four hands scraped more than twenty-five acres of cotton in one day. As in the initial plowing phase, whites on smaller operations took part in this work when necessary to keep up with the crop.[73]

Their bodies may have worked the ground, but enslaved people's hearts and minds focused on family life. While they nurtured cotton seedlings to create a good healthy "stand," love germinated and sought a solid foundation on the Ballard place in 1857, when Martha Ann, around eighteen years old, and George Turner, around nineteen, married on a Saturday. After a long week of clearing land and planting, "They are all now enjoying themselves," the overseer noted, in celebration of the union.[74] Sorrow followed, however, when an ill child, described by the overseer as "the little deformed boy," died the night after the wedding. While enslavers and overseers contemplated the profits of each year's upcoming harvest, life's turning points marked the seasons for enslaved people.[75]

With increasing acreage devoted to cotton, the spring and summer stoop labor grew each year. Enslaved farmers fought insects, bollworms, and "rust" (fungus) on cotton.[76] They thinned and worked over the corn as well, but corn never proved as demanding as cotton and could often be laid by sooner. As they did with other phases of the crop year, enslaved farmers juggled the work of chopping and scraping with other required tasks. During the first year of cultivation at Wagram, the men were so involved in the work of setting up the fences and buildings that the bulk of the late spring and summer cotton work fell to the women. The overseer explained to his employer, when altering the usual order of implements for the year's work, "The women will be the main workers of the crop and these hoes are heavier than I am in the habit of giving to men."[77]

Summers sweltered and brought on a short-lived but hectic phase of the crop year for enslaved Arkansans. The transition from spring to summer prompted many wealthy planters to vacate their holdings until cooler—and, in their minds, healthier—weather returned. The warmer season reminded whites of one of their fundamental justifications for the enslavement of African-descended people: that their bodies better tolerated heat. From the colonial period, whites believed Africans to be inherently better suited to heat, humidity, and the diseases that accompanied those conditions. Thus, slaveholders reasoned, forcing bondspeople to work in Arkansas's heat was not as cruel as it seemed, and their own avoidance of that labor was justified for health reasons (never mind that nonslaveholding whites seemed to tolerate it). The Old Southwest was in fact getting hotter, both because the massive deforestation was increasing surface heat and because the little Ice Age was ending.[78]

On the minority of farms that grew wheat, late spring signaled the time to harvest and thresh it, while those who grew oats set to tying and "shocking" them. Dry weather in June and July created challenges, as insufficient rain left the ground hard and dusty, while the heat made enslaved people's usual work especially uncomfortable. A harsh summer could stunt the crop and devastate the profits that whites anticipated, putting even more pressure on black men and women. In 1854, an exceptionally dry season reduced cotton yields in Arkansas and the entire South, placing bondspeople under even more pressure to get the most out of what acreage did survive.[79] As the crops neared the laid-by stage—when plants no longer required the constant attention but had not yet fully ripened—other work commenced. Bondspeople sowed turnips, kept grass out of the corn and peas, dug up potatoes, gathered fodder, and even cut sugar cane.[80]

During this relatively loosened phase of cotton's demanding regimen, bondspeople worked on public roads, returned to clearing land, repaired fences and implements, and engaged in lighter tasks like making baskets. Much of this work took the form of what Daina Ramey Berry has termed "working socials," in which a group completed a task together, allowing them to build and maintain social ties. As they worked, enslaved people could discuss their own lives and support each other even if their physical energy was spent enriching their oppressors. For example, summer offered reasons to celebrate when both Cassidy and Charlotte delivered baby boys at the Bozeman plantation in 1857. Nineteenth-century Americans cherished the Fourth of July, which meant that slaveholders often allowed bondspeople some respite for that holiday. Men and women at Bozeman's marked the Fourth by beginning the third pass over the cotton with their hoes, but "All hands quit a while before night."[81] Bondspeople at John Brown's plantation did not enjoy any time off for July 4, 1853, if Brown's note that he "celebrated this memorable day at home by a very fatiguing days attention to my crop" is any indication of how enslaved people spent the day.[82] As the crop year marched on, bonded farmers tended to their relationships as well. Lee and Rachel, as well as Stephen and Martha Jones, married the week before they laid by Wagram's cotton in July 1859.[83]

Finally, after months of cultivation, cotton squares began to crack open in early August, the visible slivers of fiber signaling the picking frenzy soon to follow. This was the most aggressively coerced part of bondspeople's agricultural lives in Arkansas. Enslavers obsessed over picking time and drove black men and women to the brink of exhaustion because the sooner enslaved people gathered and processed fiber into transportable bales, the sooner whites saw the fruits of their investment in acres and bodies.[84] Thus, Arkansas slaveholders and their overseers became consumed with micromanaging this payoff phase of the crop. Although picking involved tedious, repetitive stoop labor in hot weather, it did not require much strength. The pounds rolled in quickly under coercion. Planters associated better-graded cotton not only with higher profits but with personal achievement and their own honor. It was not enough to harvest quickly, then; the fiber had to be harvested cleanly. Neighboring whites rode over each other's crops to decide whose cotton was getting picked fastest and cleanest. Picking "clean" cotton required pulling the fiber free from the dry, crisp walls of the boll without allowing dirt or pieces of the boll squares and plant leaves to cling to it as it was pushed into a basket or bag. Skilled pickers made clean, quick work of the harvest, but the repetitive task created sore fingers as the sharp edges of the opened boll scraped against the skin. Enslavers and overseers set all enslaved people to this work. Older children helped by assisting adults in picking or helping to move the baskets down the rows while adults picked. Betty Robertson Coleman remembered assisting her father with field work as a child. When old enough, girls and boys worked their own row.[85] This togetherness during the frantic phase of the cotton routine allowed bondspeople to assist and support each other, but it also made them witnesses of whites' hard driving of their loved ones. The work required less muscle than it did agility and stamina, and enslaved people looked for ways to take their minds off of the repetitive strain.[86]

No matter how encompassing the harvest was for whites, enslaved people attached their own significant moments to the season. The transition to picking coincided with important turning points for the enslaved community at the Shugart plantation in 1839, for the day that the first cotton boll opened, Fanny's child died. No respite followed the tragedy, as bondspeople there worked at pulling fodder the next day, burying the child that rainy evening. At Wagram plantation Eliza Johnston gave birth at the beginning of picking season, on September 15, 1857.[87] In those harvest years, Fanny was preoccupied with her loss and Eliza focused on her growing family while the cotton routine pressed on. Enslaved people carried their grief and joy with them to the rows.

Cotton picking came to dominate all waking hours, which stretched late into the night. An oft-discussed symbol of enslaved men's and women's productivity, daily picking totals varied by gender and age and whether the entire day was devoted to picking or split between different tasks. Bondspeople hauled in fewer pounds in the beginning, when only some of the bolls had opened. Enslaved people at John Brown's brought in 100 to 128 pounds each, about 1,200 to 1,400 pounds total early in the 1853 season. The strongest pickers on the place totaled 170 or 180 pounds per day.[88] At Wagram a few years later, hands averaged a little over 100 pounds each early on in the 1857 crop, according to the overseer's account of 32 hands, "little & big," bringing in 3,255 pounds one mid-September day.[89] In August 1859, daily totals amounted to nearly 200 pounds each when everyone old enough to pick was forced out into the fields. According to the overseer, "With 41 handes I picked over 8 thousand pounds of clean cotton in one day," the best August yield he had ever seen, due to the fact that the very dry plants opened unusually quickly.[90]

As enslaved people tried to keep up with the consistently opening cotton at the demand of whites who were finally within sight of payday, their daily hauls grew heavier. In 1852, the Brown plantation had harvested about 18,000 pounds of cotton by the end of the second week of October. In November, Brown drove them harder, noting, "getting out cotton as fast as we can."[91] When Pelham at Wagram listed 9,125 pounds of cotton in one day off of 20–25 acres, he bragged that the most the bondspeople had picked in a day was over 12,000 pounds. A couple of years later, they averaged about 195 pounds each in a day's picking.[92]

Women's efforts proved crucial to the picking effort, especially when whites required men to perform other tasks. John Brown moved the men from picking to clearing new land in December, but the women continued picking well into January 1853. In fact, at Brown's, women picked longest; they were the last to stop picking the 1852 crop and the first to begin harvesting the new crop in August 1853.[93] Maggie Walker Benton of Elmwood in Chicot County tracked men's and women's daily cotton harvests over the course of 30 picking days. In the 29 days that a woman named Lithia picked, she brought in 6,752 pounds, averaging nearly 233 per day. Her haul amounted to a higher total and daily average than a man named Bill, who picked the most cotton of all the bondsmen. Bill picked 28 days out of the 30, harvesting 6,204 pounds total, averaging 221.5 pounds per workday. Bill's lighter picking days undoubtedly meant that he had other duties on those days; his most productive picking days yielded upwards of 330 pounds. Benton's diary provides a glimpse of enslaved farmers' productivity but also of the centrality of women to the harvest, especially when whites employed men at other tasks.[94]

Arkansas weather was usually still hot and dry in the early fall as the harvest continued. Picking progress slowed when cotton plants dried. During the picking season of 1853, John Brown decided that it had become too hot for him to supervise, but he kept men and women working on through the heat, though probably less energetically without a supervisor. "I do not stay with the hands now but see them every day once or twice and direct," Brown noted. "The sun is too hot to keep in it constantly picking cotton."[95] When it did rain it slowed the harvest's progress. Rain might have provided some relief from the heat, but it did not give enslaved people any respite from whites' work demands, as they were set to other chores indoors and out.[96]

Enslaved people in Arkansas brought in ever-higher yields of cotton as the years passed both because cotton varieties improved and because their captors drove them harder. According to economists, the increase in productivity by enslaved cotton farmers—fourfold between 1801 and 1862—surpassed the rate of productivity growth of laborers in the American economy overall in the same period. Around 1806, a Natchez planter brought an upland cotton type from Mexico, kicking off years of fruitful improvements in upland cotton. By 1820, whites' experimentation with upland varieties resulted in breeds that yielded more fiber, resisted disease and fungus, and boasted a higher lint-to-seed ratio. Petit Gulf and Alvarado were early favorites. By the mid-1840s, cotton planters of the Mississippi Valley lauded Sugar Loaf, Mastadon, and Prolific. Among these new varieties' sterling qualities, whites appreciated the clustering habit. The branches of the plant produced bouquets of bolls, meaning that the stoop labor required to harvest it brought greater profit. This benefit was meaningless when laborers could grow more cotton than they could pick. The new varieties eliminated that problem because the fiber clung to the plants and resisted rotting long after the squares opened. This meant that slavers could afford to grow as much cotton as acreage they could clear and black bodies they could drive. Of course, it was enslaved people who truly developed the new breeds of cotton when their toil demonstrated the potential of the new plants. While Edward Baptist emphasizes the increased labor demands placed on enslaved people and Alan Olmstead and Paul Rhode argue for biological innovations in the crop, the cause of increased yields should be credited to *both* harder driving and better cotton varieties. By the 1850s, however, the rise in picking rates had begun to slow, averaging 114.2 pounds per hand by 1862.[97]

Enslaved men and women pushed back against the pressure of picking season, both as planned and in the heat of the moment. Bondspeople on Brown's place significantly slowed the pace of the 1852 harvest. Brown left the plantation in early fall, and the men and women held there took advantage of his decision not to employ an overseer during his absence.[98] In January, when all of the cotton still had not yet been picked and baled, Brown remarked, "The negroes as I expected had not done much . . . we must try to be the more energetic hereafter."[99] On January 12, Brown complained, "We are not done ginning yet and have only sent off to Camden 15 bales of cotton." Because of the delay, that year Brown did not get his own crop ginned until February 24, and finally finished forcing bondspeople to harvest cotton purchased from a neighbor's field on March 12.[100] Black men and women may have worked at Brown's coercion, but that year they destroyed his schedule and set their own pace.

Reacting to the pressure of the harvest and understanding that their resistance packed a heftier punch in that crucial phase of the crop year, bondspeople ran away more often during the picking season. People held in slavery on the Shugart farm gave him plenty of grief during the harvest of 1839. Runaways included Nat, Henry, Elijah, and Ginnis. Susan (who had been taken to the Shugart plantation from New Orleans only four months earlier) may have also put up some opposition to the work routine, because Shugart whipped her around the same time that Ginnis and Elijah ran away. On top of that, Henry Shugart became even more exasperated when a man who had fled from another farm stopped by his place and stole a horse.[101] By withholding their valuable labor, bondspeople's picking season resistance hit whites hard at the precise time in which they hoped to reap the rewards of mastery. Men and women at the Hilliard plantation frustrated that season for whites in 1849, causing Miriam Hilliard to sullenly record in October: "Gloomy prospect, short crop, cotton opening slowly; five negroes in the woods."[102]

Enslaved people engaged in more than truancy and work slowdowns, however, when they hit a tipping point during the cotton harvest. On farms that were being built while they operated, men and women alike sometimes refused the extra strain on their labor. They pushed back so strongly against the demands of Wagram's overseer, John Pelham, during the 1857 harvest that his employer, Ballard, who believed Pelham was too easily manipulated, fired him. The strain created by the demands of picking and construction lay at the center of the incident. The quarters, corn crib, and other outbuildings remained unfinished, and Pelham had pledged, "I shall do all I can in building and picking." For example, he had planned for the field hands to have the crib and stables built before picking time but was unsuccessful. Enslaved people resisted his attempt to get all of that work at once to prove his productivity to the plantation owner.[103]

The defiance at Wagram included carpenters who had been sent from Ballard's other holdings to lend their skills to plantation construction. George Turner, John Rutherford, and perhaps more came to Wagram at the end of the summer or early fall of 1857.[104] The men knew their value and did not waste opportunities to remind the overseer that their stay at Wagram was temporary (they rebuffed his clothes ration, explaining that their clothes were made on their home plantation), to milk any sickness, and to slow the pace of their projects. The men became sick almost immediately after their arrival (which the overseer assumed was due to their not having "been acclimated") and took advantage of the chance to get out of work. As soon as the overseer put the men to a full workload, they would take sick. About John and George, Pelham said, "Neither of them can do much nor do they like to do what they can."[105] Henry, who may have been a more permanent member of the Wagram plantation but was clearly part of the construction showdown with the overseer, somehow reached Ballard with his side of the story. Pelham's defense provides some idea of Henry's success in playing the exasperated overseer. We can only guess at the supposed "double damned lie" Pelham claimed Henry had told Ballard about him; it was clearly unflattering and prompted the overseer to rage: "I suppose Henry did not tell you he was more than a month making the door & window frames & part of the shutters. I found as soon as he was put in the sun he was laid up a part of every day or two with a chill, therefore I put him to work under shelter as I wrote you. Frequently when I would stop to see his work and he had done nothing, his chill or fever had just gone off as he has lied to you no doubt he frequently lied to me for sometimes I would catch him with the fever or chill and sometimes not. I know they have no good will for me and will tell any thing they please."[106]

As a result, bondspeople at Wagram endured closer supervision and harder driving by the increasingly desperate overseer. He whipped the carpenters and forced them to make up work on Sundays. As for the rest, Pelham pledged, "I will get more out of them if it is to be had," and forced a faster picking pace.[107] He whipped them frequently, reporting to Ballard that "It requires some strap to get cotton that is pure," and "Henry requires strapping occasionally and gets it so do those who do not pick as they should." They all resented the more demanding pace and freer lash. By December 1857, after at least one man had fled, it was clear that the enslaved people at Wagram had succeeded in preventing Pelham from returning as overseer.[108]

None of the men and women imprisoned at Wagram were naive enough to believe that they had put the days of whipping and hard driving behind them forever. Slavers and their managers everywhere relied on the lash to enforce the domain of the fields, using it as a terror tactic and a physical deterrent to resistance. Peter Brown recalled waking up to the sound of brutal whippings at the Woodlawn plantation owned by the Hunts in Phillips County: "I heard that going on morning after morning." Slaveholders pressured overseers for maximum productivity, and overseers transferred that burden onto enslaved people, who lived under the constant threat of the lash. Decades later, Harriet Daniel tried to downplay the severe treatment of bondspeople by overseer Joe Hinton Scott at the Bullock plantation, but she had to admit that he whipped women mercilessly, ripped a lock of hair from one man's head, and even cut Fed—the leader of the hoe hands—with a knife across the stomach. Although Daniel supposed that the men and women held by the Bullocks harbored no ill will toward the overseer, the truth shone through when she described the black men and women there as "sullen and rebellious."[109]

Nathan, held on R. A. Brunson's plantation in Hempstead County, rebelled against first-time overseer James Martin during the picking season in October 1853. Infuriated by the man's resistance, Martin went to town that morning to drink and complain about the insubordination of the men and women held at Brunson's, who were known to be "a hard set." Martin declared that "after this if I ever do oversee again I will make the negroes obey me or I will kill them" and set off to the plantation, primed to make an example out of someone. He started to correct Nathan, who refused to be whipped, declaring that he had been whipped by the last overseer and would not suffer it again. Martin continued to threaten Nathan with his whip and a pistol, to which Nathan replied, "Shoot and be damned!" Hands still full of cotton, Nathan charged, stopped only by three shots from Martin's gun. He died a few days later.[110]

As autumn cotton labor created sore backs, swollen fingers, and hot tempers, roads and rivers carried the harvest south to a global market. Bondspeople began ginning cotton and pressing it into bales of at least 400 pounds before all of it was picked. Children often helped run the animal-powered gins that processed the fiber. Emma Moore remembered sitting at the gin as a small girl; her job was to periodically tap the mule to keep it moving. On riverside plantations, enslaved people piled bales on the banks to await steamboat pickup.[111] The bales shipped off in waves as soon as enough were ready to make a trip to entrepôts like Memphis, Vicksburg, and New Orleans. In respites from picking, black men often drove the team hauling the fruits of their labor to the nearest town or river port.[112]

While tensions associated with the scramble to get the cotton out as fast as possible raged on, Arkansas bondspeople harvested loads of corn, too. Because they often used the blades of the corn as fodder for cattle, enslaved people ripped them from the stalks, then bundled and dried them. When it rained, bondspeople often shifted from picking cotton to pulling corn; sometimes women gathered corn while men worked on fences or buildings. Men and women gathered in the corn crib to remove the husks from the ears.[113] The completion of the corn harvest could engender a feeling of celebration because it involved group work and signaled that the end of the crop year approached. Hannah Jameson described such a gathering in southwest Arkansas with a song that hinted at secret festivities unrelated to their work: "After the corn was all husked and all the white folks was gone to bed they danced the rabbit dance and sing like this:

> Early one morning, on my Massa's farm
> Cut that pigeon wing, Lizy Jane
> I heard dem chickens a-givin the alarm
> Shake yo feet, Miss Lizy Jane
> Shake yo feet, Niggers, It'll soon be day,
> Skoot along lively, Miss Lizy Jane
> Massa ketch us dancin', there'll be —— to pay,
> We got taters to dig and hoe dat corn,
> Hit dat duffle-shiffle, Lizy Jane
> You'd better be a-humpin, coz it'll soon be morn,
> Shake dat balmoral, Lizy Jane."[114]

Columbus Williams claimed that while he knew of festive corn huskings in Georgia and Mississippi, they were not allowed on "mean" Ben Heard's place in Union County, Arkansas. Similarly, while other types of seasonal celebrations came to Pate (or Pete) Newton's mind, corn huskings were unknown to him in Johnson County. Louis Davis of Pulaski County said that singing accompanied the work of shucking during the day but did not transition to a party at night (or perhaps they took place without his knowledge as a youngster). Williams's, Newton's, and Davis's testimony, paired with the lyrics of Jameson's song, suggest that corn-husking celebrations in Arkansas often had to be held in secret, if at all.[115]

Arkansas historians have well established that the emphasis on corn production lessened as cotton became increasingly important and that upland counties where conditions were not as well suited for cotton remained corn-intensive. Little explored, however, are specific corn crops grown by enslavers and how they related to the production of cotton. A few examples from the 1850 agricultural census of Phillips County, a solidly cotton-focused region, reveal a strong emphasis on corn and a wide variation in corn-to-cotton ratios at the individual farm level in the 1849 crop year. While the census schedules did not explicitly tie enslaved populations to specific farm acreage owned by slaveholders, we can infer their connections. The four bondspeople held there by R. H. Mifford produced no corn but 37 bales of cotton on 75 improved acres. In the same township, 24 bondspeople held by A. E. Addison grew 3,500 bushels of corn and no cotton on 250 improved acres. William Weatherly's 19 bondspeople produced a balance of 1,800 bushels of corn and 42 bales of cotton on his 150 improved acres. Similarly, 70 enslaved people grew 3,000 bushels of corn and 142 bales of cotton on David Thritkeld's 375 improved acres. Slaveholders often squeezed as much corn and cotton as possible out of small operations; Williamson Bonner's comparatively small 70 improved acres yielded 975 bushels of corn and 7 bales of cotton, presumably worked by the 5 people he held in bondage. Some grew only corn and no cotton, if we trust a direct relationship between slaveholdings and agricultural output across those sections of the census—8 people held by J. C. Berry grew 1,500 bushels of corn and no cotton that year. Holdings like that of John Gillem, who claimed ownership over 36 people but only grew 1,000 bushels of corn and no cotton on a mere 50 improved acres, probably indicated enslaved people's labors were split between their home farm and hiring out to others.[116] In short, the Phillips County examples illustrate what was true for enslaved farmers all over the state: those who cultivated cotton usually also grew corn, but corn farmers did not always grow cotton. Many factors influenced their ratios.

Even more so than the lighter phases offered by processing the corn and laying by the cotton, Christmas represented an important moment of relative rest for bondspeople; whites usually allowed them at least the day of Christmas "off" from work. Overseer Horace Ford noted in 1848, "Today is Christmas the Negroes are all on tiptoe. The first salute is for Christmas gifts." Men and women at John Brown's plantation enjoyed five days of respite for Christmas. Brown explained: "It is a human as well as wise regulation of society to allow them a few days as a Jubilee, and they enjoy it. All are brushing up, putting on their best rigging, and with boisterous joy hailing the approach of the Holy days." Enslaved people there must have relished this time without his "particular oversight."[117] Cindy Kinsey remembered Christmas celebrations including a large fire outside near the quarters, around which bondspeople danced. The "master" and "mistress," enslavers who believed their own fiction of the plantation as one big family, presented gifts. Molly Finley recalled that Christmas included a large dinner picnic of chicken cooked in large iron washpots. For bondspeople who were able to mark Christmas in this way, it represented one of the few moments when they could enjoy some of the fruits of their labor on the plantation—meat, root vegetables, and perhaps even some sweets. Not all people held in slavery had the chance at such a reprieve, however. Louis Davis of Pulaski County said of Christmas, "We knowed when it came, and that was all." Rather than a weeklong holiday at the end of the year, wrote planter Sterling Cockrill, "Christmas will last only from Friday morning to Monday morning, when they must go to work. Long holidays won't do when the force is large."[118]

For enslaved men and women, the holidays meant more than better food and some rest. While whites understood the ritual gift-giving and dinners of the season as solidifying their self-imagined positions as paternalists, enslaved people *expected* to enjoy the fruits of their labor and reward for their hard work at this time of the year. More importantly, the enslaved community's focus at the close of the year was not on whites at all but on their *own* leisure, family, and enjoyment of seasonal treats. The celebrations provided opportunities for black families and friends to knit their social ties and establish their sense of place. This was true for Charlie McClendon's mother, who enjoyed an extra-special holiday when he was born on Christmas Day at William E. Johnson's place in Jefferson County. John W. used his Christmas holiday to visit his wife, Rose, on a nearby plantation.[119] While seasonal holidays allowed people like Charlie's mother or couples like John and Rose to take time to build relationships, a fortunate handful had the chance to choose to work for wages. Some of the men at Brown's took him up on the opportunity to work over the holidays making and hauling rails, each earning as much as $2.37 for this extra work. They converted a seasonal rest into their own material gain, and may have used the money to buy some things they wanted or items their families needed.[120]

The cooler weather and holidays also signaled an important seasonal task for most farms large and small: hog-killing. Like corn, and linked to the production of that crop, pork provided a staple of enslaved Arkansans' diets, and as they did with corn, bonded farmers "harvested" pork toward the end of the year (or early January, if necessary). One slaughter could produce thousands of pounds of meat.[121] Harriet Daniel described the work:

> On the day before great loads of wood and several of rock were hauled to the slaughter pen, out some distance behind the Negro cabins. At four o'clock in the morning the horn, a large pink lined conc shell about the size of a calf's head, was blown by Mr. Scott and all the Negro men rolled out of bed to set fire to the previously laid heaps and to fill the vats with water from a nearby branch. These vats were made up of two pine logs about six feet long, with the side of each one sawed off. These were put in frames and wedged together,

the seams having been chinked with cotton. Rocks were put in the fire of pine knots and when red hot were thrown into the vats, thus heating the water for scalding.... Amid songs and mirth, the work of removing the hair from the slain hogs was begun and soon they were hanging in rows on long elevated poles.

Enslaved people were cheered by the prospect of pig tail snacks and the chance to acquire "a piece of liver to cook for breakfast or a maw to cook for dinner."[122] On Walworth's Southfield plantation in 1848, enslaved farmers worked at salting the meat of fifty-three hogs on a Christmas Eve Sunday.[123]

Whether it was accomplished by the time Christmas festivities began or if it lingered until February, the year did not really end for many bondspeople until they had processed the last of the cotton crop. When Henry Shugart noted in his journal on a Saturday, "finished picking cotton and I am not sorry," his opinion was likely shared by his captive labor force, who began clearing the stalks for the next crop the following Monday. The fibers of newer, hardier breeds of cotton remained on the plant into January and beyond. For example, bonded farmers at Michael Bozeman's farm in Clark County did not finish picking the 1856 crop until early February 1857. Thus, crop years sometimes overlapped, splitting black labor between completing the harvest and readying fields to begin the cycle again.[124]

Throughout the seasons of the crop year, bondspeople all over Arkansas practiced animal husbandry, a task that often pulled them beyond the fenced portions of their neighborhoods. Working stock demanded milking, watering, feeding, protection, and slaughtering in daily and yearly routine that marked and supported the central agricultural unit. Enslaved people might care for hundreds of head on one plantation. While they generally kept animals that were used for riding, plowing, or hauling (like mules or horses) in stables and pastures, stock raising in the antebellum South often amounted to turning hooved animals loose to forage in thickets and canebrakes, to be rounded up later. Hogs, particularly, roamed the brush and bottoms, to be gathered up on occasion, most notably in time to fatten them for the yearly autumn slaughter. In order to raise hogs in this manner, enslaved farmers needed access to and knowledge of vast swaths of uncultivated zones. Arkansas encompassed plenty such places, and hogs increased from only around 400,000 in 1840 to over a million by 1860. Arkansas's hog production contrasted with that of other southern states in that it increased in the antebellum period, while others fell not only in overall number but in hogs per capita. Cattle per farm unit remained high in Arkansas as compared to neighboring states but the proportion was not as high as that of hog production.[125] Although situated in a generally cotton-intensive zone, Thomas Polk of Phillips County put his bondspeople's efforts into corn and cattle exclusively by the 1859 crop year. Fifty enslaved farmers there produced an 1859 harvest valued at $30,000, including 25,000 bushels of corn and no cotton. The operation ran 100 head of cattle and 700 hogs—more by far than any of Polk's neighbors. Polk's captives also produced 1,000 pounds of butter from twenty milk cows.[126]

By comparing all of the slaveholding farms legibly listed in the 1860 census of agriculture in Izard County, in the Ozarks of north-central Arkansas, with a sample of 142 slaveholding farms from Ouachita County, in south-central Arkansas's gulf coastal plain, we can get a glimpse of enslaved people's animal husbandry in relation to crop work in two different Arkansas geographies. As table 5 shows, enslaved farmers in Izard expended effort on corn, potatoes, and stock, while Ouachita County's bondspeople's production centered around cotton, corn, and hogs. Ouachita's emphasis on cotton pulled enslaved people's efforts away from other work, especially food crops. Almost none of the bondspeople of Izard County worked cotton, however, expending their effort in animal husbandry instead. A 17:1 ratio of swine per enslaved farmer reveals a heavy emphasis on pork production by Izard's captive farmers. Their high corn production directly related to raising pork, because corn fattened hogs for slaughter. For example, eight adults and adolescents on A. W. Harris's upper White River farm worked 28 cattle, 60 hogs, and raised 1,400 bushels of corn for the 1850 harvest. Slave-driven herds in Izard County were generally larger than in Ouachita. While Izard's County's slaveholding farms averaged 15 head of cattle, the Ouachita County sample averaged 10. Similarly, the average number of hogs per slaveholding in Izard County was 41, significantly higher that of the Ouachita County sample, which averaged 32 swine per slaveholding farm. While Ouachita County's bondspeople cared for smaller herds, and the proportion of cattle and swine to bondspeople was comparatively lower than Izard's, the data still suggest that animal husbandry made up a meaningful portion of enslaved people's farm work there. A 4:1 ratio of swine to bondsperson indicates significant time and effort by enslaved drovers. In Smackover, for instance, three adults held by John F. Wilson cared for 50 sheep and 75 hogs and raised 600 bushels of corn. They split their time between that work and cotton, making 25 bales in 1859.[127]

Table 5. 1860 Ratio to Bondsperson of Cattle, Sheep, Hogs, Corn, Cotton, Irish Potatoes, and Sweet Potatoes on Slaveholding Farms

	Cattle	Sheep	Hogs	Corn (bu)	Cotton (bales)	Irish Potatoes (bu)	Sweet Potatoes (bu)
Izard	8:1	8:1	17:1	669:1	.04:1	11:1	22:1
Ouachita	1:1	1:1	4:1	88:1	2:1	3:1	10:1

Source: U.S. Bureau of the Census, Eighth Census of the United States, 1860, Productions of Agriculture.

Even free-range stock required some maintenance. Some farmers brought cattle in every night while others allowed them to roam for longer periods. The routine was determined by available grazing and weather. Periodically, bondspeople gathered roaming cattle and gave them salt. Nelson Densen explained of Arkansas's landscape, "The timber made it a good place for cattle and hogs for at that time they run out in the woods free," so when enslaved stock raisers tended herds they worked a great deal of time away from cultivated and cleared zones. They herded cattle and rustled up hogs from the woods, cane, prairies, and swamps, all the while gaining useful knowledge of the terrain. On the Bozeman place, Mart and Anthony cared for sheep and followed strays "up into the mountains" (the Ouachitas) when they wandered away from the flock.[128] The miles that enslaved people like Mart and Anthony trekked through the forested areas away from the fields added to their knowledge of their neighborhood. As with just about any of their tasks, however, herding could put enslaved people in danger in the woods and swamps. Arch, who drove cattle for the Chicot County Hilliards, got lost in the swamp overnight and was feared drowned. While Arch returned safely, Jackson, the stock driver for the Walworth holdings in the same county, was not so lucky. One winter evening, Jackson, who was already missing a leg, failed to return to the plantation at the usual time to bring in the cattle. Because his mule appeared at the plantation soaking wet, and his missing leg would have hindered his movement, those on the plantation suspected Jackson might have drowned. Bondspeople combed the area for weeks, finally discovering his body along the river more than a month later.[129] In the "immense canebrake" of southern Arkansas, it was imperative that Doc Quinn, who was enslaved on the Red River, and other hands protect the stock in sturdy pens overnight. Caring for cattle and horses came with other chores, like digging wells and building dams to hold water for them in the absence of other ready sources.[130]

A man named Peter became caught up in a dispute between neighbors in Saline County that was prompted in part by the loose roaming of the neighborhood's cattle. In 1848, neighbors caught Elihu Cornelius, illiterate and described as sixty-five to seventy years old, slaughtering another farmer's red and white cow with the help of a bondsman, named Peter, a few miles outside of Benton. Cornelius's neighbor George Keesee claimed that over the course of ten years much of his stock had gone missing and believed that Cornelius had been systematically picking them off by driving his stock close to a neighbor's herd then pulling in a "good fat one" from the other farmer's stock before heading home. According to his accusers, after gathering a stolen animal up with his, Cornelius put all the cows in the pen at night, killed the stolen cow, turned his back out, and butchered the pilfered beef in the night. To destroy the evidence, he skinned each stolen animal and sank its head and hide in a nearby lake. Keesee speculated that over the years Cornelius had stolen and processed one hundred cows that way.

Peter (the only man of the six bondspeople Cornelius held) was almost certainly the one doing most of the work in this scheme, as Cornelius is described by all parties in the dispute's surviving record as frail and weak. Not only was Peter caught up in his enslaver's illegal activity, he also seems to have been involved in the sting to catch Cornelius. The cow in question belonged to Joseph Clift, who crafted a plan with his neighbor, Whitley, to catch the old man once they were sure he had stolen another cow. One night Whitley appeared at Clift's home and gave the coded announcement, "It's a good night to catch wolves," indicating that Cornelius had struck again. Later, in answering how Whitley knew Clift's red and white cow was in Cornelius's pen, Whitley said that he had obtained the information from Peter, who freely offered it. "I never offered the negro a bribe to give me information of any kind on his master," Whitley maintained, "but I told the negro I would not begrudge $10 or $20 if I could find out when there was a cow in the pen." It is impossible to determine Peter's exact role in the dispute, including whether he profited from his enslaver's apprehension, but the saga provides a glimpse into the tension that enslaved people had to sometimes navigate in a neighborhood full of free roaming cattle.[131]

While the crop routine ordered the years and months for enslaved farmers and pioneers in Arkansas, weekly routines punctuated those seasons. Weekdays brimmed with whites' demands for crop cultivation, but while Saturdays were also usually workdays, some bondspeople enjoyed part or half of that day "off." On Saturdays at noon, the cradles of enslaved babies at the Bullock plantation were returned to their mothers' cabins. Because the babies spent so much time with designated caretakers while their parents labored, their cradles were kept in that cabin during the week. Enslaved mothers could enjoy their children in their own home, though, from Saturday until Monday morning, when Bullock forced them back into the fields.[132] While the weekdays were filled with coerced cultivation, many bondspeople's weekends provided a respite during which they could put down roots and make their own meaning out of their waking hours. After a long Saturday of plowing and hauling rails and wood in February 1839, the enslaved people held by Henry Shugart attended a dance.[133] Charley Ross remembered that black men and women where he lived in Arkadelphia could get passes to go to dances on Saturdays. Louis Davis explained, "Saturday was the only night we took for frolicing"; Saturday night was a prime opportunity for sneaking out to see friends. Louis Young claimed no experience with Saturday night parties (possibly being too young for the secret ones) until he and fellow bondspeople were sold and forced out to Texas. There, he remembered, Saturday nights were accompanied by dancing and singing, "never heard of such before."[134] For enslaved couples who resided on separate farms, Saturday night often signaled their short weekly time together. Silas Small visited Josiah McKiel's plantation every Saturday night to spend time with his wife, Eliza Bogan, departing on Monday mornings. Similarly, Rose at the Bullock plantation looked forward to Saturday evening because every other week her husband, John, came to visit from the Bozeman plantation.[135] Some people chose to attend religious meetings on Saturday evenings. John Bates said that the faithful used to attend preaching on Saturday nights only "if we wasn't in the grass"—meaning if the cotton had been scraped and hoed clean of weeds. Some operations distributed food on Saturdays or Sundays, so enslaved people who had run low looked forward to replenishing their meager food stores for the week.[136]

While Saturdays might mean rest for some, enslavers more often thought of the Sabbath as an appropriate day of repose. But although Arkansas law dictated that bondspeople could not be compelled to labor on Sundays, whites routinely violated the statute.[137] As seen earlier with the Wagram carpenters, people who fell behind on the tasks demanded of them might be made to complete that work on Sundays. The nine bondspeople on the farm where Louis Young lived in Phillips County never enjoyed Sunday respite.[138] Lucretia Alexander remembered that enslaved workers hired to other whites had to toil until noon on Sundays in her neighborhood in Chicot County, after which they attended church. Because "Old man Bill Rose" kept his hired group right up until the last minute, they were forced to attend the service while still dirty from their work. Bondspeople's own household chores might keep them busy on Sundays, if there was no time to complete them during the week. As discussed in the following chapter, those routines of homemaking contributed to enslaved people's efforts to make their own meanings of the places where they were held. White observer James Speed noticed that black families had to cut wood for their fires and wash their clothes on Sundays on one Arkansas plantation because whites allowed them no other time for those tasks.[139] Thus, while not universally protected, Sundays were the only days that many of the enslaved were allowed time free from labor and could enjoy the slightest bit of leisure time with those they cared about. Sunday's sanctity gave way to Monday's monotony, though, when bondspeople's hard work began again. Whatever Christian kindness enslavers might have professed on Sunday did not eliminate their labor demands come Monday. Recalling this weekly routine, George Kye scoffed, "Old Master was baptized almost every Sunday and cussed us all out on Monday."[140]

Punctuating the weekly rhythm, bondspeople's daily work routines varied across the southern periphery. Essential to the regime everywhere, however, were whites' expectations for black bodies to be at the right places at the right times, performing the required tasks with due attention throughout the day. At sunrise, tens of thousands of captive laborers set out for fields, kitchens, mills, roads, rivers, and workshops across the state. Some family members went their separate ways for the day, while others stayed together. Daylight often initiated the workday, but whites did not hesitate to call laborers to work before the sun's rays appeared. On plantations large enough to be managed by an overseer, he blew a whistle or horn to summon men and women to work.[141] Columbus Williams remembered the morning signal: "When that horn blows, you better git out of that house, 'cause the overseer is comin' down the line, and he ain't comin' with nothin' in his hand." Competitive managers, or those fearful of disappointing their employers, called enslaved people to work extra early. The daily routine on the Trulock plantation reflected black enslaved overseer Reuben's sense of ownership over the operation's productivity. Noticing Reuben's success as overseer, one neighbor declared that Reuben blew his horn so early in the morning that he was "gaining two days in every week."[142] Inside the Bullock home, domestic laborers were required to begin their day with morning prayers led by the planter. Some bondspeople started their workday with their own secret prayer, however, surely asking for very different things than "master" Bullock prayed for in his house. Minnie Johnson Stewart's mother told her how bondspeople in Howard County would drop to their knees in prayer at daybreak, with such fear of being caught by the overseer that they would "be watching for him with one eye and looking for God with the other."[143]

Enslaved children experienced especially difficult mornings as they often endured separation from their parents during daylight hours. Dinah Perry's mother had already left for the fields every day by the time she woke up each morning. Mandy Tucker explained, "I didn't know nothin' bout my mother and father cause it was night when they went to work and night when they come in." Harriett Payne experienced a similar scenario on the Chaney place in Arkansas County: "We wouldn't see our mammy and daddy from early in the morning till night when their work was done." The work routine infringed on enslaved families' ability to exist as a household. At the Bullock plantation, black children filed into Rose's cabin each morning for the day. Their mothers, in order to allow their children to sleep as long as possible, sometimes sent them with their breakfasts in a tin bucket for later. George Kye remembered spending so much time in a cabin with the rest of the plantation children that he did not even recall living in a cabin with his mother, Jennie, on the place owned by Abraham Stover north of Van Buren in western Arkansas.[144] Cotton took up many parents' daylight hours, meaning that the work of placemaking and nurturing family had to wait until dark. Slavery's children often looked to elder women for care and comfort during the day.[145]

This daily separation pained parents. Becky, a bondswoman on the Bullock plantation, came in from work at about 10:00 a.m. each morning to feed her baby in the "big house," presumably stopping in for more feedings throughout the day.[146] James Speed, a white Kentuckian who was interviewed after the war by the Freedmen's Inquiry Commission, told of bondswomen in Arkansas having to walk a mile to the house to nurse their babies only once during the day. On two occasions, he claimed, a mother came to the house to find her infant dead. "She was just ordered back to the field again, & did not attend the funeral at all. The child was just boxed up & buried."[147] While it is possible that Speed exaggerated his testimony for the commission's benefit, his story, even in a milder form, expresses the helplessness and sorrow enslaved mothers must have felt when forced to leave their children in the care of others, especially if tragedy struck.[148]

After their long workdays, family and friends came back together, too tired to do much more than eat and sleep. Bondspeople returned to their quarters, where families sat down together for an evening meal from their weekly rations. Women often left the fields early to prepare evening meals for their families, while sometimes men hunted at sundown to supplement their family's diet. After a long day of toil, enslaved women bore the added burden of what Stephanie M. H. Camp termed the "second shift"—evening hours spent completing chores necessary for the upkeep of the family and their cabin. While men might *choose* to hunt and fish at night to supplement their family's diet, women *always* had the "greater and more consistent" chores of cooking supper, cleaning the cabin, cleaning and mending clothes, and providing any of the extra articles such as linens, bonnets, or socks that their families might use to supplement textiles provided by their enslavers. This tiring and necessary routine revealed a sense of home.[149]

After they finished their work in the field, however, sometimes men and women sat down to additional assignments such as washing or spinning cloth. Enslaved children could be seen by the fireside completing smaller tasks. Hannah Allen remembered being required to pick a shoe full of cotton from a pile of bolls while the white children had their evening lessons. She explained, "You did a lot before you got that shoe full of cotton when it was pressed down. This was almost enough to pad a quilt with."[150] Women working in the house wrangled their children and the white children in preparation for bed before they could rest for the night. In the Bullock home, domestic servants had to endure nightly prayers with the white family before they could get away to rest for the night.[151] At Wagram, a young man named Jesse had the job of sitting up at the steamboat landing to keep a light burning when the overseer anticipated a delivery of supplies.[152]

Although often encroached upon by unwanted work, evenings held special moments, too. Scott Bond, who would become an influential black leader in Arkansas, remembered that his mother's domestic duties kept her so busy that she was unable to spend much time caring for her son during the day. But late at night, after Bond's mother finished her work, she would check in on him, sharing tender moments with her son that he would cherish for the rest of his life. Evenings for Sweetie Ivery Wagoner's mother carried special anticipation because that was the time of day that her "mistress" taught her to read and write. And just as secret prayer might begin their day, some enslaved people ended the day with prayer after dark. Ellen Briggs Thompson's grandmother used to take her along when she crept away for prayer after nightfall. In these ways, black men and women imprisoned on the cotton frontier claimed meaningful time in the late hours for themselves.[153]

While enslaved people might wind down with family or prayer, for the adventurous, the cover of darkness also allowed for secret parties. The security of clandestine gatherings required their placement out of and away from the "big house" and the quarters, in nearby woods. This made it unlikely that many people held to domestic service, because they were so easily missed, would be able to take part.[154] Gatherings might take the form of prayer meetings, and if they were small and quiet enough, they could be held in one of the cabins. Lucretia Alexander explained that enslaved people, unsatisfied with the sermons they received from white preachers on Sundays, peppered their weeknights with their own prayer meetings: "My father would have church in dwelling houses and they had to whisper.... Sometimes they would have church at his house. That would be when they would want a real meetin' with some real preachin'. It would have to be durin' the week nights.... They used to sing their songs in a whisper and pray in a whisper." Bondspeople remained on guard, careful with their activities after dark, because whites carefully watched their night hours. At Wagram, overseer John Pelham read or napped in the early evening then made a round at about 10:00 or 11:00 to be sure that no one was out of their cabin and that no outsiders lurked on the premises.[155] Although secret rendezvous of various sorts sometimes transpired, the close of the workday during the week was more often than not pretty ordinary. Used to the routine of hard work and short rest, weary men and women settled down for the night to "talk awhile before going to sleep" in their crude beds. After all, only a handful of hours separated bondspeople from the next occupied day.[156]

And so it went, day after day, week after week, year after year, as men, women, and children retraced their steps, filed to and from the fields, wore paths through the brush and cane, and maintained the ground upon which they were tied. The routine only increased in intensity as their work transformed Arkansas's landscape. The 1850 and 1860 censuses give some idea of the agricultural changes that slavery wrought as the state's population climbed: bondspeople per 100 Arkansans rose from 22 to 27; cattle per 100 people dipped from 139 to 131, hogs from 399 to 269, and corn declined from 4,237 bushels per 100 Arkansans to

4,093. Bales of cotton per 100 people in Arkansas, however, shot up from 31 in 1850 to 84 in 1860. From the 1849 to 1859 cotton harvests, Mississippi and Alabama held fairly steady in their share of the South's overall cotton crop, while Arkansas, Texas, and Louisiana each increased their share of cotton bales grown in the South. Enslaved men and women bore the brunt of cotton's expansion to and intensification within Arkansas, suffering increasing demands and a crop cycle that infringed upon their family lives. The daily, weekly, and yearly farm routines that enriched enslavers also created bondspeople's intimacy with cultivated spaces and crop cultures. This closeness, however, remained coerced, and the rhythm of enslaved farmers' labor reinforced the relationship of race and power on the land. Arkansas's ground bore the imprint of that cadence.[157]

Enslaved women probably made this "Carolina lily" pieced quilt around 1850 in Nevada County. From the Permanent Collection of Historic Arkansas Museum.

Unnamed women pause their work outside an unidentified home near Helena during the Civil War, while a white figure on the porch observes. Butler Center for Arkansas Studies, Central Arkansas Library System.

An unidentified woman poses with her charge, circa 1857–60. From the Permanent Collection of Historic Arkansas Museum.

Photographed in 1865, the grounds of the Tappan house near Helena encompassed the white residence, enslaved people's cabins, and several outbuildings, including a separate kitchen. According to the 1860 census, fifty-five enslaved people resided in the eight cabins. The Tappans held ten more bondspeople in town. From the Permanent Collection of Historic Arkansas Museum.

Aaron Brooks fled slavery in Bradley County in 1863, enlisting in what would become the 54th USCT. National Archives and Records Administration.

5 /   The Material of Survival

Enslaved people's restrictions and opportunities relating to spaces and places were linked to their struggle to control the substance of their surroundings—the access to and use of objects and resources, including the bounty of cultivated and uncultivated zones. A ground-level look at their day-to-day material lives highlights enslaved people's limitations and abilities in placemaking. The "power of place," as Edward Casey theorized, links where a person is with *how* they are and *who* they are. Producing and consuming food and goods for themselves helped enslaved people find some grounding. As Kimberly Smith explains, "[Bondspeople's] homemaking and food production established their own sense of right and belonging to the American landscape." This placemaking was inherently social.[1] Enslaved Arkansans related to each other and with the space around them through the food they consumed, the shelter they relied upon, the clothes they wore, and the objects they treasured. Their histories include the feel of the earth under bare feet, the taste of meals that provided adequate calories but little nutrition, the secret satisfaction that came with a hidden stash of fine cloth, printed material, or cash tucked away in their cabins, and delight in the materials used to personalize their homes or appearances. Their stories are found in the gentle application of a grease dressing to soothe wounds left by the lash and in the earthy warmth of herbal tea on a sore throat. When they could, enslaved people converted what they procured from Arkansas's ample uncultivated zones into goods and assets—both literally and socially.

They exchanged with, shared with, and stole from others. Whether they were forced to spend their waking hours cultivating corn outside of Batesville or cotton on the Red River, men and women held in slavery lived a *relational* material life. The tangible parts of their daily lives linked them, whether in the cooperation that built relationships or in strains that sundered bonds.[2] Enslaved people also endured the humiliation of being held at arm's length from the physical comforts that their labor created. The difference in material widened the gulf between their status and that of their oppressors. "We earned lots of money durin' slave days," declared John Bates of Pulaski County, "but we never did get paid any." One of the ways slavers extracted labor was to threaten the deprivation of material comforts or necessities. Thus, bondspeople's acquisition and use of material always held the potential for a political element—simply purporting to own property when held as property themselves complicated the system. Generally, enslaved people's daily material existence focused on making do, together.[3] Enslaved people created a sense of place and made meaning out of Arkansas's landscape via their relational material life and the political nature of their acquisition.

One of the most immediately recognizable and significant sites of enslaved people's daily material existence was their homes. While some enslaved people were housed in frame buildings, most living under slavery in Arkansas inhabited crude shacks made from logs, mud, and grass gathered on-site. Thinking back on his father's life in Ouachita County, Oscar Junell asserted, "Even in *my* time, there was hardly a board house" in the area.[4] Sometimes builders hewed logs on one side to give them the appearance of flat sawmill boards. Grass and dirt provided the "chink and daub" for these typical residences. Brick homes were rare in antebellum Arkansas, especially for enslaved people, although R. C. Ballard considered them for his Chicot County plantation. The overseer worried that "they were close and the negroes would have large fires and get too warm and then going out in the cold or rain would likely bring on Pneumonia, cold, &c." If their further deliberations are any indication, the cost and extra labor prevented planters like Ballard from using brick for enslaved people's houses.[5] Joe Ray described typical one-room log huts with tar roofs housing bondspeople near Fulton, in southwest Arkansas; the "master's" house was made of sawed cedar logs. Formerly enslaved people interviewed in the 1930s recalled rough plank or dirt floors; some remembered windowless cabins while others recalled large windows. Similarly, some described drafty homes while others remembered more substantial construction.[6] Many did not live separately from the slaveholding family at all. Families who resided in a back room of the "big house," like R. C. Smith's family in northwest Arkansas, might have enjoyed a little more comfort, but they lacked the relative privacy of a cabin set back from the whites' residence. Enslaved people who slept in their captors' home rested as well as they could on flimsy beds rolled out from their daytime storage. On some plantations, whites gathered enslaved children together in one cabin for the night without their parents.[7]

On operations large enough to work more than a few enslaved people, they most often slept in cabins housing one or two families. Candles fashioned from twisted wicks in animal fat or beeswax lit their evenings together, along with a fireplace vented by "stick" chimneys plastered with mud. If they slept on beds, rather than pallets on the floor, those were often attached at one or two sides to the cabin wall. A crude mattress—often consisting of a cotton bag stuffed with corn shucks or straw—lay on top of ropes stretched across the bed's crude frame. Columbus Williams described a stark setup with the bed attached to the wall in Union County, south Arkansas: "The bed would have two legs and would have a hole bored in the side of the house where the side rail would run through and the two legs would be out from the wall. Didn't have no springs and they made out with anything they could git for a mattress. Master wouldn't furnish them nothin' of that kind." This was not just a place to rest between workdays, however. Harriet McFarlin Payne remembered the centrality of the family home, pronouncing that "everything happened in that one room—birth, sickness, death, and everything."[8]

How did the sites over which enslaved people had no real control in terms of the quality of building materials, layout, or crowdedness—buildings in which they were *forced* to live—become homes? How could they possibly have served as what theorists of space understand to be true *dwellings* imbued with a sense of safety and intimacy rather than simply a place to sleep? The "quarters" have long been discussed by scholars as the nexus of black social life under slavery. "In the quarters" has even been used as a synonym for the enslaved community. Some recent scholarship (re)emphasizes hardship and displacement associated with those spaces, however. So how can we understand enslaved people's housing both as sites of production *and* as dwelling places? Stephanie Camp's work provides a model by exploring the double character of the slave cabin as both public and private. For scholars of space, what makes a site a meaningful dwelling, a place in which people can feel *insideness*, are the daily "habit memories." Daily life with other people and, as exhibited in Harriet Payne's words above, the experience of life's many milestones there added layers that culminated in a sense of meaningful place. This process of placemaking included an element of physicality. Daily repetitive activities like preparing and consuming food, wearing and mending clothes, and keeping house created enslaved people's experience of home. Edward Casey described the body as an "engine of exploration and creation as well as an agent of habit." But because enslaved people's bodies were also commodities, this daily process of inhabitation was also an experience of oppression.[9]

Enslaved people's abodes, whether separate cabins or nooks in the back rooms of white homes, offered at least some small place for bondspeople to store their few possessions. Mollie Barber remembered that her mother, who enjoyed little space of her own, kept a small bundle of clothes tucked away in the back of the "big house."[10] Near DeWitt, Sam Word's mother had more belongings and more room for them. According to Word, she owned "lots of nice things, quilts and things, and kept 'em in a chest in her little old shack." Scott Bond's mother, a domestic laborer in Little Rock, kept a trunk of possessions including the dresses she aired out on Sundays. Among her treasures was a pair of tiny red shoes that Bond's biological father, a white man, had given her when Bond was a baby. Bond's mother cherished the little shoes, and the memory of her son as an infant that they recalled, long after he outgrew them.[11]

Certain objects, especially handmade ones, enlivened bondspeople's community. Enslaved people's production and experience of material culture formed the foundations of their sense of place. As Casey explained, "The culture that characterizes and shapes a given place is a shared culture, not merely superimposed upon that place but part of its very facticity." When an enslaved artist crafted a musical instrument—like a mouth harp, fiddle, or banjo—the musician created a meaningful nexus for folks to seize moments of diversion together in the yard, among the cabins, or perhaps in more secluded places away from the farm. As Solomon Lambert put it, "We made our music." Black men and women carved out a rich cultural and social life that coexisted with their hardships when they gathered to sing, dance, and enjoy one another's company. For many, this kind of socialization might be the only kind of amusement that whites did not try to suppress. Columbus Williams remembered a bleak material existence and closely monitored social life in Union County, southern Arkansas. He said, "Didn't have no quiltin's. Women might quilt some at night. Didn't have nothin' to make no quilts out of." Even when quilters could not gather in large festive groups to practice their craft, quilting constituted a valuable form of expression. Alice Trammell, enslaved near Magnolia, made quilts later in life in a style that fiber arts experts trace to the southeast coastal region. Trammell's mother, Handy Young, was probably enslaved by John and Eliza Young, planters who came from North Carolina, or by one of their sons, Norburn and William Young. Handy likely taught her daughter Alice to quilt, and the resulting artistry reflected the women's eastern roots.[12] More mundane objects could have meaning for enslaved people's social connections. Adeline Blakely's mother, Liza, enslaved in the Ozarks, kept a brass ring "about the size of a dollar with a handwoven knotted string" that she used to tell the fortunes of young people from all over the neighborhood. The ring symbolized enslaved people's hopes and fears for the future, and it connected them to each other, for those sincerely hoping for an indication of what the future held as well as for those who simply enjoyed the game. For children, toys like dolls or marbles enriched their play and forged friendships.[13]

Everyday necessities like clothing also offer a window into the lives of those imprisoned in Arkansas. Their garments varied in quality and origin but were almost universally sewed by enslaved women. Sometimes whites ordered cloth and had items sewn on the farm or plantation, while on other places bondspeople created their own clothing from scratch—spinning, weaving, dying, and sewing the cloth into finished articles on-site. Joe Bean described the elaborate process of weaving and dying clothes on Mark Bean's plantation in Washington County. Bondspeople gathered "walnut bark for black, the post oak bark that mix[ed] in with copperas [iron sulfate] for yellow, [and] the log-wood mix[ed] in with alum for red-brown colors." Roots from ivy created a red hue, while hickory bark rendered yellow, plum root made brown, and poke berries yielded magenta. Rebecca Thomas helped make clothes on Jake Saul's plantation in Little Rock but her "mistress," Sukie, kept her away from the silkworm operation, distrusting the girl with the production and handling of finer material. Like clothing, shoes worn by enslaved people varied. Sometimes whites ordered them ready-made, and sometimes they had enslaved craftsmen fashion them. On the Bullock plantation, Macklin made shoes. During the Civil War years, he made do with what was available—leather from discarded carriage seats, lasts made from maple, finishing his products with pine wax—to craft shoes for bondspeople and the white family. Mack Bertrand made the shoes for the whites and blacks where he was enslaved, and then passed that skill on to his son, James Bertrand, who was born near Pine Bluff a few years after the Civil War ended.[14]

Seamstresses and shoemakers generally created the garments donned by enslaved people on an as-needed basis, with some craft involved. However, sometimes whites strictly regimented the supply and distribution of shoes and clothing, essentially reducing their operation's production costs. Bondspeople's acquisition, storage, sharing, and mending of clothing was a productive as well as domestic process. Many larger slaveholders rationed uniform garments, distributing them among their captive workforce twice per year. An important aspect of merchants' business was supplying clothing for slaveholders to issue to bondspeople. Benjamin Britton's store in Washington, southwest Arkansas, advertised "Negro Cloths—Kerseys, Linseys, Jeans" and "Negro Blankets."[15] Enslaved people wore long-tail cotton shirts or dresses in the warmer months and jackets over woolens in the cooler part of the year. Formerly enslaved people recalled caps with ear flaps for warmth in the cold months. The distribution of clothing and shoes directly related to how whites perceived black adulthood and work. Boys wore long shirts without pants until their enslavers decided they were big enough to do adult work, at about twelve to fourteen years old. Graduating to pants was to become a full hand. This was also the age at which their captors issued children their first shoes; youngsters usually went barefoot up to that point. Scott Bond remembered the damaging lack of shoes; he left trails of blood as he walked because his feet were so badly cracked. His mother, a seamstress, made him a pair of shoes from discarded boot tops, which felt awkward on Bond's feet, because he was so unused to wearing shoes. Charley Ross remembered being given a pair of hand-me-down shoes as a child; like Bond, it took time for him to get used to the feeling of protection on his feet.[16]

Clothing inferred status, served as a canvas for enslaved people to express themselves, and added definition to place and time. While many bondspeople routinely received the commonplace set of simple osnaburg or homespun garments twice per year, the acquisition of additional or nicer clothing broke up the drudgery. Youngsters cherished special garments of higher quality or of interesting colors, even if they came as hand-me-downs from whites. Hannah Allen recollected that some enslaved people lucky enough to be able to work on the weekend for themselves used the money they earned to purchase clothes and shoes.[17] Self-purchased apparel was a material manifestation of bondspeople's agency and resourcefulness. Black men and women wanted to look their best on occasions they valued and in spaces of importance. Callie Washington recalled, "Our Sunday clothes was striped, in the prettiest colors you ever seed." Attendees of the yearly Manchester revival in south Arkansas donned their best clothes. One free black woman from "down river" gained special attention for her finery but so did other black women who chose to present the best outfits they could muster. This was one of the few times enslaved people could express themselves in this way, so they treasured the clothing worn for the occasion. They also knit social ties when they shared. When Jenny accidentally ripped Beck's dress during the emotional service at Manchester, she had damaged a garment borrowed especially for the occasion, angering her friend and creating a rift between them.[18]

Indeed, enslaved people, like southerners everywhere, especially cherished "Sunday clothes" if they could get them. Cindy Kinsey beamed with pride over a red cotton Sunday dress dyed on the plantation. When bondspeople held by Abraham Stover north of Van Buren were allowed to walk to a white church to listen outside (they had no other place to attend, although they could have singing on their place), the group protected their shoes by walking barefoot, with their footwear slung by the laces over their shoulders. Upon nearing the church, they stopped to put their shoes on, looking their best as they sat outside the building to listen. Donning finer apparel solemnized the experience and defined the space as special. Subject to countless humiliations in bondage, enslaved people sought dignity in dress and, if they were lucky enough to have them, observed a separation between "good" clothes and work clothes.[19] Yet, when bondspeople possessed nicer clothes or other items, they did not necessarily want whites to see them wearing such things. Evelyn Jones's grandmother told her about how she would carry her good clothes in a bundle when she walked to church, stopping to change when she got close, stuffing her "old clothes" under a rock somewhere along the way. On her way back to the Jordans in Lonoke County, she changed back into her old clothes. "She didn't dare let the white folks see her in good clothes." This reluctance did not necessarily indicate that the items had been stolen but instead revealed an acute awareness of clothing as communicating status. Bondspeople who wore clothing of quality above their station could draw whites' ire.[20] Enslavers dictated the terms upon which enslaved people improved their dress. They might choose to hand down clothing items that, even if worn out or stained, would have exceeded the quality of bondspeople's usual clothes. Women held in domestic service enjoyed the most access to new garments. In an exceptional example,

Rose, on the Bullock plantation, had knitted her enslaver a pair of gloves; he brought her a red and black dress from New Orleans.[21]

In fact whites often figured enslaved people's clothing into the performance of their own wealth, status, and power, usually by making sure that their domestic servants wore relatively higher-quality clothing, especially when hosting company or on visits to other wealthy white households. The quality of bondspeople's garments proclaimed their captors' status, defined the space of their enslavers' homes, and marked the significance of whites' occasions. From time to time, slavers ordered their captives "dressed up" for special events, such as the weddings of their children. Mary Overton said the only time she ever laid eyes on her first enslaver, named Kennard in Crawford County, was after he had fallen seriously ill and ordered the enslaved children "dressed up and brought in to see him." What enslaved people wore and where they wore it reinforced meanings of race, power, and space.[22]

Keeping clothing and linens clean made up a hefty component of the daily habits of home and community, an arduous chore that enslaved women often completed together. On Saturday nights and Sundays, Hannah Jameson recalled, bondswomen hauled their clothes and bedding down to a nearby spring. Washing clothes at the spring away from the house made sense in terms of the ready supply of clean water, but, as with other tasks performed away from the main yard, the distance had the added benefit of allowing the group to lower its guard as the women talked over the events of the day. By the light of a pine torch, Jameson remembered, they washed the heaps with homemade soap, hanging the clothes to dry on ropes stretched between trees or draped on bushes. After the women finished, children bathed in the warm soapy water left over.[23]

Enslaved people also cleaned and cared for their modest homes, scrubbing plank floors with sand and ashes and scouring them with mops made of corn shucks. Their own acts of homemaking, reflecting their sense of order and hygiene, always took place under the shadow of their enslavers' sense of dominion. Owners or overseers inspected their rooms or cabins and gave orders about cleanliness, a constant reminder that enslaved people's domestic space was also productive—storage for human assets, to put it crudely—and never completely private. In a notebook kept by southern Arkansas planter Sterling Cockrill, likely meant for an overseer, comments on cleanliness were embedded within instructions for order and productivity: "Keep all their clothes clean when they are sick, get all the work out of them you can, and the way to do that is to stay with them early and late. Keep their houses and skins clean."[24] What to enslaved families were daily habits to create a healthy and comfortable home life were for slaveholders and their managers essential components of a streamlined production. Women and children swept dirt floors and yards with brooms made of dried grass, which were wrapped with string to create a handle. According to Solomon Lambert, broom makers used "sage grass," which grew almost to the height of a person, cut and "cured like hay."[25]

Young couples might jump those same brooms and set up house to mark their new lives together. Ellen Briggs Thompson described wedding feasts on the farm officiated by a preacher, "just like they do now."[26] Sometimes their enslavers performed the ceremony, in which case men and women would "dress up as nice as they could and go up to the big house and the master would marry them." Whites who hosted wedding ceremonies in the big house might do so to improve their self-image as masters; they often held a patronizing attitude toward the marriages, which everyone understood had no legal standing. Enslaved people welcomed the public acknowledgment of their unions but likely felt uneasy about their oppressors' presumptions at the same time. Cora Scroggins's mother was married inside the white family's home in Batesville.[27] Harriett McFarlin Payne described wedding ceremonies at the "big house": "When two of the slaves wanted to get married, they'd dress up as nice as they could and go up to the big house and the master would marry them. They'd stand up before him and he'd read out of a book called the 'discipline.' . . . Then he'd say they were man and wife and tell them to live right and be honest and kind to each other. All the slaves would be there too, seeing the 'wedden.'"[28] Payne's account showcases the importance of marking the occasion with a degree of formality brought on by the setting, the couple's best clothing, readings from the Methodist Book of Discipline, and the presence of other bondspeople.[29]

While the "big house" might be the site of the marriage announcement and accompanying festivities, setting up house in the quarters, for couples who were lucky enough to live on the same place, truly solidified the milestone. That process might even be the extent of the ceremony. The couple's daily habits in their home together helped solidify their bonds. As Edward Casey phrased it, the process of making a home, a dwelling place, "localize[d] caring." Living together signified enslaved couples' commitment in a world that denied them legal marriage. "You moved in and there you was. You was married," said Lou Fergusson of southwest Arkansas, who had gotten married before the end of the Civil

War. Columbus Williams of Union County had heard of "jumping the broom" but never witnessed any such wedding ceremonies under slavery himself. Couples simply "took up with" each other without much ado. This is not to say that bondspeople like Williams held any less respect for marriage but that like all people, enslaved couples might take part in relationships that were more serious than courting but less so than marriage, and not all enslaved people solemnized their marriages with ceremony.[30]

Enslavers encouraged these unions because they could watch their investment and their children's inheritance multiply before their eyes as enslaved couples began their families. When bonded couples set up house together, their oppressors expected children to follow. As chattel, even the most intimate moments of enslaved people's lives were linked to whites' profit. Sterling Cockrill's plantation book included the births of black children in his anticipated yield for the crop year, expecting "400 bales of cotton, 40,000 pounds of pork, etc. and 10 negro children." The U.S. Army official who recorded the notes wrote down Cockrill's plan: "He arranges for the producing of 10 negro children and orders the following marriages. Henry & Susan, Cambridge & Matilda, Sally & Yellow Kitty, George & Harriet or Mary, Floyde & Julia, Robin & Caroline, Granville & Diana, Joe & Harriet, Edmund & Nelly, Middleton & Dorkey, Jordan & Fanny, Argus & Elizabeth, Juley & Alsey, Bryant & Susan, Benton & Sarah Ann, Jack & Harriet, Green & Sylvia, Black Jim & ____, Joe & Helen."[31]

Plantation owners like Cockrill could devise crude plans, but enslaved people considered their own commitments to each other as binding and meaningful. Referring to the years during and after the Civil War, Hueston Blackburn recalled: "The soldiers had to marry if they lived together with their wives. When the law first came out that old marriages were no good, I married under the new law."[32] Significantly, Blackburn did not consider this second act as legitimating the marriage for the *first* time but as a *renewal* of the "old marriage" under the "new law." Similarly, Walker Frazier explained, "I had a wife that I had in slave times & we were married again."[33] Their conviction about the legitimacy of their marriages remained so ingrained that John Holt's explanation to a WPA interviewer caused him to note that his parents had been "legally united at the time, but after the War was over, they were remarried, according to a new law then put into effect regarding ex-slaves."[34] That is exactly how the Holts and others understood their unions: the marriages had already been binding; post-slavery weddings were simply a matter of compliance with *new* rules. Enslaved couples struggled to maintain nuclear family units, however, against the backdrop of the cotton frontier. Carl Moneyhon found two-parent family units to be less common in Arkansas's enslaved families than in those of other southern states. Sixty percent of formerly enslaved Arkansans interviewed by the WPA remembered a family with both parents. In 20 percent of these cases, their parents lived on different farms. After they expressed commitment to each other in ceremony or in secret, enslaved couples knew that their families faced constant threat.[35]

Like housing and clothing, food was heavily laden with social meaning and provided a constant reminder of the inability of enslaved people to have complete control over their bodies. Yet, enslaved families bonded over dinner, shared special treats, and looked out for one another's nutrition. All the while their consumption of food also amounted to input into their enslaver's investment. On small as well as large operations one woman usually handled the preparation of food for whites and blacks alike. But although they often ate much the same fare, she placed the food on segregated tables.[36] Hog meat reigned as the staple protein, dried and salted or in a stew with potatoes or other vegetables. They also ate greens, pot liquor, corn bread, buttermilk, and various garden vegetables. Expensive or rare products of the farm were off-limits, especially to children. Some people had limited access to fruit, for example, such as pears or peaches, but whites closely monitored the consumption of these treats.[37] The consequences of "stealing" that food could be severe. T. W. Cotton remained haunted with regret for years by an incident from his boyhood involving fruit in Monroe County. T. W. and Walter, who was the son of his enslaver, Ed Cotton, had caused a bondswoman on the place to be whipped for supposedly taking a pear without permission. It was in fact Walter who had knocked the pear off the tree and shared it with T. W. When Ed Cotton asked about it, Walter told his father that "Aunt Sue" had taken it. "I was scared then to tell on Walter," T. W. remembered. Ed whipped Sue even as she cried that she had not gone near the pear tree, much less eaten from it. Ed Cotton may have dealt especially brutal whippings there, as T. W.'s Aunt Adeline killed herself on that same place to avoid one.[38]

Some formerly enslaved people described plenty of food, like fresh meat and vegetables, along with various types of corn bread, while others remembered privation. Joe Bean said that food stores on the Bean plantation in Washington County, northwest Arkansas, remained "wide open" for bondspeople to take what they needed. Laura Shelton, however, remembered that many bondspeople "didn't have half enough to eat and were half naked and barefooted all the time." Whites did not guard food distribution as strictly on smaller operations. Cyntha Jones, held in slavery on Simpson and Adeline Dabney's farm in Drew County, south Arkansas, claimed that bondspeople simply took what they wanted and needed from the smokehouse. Only four of the enslaved people held there were over twelve years old. Larger holdings usually meant more restricted access and a locked smokehouse, as on the Bullock plantation. Letters sent by R. C. Ballard's overseers as they struggled to make his Wagram plantation self-sufficient reveal the inconsistency of provision for bondspeople held on operations that relied on food shipments. Pelham wrote to Ballard in Vicksburg, "I weighed out the last of the meat last night. There are a few middlings hanging in the smoke house, enough to last a few days"; he mentioned the problem again in another letter a couple of days later. Undernourishment is evident in the fact that infant mortality was more than two times higher in black families than white families and that enslaved people reached a shorter stature than whites. Bondspeople shared food with loved ones to ease their privation. Adrianna Kerns's mother told her the story of a woman who did not get adequate meals whose husband walked three or four miles to bring her his supper.[39]

Children were often undernourished. Because they did not (yet) amount to full labor "hands," enslavers provided them with the least sustaining meals. In economist Richard H. Steckel's calculations, feeding meat to children did not profit enslavers. Many youngsters' privation began at birth in instances where whites had enslaved women feed their own babies with bottles and breastfeed whites'.[40] Sallie Crane remembered the unappetizing diet of enslaved children: "Mush and milk. Didn't know what meat was. Never got a taste of egg. . . . Weren't allowed to look at a biscuit." Whites fed their own children lighter, often meatless meals and thus were especially reluctant to diminish their meat stores for black children's benefit. People who remembered childhoods under slavery often remarked upon whites' refusal to allow enslaved children meat, but because they wanted visitors to believe that the children *had* been consuming meat, they would "grease" their mouths. This peculiar practice must have been a performance of bounty and generosity for the benefit of their peers. Enslaved parents looking to provide meat for their hungry children sometimes had to appropriate some from the stock, a theft— though it is unlikely bondspeople thought of it that way—that incurred harsh penalties if they were caught. Emma Moore remembered watching her parents cook "stolen" shoats. "When that pot was on the rack," she recalled, "you better not say nothing 'bout it."[41] Although geophagy, or dirt-eating, does not seem to have been a common practice for enslaved people on the cotton frontier, Tom Haynes remembered being scolded for eating dirt in the yard when he was a small boy on the Franks plantation in Drew County. According to the record of his interview, Haynes did not mention that he had been hungry, but geophagy is known to be practiced by those who are.[42]

If whites in Arkansas often kept meat out of the reach of enslaved children, they dangled wheat flour as a rare delicacy for all. While bread made from wheat flour was a rare treat for most bondspeople, they routinely consumed many different types of corn bread in the form of hoe cakes, ash cakes, and more. Formerly enslaved people remembered biscuits as a once per month or once per week treat, to be enjoyed on Sundays, or on special occasions like Christmas.[43] Jane Osbrook said of her meals under slavery near Camden, "Some of the folks said they never seed a biscuit from Christmas to Christmas but we had 'em every day." The way Osbrook discussed the topic suggests that she understood her experience to be less than common.[44] On smallholdings bondspeople's fare was tied more closely to that of the white family. Mary Myhand and her family lived in the main house with the white family on the edge of Washington and Benton Counties in northwest Arkansas. She said, "We ate what they ate and when they ate."[45] Similarly, Louis Lucas, who was held by the Brumbaugh family in Jefferson County, where only a few bondspeople resided, remembered that everyone ate the same food at the same time.[46] The spaces in which these meals were consumed, however, reinforced enslaved people's oppression. Farm laborers often ate their breakfast and lunch in the fields during a short respite from labor, drinking from barrels of water hauled out on a cart under the trees. Although their midday meals often took place in a hurried fashion during the workday, enslaved people looked forward to suppers together as a family, and all meals together on Sundays. Callie Washington remembered that each family cherished cooking and enjoyed their own evening meal in their own cabin on Christmas. Joe Bean remembered sitting on the floor next to the fireplace eating off of wooden dishes with his family.[47]

Yet food, like housing and clothing, should be understood as both domestic and productive. Whites enforced a regimented distribution of food, usually issuing rations to enslaved people once per week, every Saturday or Sunday. Amounts varied but slaveholders usually allotted about three pounds of meat per working adult. For example, on the Hawkins plantation near Fulton, in southwest Arkansas, enslaved people received "4 pounds of fat meats, a quart of molasses, a 'peck' of corn meal, and some bran for flour." If it did not last, "You was just out until Saturday night come around again." Norman Burkes remembered weekly rations of three pounds of meat, a peck of meal, and a half gallon of molasses in Union County. Burkes's rations can be considered typical, including his mention that bondspeople received no sugar or coffee. Burkes and his compatriots received some flour on Saturdays with which to make Sunday morning biscuits. Overseer Pelham on the Wagram plantation felt he had to justify handing out flour to bondspeople there. "I gave the negroes a cup of flour each this morning," he wrote on a Sunday, "as it is rather coarse for any other use." When he was twelve years old, Louis Young was sold to Hampton Atkinson (who held about ten bondspeople in all), a man he described as "long" on work and "short" on rations, listing an allotment of seven pounds of meat, one peck of meal, and one quart of molasses. Although Young did not specify how many people this supply intended to feed, he remembered that once it ran out, that was it. Whites' regimentation of plantation food also extended to the spaces in which people consumed it. Sweetie Ivery Wagoner described a "long house made of rough brick" where bondspeople ate together even though they had their separate cabins at the Tittsworth farm. The rations and the rituals of their allocation and consumption reinforced enslaved people's race and status.[48]

Formerly enslaved people interviewed by the WPA in the 1930s remembered especially degrading meals as children. In Calhoun County, enslaved children spent the workday in a cabin together, where they might look forward to a visit from the cook who would hide food under her apron and sneak it to the children through a chink in the wall.[49] On the Stover plantation north of Van Buren, George Kye and other enslaved children spent their days crowded together in a cabin. "You couldn't stir us with a stick," he remembered. Enslaved children could look forward to a meal of gruel, stew, or bread with milk poured over it in a large trough or pan from which all the children ate at once. Charlie Hinton, who had his meals as a child in slavery at Jefferson County, recalled, "They pretty near raised us with the pigs. I remember they would cook a great big oven of bread and then pour a pan full of buttermilk or clabber and we'd break off a piece of bread and get around the pan of milk just like pigs." Some used a wooden spoon or other tool to get what they could as fast as they could from the trough or pan. George Kye remembered the scramble when all of the food was poured into one large pan for the kids:

"One what ate the fastest got the most." Formerly enslaved people routinely likened childhood meals to the feeding of livestock.[50] The children on the Bullock plantation clamored to eat peas cooked with a chunk of meat by Rose in a large pot over a fire. Harriet Bullock, the planter's daughter, was allowed to eat these meals with the enslaved children, who used mussel shells for spoons. Her mussel shell was stored apart from the others. If her father came around, Harriet fled. On smaller operations whites kept enslaved children in the house with the white family and simply sent them off to the kitchen as a group when it was time to eat. Parrish Washington of Jefferson County spoke for everyone when he remembered, "We just got what we could."[51]

Enslaved people used food and foodways to mark time, strengthen social ties, and make meaningful homes out of the sites where they were held, even as those meals involved white slaveholders and overseers. They cooked and ate together to celebrate breaks in the crop routine and marked special occasions with picnics or other casual gatherings. Bondspeople on one farm between Arkansas Post and Pine Bluff enjoyed large pots of chicken in these instances—a food rarely mentioned by the formerly enslaved. Yearly hog killings provided some excuse for festivity, even if the meat stores that resulted were often strictly rationed for the next twelve months. Cindy Kinsey remembered a big fire around which bondspeople danced. Children made toys out of hog bladders blown full of air.[52] Near Booneville, then part of Scott County, a months-long hunting competition took place annually from June to October, in which participants accumulated certain points depending on the animals they harvested. While it is unclear whether enslaved people were able to take part in the competition, they were present at the barbecue that celebrated its culmination. Belger Cauthron and wife, Silvia, two of the bondspeople held by Walter Cauthron, cooked the celebratory meal. Whether in cooler or summer months, a table laid out for the group, however festive, represented many hours of labor. Food was work. Every dish was the result of immeasurable toil from farm to pantry or smokehouse. Enslaved farmers dug pits or stored potatoes under the big house. They hung onions to dry. They lowered butter and milk into a well to keep it cool. Other than special occasions, bondspeople were consistently surrounded by food of their own creation that they were not allowed to freely consume.[53]

Enslaved Arkansans' foodways cannot be separated from their interactions with the wider landscape, specifically the uncultivated spaces around them. They supplemented their diets by hunting game like turkeys, deer, squirrels, opossums, raccoons, and rabbits. They fished the streams and rivers around them as well.[54] Observers then and in later decades consistently emphasized the bounty of Arkansas's game. It was indeed plentiful, though probably not quite as abundant as the Kentucky friends of the Chicot County Hilliards believed; after having heard "such accounts of the game of our country, they imagine a fire at the gatepost, or in any direction, will 'bring down the buck.'"[55] Animals valuable for their flesh or skins—such as wolves, bears, deer, and turkeys—were so abundant in the Ouachita Valley that Moriah, the cook at the Bullocks' frontier plantation, stepped out the door and killed a wild turkey with a stick.[56]

The structure of nineteenth-century southerners' fields created plenty of interstices supporting "microhabitats" for small game animals like raccoons, rabbits, squirrels, opossums, and quail, and even provided food and cover for deer. The clearance of forests dispersed bears, wildcats, and wolves but not the smaller game. Enslaved hunters focused their efforts on smaller quarry that did not require a gun but instead could be taken in traps or snares. A profitable strategy for night hunts, "fire hunting," involved using light to catch the reflection in animals' eyes.[57]

Accounts of hunting by formerly enslaved people and contemporary accounts suggest that some enslaved people had access to firearms with whites' permission for that purpose. In one well-documented example, court records from Benton County, northwest Arkansas, reveal that a man named Wagoola and two other enslaved men from Sarah Ridge's place "frequently carried guns; that used by Wagoola, being a large rifle." This practice owed in part to the benefits enslavers incurred from enslaved people being able to hunt and defend themselves from animals on Arkansas's densely forested landscape. This access, however, probably amounted to more of an understanding of use rather than ownership; the above quotation, for example, uses the word "carried," not "owned." Hunting and fishing helped stave off hunger, provided relief from the crop routine, and held cultural and community value by offering enslaved people a way to push back against their bondage by claiming time and resources for their own.[58]

Family members who hunted or fished together strengthened bonds. For example, Mittie Freeman cherished memories of fishing with her father in Ouachita County. For enslaved families, game and forage supplemented their food sources, and sharing nature's bounty forged ties in the quarters. When Betty Brown's mother hunted and trapped in Greene County, she fulfilled part of what whites expected as masters but also provided for her family's material needs. Children gathered nuts from the woods in the fall that they could crack and eat around the fire in the winter.[59] Friendships and social ties were forged and strengthened on these excursions, like those between Scott Bond and other young men and boys during frequent nighttime expeditions with dogs for opossum and raccoons in the woods of Cross County.[60] Their time together in natural spaces away from the main sites of their labor created adventures and lasting memories. Doc Quinn remembered fishing near the Ogburn plantation with another enslaved man, Jerry, in Miller County. When the men encountered a bear, Jerry stabbed it with a knife so that they could escape. Apart from the exciting tale, Quinn's story represents the autonomy and use of weapons that enslaved people took advantage of when hunting and fishing Arkansas's woods and streams.[61]

Men hunted with their enslavers, too, which, while it might have been a welcome respite from other tasks, still meant work. In doing so, however, bondspeople learned the terrain, built trust with their enslavers (which could come in handy), and surely valued some time away from the drudgery of their usual labor. Joe Bean squirrel hunted on horseback with his enslaver in the woods of Washington County. "Little Bill," trusted with more autonomy than others held by Henry Shugart in southern Arkansas, accompanied Shugart to the swamps on duck-hunting excursions. It is not clear, however, if Bill simply carried supplies or shot birds himself. Bondspeople held by the Bullocks hunted with whites for opossum and other small game. When the planter and his sons or guests hunted deer there, they sometimes forced enslaved people to run through the woods to flush the deer and drive them to run under the stands upon which the hunters perched.[62] When the planter allowed his daughters to accompany white men and enslaved men as they set out on a nighttime hunt from the Bullock plantation, Belle and Ida, their enslaved maids, had to go with them. For children on that place, these excursions, even as they supplemented diets, were play. White children and enslaved children on the Bullock place caught minnows and brought them to the cook, Rose, to fry for a snack.[63]

Bringing in meat, fish, and skins could endear bondspeople to whites who benefited from their success in Arkansas's woods and streams, as when Rob's fishing helped Miriam Hilliard impress her out-of-town guests.[64] It is possible that enslaved hunters might have even brought in some cash to whites in early Arkansas's morass. The law allowed county courts to set bounties for wolf "scalps," specifying that slaveholders could collect bounties for wolves hunted or trapped by enslaved people, although it is not known how many wolves might have been killed by bondspeople.[65] Autonomy in other regards and privileges to hunt or fish might have been mutually reinforcing. For example, Thom, who performed much of the important business for the Browns, such as errands to town, sometimes fished for the family, too. He may have initially been given opportunities to go out fishing because the Browns had deemed him trustworthy in other business, or Thom may have helped secure those other opportunities by bringing in fish for the white family.[66] The ability to go out into the woods without the oversight of whites could be a perk of relatively privileged status under slavery, while profitable hunting or fishing created its own rewards.

Food and goods figured prominently in the ways enslavers performed mastery—sometimes to the annoyance of bondspeople and sometimes to their pleasure. Practices and rituals of allotting food and other provisions reinforced the divide between enslaver and enslaved. When Miriam Hilliard hosted friends at the plantation, they passed the time by walking through the quarters inspecting quilts displayed by enslaved women. It is impossible to know for sure whether the women enjoyed showing off their handiwork or if they rolled their eyes at having to haul out their quilts, which Hilliard condescendingly described as "curiously patterned." Miriam Hilliard also distributed treats and clothing in the quarters before she left town in May 1850, including "pickles, honey, preserves, groceries, baby clothes." She had bondspeople lined up to see her off, and she went down the row handing out slices of ham, biscuits, cakes, figs, and raisins. Some of these things, like clothing and groceries, may have been given to make sure bondspeople were adequately supplied for a time while Hilliard was away, but Hilliard bestowed them in a ritual that solidified her self-image as a plantation mistress. Regardless of her pretensions, the bondspeople there must have enjoyed the goods.[67] Sometimes whites made much ado about presenting Christmas goodies like ham, molasses, fruit, candy, cakes, clothes, and even cash. Cindy Kinsey remembered gifts like red wool stockings or shoes at that time of year while the older men and women received a "hot toddy."[68] Sterling Cockrill Sr. of Jefferson County came down to the quarters bearing gifts of candy or apples to enslaved children on his plantation each Sunday. Once bondspeople became big enough to labor in Cockrill's fields, they stopped receiving these treats.[69] Other enslaved people did not enjoy a material benefit from whites' performances of generosity, though, especially if they lived on absentee-owned operations.[70] Whites used the gifting of food, especially treats, to demonstrate their power and entertain themselves. Sallie Benford in Union County treated enslaved children to sugar in a way that degraded them and made her feel maternal and powerful. "'Come on here, you little niggers,'" she'd call, as Bob Benford remembered, "and she'd sprinkle sugar on the meat block and we'd just lick sugar."[71]

Enslaved people viewed "privileges" of certain consumables as rightfully theirs and owed to them. It was common for enslaved men to be rationed some tobacco and even whiskey from time to time. It was one small thing for youths to look forward to when they transitioned to wearing pants and working as a full hand. At Wagram, bondsmen expected this provision. Overseer Pelham wrote, "I have put a stop to giving tobacco to some of these chaps. Rather young to chew tobacco I think. . . . There was some one said you had all ways allowed tobacco to all who worked out. They seemed to think you gave it as extra to workers &c. I stopped all by telling them you would decide and if youngsters were to have any thing something else would do better than tobacco."[72]

While enslaved people's access to delicacies or other pleasures brought some gratification, other aspects of their material lives carried higher stakes, particularly items related to health and healing. The edges of fields and pastures supplied the herbs and roots that men and women used to care for each other's ailing bodies. White doctors were usually both expensive and far away, so enslavers and their managers normally avoided calling in a doctor to treat bondspeople unless the ailment seemed grave. Doctor visits usually cost planter Henry Shugart two dollars each in the 1840s, depending on the distance the doctor traveled and the amount of medication prescribed. Eight miles and two prescriptions might cost ten dollars. As Molly Finley put it, "If a doctor was had you know somebody was right low."[73] Like other nineteenth-century Americans, enslaved people often took mercury, in the form of calomel or "Blue mass" pills, to prevent illness and treat it.[74] They also passed the knowledge of harvesting leaves, berries, and roots down generations and carried on traditions of applying them as medical remedies or even in the practice of conjuring.[75] Black men and women applied their knowledge of herbal teas and poultices for minor illness. But while many might have basic knowledge of "natural" remedies or wore charms to ward off disease, they deferred to those wealthiest in healing knowledge. Liza Smith remembered that if someone on the place in Jefferson County took sick, "the master would send out for herbs and roots. Then one of the slaves who knew how to cook and mix 'em up for medicine use would give the doses."[76]

Some of the herbal remedies used by white and black Arkansans were no doubt learned from Native Americans, and although the specific *species* of plants used by the Choctaw, Creek, Cherokee, and Chickasaw changed somewhat from the early to late nineteenth century, their preparation and uses remained largely the same.[77] Jerusalem oak, which has a well-documented historical use by Cherokees for worms and to treat colds and "fever diseases," was also used by enslaved Arkansans, especially to prevent and treat worms in children. Enslaved people also used worm-seed, related to Jerusalem oak and employed by several eastern native groups, in the same ways.[78] Native Americans shared with whites and African Americans the many uses for the bark of the Slippery Elm (or Red Elm), a tree native to Arkansas and the eastern United States. The bark had many uses, including easing labor pains. First the bark was removed, then the inner portions scraped off. Those fibers were dried and used in a poultice to treat inflammation and heal wounds. People also boiled the inner bark to make a tea that relieved coughs and sore throats, and it was sometimes used as a laxative or to relieve urinary inflammation.[79] White and black southerners knew Slippery Elm well. When George Washington Bond forgot to gather some of this tree's bark for his enslaver in Jefferson County, he was whipped to "give [him] a little piece of remembrance" while the white neighbors watched and laughed.[80] These remedies were mixed with less "natural" ones. Enslaved people experienced a combination of folk remedies and "modern" medicine. Eda Rains of Little Rock recalled being vaccinated for smallpox; she also remembered how enslaved people would "make medicine" out of black willow, black snake root, and boneset, all of which are native to Arkansas.[81] Callie Washington described a combination of white doctor visits for serious illness and "old women" treating less serious ailments like colds with herbal teas near Red Fork in Desha County.[82]

By the nineteenth century, Americans, including enslaved Arkansans, widely used asafetida, a medicinal plant known in other parts of the world since antiquity. Stories of its use are common in the WPA interviews of formerly enslaved people, although it is clear from those documents that the term "asafetida" (or "akerfedity") came to be used by southerners as a shorthand for any bag of herbs worn for medicinal purposes. The contents of the bags worn around the neck hint at the blurred lines in enslaved communities between medicine and conjure. Cindy Kinsey remembered children on a plantation near Little Rock wearing the left hind foot of a rabbit and a pungent asafetida bag around their necks to ward off fever. Louis Davis recalled that wearing asafetida bags and lead were popular methods to prevent disease. Callie Washington claimed that all the enslaved children wore asafetida bags as disease preventatives; she was so convinced of the effectiveness of worn charms for disease prevention that when she was interviewed by the WPA she was wearing a penny and a piece of lead around her neck for "heart trouble."[83] Liza Smith recalled that all the men and women on the Mason place (who came to Jefferson County from Virginia) wore charms to ward off disease. Joe Ray of southwest Arkansas wore a charm around his neck—a needle with a blue velvet string through the eye—for "sharp luck."[84]

Folk medicine and midwifery were highly valued, so bondspeople with those skills, usually women, enjoyed special status in their neighborhood. Often these experts, such as the "old doctor woman" that Mandy Tucker remembered on the Cockrill plantation, provided the most consistent medical care for enslaved people. At the Bullock plantation, Rose was respected as an authority on medicine by black and white alike. She kept a trunk containing (at least) the following: turpentine, castor oil, Jerusalem oak, worm-seed syrup, and sulfur. She treated children's cuts and sores, as well as other ailments that cropped up, but she also administered a preventative routine. Every so often Rose gathered the plantation's children—one row of white children and one row of black children—and made her way down the lines administering sulfur and molasses to maintain the youngsters' health.[85] Sharla Fett established the historical importance of such women, explaining, "It was they who administered food and medicines, eased pain, caught the babies, soothed and wrapped injuries, and prepared the bodies of the dead for burial." Bondspeople's concept of healing included a "relational vision of health" in which medicine, conjuring, superstition, personal relationships, and community dynamics all figured.[86]

These connections reveal themselves in Cindy Kinsey's description of the power of her mother, Zola Young, in Pulaski County. Young presided over the enslaved community's funerals, wearing a veil that was altogether beautiful, protective of evil spirits, repellent of ghosts, and imbued with healing power. Zola Young's enslavers knew to allow her time away from work for such occasions, because only she could lead the plantation's black men and women through such distressing times. Remembering her mother's veil as an elderly woman, Kinsey groaned, "Wisht I had me that veil right now, might help cure dis rheumatism in my knee what ailin me so bad." The spiritual power of healing also related to enslaved people's use of natural remedies. Mart Stewart explains, "Some plants, indeed, saved both body and soul" by the reckoning of enslaved people.[87]

Bondspeople understood disease differently than whites, who did not connect health with spirituality or fortune in the same way. The relationship between medicinal skills and conjuring or root work, often feared by whites, sometimes caused power struggles over what methods defined appropriate practices and who could administer them. Many bondspeople freely used herbs and roots from their surroundings to treat ailments, but others had to exercise caution, especially if the practice looked to whites like superstition. George Kye, who grew up on a farm in western Arkansas bordering Indian Territory, said that his enslaver prohibited herb medicine but "I wore a buckeye on my neck just the same."[88]

Although enslaved women often held a special status as healers, whites sometimes tried to exert a measure of control over their practice. O. W. Green's grandmother had a knack for the art of medicine and moved between two worlds: the provenance of white men with official training and the realm of folk medicine where a knowledge of natural remedies ruled. Green described her methods and record as a healer: "Grandmother used herbs fo' medicine—black snake root, sasparilla, blackberry briar roots—and nearly all de young 'uns she fooled with she save from diarrhea" (the latter of which was a nineteenth-century killer). She worked under her enslaver as a nurse for thirty-seven years and learned his methods as well. Threatened by her knowledge, however, the doctor would whip her to intimidate her from sharing his medical secrets.[89] Overseers and slavers might altogether avoid consulting black men and women with medical knowledge. Two women at Wagram plantation, Jane and Pauline, who suffered from prolapsed uteruses (an ailment that plagued them for years), endured the overseer's attempt to treat them according to a home health manual in 1857. They likely also received care from their fellow bondswomen in addition to whatever procedure the overseer subjected them to.[90]

Pain was a constant reality for men and women held in slavery, and they relieved it with the creative use of everyday items around them, including a simple poultice of corn shucks and ashes. Pork grease had many uses for soothing and protecting wounds incurred as a result of their heavy labor on the cotton frontier. As Scott Bond said, "Tallow was the cure all"—bondspeople used it for burns, cuts, and cracked feet.[91] They also applied warm tallow to the chests of asthma sufferers and others who had difficulty breathing.[92] Pork grease was a go-to when enslaved people helped each other recover from whippings. Katie Rowe's description of overseer Saunders's whipping routine in southwest Arkansas was not atypical. First his victims had to strip to the waist, then they received lashes that created blisters, which the overseer proceeded to burst with a leather strap. To treat these wounds, other enslaved people procured "a sheet and grease[d] it with lard and wrap[ped] 'em up in it." The injured person wore the greasy wrap under his or her clothing for several days of their recovery.[93] Sallie Crane never forgot the periodic whippings she received in southwest Arkansas. She was held by Harmon Bishop, then was passed to his daughter Evelyn, but for a time stayed with Jenny and Joe Nelson—Bishop's daughter and son-in-law. "They kept a bowl filled with vinegar and salt and pepper settin' nearby, and when they whipped me till the blood come, they would take the mop and sponge the cuts" to increase the pain. Enslavers routinely salted the gashes they opened on black men's and women's backs with the lash, often following up by scraping a corn cob over the flesh to further increase the pain of the attack. Sallie Crane recalled, "They would whip me with the cowhide part of the time and with birch sprouts the other part," which left splinters "long as my finger" in her flesh. Like countless others, Crane benefited from the kindness of other bondspeople who helped her to recover. In Crane's case, Betty Jones would come over and soak the splinters out of her back.[94] Vinegar, salt, pepper, corn cobs, animal fat and hides—all pantry items or by-products of agriculture—were ubiquitous in the histories of the most brutal symbol of slavery's horror in Arkansas.

Indeed, enslaved people's oppression was inseparable from many of their everyday items. Removing one's shirt was a symbol of the violent beatings that reinforced mastery because it was often the first step in receiving a whipping. As Columbus Williams remembered the brutal whippings dealt by Ben Heard of Union County, whether they were men or women, "Strip 'em to their waist and let their rags hang down from their hips and tie them down and lash them till the blood ran all down over their clothes." And afterward, "they would put their rags on and go on about their business. There wouldn't be no such thing as medical attention. What did he care."[95] To demand a bondsperson's shirt was to declare that they must submit to this degradation. In 1853 in southwest Arkansas, Nate refused to do it and paid for that refusal with his life. When the overseer, James Martin, demanded Nate's shirt, he shot back that he had "given his shirt" to the last overseer and was not going to do it again. Martin shot him to death.[96] While giving over his or her shirt was practically synonymous with whippings, enslaved people did not always experience those attacks in that way. Sometimes whites whipped them with their clothes on until they became slivers of cloth clotted with blood. This further complicated victims' recovery because the cloth had to be soaked out of the wounds.[97]

While various materials figured prominently in the history of enslaved Arkansans' oppression, others took center stage in their struggle to define some breathing room for themselves and make a home. The luckiest of those acquired some property, often rooted in bondspeople's harvest of the fruits of the natural world around them. This acquisition required effort, which usually reinforced bonds between those in deprived circumstances but sometimes strained them.[98] On the margins of the South, especially away from Arkansas's few urban areas, bondspeople's opportunities to acquire items of their own were most often related either to their extraction from the vast wooded zones around them or the ability of domestic workers to secure household goods. Betty Brown's mother, for example, hunted and trapped in the forests of northeast Arkansas, converting skins into the goods she wanted. When peddlers came around, she was ready with piles of raccoon, deer, beaver, and mink hides to trade for calico printed cloth and trinkets. Because they were the only enslaved family on the place, her activity did not compete with other family economies.[99]

Sam Word's mother did no such hunting, but she acquired desirable goods, like quilts stored in a chest in her cabin, by way of her work in the house.[100] Rachel, who worked in the Bullock home, secured some quilt pieces from the planter's young daughter (who got them from her mother's bag of fabric scraps while she was out of the house) by promising not to report her misbehavior. Betsey, another domestic worker, acquired material from the same little girl, who was able to hide her antics that led to a ripped calico dress by offering to give the ruined dress to Betsey for a quilt. Women who had access to these kinds of goods gained not only material to create improved clothing or bedding but also useful trading items that could be exchanged for other goods they desired.[101]

For those who could engage in it, like R. C. Smith's father, independent economic activity offered opportunities to make meaning out of their labor, exert some measure of power over their material lives, relate to one another, and establish a sense of rootedness in place. Proximity to town increased these chances. Smith was held in the Ozarks near Fayetteville by Presley R. Smith, who allowed him to work out at jobs, likely relating to his skills in stonemasonry, for wages.[102] Some bondspeople near Pocahontas in Randolph County enjoyed some time to labor for themselves, using the money to buy shoes and clothes. It is possible that their enslaver relied on this system to shift the burden of clothing supply onto bondspeople, a common practice for the task system used in the older, eastern South.[103] In Phillips County, Mollie Barber's father made boots and shoes for "out money" in the evenings; his enslaver, Nat Turner, took a cut of the money and Reuben Turner got the rest. Part of Reuben's job was to haul the farm's cotton four miles to Helena—this was likely when he had the best chance to sell what he made.[104] When they were assigned to pick neighbors' cotton, people held by John Brown could earn 50 cents per hundred pounds picked. At least once, Brown paid bondspeople money for all cotton above 100 pounds picked (he raised this number for better pickers).[105] According to Ellen Briggs Thompson's testimony, whites may have actually purchased things from enslaved people on Joe Mitchell's place in Howard County. "When they had a supper, they would usually sell the things," she recalled. "Then the whites folks would come and buy from them. There would be nice looking things on the table."[106]

Enslaved people provided food and resources for themselves when their captors allowed them to tend gardens after the end of the day's work or on weekends. If, as Kimberly Smith argues, enslavement caused African Americans to connect possession/control of land to possession of self, then much more was at stake for enslaved Arkansans who were allowed to cultivate gardens or cotton patches than simply the vegetables or cash those efforts could generate. The chance to garden meant gaining some autonomy in their relationship to nature, improving their material existence and that of their families, and leveraging that into their sense of rootedness and home. The ability to modify the landscape for their own benefit was a rare opportunity but a meaningful one. Bondspeople at Ed Lindsey's place, who had moved to Pine Bluff from Virginia shortly before the Civil War, could sell cotton that they grew in their own gardens. There does not seem to have existed anything like the slaves' farm market activity (selling eggs, etc.) in Vicksburg and Natchez, however. Hannah Jameson's experience, that "there was no chance to have their own gardens," would have been more typical.[107] Thus, enslaved people's activity in peddling their own farm goods seems to have been rare in Arkansas, but it is also probably underrepresented in the available documents.

Enslaved households connected to the wider neighborhood by the threads of economic exchange, but bondspeople in the possession of contraband had to choose their friends wisely. Sometimes goods like alcohol, tobacco, and clothes linked bondspeople with whites in extralegal economic activity.[108] Pleasant, a bondsman in South Arkansas, must have had some friendly interaction with a poor white woman named Sophia Fulmer before he was accused of attempting to rape her. Because Sophia testified that the altercation began with Pleasant entering her home looking to acquire some liquor and tobacco, it seems that exchanging or sharing those items might have been a regular part of their interaction. Whether or not their friendship or acquaintance had actually turned violent as Sophia claimed, the fact that they already knew each other and that Pleasant felt comfortable going into the home looking for those items suggests that they had traded or shared them before.[109] The possession of alcohol may have made for a deadly stunt on Isaac Jones's plantation in Hempstead County, southwestern Arkansas. Bondspeople there were able to get their hands on some liquor and left a half-drunk jug outside the cabin of the black foreman named Sandy. When the overseer spotted the flagon, he became enraged and, according to the story, took Sandy out into the woods and beat him to death, while the others huddled in their cabins in terror.[110]

While consumables might pass muster in certain circumstances, most whites considered enslaved people's access to books and paper unacceptable. Arkansas law did not prohibit teaching enslaved people to read and write, but most whites discouraged it. Exceptions existed—the WPA interviews include accounts of white schoolchildren teaching enslaved youngsters their lessons—but they proved the rule. Generally enslaved people were prohibited from accessing printed material and learning to read. Laura Shelton's mother, Susan Bearden, told her how "they didn't allow them to pick up a piece of paper in slave times for fear they'd learn." This was in Drew County where she worked in Tom Barnett's house. Annie Page declared, "I can show you scars now" from being whipped for hiding out in the yard with a Blue Black Speller book, learning from the enslaver's granddaughter, Mary Jane, in Union County.[111] Books and literacy represented dangerous challenges to slavery's regime. Ben, held on Harry Hogan's farm in Pulaski County, read the Bible to himself and other enslaved people, interpreting the scripture in subversive ways. In Ben's reckoning the Good Book clearly foretold freedom for enslaved people. At first, this earned him his enslaver's condescension, but Hogan's fear showed through when he taunted, "Hell no, you never will be free, you ain't got sense enough. . . . you'll be a slave as long as you live." Hogan took Ben's Bible and banned bondspeople from church services altogether. Ben eventually got his hands on another Bible, but he kept it and his rebellious faith hidden from whites from then on.[112]

Indeed, the story of acquisition, consumption, and independent economic activity in Arkansas is a story of scarcity, restriction, and risk. It was very difficult for bondspeople on the margins to purchase and trade for the material things they wanted, relative to those in more populated, urban, or longer-settled areas. For Arkansas pioneers in the early days (and for many, for the entire duration of the antebellum period), "neighbors, general stores, and itinerant peddlers were nonexistent."[113] Because population centers were small, few, and far between, it was more difficult—though not impossible—for enslaved people on the fringes of the cotton frontier to take part in the market. Anthony Kaye and Anthony Gene Carey find much more market activity among bondspeople in the Natchez and Chattahoochee regions than the WPA interviews and Southern Claims Commission records suggest for most of Arkansas. Both locales studied by Kaye and Carey had higher population concentrations as well as larger percentages of enslaved people in their populations than Arkansas did overall in 1860.[114] For example, anything like what historians describe as the "slave gentry" of Virginia, a group of finely dressed enslaved men whose public demeanor infuriated some whites, was unknown on Arkansas's cotton frontier.[115] As was the case in many other states, Arkansas law prohibited enslaved people from buying commodities, especially alcohol, from whites without permission from their enslavers. Slaveholders closely monitored trading activity among enslaved people as well. Whites inconsistently enforced these laws and conventions, however. To test whether passing boats would break the law against selling to bondspeople, Walworth, in southeast Arkansas, sent an enslaved blacksmith with a dime to try to buy some whiskey. To Walworth's relief, he was denied. The law also barred bondspeople from hiring out their own time. But enforcing that restriction proved difficult and seems to have been routinely ignored.[116] The few relatively urban areas in Arkansas, such as Little Rock, Helena, and Fayetteville, provided bondspeople, especially those with skills, more access to the market than in places dominated by plantation agriculture. Many enslaved people in Little Rock were able to use their skills to acquire finer things to supplement their material life. However, only about 3.5 to 4 percent of Arkansas's enslaved population lived in towns.[117]

Bondspeople who openly acquired property and traded goods for profit did so at the pleasure of their enslavers. Wesley Dodson, held by Miram Dodson about twelve miles south of Fayetteville, enjoyed a particularly broad ability to acquire and dispose of the fruits of his labor on the land. When her husband, John, died, Miram Dodson recognized how heavily she relied on Wesley and seems to have realized that she could profit and wash her hands of the management of the farm by giving Wesley a great deal of control over it. By 1860, sixteen enslaved people labored there for Miram, who had no children. The enslaved people assumed that her childlessness contributed to her practice of allowing them relative autonomy in property ownership—as John Dodson put it, Miram had "no children to leave her property to" anyway. The men, at least, on Miram's farm kept "all the stock we wanted and we always raised stock & bought & sold & traded about just as if we were free men." The arrangement transformed Dodson's farm into more than a site of captivity; the fields and barns became a source of opportunity as well. Wesley and his compatriots at Dodson's leveraged their ability "to raise individual property of [their] own" as soon as the war began, when Miram granted their freedom.[118] However, as Damien Pargas argues, the "internal economy" that Wesley and the others enjoyed in the antebellum years should not be understood as occurring outside of or in spite of the slave system, because it was "inextricably interwoven with the broader demands of slave-based agriculture." Miram Dodson benefited from the arrangement she made with enslaved people and always reserved the right to change the rules. And at the end of the day, it was enslavers who had the final say in bondspeople's ability to acquire property above the table.[119]

Because of the precarity of acquisition and trade, enslaved people had to manage risks and guard their gains. For example, in 1857, the bondspeople at Ballard's Wagram plantation, having been promised payment for information about runaways, exposed an escapee from another farm. A couple of months later, however, when a seamstress fled one of Ballard's other plantations, the new Wagram overseer believed that bondspeople there harbored her, writing, "I will double my diligence now and hope to meet with her if she is about. I am confident there is not one here too good to harbor her."[120] Though it is not known whether the men and women truly did help the seamstress, the difference between the two scenarios is important. In the first instance, a stranger was quite literally "sold out" by the bondspeople at Wagram who would rather have had cash than solidarity with the runaway, but, in the second, they were more apt to hide a woman who might have been known to them (they may have lived with her on another of Ballard's plantations). Such incidents did not indicate failed solidarity, as Eugene Genovese supposed. While they suffered common trials, bondspeople did not necessarily feel loyalty or share aims with other enslaved people, especially if their own safety or material gains were at stake. Walter Johnson elegantly explains that solidarity "was less an achieved state than a continual terrified request: Can you help me? Do you know the way? Will you share what you have? Will you risk your life to save mine? Many were the individuals whose supplications were unsuccessful." Constant implied and real requests for solidarity by others asked bondspeople to risk what they had built for themselves.[121]

At the end of the day, all of the products of the farms and plantations upon which enslaved people labored were the result of *their* efforts, from the felled trees hewed into logs forming their cabin walls to the corn in their bread. Enslaved Arkansans were the producers of goods and resources that they were denied control over. In turn, many of them carefully appropriated the fruits of their labor. Cyntha Jones of Drew County explained, "I thought what was my white folks' things was mine too."[122] And although Jones was speaking of her indignant reaction to Union soldiers' seizure of her enslaver's belongings during the war, the sentiment held some truth beyond that context. Bondspeople who took from the food stores or goods of the operation on which they were held may have simply reckoned that they created the wealth and thus had a right to it. Others may not have felt the need to rationalize at all, knowing full well that the world in which they lived was not fair, and that resourcefulness and risk could pay off. A biscuit plucked from the kitchen could soothe a rumbling belly, while something bigger might offer a greater advantage. Snatching items from a tool shed or a chest of drawers facilitated bondspeople's fun and sociability, at the expense of whites for once. Manuel, owned by the Fultons just outside of Little Rock, stole a bridle and saddle from his wife's enslaver and lost them both while gambling.[123] Stephen, at one of Walworth's plantations on the Mississippi, stole shoats and sold them to purchase clothes, but was caught and whipped for it. (It is not clear if the bondspeople there were inadequately clothed, if Stephen wanted to resell the clothes to others, or if he simply desired new clothes.)[124] Solomon Lambert claimed that stealing was a prime reason for whippings: "They trust 'em in everything then they whoop 'em if they steal. They knew it [was] wrong. Course they did."[125] Theft—if people held in bondage even thought of it that way—provided a means for black men and women to share a treat together, acquire clothes for an occasion, or have some fun at the card table on the old master's dime. Beyond materials of survival, their contraband amounted to the substance of everyday resistance.

Food, goods, material culture, property, and exchange connected and divided bondspeople in Arkansas, as they acquired, shared, traded, and disputed. They strengthened ties of family and friendship and rooted themselves in their homes and neighborhoods when they treated illness and injury, shared food, and enjoyed objects like musical instruments together. They achieved a sense of place rather than alienation through their daily material habits. The nuclear family household worked as the major unit of distribution and consumption of goods, but sharing had its rewards. Sharing game and the fruits of the land may have been more frequent forms of this interaction than accumulating stock, large items, or valuables on the edges of the cotton frontier. But although the "slaves' economy" on the periphery paled in comparison to the older and more settled sections of the South, as Steven Hahn points out, the differences would have been a matter of "degree rather than kind." Earning, trading, and sharing still proved meaningful to bondspeople on the periphery—perhaps even more so.[126] While the produce of the forest (like skins or nuts) and items "stolen" from their captors' farms seem to have been enslaved people's primary source of items to trade or share, every once in a while enslaved people could earn a little money working extra. Chances to create their own produce via gardening or small personal cotton patches came to enslaved Arkansans rarely, making the ability to leverage the cultivated landscape for their own benefit all the more significant. Circles in which enslaved people exchanged money, goods, skins, toasts, bets, and laughs were important aspects of their society, made all the more precious by their rarity. As Walter Johnson phrased it, their ties were "expressed in material form." All of the above-listed activities contributed to enslaved people's sense of implacement—the connections they made to each other and to place via shelter, food, clothing, other necessities, and extra goods made meaning of the landscape. Consideration of quotidian material lives of bondspeople, however, also brings the brutality and humiliation of enslaved life into sharp relief, as men, women, and children suffered privation, scarcity, and pain. Yet to find a sense of place is not necessarily to live in harmony or free of trauma. Enslaved people in Arkansas would have understood all too well the explanation offered by Barbara Fields: "Ties of place, like ties of family, do not signify an absence of evil, injustice, or suffering. . . . In common with other relationships that matter . . . the relationship of human beings to place may involve oppression, betrayal, suffocation, and outrage as much as comfort, contentment, and peace."[127]

6 / Battlegrounds

In his attempt to convince white Arkansans to remove their state from the union to protect slavery, Governor Henry M. Rector articulated a vision for Arkansas's ground linked to the labor of black men and women as chattel: "That institution [slavery] is now upon its trial before you," he warned, "and if we mean to defend and transmit it to our children, let us terminate this northern crusade, by forming a separate government, in which no conflict can ensue." Rector explained, "The extension of slavery is the vital point of the whole controversy between the North and the South," but he pushed for the unity of white Arkansans. Although slaveholdings looked different across the state, he asked, "Does there exist inside the borders of Arkansas any diversity of sentiment, as to the religious or moral right of holding negro slaves?" In Rector's vision the captive labor of black Arkansans linked the economies and destinies of Arkansas's upcountry, river valley, prairies, and delta. He invoked Providence in this relationship. "God in his omnipotent wisdom," Rector declared, "created the cotton plant—the African slave—and the lower Mississippi Valley to clothe and feed the world, and a gallant race of men and women produced upon its soil to defend it, and execute that decree."[1]

Although many hesitated, eventually enough white Arkansans agreed that this destiny was worth protecting with their lives and they pulled Arkansas from the United States—of which it had been a part for only twenty-five years—to enter the newly created Confederate States of America (CSA). Ironically, this "slaveholders' rebellion" accelerated slavery's demise. In only a few decades after its establishment, chattel slavery ended in Arkansas. Westward expansion had broken the system as increasingly paranoid slavers rejected any criticism of slavery's spread. Arkansas whites joined slaveholders all over the South in their growing fear of abolitionist plots, clamoring for federal safeguards of mastery. Even the tougher Fugitive Slave Law had not been enough to satisfy their intensifying cries for not only national toleration of the institution but active federal protection of it. Some of the most rabid proponents of reopening the African slave trade were white Arkansans. By the time the election of 1860 came around, tensions had reached a fever pitch.

Enslaved Arkansans well understood the stakes. Some proceeded with caution while others embarked on bold courses toward freedom.[2] The same themes that informed their lives under slavery continued to be important, but with greater risk and more promise. William Smith, born into bondage in Ozan, Hempstead County, described the war years as "Stormy times for everybody."[3] Some bondspeople navigated the war under tight restrictions, while others took advantage of wartime upheaval to undermine the regime that had ordered their entire lives up to that point. The war changed the meaning of space. Forests and uncleared zones where enslaved men and women used to go for respite now brimmed with soldiers and guerillas, while some bondspeople achieved greater autonomy in public spaces than they had ever known.[4]

White and black Arkansans interpreted the meaning of Abraham Lincoln's election in much the same way: that slavery's days were numbered. Although slavers tried to limit their captives' access to information, or spin news to their own benefit, bondspeople knew enough to craft their own understandings of the events leading up to the war, concluding that Lincoln would use his army to free them. Folk stories of Lincoln emerged in black communities everywhere as enslaved people tried to explain his role in their destiny. Adrianna Kerns recounted her mother's theory: "My mother used to say that Lincoln went through the South as a beggar and found out everything. When he got back, he told the North how slavery was ruining the nation."[5] Bondspeople who looked to Lincoln with hope ran up against the interpretation of Arkansas whites, not because they disagreed with their assessment of Lincoln but because they *also* saw him as an abolitionist. Whites, particularly from the Mississippi River region, warned that white people of all classes would suffer economic ruin from the destruction of slave property.[6]

After taking a wait-and-see stance until the firing on Fort Sumter, a second convention of whites in Arkansas voted to secede from the United States on May 6, 1861. Less than two months earlier, the vice president of the Confederacy, Alexander Stephens, had articulated the basis of that government, famously declaring, "Its foundations are laid, its cornerstone rests, upon the great truth that the negro is not equal to the white man; that slavery, subordination to the superior race, is his natural and moral condition."[7] As the state delegation embraced secession, they drafted a new constitution. The document looked almost identical to the 1836 statehood document, with a few important differences, including the declaration that "all *free white men*, where they form a social compact, are equal, and have certain and inherent indefeasible rights"—a change from simply "all free men" in the 1836 version.[8]

At first glance, the state boundary looked more important than ever, as Arkansas's neighbor to the north had not seceded. Not enough Missouri whites backed the Confederacy to enable its support there to take hold officially, just as Arkansas's white Unionist minority had failed to prevail in Arkansas. Some pro-Confederate Missourians took refuge in Arkansas while others remained to challenge federal control, buoying CSA officers' hopes to take Missouri. As was the case in Arkansas, much of Missouri's ground remained bitterly contested. White Texans and Louisianans more easily swept their governments into the Confederacy, abandoning the union even before the attack on Fort Sumter. While many of Arkansas's white Unionists refugeed to Missouri, when federals arrived, waves of Arkansas's Confederates would seek safe haven in Texas.[9]

To Arkansans' west, federal forces in the spring of 1861 vacated troops from Indian Territory, pulling them north to Kansas. One united view of the Civil War did not exist among Native Americans in the Territory, whose governments held complex relationships with the U.S. government yet did not enjoy its citizenship. Few succeeded in remaining neutral; many threw in their lot with the Confederacy. Residents of Indian Territory had never been isolated from the conflict related to slavery, especially considering the previous years of bloodshed in Kansas and slaving raids into Indian Territory. Albert Pike—an Arkansas slaveholder, nationally prominent Freemason, and former agent for the Choctaw, Chickasaw, and Muscogee Nations—served as Jefferson Davis's representative in the Territory. As a result, Cherokee, Chickasaw, Choctaw, Creek, and Seminole nations, all of whom practiced slavery, provided Confederate units. The Chickasaw and Choctaw in particular proved amenable to a partnership with the Confederates. Indian alliances with the Confederacy reflected both their commitments to race-based slavery and their struggle for tribal sovereignty.[10] Arkansas's bondspeople, then, entered the conflict on ground officially associated with a militant commitment to preserve black slavery, supported to its south and west. Increasingly fierce guerilla warfare contested Confederate control in Arkansas, however, especially in the northwest.

Everyone in Arkansas understood the war's threat to slavery. Bondspeople bore tighter restrictions as whites mobilized unprecedented watches and patrols across the state. Sterling Cockrill went as far as suspending enslaved people's religious meetings, recording, "I have stoped the negroes from preaching and it is not to be commenced again, also prayer meetings." Whites of Chicot County became so apprehensive about a possible revolt that each township organized guards, and the county put up $20,000 to arm them. The Planters Township Guard drilled in an empty cornfield on Saturdays with canes and sticks. Over the summer, the zeal of Chicot County home guards waned but white fears never fully subsided.[11] In another area with a high enslaved population, Camden, white residents aimed angry suspicion at "Dutch" merchants in their town, whom they suspected might be sympathetic to the cause of abolition. To the north, Searcy whites lynched several enslaved men accused of planning a rebellion along with a white tanner accused of inciting them. Angry residents followed up by driving additional bondspeople from the area.[12]

Whites worried that economic activity could facilitate more subversive aims. Pulaski County bondspeople associated with J. T. Pendergrast, a poor white man from Alabama, to buy whiskey and perhaps also to socialize. Early in the war, authorities indicted Pendergrast for selling alcohol to enslaved people, adding the charge of "encouraging slaves to rebellion" in the fall of 1862. An essential witness's absence allowed Pendergrast to escaped the alcohol charge, and the case against him for inciting enslaved people to rebellion seems to have eventually been dropped as well.[13] Area whites, affronted by Pendergrast's actions, probably simply wanted to raise the stakes for those who broke codes meant to regulate bondspeople, but it is possible that enslaved people might have been making plans with Pendergrast for something bigger than booze. Pendergrast's charges occurred around the same time that authorities accused Mary, "a colored woman, slave for life," of setting fire to "a certain dwelling house . . . with intent thereby then and there to injure the said William Murray." There is no evidence that this incident had any connection to Pendergrast's activity with enslaved people, but the surviving documents related to both cases are slim. Mary's guilty verdict came with a sentence of five hundred lashes "well laid on" her bare back, a punishment that the courts later reduced.[14]

While bondspeople already in Arkansas came under closer scrutiny at the advance of the war, the beginning of the conflict initiated a flood of forcibly migrated men and women into the state, as whites in the Southeast and seaboard South feared the loss of their human property and sought to remove them as far away from federal power as possible. Some arrived early. Slave trader A. M. Boyd drove Robert Houston, born in Buckingham County, Virginia, to Memphis at the beginning of the war, with forty or fifty others, then sent them to work on Boyd's plantation in Chicot County in early 1861. Mingo Scott, born in Hinds County, Mississippi, suffered a forced relocation to Arkansas in 1861 as well.[15] Many bondspeople's trips amounted to yet one more move among others in their lives as chattel. Mary Estes Peters recalled that whites sold her mother from Missouri to Mississippi, before taking her to Arkansas during the war years.[16] Bondspeople pushed to the southern margins during the war likely resented the journey *and* the destination, many arriving from much more settled zones of the South. Doc Quinn marveled at the ruggedness of the Red River Valley when he arrived in Arkansas with other bondspeople forced there by Colonel Ogburn from Monroe County, Mississippi. "When we first came here, this place, as well as the rest of the Valley," Quinn observed, "was just a big canebrake.... The folks didn't go gallivantin' round nights like they do now or the varmints would get them."[17]

While refugeeing slaveholders forced black families into Arkansas, resident whites forced bondspeople into hiding, often within their own neighborhoods, to keep them out of freedom's reach. Previous years of bondspeople's flight, when fugitives had much less reason to hope their journeys would pay off with freedom, taught whites that proximity to U.S. soldiers, especially after the Emancipation Proclamation, threatened mastery. Thus, upon the approach of federals, many slavers forced their captives to the very places where they were normally exasperated to find them—the woods and swamps. When Union soldiers neared, Solomon Lambert recalled, "Lambert then hid the slaves in the bottoms. We carried provisions and they sent more 'long. We stay two or three days or a week when they heard a regiment comin' through.... We didn't care if they hid us. We heard the guns. We didn't want to go down there." The same cane, woods, and brush into which black men and women had long sought refuge from enslavers and their overseers now became destinations for whites looking to hide bondspeople. While they used to follow trails into the cane to find runaways' hideouts, now slavers and their hired managers created similar paths themselves as they provisioned black men and women hiding in those spaces.[18]

As it had been from the earliest days of white mastery on Arkansas's ground, the Mississippi River served as an interstate for men and women fleeing their enslavers. Only now the stakes rose higher than ever. Walke, commander of the USS *Carondelet*, reported in July 1862 that black men and women seeking refuge were "very numerous, standing under the banks of the river and making signals to us at night, asking to be taken away."[19] Knowing the danger of keeping bondspeople so near the tempting river within easy access of U.S. soldiers, riverside planters often drove their captive laborers into the interior of the state. When U.S. gunboats appeared on the Mississippi River near the Hilliard and Rayner places in late 1862, Isaac Hilliard boasted that within half an hour all of the enslaved people, about 350 total, had been successfully spirited away from the federals. Moving west away from the river about twenty-eight miles, Hilliard and his group had placed "an impassable swamp between" them and the access to freedom that the Mississippi River represented. The displaced bondspeople huddled in shanties and lived off corn hauled from the Hilliard and Rayner fields. As Lambert explained above, bondspeople who complied with their concealment did so out of fear—both of their enslavers and of the unknown that might await them with federal soldiers—which helps explain the ease with which so few whites were able to move a great many people in such a short time. Indeed, Rayner boasted that his captives "fled *from* the Yankees" rather than toward them. In contrast, at Ringo's plantation nearby, nine enslaved men and boys took off with the federals. Although Rayner said that the men did so "against their will," they likely connected the U.S. presence with freedom and safety.[20] Forcing valued labor away from the riverside fields might have cost slaveholders in the short term in lost productivity, but they focused on the overall payoff if they managed to preserve their investment in captive farmers. Chicot County planter Charles C. Stuart complained, "We have all moved our hands some distance from the River, but have no work of value to do." Seventeen relocated bondspeople worked for William E. Woodruff in Little Rock in 1862. Within eight months after the group's arrival, four died and another fell gravely ill. One Confederate official surveyed the situation early in eastern Arkansas, recording, "the plantations seem to be almost a waste, the slaves have nearly all been moved back, further in the country, & elsewhere." Enslaved people's tendency to rebel when they had the chance had inspired whites to take a preemptive strike to protect mastery in the plantation districts.[21]

Slavers' fears were well-founded. Not only did Mississippi Valley bondspeople tend to gravitate toward federal lines rather than away from them, they spoiled enslavers' plans when they disclosed the hiding places of those whom whites had hidden from federal forces. Johnson Chapman of Columbia explained to William Woodruff that federals discovered secreted bondspeople "invariably through bad faith of some of the Negroes." Slaveholders near Union forces sought to keep their captives out of reach because they knew that their enslaved labor force interpreted the presence of federals to mean at the very least a weakening of their bondage.[22] While it is impossible to know exactly how many and from exactly what places, sources show that thousands of bondspeople took charge of their own movement to seek freedom with the federal army. As Thomas DeBlack explains, "Black Arkansans along the route of the [Union] march were not inclined to wait for an official proclamation."[23]

The weakening of bondage associated with the federal presence that began in 1862 affected bondspeople in northwest Arkansas, too. In January and February 1862, Union forces driving Confederates out of Missouri met Confederate efforts to repulse them, leading to the Battle of Pea Ridge in early March, the conclusion of which established a lasting, if shifting, federal presence in northwest Arkansas. The Prairie Grove campaign at the close of the year proved that hold would not be easily relinquished. Like their counterparts in the Mississippi Valley, enslaved people in the Ozarks faced the possibility of forced removal. At one point in the conflict, perhaps as federals neared Cane Hill in November 1862, Tandy Kidd drove enslaved people south, away from Union forces as far as Mulberry, only to give up and drag them back, reckoning, "If they was lost they was lost." Although Union forces in northwest Arkansas maintained a presence there, the challenge of supply caused them to move in ways that kept them open to attack. The U.S. presence in the Ozarks faced consistent harassment by both Confederate guerillas and unaffiliated vagabonds whose practices of raid and retreat were facilitated by the mountainous terrain.[24]

The realities of war made it increasingly clear that the conflict was not about enslaved people only in the abstract—their labor and their movement held great power in determining which side would prevail. Frustrated that Confederates had employed enslaved labor to obstruct his advance across Arkansas in the spring and summer of 1862, and acknowledging that hundreds of black men and women descended on his army seeking freedom, U.S. general Samuel Curtis recognized an opportunity to undermine the Confederate effort. Concerned that Confederates would recapture fugitives and use their labor against him, and increasingly interested in employing them for the federal cause instead,

Curtis claimed the authority of earlier Confiscation Acts. Issuing certificates of freedom to hundreds of the "contraband" fugitives, Curtis proclaimed permanent freedom for enslaved people whose labor had been used in rebellion against the union. The term "contraband," in its characterization of men, women, and children as confiscated property, however, revealed the limits of U.S. policy before Lincoln's Emancipation Proclamation.[25]

Word spread among captive Arkansans, and when Curtis's army arrived at Helena, so did crowds of escaped black men, women, and children who had been following the army.[26] C. C. Washburn, commander of the post of Helena, understood that the fugitives could not return to their homes and that it was both wrong and dangerous for Union forces to turn away people who had risked so much. The U.S. Army struggled to provide for refugees but also faced obstructions in their attempts to transport them out of eastern Arkansas to places like Cairo, Illinois. Northern whites did not look kindly upon the prospect of large numbers of black southerners flooding their cities. Eastern Arkansas remained a draw for runaways, and freedpeople's settlements multiplied. Recent works by Jim Downs, Chandra Manning, and Amy Murrell Taylor have helped clarify the experience of African American Civil War refugees, still a relatively little-explored aspect of the war.[27]

President Lincoln, whom countless black men and women had already instinctively trusted, clarified the landscape of freedom when he issued his famous order. Lincoln's initial Emancipation Proclamation, announced in September 1862, warned that areas still in rebellion at the beginning of the following year would see their enslaved population officially freed in the eyes of the U.S. government. Lincoln and his advisors designed the measure to weaken the Confederacy and strengthen the moral high ground of the United States. For African Americans, however, the war had always been about freedom. On January 1, 1863, the Emancipation Proclamation went into effect, and black men and women continued to overwhelm the U.S. Army with their numbers. The Emancipation Proclamation would have been practically meaningless without enslaved people's willingness to act on it. And they did so all over Arkansas when they felt it was safe enough to flee.[28]

And so, working their way through the woods and hollows, escapees relied on old traces through cane and brush, this time with a plan not to lay out for only a few days but to put their bondage behind them forever. Here, Mart Stewart's contention that "fugitive environments" relied on knowledge of the natural environment is instructive. As before the war, runaways relied on a double-layered understanding of the natural world around them—an eye for the best paths and locations for concealment as well as an intuition of their pursuers' movements. Enslaved people's confidence in their flight was grounded in their experience in the brush, woods, and swamps. Boston Blackwell described the journey from the Blackwell plantation to Pine Bluff in October 1863: "We made the stream for a long piece. Heard the hounds a-howling, getting ready for to chase after us. Then we hid in dark woods. It was cold, frosty weather. Two days and two nights we traveled. That boy, he got so cold and hungry, he want to fall out by the way, but I drug him on. When we gets to the Yankee camp all our troubles was over."[29]

Men and women fled enslavers all over the state when they could, pulling the rug out from under the slavers' economy and war effort. Nearly 100 people fled Lycurgus Johnson's plantation between 1862 and 1863. All of planter James Peak's captives ran away to freedom, forcing him to cook and wash for himself.[30] Amanda Trulock complained that all the bondspeople on her place had been "taken" from her, except America and her children, by the summer of 1864. By then, Reuben, her enslaved overseer, had gone to work on a nearby farm owned by the Roane family. To Freedmen's Bureau officials, Reuben dated his flight from Trulock at October 1863. As idyllic as his work for Trulock seemed on paper to those who would offer an apology for slavery, Reuben seized the chance to escape Amanda Trulock's clutches and found himself managing federally leased plantations.[31] One man explained decades later, "We all called ourselves free after we ran away and came to the Yankees." As Amy Murrell Taylor's work has shown, fugitives' arrival to Union camps and their continued presence and movement in relation to them "flaunt[ed] newfound leverage."[32]

Not only did bondspeople transform their lives when they fled for freedom, but many also determined to risk it all and join the fight. More than 5,000 of Arkansas's black men succeeded in breaking their bonds to enlist in the U.S. Army. American service pension files show that such men often made this move in groups of friends and/or family. For example, in Bradley County, young men crept away in twos and threes from neighboring plantations about thirty-six miles from Pine Bluff and forty miles from Camden. Simon Frazier, Walker Frazier, Emanuel Frazier, Wright Allen, and Aaron Williams fled together to join the U.S. forces in December 1863. While the Fraziers and their neighbors joined what became the 54th United States Colored Infantry, African Americans from Arkansas also proudly served in the 46th, 56th, 69th, 112th, and

113th USCT regiments, joining the ranks of black men who would make up 10 percent of U.S. manpower in the conflict.[33]

Many men who stole away from their enslavers felt reluctant, though, to become involved with soldiers or become soldiers themselves, whether because they distrusted outsiders, had heard stories of rough treatment and discrimination in the ranks, sought to avoid battle, or simply desired, like other men, to stay close enough to their home bases to protect their families. Men knew the risks that fighting posed and they also knew better than to assume that U.S. Army posts were impenetrable. Steven Hahn expresses compelling reasons why black men might avoid U.S. lines and camps altogether: "They only had to rely on their own intelligence networks to learn that fugitives could be denied entrance, surrendered to demanding owners, impressed into military service, contracted to profit-hungry lessees, physically abused and sexually violated by Yankee soldiers, and generally treated with contempt."[34] Some black men who enlisted in Helena were betrayed by Union soldiers who accepted bribes to turn them back over to their enslavers. Jim Downs's work further elucidates the extreme health risks black individuals and families incurred when they arrived at U.S. lines. Camps cultivated devastating disease rates among people already weakened by the journey to reach them. Amy Murrell Taylor has well documented that the U.S. Army acted first and foremost on military necessity, which changed based on several factors including enemy movements and supply line disruptions. Black Arkansans could not place unqualified trust in the presence and stability of federal troops.[35]

Black men who did not want to enlist often had to keep themselves hidden to avoid increasingly aggressive recruitment and impressment. One soldier recalled, "They hide from us like chickens from a chicken hawk."[36] Slaver Robert Mecklin of Washington County claimed that three black companies of the U.S. Army swept through his neighborhood "conscripting such as were unwilling to join. They got some five or six, all of whom they had to take off in strings. One fellow they ran down, caught and tied his hands together, also his feet, then placing a rail between them he was carried swinging in this painful attitude to the guard house by two buck negroes, amidst the shouts and roar of laughter of officers and soldiers."[37] While this particular incident was witnessed through the eyes of a man looking for confirmation of his own racist conviction that freedom and responsibility brought out the worst in African Americans, the incident indicates that African Americans had varying ideas of how best to navigate the war. Like other young men during the conflict, they had their reasons for resisting military service.

While thousands of men and women moved from slavery to some kind of freedom, most remained the commodities of increasingly desperate enslavers. The Emancipation Proclamation provided more incentive for them to relocate. Countless bondspeople endured forced flight from the state, mostly to Texas, with captors who looked to put as much distance between them and federal lines as possible. Bondspeople from all over found themselves trudging toward Texas with their enslavers or overseers; those situated in western Arkansas did not have as far to go, such as those held by Frenchman Anton Neice. The three people held by James P. Spring and the five held by E. B. Bright, both of Sebastian County, also relocated to Texas.[38] At least half of the men and women held by Arkansas's largest slaver, Elisha Worthington, made the forced move with him from Chicot County to Tarrant County, Texas. James Mason and his sister Martha (the children Worthington had with an enslaved woman named Cynthia) stayed behind, where Mason managed his affairs.[39] The families held at Peter Van Winkle's lumber operation in Benton County were driven to Bowie County, Texas, by 1864, before Union forces burned the entire complex to the ground. One contemporary estimated that "150,000 slaves had crossed the Red River by the middle of the war."[40]

Bondspeople understood very well why they were "drove off" as white anxieties mounted. Molly Finley's parents' enslaver sent bondspeople all the way to Houston because "he didn't want the Yankees to scatter them and make soldiers of them."[41] In addition to protecting their investments, slavers wanted to escape the horrors they believed would accompany federal control and black freedom. The *Arkansas True Democrat* fanned whites' fears, claiming that U.S. soldiers "permitted a number of negro teamsters to seize the daughters of Mr. Anthony, and ravish these unprotected females. Their mother besought the protection of the officers, but these brutal men only cursed her as a d____d rebel. . . . It is a saddening, sickening picture of the condition to which society is reduced wherever the vandals of the North pollute our soil." Even if the incident never occurred, the story likely ratcheted up white anxieties and cast increased suspicion on enslaved people.[42]

Most importantly, the forced movement of bondspeople out of Arkansas distressed and disrupted their lives, as it often meant families were separated, amounting to yet another painful parting in a lifetime of upheavals. Sometimes all of the bondspeople held on a place made the move, but others parted when their enslavers chose to leave behind a skeleton crew to maintain their farms or plantations, or when they chose to take only men and leave women behind. Mary Myhand, of Clarksville, Arkansas, recollected her near separation from her brother. Only a young girl when her enslaver "took my brother and a grandson of his and started South," the frightened child "followed them about a half mile before they found me and I begged so hard they took me with them." Moses Mitchell was only twelve years old when whites forced him out to Texas as Arkansas Post fell to federal forces. Mitchell never laid eyes on his mother and infant sister again.[43] Enslaved people who suffered forced refugeeing became separated by death, too. John Wells's mother died—either giving birth or after delivery—while on the road with their enslaver to Texas. The infant perished, too. Senia Rassberry's mother succumbed to a "congestive chill" during a three-year stay in Texas.[44] Mary (or Martha) Allen McGehee was "ran down into Texas" with her brother John McGehee to Grayson County. Whites sold her away from her brother; she did not survive the war.[45]

One of the most immediate problems for bondspeople making the forced journey was the quality of the roads. Crowds of refugees trudging down the same poorly maintained roads made for excruciatingly slow travel.[46] In addition, men and women moving west out of Arkansas fought "heat, dust, wind, insects, reptiles, and boorish neighbors." Scarcity of water posed a problem, too. The long, dry stretches between rivers made bathing and washing a luxury. The only food and goods bondspeople could be sure to have on the way were what they were allowed to take with them. All of these inconveniences of the journey created the most serious hardships for enslaved people rather than their drivers, as it was bondspeople who were most likely to have to walk, to be the last to enjoy a break or to eat and drink, and to be the first to have to keep up chores like gathering water while encamped. Just as they and their parents had done on the way to Arkansas, so did these men and women have to suffer forced migration in the worst of circumstances.[47]

These journeys proved dangerous, not just inconvenient. The countryside crawled with ruffians who claimed allegiance to either the United States or the Confederacy, depending on whom they happened to be terrorizing at the moment. These "lawless bands abroad in the land" stole and destroyed property and engaged in acts of indiscriminate violence.[48] "Every steamer and wagon train leaving Fort Smith and Little Rock" became inundated with "families compelled by the ravages of war to seek a place of safety."[49] The danger is clear in DeBlack's assessment:

"In large areas of Arkansas beyond the Confederate-controlled southwest and the Federal-occupied towns, the last remnants of civil government and the rule of law had disappeared, guerillas and desperadoes roamed the countryside, and the only authority came from the barrel of a gun."[50] A few enslaved people of Yell County, held by Henry W. Maynard (who enslaved three young adults and two children by 1860), were "jayhawked" in the course of the war. Their captors took two of them to Clarksville, Texas, by May 1864. A few found themselves in the hands of partisan ranger Captain James Fitzwilliam's family; others were taken to Indian Territory. No one ever heard from Maynard again, who was suspected to have been murdered. Fitzwilliam's company sold the rest of the bondspeople, dividing the money among them.[51] Such groups consistently preyed upon bondspeople heading west. Mary Ann Brooks summed up her journey as a child, in which the party forded the Saline River: "We had six wagons, a cart, and a carriage. Old Dr. [Asa] Brunson rode in the carriage. He'd go ahead and pilot the way. We got lost twice. When we came to the Red River it was up and we had to camp three weeks till the water fell. We took some sheep and some cows so we could kill meat on the way." Before journey's end, the group experienced two run-ins with guerillas.[52]

After successfully completing the trek to Texas, bondspeople endured uncomfortable, crowded living arrangements.[53] Arkansas refugees settled primarily in the northeast portion of the state. The cities of Bonham, Clarksville, Jefferson, Marshall, Sherman, Tyler, and Henderson served as popular points for temporary homes. Some Confederate Arkansans already had connections in northeast Texas through family and friends and simply relocated to be near those people.[54] Others who shared the same hometowns in Arkansas, like those from the Camden area who were temporarily located near Tyler, clustered closely enough to each other that visitation was possible. Thus, some enslaved people might have been able to see friends and acquaintances and enjoy some reconstruction of their home neighborhoods while in east Texas.[55]

Black Arkansans' removal offered no kind of respite from work or from the usual uncertainties that characterized life under slavery. The farther west bondspeople moved out of Arkansas, the farther away they were from the potential freedom of federal lines. Slavery was well protected in Texas (only forty-seven men from that state managed to escape their captors and enlist in the U.S. Army), leaving relocated bondspeople few options. The risk of separation through hire or sale climbed with the prices their bodies commanded. Men and women continued to toil, many having to adjust to new tasks. "What *didn't* we do in Texas?" exclaimed John Wells in remembering his labor there. Relocated near Greenville, Wells learned to herd sheep. He was responsible for five hundred head, on which he commented: "Carry 'em off in the morning early and watch 'em and fetch 'em back b'fore dark." Wells enjoyed the novelty that came with chasing after sheep as a boy but described cactus and snow as harming his young bare feet. Not everyone's jobs changed as drastically, however. Wells's uncles made shoes and farmed cotton, corn, and wheat. Lou Fergusson and other bondspeople "settled down and made a crop" on land rented by her enslaver in Texas.[56] Whites frequently sold or hired enslaved people to other whites. These arrangements served to keep bondspeople busy and provided whites with income. Forced to Texas from Camden, Lucky, Nat, and Fin hired for $150 each, while Rachel and her children's labor went for $50, as did Flora's, Nancy's, and Fannie's, according to a letter written by their enslaver's daughter. She recorded, "Women without children hire for $100.00. I think they will all hire without any trouble, except the women with little children." Sale prices continued to rise. For example, Moses Mitchell was sold in Marshall, Texas, for $1,500.[57]

Back in Arkansas, bondspeople in areas under Confederate control worked harder and endured greater deprivation than ever. As Chandra Manning explains, "no amount of human courage, determination, or resilience" could overcome the overwhelming military and state power mounted against so many black southerners. Josephine Howell's mother, Rebecca Jones, remembered rough times on Gabe McAlaway's plantation near Augusta in Woodruff County. She told her daughter that "during the War women split and sawed rails and laid fences all winter like men. Food got scarce. They sent milk to the soldiers. Meat got scarce."[58] To the south, the bondspeople at the Bullock plantation made a large crop the first year of the war, harvesting the "white oceans" of cotton and storing many of the bales in the very woods where runaways from that plantation had a habit of hiding. Toward the end of the war, however, most of the maids there had been moved from housework to the fields as more and more men escaped. This did not exempt them from the pressures of domestic work, which became even more difficult in the wake of widespread shortages of foodstuffs. Moriah, a cook who had, at least by Harriet Daniel's account, always enjoyed a place of relative privilege at the Bullock place, bore the brunt of her enslaver's wartime frustrations. Her makeshift coffee of parched wheat and sweet potatoes angered Bullock, who beat her over the shoulders with a horse whip.[59] When soldiers passed through their neighborhoods, whites expected domestic workers to feed and attend to them, even as battles raged around them. Virginia Sims of Jefferson County remembered: "General Shelby's troops was comin' on this side of the river. That's one time I was scared. Never seen so many men in my life. They wanted something to eat. Mama cooked all night.... I toted canteens all night long."[60]

Confederate whites expected to use bondspeople's labor to support not only white families but the rebel cause overall. The Confederacy relied on enslaved people's work on farms, in homes, and in construction. When Confederate authorities passed draft exemptions for planters in order to free up men to supervise enslaved people at work, John Eakin of southwest Arkansas's *Washington Telegraph* approved. "Some one *must* be with the slaves," Eakin rationalized, to keep them in place, at work, and too fearful to stoke rebellion against their enslavers. And further, Eakin explained, "by the products of their industry, support our armies." Bondspeople drove wagons, fortified Confederate positions, and worked as blacksmiths for the Confederates. Those held in and around Little Rock might work in the hospital or at the salt works. Enslaved people from the Bullock place mined and bagged salt for some time during the war. Bondspeople at work for the Confederacy suffered the usual dangers of falling ill or becoming injured. Some managed to escape.[61]

Confederates also put bondspeople to work converting Arkansas's natural resources into products to aid the war effort. Peter Van Winkle contracted his Ozark lumber mill to the Confederate government, setting enslaved people there, including Aaron Anderson Van Winkle, to build barracks and stables for Confederate troops. Enslaved people extracted and processed niter in Marion, Newton, and Searcy Counties. They also mined potassium nitrate (saltpeter) from Arkansas's limestone caves and converted the mineral into gunpowder for Confederate guns. This work greatly increased the number of bondspeople in Newton County, where those of taxable age rose from 24 in 1861 to 46 in 1862. About 100 bondspeople worked the mines in Marion County, guarded by one company of soldiers until General Henry Halleck destroyed them in 1862, taking the enslaved people who had labored there. The proximity of federal troops to Batesville early in the war emboldened bondspeople working in the Searcy County munitions operation to flee.[62]

Confederates' need for labor only increased, a problem that actually served to chip away at the institution of slavery. In 1862, the state legislature approved the impressment of one enslaved man for every six between the ages eighteen and forty-five for the Confederate cause. Jerry White was one of the many men in Arkansas pressed to serve the Confederate army, later to be "confiscated" by General Curtis. Daniel Rhone of Phillips County went as a "bodyguard" for Tom Jones. Years later his son explained, "My father stuck with him till peace declared—had to do it."[63] Confederates impressed more bondspeople than the measure called for, however, as labor-strapped officers took as many men as they needed rather than adhering to a quota. In the summer of 1864, Confederate military authorities announced the conscription of *all* enslaved men between eighteen and forty-five—not as enlisted soldiers but as laborers.[64]

Slavers and enslaved people alike balked at these orders. Black men did not want to risk injury or separation from family, especially for such a cause, while for their part, enslavers worried about property loss in a war that was already proving economically devastating. Bondspeople and their captors, then, worked together to avoid the impressment of black men by Confederate officials. In response to a call for enslaved people to work on breastworks, slaveholders in eastern Arkansas sent as few as they could get away with. A. M. Boyd's father-in-law sent only one man, and then went to Lake Village to make a speech against the conscription of enslaved labor, declaring it too deadly for bondspeople to work in the unhealthy swamps. When authorities repeated the requisition for enslaved manpower, Boyd's overseer, Hedspeth, gave up. He instructed his charges to "put out to the woods and he would send us provisions till we could get to the Yankees. And he had to leave the country. We stayed in the woods about three weeks." The group then made their way to the Mississippi River.[65] Similarly, James Pine, an enslaved driver at the Joseph Deputy plantation, remembered, "The rebels tried to press some hands from Deputy to work on Fort Pillow up the river, but Deputy had us colored men posted to give notice when the pressers were coming, so we could get back in the woods and run the horses and mules in the cane."[66] These evasions redefined the spaces at the seams of Arkansas's corn and cotton fields. Instead of truant and runaway black men and women hiding in the forests and brush awaiting provision from sympathetic compatriots, hidden bondspeople did so at the urging of whites, and waited for their enslavers and overseers to provision them (as they did in instances where whites hid bondspeople from Union soldiers). Slavers hated to see their investments working in the malarial swamps out of their sight, and bondspeople looked out for their own safety and security.

Growing increasingly desperate, the Confederacy eventually considered arming enslaved men in 1865, in a plan that would grant freedom in return for military service. Confederates developed the scheme too late to implement the plan, however. "Use all the negroes you can get, for all the purposes for which you need them," one Confederate official famously warned, "but don't arm them. The day you make soldiers of them is the beginning of the end of our revolution. If slaves will make good soldiers our whole theory of slavery is wrong." Some Confederates welcomed the idea of potential help, but by and large, white Arkansans reacted to the proposition with horror. John Brown of Camden declared, "It is virtually giving up the principles upon which we went into the war." Although many black men labored directly and indirectly in support of the Confederate effort at the direction of whites, the Confederate States of America never enlisted enslaved men as soldiers.[67]

While whites tried to direct their captives' activity during the war, bondspeople carefully navigated the conflict, weighing their options. They exercised caution as they continued to move and work in communities undergoing unprecedented change. Winfield Scott treaded delicately on the Rapley plantation just south of Little Rock, describing the white family there as "bitter rebels."[68] Bondspeople still in Confederate zones bided their time and did what they always had: survived the best they knew how, but under increasing risks. When Virginia Sims's husband, who was sent to Confederate lines, came down with the measles she pulled on a pair of boots and waded to his camp to attend to him. As the war shifted the meaning of wild spaces in Arkansas, bondspeople trudged out into the brush and bottoms when forced to assist rebels hidden in the woods. Enslaved women brought provisions and ran errands. Fannie Sims recalled washing clothes for soldiers in a spring near the Ouachita River in Union County, then taking the clean clothes to the hidden men after dark. Bondspeople might hide in the woods themselves with Confederate horses or livestock in order to prevent passing soldiers from taking them.[69]

The shifting nature of uncultivated spaces contributed to keeping bondspeople on-site. The places they had used before to hide and flee now teemed with whites animated by a spectrum of motivations. Bondspeople had to be careful of whites on both sides, and everyone in between. Matilda Hatchett explained that her father's predicament in going along with whoever held power in his neighborhood: "The Secesh wouldn't go far. They would just hide. One night there'd be a gang of Secesh, and the next one, there'd come along a gang of Yankees. Pa was 'fraid of both of 'em. Secesh said they'd kill 'im if he left his white folks. Yankees said they'd kill 'im if he didn't leave 'em. He would hide out in the cotton patch and keep we children out there with him."[70] Arabella Wilson described Confederate guerilla activity at Pine Bluff: "There is a party of Bush Whackers all round in the woods . . . . they have still escaped detection & are continuing the same work stealing negroes & destroying generally." Matthew Stith has demonstrated how the topography and vegetation, particularly of southern Missouri bleeding into Arkansas, harbored guerillas and facilitated their tactics. While federal forces nominally controlled the Mississippi, Arkansas, and White Rivers during much of the war, guerilla forces populated those watersheds and continually harassed the Union presence there. This activity made it incredibly dangerous for black Arkansans to strike out away from their enslavers on principle. As Amy Murrell Taylor has explained, freedom was a slow-motion process that happened in fits and starts for many people. Black southerners were often reluctant to leave their homes during the war if they could possibly stay and be free, or free*r*, there. Because many enslaved men and women had set down roots, it served their immediate interest to stay in place.[71]

Men and women held by Robert Mecklin just outside of Fayetteville, Washington County, for as long as they stayed, took on an air of confidence during the war. Wesley, Net (a cook with two children), and Rindy (Merinda, who took up cooking after Net left) lived and worked at Mecklin's house on the campus of the Ozark Institute. Mecklin complained, "Net, her children and Rindy are all well, fat, saucy, and feel much inclined to make declaration of their independence." Few bondspeople remained on these farms outside Fayetteville; they knew that their labor was of great value. Mecklin speculated, "They all seem to be enjoying themselves finely. Our own have done well when we consider the influences which have been operating on them to get them away from us."[72]

Slavery and freedom, then, included a gray area in between. Wesley Mecklin enjoyed a considerable amount of autonomy, even maneuvering himself into a state of quasi-freedom. He moved freely about his Fayetteville-area neighborhood, including visits to his wife, the cook at Mrs. Nolen's, on a nearby farm, every weekend.[73] He did his usual work at the Mecklin farm but took on added tasks like hiding wheat from the federals. Wesley also took the chance to convert the bounty of nature into economic gain. He trapped pheasants and sold his game to Union soldiers in town. But Wesley claimed public spaces, too. He rode about the roads of his neighborhood conducting his own business as well as running errands for whites. On one occasion, he drove a family to retrieve the body of their son, and then transported them to Benton

County for the burial. His enslaver, acutely aware that he had lost his grip on Wesley, grumbled, "Wesley does a little work for me and a little for himself, smokes and chews his new tobacco, spits, struts," carrying himself "with an air of independence not known to the common soldiers of Lincoln's army; and really enjoys more freedom, ease and comfort than any of those darkies who went off with the Federals."[74] Wesley's status was made possible by his volition, of course, but, as Rebecca Howard notes, also by the fact that the only people left in his neighborhood were women and older men. Northwest Arkansas's guerilla war raged with particular intensity, frightening Wesley's enslaver (who was too old for military service but still deemed a threat by enemies). Howard's work reveals that the vacuum left room for Wesley to become the responsible able-bodied man of his neighborhood. While his "master" hid at the sound of approaching horses, Wesley moved about as he pleased.[75]

Net, the cook at Mecklin's farm, bided her time. Assisted by another bondswoman, Net borrowed a horse from a neighbor to go to town to make her arrangements, returned for the rest of her things, and began work cooking for a woman in Fayetteville for board and wages of two dollars per week. Mecklin fumed that the "impudence is not bearable." While Net started out on her own as a free woman, Merinda stayed on with the Mecklins, for the time being, taking on the position as cook, with control of her own kitchen. Mecklin wrote, "Rindy has cleaned up her kitchen very neatly and seems to be getting on well in doing our cooking." The old patriarch knew he was on borrowed time, however, and may have treated Rindy differently out of fear that she might also decide to leave. "I do hope that none of Abe's abolition minions will put it into Rindy's head that she would do well to leave us," he fretted.[76]

While Rindy made do with a northwest Arkansas Confederate, Jack and Eliza Bradley of Des Arc lived with a Unionist widow, Martha W. Bradley. Confederates closely watched the Bradley place, fearing she would head to federal lines with her bondspeople. Years later Eliza testified that Mrs. Bradley endured threats on her life but refused to support the Confederacy. An enslaved neighbor, Sylvester Caldwell, who partly attributed his awareness of the gravity of the war to the fact that his enslaver read him newspapers, talked politics with the widow. He explained their exchanges that predated the war arriving at their doorsteps: "Our fences joined. I was well acquainted with her. I knew her sentiments about the Union for she told me she proposed to be a Union woman. She said to me, 'Sylvester people that is Union is far better than secessionists' and I said 'Miss Martha those that are Union is on the right side and they ought to stand fast.'" When Caldwell explained that "the colored people lived in regard to her being a Union woman," he revealed much. Enslaved people held by Bradley knew that they could support and exchange news about Union forces' success in Widow Bradley's presence without fear. Jack and Eliza may have determined that it could be safer to ride out the war with the widow than to risk being kidnapped and dragged deeper into Confederate territory, or worse.[77]

Some whites in war-torn Arkansas became wholly dependent upon bondspeople, not just for the profit of their labor. Wesley Mecklin fell very ill with typhoid pneumonia on one of his weekend visits with his wife in the fall of 1863. He was not well enough to travel and did not return to Mecklin's for at least a week. Robert Mecklin did not write on those days because he was too busy doing all the work Wesley would normally have taken care of but could not. On the day Wesley returned, Mecklin wrote, "I have been pulling, hauling and husking my corn and putting it away for our bread. Worked a little too much like a young man and am pretty well worn out." Suffering from some type of tumor in addition to recovering from fever, Wesley remained weak into November, when it was time to plow winter wheat. Robert Mecklin tried to plow and prepare for planting but could not do it on his own.[78]

It remained relatively easier for enslaved men to claim public spaces than it was for women. White women loaded more and more responsibility on enslaved women who remained with them, a role bondswomen may have tolerated when it came with some increased power. Rindy spirited Mrs. Mecklin into grown-up pasture and brush when the approach of Union soldiers near Fayetteville disrupted her visit to a friend. Mecklin described the scene: "The weeds were nearly as high as she was on her pony and much higher than Rindy on foot; but they weeded their way through. . . . got home safely but much fatigued."[79] Stories of the river valley mirrored the dynamic at the Mecklins'. The cabins that usually housed enslaved people on the Howell place in Pittsburg, Johnson County, made up a little ghost town by early 1865, when Seth J. Howell vacated with his entire captive labor force to Texas, leaving his wife and sister behind. Union soldiers harassed Lutetia M. Howell and her sister-in-law, Susan Willis, locking the women in one of the slave cabins. Out of a sense of humanity, three neighboring bondswomen came to their rescue and brought the frightened women to rest back inside the house. The bondswomen walked to a spring to wash clothes and when they returned, they found the white women lying in the yard and the home ablaze.[80] In the same neighborhood in January 1865, Lucy helped white women save another who had allegedly been pushed into the fireplace by men described as Union soldiers but who might have been guerillas, considering their blatant brutality. Lucy also helped the women bury their men who had been killed by the federals.[81] As the war raged, white women increasingly clung to enslaved women. Failing to recognize it was her husband and friend who approached her home, when Mary Bullock spotted soldiers outside, she panicked, ran out into the yard to her enslaved maid, and "flinging herself into Betsey's arms, she cried, 'O save me, Betsey! Save me and my children!'" In wartime, black women carried the extra burdens piled on them by white women who looked to them for protection and continuity. Black women who weathered the conflict with white women did so not because they embraced servitude but because they were afraid, too. As Thavolia Glymph writes, the concept of "loyalty" does not accurately describe their relationships with white female enslavers; it does no justice to enslaved women's "political sensibility" during the war. Their sense of humanity and strategic self-preservation did not make enslaved women forget the wrongs done to them by whites.[82]

Eva Strayhorn navigated these treacherous waters in Johnson County, an area that blurred the Arkansas River Valley and the Ozarks. Strayhorn, her sister, and her mother became increasingly relied upon by white women left in the countryside. As she remembered, "The white men that was not too old was in the army and the colored men and boys had been refugeed to Texas." As older men drove bondspeople to Texas, this left women enslavers and bondswomen together. Some of their goals conflicted, but their major objective to survive with families intact often encouraged cooperation as they called the same place home. Strayhorn remembered her mother's hard toil at tasks commonly considered men's work: "Mother had to work mighty hard as she had to cut wood and haul it in with a team of oxen. Us children helped her all we could." On one occasion, Strayhorn and her sister were posted as watches for federals who might be pursuing the son of their enslavers. The little scouts fell asleep, though, failing to warn their mother who was taking food and coffee to the hidden man, somewhere beyond the field. She narrowly escaped injury.[83]

Despite the hard work and dangerous tasks asked of her, Strayhorn's mother remained with her enslaver, even after being encouraged by federal soldiers to leave. She knew her best hope of reuniting with her husband lay near their home where he had last seen her; she feared the two would never be reunited if she left the area. She chose to take an oath of loyalty to the union in order to secure safe movement about the neighborhood, making the twelve-mile trip to town to do it. Strayhorn recalled, "I know mother was scared but she was determined to take the oath so she could stay on with old Miss Tessie." But when they returned, bushwhackers had burned the place to the ground and Strayhorn's enslaver had gone to stay with her daughter. Strayhorn's mother took the girls to live in a cabin on the side of the mountain, never straying far from the home farm. When her enslaver turned up, Strayhorn's mother and sister went with him and his wife to Texas. "We found father and we was all happy again," Eva Strayhorn recalled. Her mother went to great lengths to keep her family together and reunite with her husband, leveraging her ties with the white family, and it worked.[84]

Arkansas's towns fostered their own kind of tension during the war. Bustling and often disorderly, they provided a place to congregate and secure resources and information. When the U.S. Army presence made it safe to do so, slavery's fugitives crowded towns in search of safety, work, and reunions with their loved ones. As Taylor explains, the spatial order of freedom was linked to the social order of freedom.[85] For example, James Jackson's baking business boomed even in Confederate Little Rock. One of the few enslaved Arkansans who enjoyed a level of urban autonomy in the antebellum period, Jackson simply continued what he had begun before the war, but now to greater profit. Hungry soldiers funded the Jackson family's future. He recalled, "I made considerable money after the war broke out. I baked cakes and pies and sold to the Confederate soldiers, and with the Confederate money obtained this way I carried on my business, and whenever I had a chance I bought gold and silver with it, and laid that away." Jackson also did favors and ran errands for federal prisoners in town for a price.[86] Bondspeople like Jackson had long enraged some whites because they threatened the boundaries of chattel slavery. Now that opposition became more urgent. The *True Democrat* lamented the numbers of enslaved entrepreneurs in Little Rock like Jackson who "have cookshops, beer holes, and other pretended means of support. They are flush of money; buy pistols and horses and get white men to bid for them at auction." The underground black economy grew stronger and more public in urban areas like Little Rock and Helena.[87]

For its part, Helena, occupied by Union forces since July 1862, provided a base of federal power in the area surrounded by Confederate guerillas as well as indiscriminate ruffians. The U.S. Army weathered a major Confederate attack in July 1863 and endured lingering Confederate harassment. The Bogans, whose broader story is elegantly told in Amy Murrell Taylor's recent work, represent the complicated choices the war forced on black Arkansans and the careful ways in which they interacted with federal posts. Eliza Bogan, enslaved on the McKiel plantation north of Helena, had always lived apart from her husband, Silas Small, but nearby. In 1862, Small fled his enslaver and refugeed to Helena but Eliza stayed with hers. Upon hearing that her husband was sick, however, she traveled the fifteen miles into town to convince her husband to leave the Union fort and come back to "my house"—and back to slavery. Frederick Steele had rolled back enforcement of Samuel Curtis's policy of accepting refugees (and the Second Confiscation Act of that summer) and expelled from Helena enslaved men and women who could not work. Many had no choice for survival except to return to the farms and plantations they had fled. Eliza prevailed upon her husband that to return to her home in slavery represented the safest place for him, for now. After Silas became stronger, his mother, Indiana, took him to the plantation of his enslaver. These difficult choices did not dim Silas Small's conviction that Union lines represented freedom in the long run. By the end of 1863, he had returned to Helena and enlisted in the U.S. Army. Eliza waited until the right time before joining him at Helena's federal post.[88]

Men and women held on Joseph Deputy's plantation near Helena seemed to employ a similar strategy of preferring to negotiate the known rather than the unknown until real gains could be made. Not all from Deputy's plantation immediately fled to the federal presence in Helena. Those like Aleck Castile may have wanted to navigate the war without being drawn into battle or crowded into camps riddled with disease if they could help it. Castile said that his enslaver, a Unionist from Indiana, recognized that his bondspeople would be free eventually but wanted them to stay on the place with him in the meantime. Black men and women there might have reckoned that if they stayed through the war, they could achieve good arrangements with Deputy as free laborers when the war ended. Running from Deputy's place would have been risky anyway. Southern Arkansas's forests and swamps, like so many other places, teemed with Confederate bands who would kidnap freedpeople back into bondage. Pine related that black men and women remained wary of the danger of venturing into the woods, "as there might be rebels in the woods, they were always hanging about bushwacking." Many remained on the place, then, laboring and helping Deputy avoid Confederate impressment and guerillas. Castile recalled, "One time I was out with his stock for over two weeks in the timber to keep them out of the way of the rebels."[89]

All bets were off, though, when Deputy died. There were Feds in town, Rebs in the woods, and an overseer on the place. Peggy Deputy remembered the fear that radiated on the dead man's plantation, especially among women: "The men was so bad, the women had to keep out of the way, if they hadn't they would not have been worth two bits." The overseer tried to keep the plantation running for a while but began spending more and more of his time with Confederate guerillas. He "would go off to the bushwackers sometimes and stay a few days and then come back." Eventually, most of the black men and women as well as the overseer left the plantation for good. But Castile didn't. He stayed on the place to survive and take care of his two little boys and even took up residence in Deputy's empty house. This proved too bold for Confederate guerillas who lurked in the area, always watching. Castile's recollection is chilling: "I moved up in his house, and tried to stay there, but the rebels went for me there one night." Castile then finally came in to Helena to Union lines.[90]

Near the Deputy plantation, an enslaved family's business facilitated the Unionist element in Helena. Even before the arrival of Union troops, there was a small but fiercely Unionist element in Helena, who gave voice to their sentiments in the safety of a slave-owned and operated barber shop. James Milo Alexander's father owned the shop. Alexander's enslaver was related to Deputy. Young Alexander learned his father's trade and worked at the shop from 1857 to May 1863. Alexander's father's customers included a handful of Unionists who stopped in a few times a week. Alexander explained, "I would see them meet in our barber shop and knew there was a secret understanding between them, they would congratulate each other over Union successes when there was none other but colored men in the shop. This was in 1861, and 1862."[91] Moses Clark, enslaved by J. U. Childers in Helena, crossed paths with Alexander and no doubt shared some winks at Confederates' expense when he was sent there to learn the barber's trade. Childers had Clark apprenticed "as he desired to make me a valet so that I could travel about with him." Clark came to the Helena barber shop in 1857, stayed until 1859 when he moved to Nashville, and returned to Helena in 1860. Clark spoke for all bondspeople who waited for freedom when he explained that "at that time every body had to pretend to agree with the popular sentiment" and "had to seem a good rebel if he was not."[92]

Those far from federal lines in southwest Arkansas enjoyed no such luck, remaining with their enslavers and out of easy reach of the liberating power that federal forces represented. In Hempstead County, for example, the power structure remained largely intact and the presence of Confederate forces meant that most bondspeople held there had to ride out the war, as flight posed greater risk. In fact, when Little Rock's Confederate government vacated Little Rock upon the U.S. Army's arrival in the capital in September 1863 they reconvened in Washington, Hempstead County. Ensconced by Confederates, enslaved men and women in southwest Arkansas continued to work, but some indication of their wartime insubordination is revealed by the *Washington Telegraph*'s story of a woman who had trouble keeping her house workers focused on their duties. Servants in that household felt "above their business" and clearly awaited the arrival of the federals, their enslaver lamented.[93] Bondspeople at Isaac Jones's plantation in Hempstead County endured their belligerent enslaver's angry ravings against any notion that the fighting in other parts of Arkansas might mean freedom for black men and women on his place. Jones taunted, "Them Yankees ain't gonna get this far, but if they do you all ain't goin to get free by 'em, 'cause I'm goin to free you before that. When they get here they going to find you already free, 'cause I'm going to line you up on the bank of Bois d'Arc Creek and free you with my shotgun!" Resenting any hint that the old regime was fading, Jones threatened, "Anybody miss just one lick with the hoe, or one step in the line, or one clap of that bell, or one toot of the horn, and he's going to be free and talking to the devil long before he ever sees a pair of blue britches!"[94] Jones was killed in an accidental gin explosion, though, freeing the bondspeople from his abuse, at least. When Annie Page's temperamental enslaver died while on furlough, the lore of his death included the story that he requested to be buried "by the side of the road so he can see the niggers goin' to work." Enslaved men and women sustained hope, however, by news they received about the progress of the war.[95]

Navigating the treacherous landscape of Civil War Arkansas proved difficult, but Moses Mitchell summed up the attitude of bondspeople when he stated: "Here's the idea, freedom is worth it all."[96] After the Confederate capital in Little Rock fell to Union forces, Arkansans lived to various degrees under one or the other of two state governments: one controlled by the United States in Little Rock and the other the languishing Confederate government in the southwest corner of the state in Washington. Slavers tried desperately to keep the institution alive as bondspeople destroyed it. They did so because, as Henry Rector articulated at the beginning of the conflict, it provided so much of Arkansas's economic and social foundation and the meaning of Arkansas's very ground. "Without it," Rector was convinced, "her fertile fields are deserts, and her people penniless and impoverished." One U.S. officer wrote from Helena describing the reluctance of white Arkansans to let go of slavery as late as December 1863:

> It is said that the state of Arkansas is ready to come back into the Union. It is not true. Every slaveholder sticks to the institution as his only hope for fortune respectability and means of living. The non-slaveholders are afraid of negro equality and feel as savage a hostility to the *Race* as animals that by nature devour each other. In my vicinity a few of the slaveholders contrive to live on their plantations, and feed and clothe their negroes though the[y] produce nothing, in the hope that slavery will be restored, while the greater portion of them have removed their slaves to the southwest part of the state, or into Texas, Mississippi, and Alabama. No one yet submits to the idea of its abolishment.[97]

Confederate Arkansas fell into disarray in the spring of 1865, and the Confederate forces of the Trans-Mississippi officially surrendered to the United States on June 2, 1865.[98] The war turned most neighborhoods in Arkansas on their heads, rewriting the rules as to which types of spaces put enslaved people on guard and which might allow for breathing room. Bondspeople's use of the places around them took on an unprecedented political element—sometimes they complied and at other times rebelled. The seams between farms and plantations—formerly the domain of runaways, truants and their pursuers, or bondspeople's covert religious meetings or parties—became flooded with whites who now found reason to hide. Federals, rebels, guerillas, and opportunists took to the mountainsides, cane, and brush. But bondspeople did not necessarily give up those spaces. Fugitives from slavery traversed Arkansas's river bottoms in their treks for freedom and security behind Union lines, which also tended to move along the waterways. Men and women still held by the chains of slavery were hastened into uncultivated zones by whites looking to keep them out of reach of U.S. soldiers who wanted to free and arm them, and away from Confederates who wanted them to dig trenches and build breastworks. Others endured driving like cattle out of the state altogether. This shifting landscape required bondspeople to make difficult choices. Some achieved increased autonomy and occupied public spaces like never before, while others had to lie in wait until the time was right. Overall, the conflict stimulated black Arkansans' desire to leverage the landscape and resources around them for their own benefit.[99]

Conclusion

When Reuben Johnson composed his first letters to his wife and father (whom he had not seen in twenty years), he reaped the rewards of years of hard work and sacrifice. Following the war, his studies allowed him to take a job as a teacher at a "pay school" outside of Little Rock. Johnson recalled that although he worried his lack of *formal* education might hinder him as a teacher, "I pitched in to do the best I could and I got along very well for a while, and kept the people in good spirits." By the time he told his story of persistence to the *Christian Recorder* in 1878, Reuben Johnson was enjoying a successful career as an educator and clergyman in Arkansas. What he had begun in stolen moments in the woods of central Arkansas lived on in his efforts to educate the next generation of African Americans there. By the time Johnson mustered out of the U.S. Army in 1865 more people had become clustered in Arkansas's towns in more concentrated populations than ever before in its history. Hundreds of black men like Johnson who had fled their enslavers and fought for their country joined with as many black civilians, women, and their families to remake their lives together in their most public and urban existence up to that time. *Harper's Weekly* published a glimpse into that immediate postwar landscape via a short report in June 1866 about a modest neighborhood of freedpeople's log houses and shanties in the middle of Little Rock. Families and friends had constructed the village to be near USCTs in garrison. When the men mustered out, their loved ones welcomed them "home" to this little enclave optimistically dubbed "Blissville."[1]

Arkansas's ground had been carefully and brutally marked off and built up as a slaver's empire from its days as the southern portion of the Territory of Missouri. The morass proved a speculator's dream and a trafficker's paradise. Its rich soil and reputation for lawlessness attracted opportunists with all sorts of designs. As in other rural parts of the South, enslaved people struggled against whites who sought to direct their activity and movement toward their own profits. Black life in Arkansas transformed as the frontier exchange economy gave way to the second slavery. Their labor supported early trading posts that would pave the way for slaveholding farms and plantation districts, enriching white Arkansans into the antebellum years. Arkansas's "charter" generation witnessed ever-harsher demands on their labor in staple crop cultivation. Harvest yields and forced migrations only increased as the years passed.

Whites trafficked thousands of bondspeople out to this region of the South where, although the legal and financial scaffolding supporting the second slavery had hardened, the physical terrain remained lightly populated and the infrastructure little developed. Whites marched tens of thousands of men, women, and children from older parts of the South to this periphery as chattel, inheritances, gifts, and merchandise. The domestic slave trade combined with the migration of white families to push enslaved populations out to the margins in waves, continuing through the Civil War. This process tore families apart and destroyed relationships. It required long treks in uncomfortable conditions. Some enslaved farmers adjusted to a new agricultural routine while others took up farming for the very first time. Displacement threatened and destroyed the health of people who endured a brutal "seasoning."

The crop routine on the edge of the South, as in other regions, ruled the days and seasons of enslaved farmers. Bonded pioneers carved corn farms into hillsides, drained cotton plantations along rivers, and built homes, barns, and roads. The clearest differences between the work routine in the Old Southwest and in older, longer-settled parts of the South are related to the condition of the land. Southern whites brought their habit of shifting cultivation to Arkansas's fresh ground. Enslaved farmers in Arkansas worked under increasing pressure to produce profits from existing acreage while carving new fields out of the woods and brush. The cycle of planting, cultivating, harvesting, and clearing increased in scale from year to year as enslaved Arkansans in cotton districts put increasingly more acreage into production. Bonded black farmers across the state developed a deep knowledge of the land and its use, living out a contradiction in which whites leaned on their knowledge but also relied on their status as chattel. Even when bondspeople's work occurred alongside their enslavers it was not intended to translate to power over the ground, its use, or its fruits.

The same fresh land that hosted the increasingly harsh second slavery in Arkansas also provided opportunities for bondspeople in their contest with their captors. Bondspeople crisscrossed the Old Southwest as fugitives for freedom, hid in the woods as truants, and assisted each other in the effort to use the woods, brush, and swamps as cover for both temporary and final escapes. Rivers, especially the relatively populated Mississippi, served as runaway highways. While whites moved newly purchased bondspeople and supplies upriver and shipped the fruits of their labor downriver, their captives used those very same channels in attempted escapes.

Enslaved families and individuals forced to Arkansas managed to make a home. Bondspeople marked marriages, births and deaths, firsts and lasts while negotiating demands on their labor. In Arkansas, multiple generations of an enslaved family living in one place was unlikely; for most, living in Arkansas meant having already endured a seismic disruption. Communities consistently added newcomers and lost old friends and relatives due to sales and moves. Under this regime men and women countered displacement, crafting a sense of home and rootedness by mapping out neighborhoods of meaning. Forests and cane facilitated that quest as they met to pray together, socialize, court, share news, and relax. Those who were unable to freely worship built their faith communities in the wild spaces between farms and fields. The woods and brush also served as a conduit for bondspeople's news and rumor networks. They experienced and offered friendship and kinship through food, material goods, and personal property. Opportunities to engage in the "slaves' economy," however, were not easy to come by, but the difficulty of access made such victories that much more uplifting and sharing that success with family and friends all the more meaningful.

The coming of the Civil War only intensified the mobility of an already dynamic population as whites drove untold numbers of black men, women, and children westward out of the way of federal forces. These migrations brought even more newcomers to the state, as well as through and out of Arkansas to Texas and northern Louisiana as whites sought to protect slavery for as long as possible. The war upended the ways in which enslaved people and whites in Arkansas had been negotiating space on the edge of the South. Wartime changed the map, opening new opportunities for some bondspeople in open, public zones but often creating increased danger in uncultivated ones. For some, the upheaval of war completely reversed the use of space as whites took to the woods while the men and women they purported to own might more freely do business in town. Runaways increased and continued to trust the woods and river bottoms for their getaways, only now with greater danger, yet increased hope. Most had to bide their time until the opportunity for freedom safely reached them.

Kimberly Smith has posed essential questions about the toll that the experience of slavery must have exacted on African American concepts of land and nature. Because their intimacy with agricultural land took place under brutal coercion, could enslaved Arkansans have established a sense of identity or even stewardship on that ground? In part because nineteenth-century Americans forged their basic connections with the landscape surrounding them in the form of "the labors of planting and harvest that shaped everyday life," enslaved people bought into the nineteenth-century convention that space was something to be ordered; to create and produce upon it was the ideal. Black Arkansans incorporated an identity as pioneers of the frontier. They did not reject agricultural production, only the power structure that had ordered it. Enslaved people's intimacy with "wild" zones was forged out of necessity. They were "creative and sensitive" in their engagement with land and sought to modify and interpret the landscape and spaces for themselves. This was an essential part of their placemaking and sense of rootedness. Liberated Arkansans defined their freedom as the ability to make a place on their own terms, independently farm their own land, and modify the landscape for their own benefit. Take, for example, Reuben, the enslaved black overseer on the Trulock plantation who worked with such autonomy as the manager of Amanda Trulock's operation. Although he had clearly developed a proprietary attitude over the place, Reuben jumped at the chance to become a plantation manager as a free person. Reuben secured the position as "head man" at a plantation of Patrick Benjamin & Co. in Jefferson County by bragging to federal authorities about his excellent management of the Trulock operation under slavery—paying off $20,000 of debt in the three years after George Trulock's death.[2]

Black Arkansans made it clear that they also defined freedom as the ability to pick up and try again somewhere else. An organized group in western Arkansas exhibited such desires in September 1866. Envisioning a future in which their toil on the land would translate into economic independence, freedpeople from nearby counties gathered in Fort Smith and resolved to fashion an agricultural settlement plan to pitch to the federal government. They compiled a list of 500 men, women, and children who had confirmed their interest in participating and estimated that about 150 more men would join them. The group petitioned the U.S. government for the loan of "Rations, and some agricultural Implements" to be repaid after one or two years. The Fort Smith farmers possessed the knowledge and the will but lacked the place, requesting permission to settle public land or, even better, they said, to colonize in a western territory. The group did not seek to remain in Arkansas but prioritized economic stability and rootedness together on any land that they could transform for themselves. Their rejection of Arkansas as the future site of their farming community did not mean that the bondspeople in the Fort Smith area had failed to achieve a sense of place or home under slavery. As Barbara Fields put it, "Revolt against a place is not placelessness.... The rejection may start roots growing elsewhere out of a quest to supply the deficiencies of the rejected place."[3]

Others also sought to set new roots but in familiar places. The group of enslaved people whom Kenneth Rayner had forced out to Texas during the war made heading back to his plantation a priority. They sent Rayner "earnest and repeated solicitations" requesting that he pay for and arrange their return. Rayner claimed it was a "considerable expense." The group was motivated by a desire to return to what was familiar, where they had a sense of place and home—but not, however, to return to the same power regime. Their commitment to a new order in agricultural labor frustrated Rayner's overseer, who wrote to Rayner in 1869 about their "idleness and insubordination." Formerly enslaved Arkansans had not been successfully alienated from agricultural land in Arkansas but did reject the power structure that had dictated their interaction with it. "What a miserable set of ungrateful wretches they are!" declared Rayner, who eventually suffered financial ruin.[4]

Aaron Anderson Van Winkle made a similar calculation in the Ozarks, returning to a familiar landscape but expecting new rules. He had worked Peter Van Winkle's mill under slavery, and returned to labor for his former enslaver as a free man, probably helping rebuild the complex that had been razed during the war. Aaron and his wife, Jane, raised their family of four children there. Significantly, the young black Van Winkle family did not set up house in the old "slave quarters" but among a cluster of worker housing closer to the mill. Archaeologists' work at the site has revealed a significant difference in the material evidence left behind at the two sites. The material record of the quarters revealed a spartan existence, with little evidence of personal household goods. The site occupied by Aaron and Jane (among other workers), however, included evidence of consumerism not enjoyed under slavery—personal effects like dishes and fragments of toys. Earning wages at Van Winkle's mill was not only about compensation as free laborers but about black families' ability to build a domestic life on their own terms.[5]

In their early years of freedom, black Arkansans struggled to define the terms of their new status in the face of consistent assaults on their liberty. Countless black Arkansans made a living in those early years converting Arkansas's forests into fuel. Anthony Hanna, a veteran of the 49th USCT, chopped wood and took deliveries at the landing at Sunnyside Plantation, which continued to be managed by James Mason (the son of the planter and an enslaved mother). Hanna and the other men and women who worked there suffered under an increasingly bold terror campaign launched by local whites. While Mason was away in New Orleans on business, whites placed his workers under arrest because, they claimed, as a black man Mason did not have the right to hire laborers, meaning the people there had no real gainful employment and thus violated the law against vagrancy. For whites, black men and women only existed in place when tied to whites' land. To be without this legitimate tether was to drift aimlessly and dangerously. For three days and nights, the two white men, Cleary and Johnson, held the Sunnyside men and women in separate rooms, where the women endured daily rapes. The problem stemmed from corruption within the very institution that had been created to help protect recently enslaved people: the Bureau of Refugees, Freedmen, and Abandoned Lands. Known simply as the Freedmen's Bureau, the agency had been established by the War Department in March 1865 to provide some order to the loose ends created by the war and help ease the humanitarian crisis. Cleary and Johnson operated under orders from Thomas Hunnicut, a civilian working as a Freedmen's Bureau agent. Administered as part of the U.S. Army, the agency did not facilitate redistribution of confiscated lands of traitors to formerly enslaved people, like so many in the more radical camp of Reconstruction reformers had hoped. Rather, Hunnicut, who kept "nigger dogs" to hunt down African Americans and terrorize them into submission, represented Arkansas whites who sought to prevent a remaking of the landscape in freedom. After the Bureau's assistant commissioner sent officers to investigate Hunnicut, he was relieved of his post; the investigation uncovered a whole host of wrongdoing. Hunnicut's predations included moving African American farm laborers from plantations where they were contracted to places where he held financial interest. Hunnicut also extorted fees for labor contracts and marriage certificates, which Freedmen's Bureau agents were supposed to facilitate. Although Hunnicut was certainly a "bad apple," antithetical to the spirit of his post, he and his accomplices represented forces that sought to hold the order of land and labor in Arkansas as close to that of the pre–Civil War era as possible.[6]

While newly freed Arkansans tried to make their place on the uncharted and volatile landscape of free postwar Arkansas, some fell prey to the machinations of predatory landowners. The Freedmen's Bureau superintendent for Ashley County wrote from Hamburg in December 1866 that twenty freedpeople had been swindled by a white man named A. C. McClendon. McClendon managed the plantation owned by J. D. Christian (in partnership with a man named Willoby). In Christian's quest for labor, he promised McClendon a bale of cotton for every hand he could bring in to sign a contract. McClendon headed west to Union County to recruit, claiming to prospective workers that he had purchased the Christian plantation. The men and women who decided to accompany McClendon to work under contract had been partly enticed by the promise that they could "have guns" and "go hunting whenever they pleased," a crucial aspect of African American Arkansans' designs for freedom. After the arrival of the new laborers, to keep up the ruse, McClendon instructed the true landowners to allow him to continue pretending to be the proprietor. The newcomers signed a contract with McClendon, who always stuck around to "Trade with the hands nights and Sundays" as if he owned the plantation's stores. In McClendon's scam, he would sell the same barrel of flour to more than one person and mark up supplies by 50 to 100 percent. In time he informed the workers that they owed $1,400, due by the middle of July. The Freedmen's Bureau received and acted on the complaints of McClendon's victims, but by then he had gone to Texas and gotten killed; in September Willoby died; in November Christian died. The Bureau successfully defended what was owed to the cotton laborers—half of the harvest. Their part amounted to nine bales, minus their more fairly calculated debt (about $500), the rest to be divided among them.[7]

Thieves like McClendon reeled in freedpeople from other parts of the South who took a chance on Arkansas as a place to make a fresh start and enact some agency over the landscape. For example, Edward Smith, a freedman, entered into a contract with C. A. Norton in Alexandria, Virginia, "who represented himself as a proprietor of a Plantation in

Arkansas." Smith moved there and found himself in a nightmarish situation when he arrived to Laconia Landing, which was not owned by Norton but by George Flournoy. Nineteen workers lived in two rooms, one of which also served as the kitchen. About two-thirds of the laborers had already taken sick. Smith and three other men, William H. Morton, John Giles, and Morris Smith, "becoming tired of the treatment" they were receiving, took off in order to report the conditions to the Freedmen's Bureau in Helena. They got about fifteen miles away before being intercepted by a posse that included George Flournoy, Paul Rice, and M. P. Hunter, armed and accompanied by dogs. They caught Morris Smith and John Giles, but Edward Smith and William H. Morton made an "escape through the woods," where they hid out for a couple of nights. When Smith and Morton set off again, Flournoy's party overtook them and started them back toward the plantation at a quick clip with their hands tied behind their backs. Flournoy took Edward Smith's papers—which included his contract and records relating to his labor—and his money. The men threatened a black woman who had fed them on the run in assistance all too reminiscent of African Americans' flight in bondage, vowing to "learn her better than to feed run away niggers." The whites led the men as far as Casteel's plantation when a party of five black men—who had been hunting and were armed—appeared and demanded their release. The black hunters, including a man named James Finlay, "ordered Flournoy & Party to leave us which they did at full speed." The terrain of struggle had shifted. Finlay and the other men escorted Smith and Morton to Helena. Finally, it seemed, black Arkansans had some hope of leveraging a freedom of movement and interaction with their natural surroundings into the typical nineteenth-century claim of independence and security that chattel slavery had denied them.[8]

Yet too few things had changed since the days of slavery, even if major gains were undeniable. One of the ironies in the story of Arkansas's ground is that over time it continued to draw African American families from elsewhere in the South who believed Arkansas represented a land with fewer restrictions on their independence, particularly in terms of acquiring land and extracting bounty from the soil. Boosters touted the productivity of Arkansas's acreage to frustrated black farmers in the east, drawing groups as large as five thousand who made the journey together on foot. In their first ever unforced migration, more than two hundred thousand black Southerners arrived in Arkansas between the Civil War and World War I. Many of their hopes wilted, however, as the place they sought to make their own would only continue to harden against their opportunities.[9]

Notes

Introduction

1. Reuben Johnson, "My Struggles for Education," *Christian Recorder*, May 23, 1878.

2. Although his account does not specify where he cut the hay he sold for books, Johnson's nighttime gathering suggests that he cut it from grassy zones where whites would not have missed it. Johnson, "My Struggles for Education."

3. The works of Ira Berlin and Anthony Kaye represent two examples of how notions of space and place have influenced the story of slavery in the past twenty years. Berlin, *Generations of Captivity*, 93, 215; Kaye, *Joining Places*.

4. Johnson, *River of Dark Dreams*.

5. Some context is available for the stories of people on the edge of the South, like enslaved Texans and bondspeople on Missouri's smallholdings, but the stories of their neighbors in Arkansas are *relatively* untold. Campbell, *Empire for Slavery*; Torget, *Seeds of Empire*; Burke, *On Slavery's Border*; Epps, *Slavery on the Periphery*.

6. Taylor, *Negro Slavery in Arkansas*. Donald P. McNeilly's study of Arkansas's cotton frontier, *Old South Frontier*, highlights the planter class, the rise of cotton, and slavery as an institution rather than the ground-level experience of the enslaved.

7. Kolchin, *American Slavery*, 177.

8. James W. Bell, "Little Rock," in *Encyclopedia of Arkansas History and Culture*, ed. Lancaster (accessed January 1, 2019); Moore, *The Emergence of the Cotton Kingdom in the Old Southwest*, 190; U.S. Bureau of the Census, Eighth Census of the United States, 1860, Free Inhabitants, Warren County, MS.

9. W. E. B. DuBois's *The Souls of Black Folk* emphasized the suffering of enslaved people as expressed in spirituals, for example. Kenneth Stampp broke ground with *The Peculiar Institution* in 1956, blasting the myth—perpetuated by slavery apologist U. B. Phillips and his students—that slavery was a benevolent and civilizing institution. Historians after Stampp resented the emphasis on the brutality of slavery, prodded in

good part by Stanley Elkins's infamous "Sambo thesis" (wherein bondspeople became numbed, dependent "Sambos") in his comparison to victims of Nazi concentration camps. Scholars reacted with accounts emphasizing agency—what enslaved people were able to do for themselves. Historians at the helm of this burst of scholarship in the 1970s include Herbert Gutman, John Blassingame, Eugene Genovese, and Albert Raboteau, all of whom sought to orient the focus of slavery studies toward the enslaved people themselves. Elkins, *Slavery*; Stampp, *The Peculiar Institution*; Phillips, *American Negro Slavery*; Gutman, *The Black Family in Slavery and Freedom*; Blassingame, *The Slave Community*; Genovese, *Roll, Jordan, Roll*; Raboteau, *Slave Religion*; DuBois, *The Souls of Black Folk*.

10. Berlin, *Many Thousands Gone*; Berlin, *Generations of Captivity*; King, *Stolen Childhood*; Fett, *Working Cures*; Penningroth, *The Claims of Kinfolk*.

11. Camp, *Closer to Freedom*; White and White, "Slave Hair and African American Culture in the Eighteenth and Nineteenth Centuries"; Meacham, "Pets, Status, and Slavery in the Late Eighteenth-Century Chesapeake"; Forret, *Slave against Slave*.

12. For a few examples, see Baptist, *The Half Has Never Been Told*; Schermerhorn, *Business of Slavery*; Beckert and Rockman, *Slavery's Capitalism*.

13. For an example of a recent landscape study, see Swanson, *Remaking Wormsloe Plantation*; Paul Sutter, "Introduction: No More Backward Region: Southern Environmental History Comes of Age," in *Environmental History and the American South*, ed. Sutter and Manganiello, 1–24; Hersey, "Environmental History in the Heart of Dixie"; Stewart's most well-known work remains "*What Nature Suffers to Groe.*"

14. McNeilly offers a mostly bird's-eye view of the economic and social structure of Arkansas's society as dominated by an ever-strengthening planter class. McNeilly, *Old South Frontier*; Bolton, "Slavery and the Defining of Arkansas"; Moneyhon, *The Impact of the Civil War and Reconstruction on Arkansas*.

15. Whayne et al., *Arkansas: A Narrative History*; Bolton, *Arkansas, 1800–1860*, 125–44; Van Deburg, "The Slave Drivers of Arkansas"; Lack, "Urban Slave Community"; Moneyhon, "The Slave Family in Arkansas."

16. Bolton, *Fugitives from Injustice*; Bolton, *Fugitivism*. Other more recent studies focusing on bondspeople's agency include Lankford, "Austin's Secret"; Kelly Houston Jones, "Bondwomen on Arkansas's Cotton Frontier," in *Arkansas Women*, ed. Jones-Branch and Edwards; Jones, "Chattels, Pioneers, and Pilgrims for Freedom"; Jones, "'A Rough, Saucy Set of Hands to Manage.'"

17. Houston, "Slaveholders and Slaves of Hempstead County, Arkansas"; Otto, "Slavery in the Mountains"; Battershell, "The Socioeconomic Role of Slavery in the Arkansas Upcountry"; Smith, "Slavery in Washington County"; Duncan, "Manumission in the Arkansas River Valley," 422–43; Duncan, "'One negro, Sarah.'"

18. Lefebvre, *The Production of Space*, 15, 73, 116; Pargas, *The Quarters and the Fields*, 8; Paulette, *Empire of Small Places*, 2, 5–6. Anthony Kaye profitably employed this approach in *Joining Places*.

19. Stewart, "If John Muir Had Been an Agrarian"; Stewart, "Rice, Water, and Power."

20. Smith, *African American Environmental Thought*, 19, 28.

21. I prefer the use that Kristen Epps employs in *Slavery on the Periphery*.

22. Relph, *Place and Placelessness*; Smith, *African American Environmental Thought*, 28.

23. Historian Nan Woodruff coined the term "alluvial empire" to describe Jim Crow in the Mississippi delta in *American Congo*.

24. Taylor, *Embattled Freedom*, 16.

25. Eva Strayhorn interview in Lankford, *Bearing Witness* (hereafter *BW*), 222. Like some other scholars, I have made the choice in this book not to re-create some WPA writers' efforts to convey southern African American speech, in part for clarity and also as a corrective to racist choices made by those who produced notes on the interviews. For example, there is no benefit to readers in transcribing the pronunciation of "was" phonetically as "wuz," or "from" as "frum," because every speaker of American English would have pronounced those the same. By recording the interviewees' stories this way, interviewers reproduced the racist language ideologies they had been socialized to hold, probably without even realizing it, an injury that need not be perpetuated here. Keri Leigh Merritt similarly lightly altered WPA interview quotations in *Masterless Men*. See also Rosa and Flores, "Unsettling Race and Language"; Jaffe, "Transcription in Practice."

1 / The Morass

1. Rothman, *Flush Times and Fever Dreams*; Casey, *Getting Back into Place*, xxv, xxvii; Valencius, *Health of the Country*, 145–46, 151.

2. Toudji, "Intimate Frontiers," 177, 192; Arnold, *Colonial Arkansas*, 7–12, 16–17; Bolton, *Territorial Ambition*, 12.

3. Arnold, *Colonial Arkansas*, 8, 16, 58–62; Kathleen DuVal, "Arkansas Post," in *Encyclopedia of Arkansas History and Culture*, ed. Lancaster (accessed April 17, 2019); Bolton, *Territorial Ambition*, 16.

4. Arnold, *Colonial Arkansas*, 58–62; Bolton, *Territorial Ambition*, 14.

5. Arnold, *Colonial Arkansas*, 16, 58–62; Bolton, *Territorial Ambition*, 14–16; Toudji, "Intimate Frontiers," 192–93.

6. Toudji, "Intimate Frontiers," 185; Bolton, *Territorial Ambition*, 15–16.

7. Winter's descendants argued that the grants were much larger but after several years of litigation were only able to legally claim a small chunk of the Winter land. Hempstead, *Reports of Cases Argued and Determined in the United States Superior Court for the Territory of Arkansas*, 345–47, 351–52, 359; Bolton, *Territorial Ambition*, 61–62; Adam Miller, "Spanish Land Grants," in *Encyclopedia of Arkansas History and Culture*, ed. Lancaster (accessed October 23, 2020).

8. Stewart, "What Nature Suffers to Groe," 148, 174.

9. Whayne et al., *Arkansas: A Narrative History*, 97–99; McNeilly, *Old South Frontier*, 33; *Morine v. Wilson*, 19 Ark. 520 (1858).

10. Taylor, *Negro Slavery in Arkansas*, 21–23; Bolton, *Arkansas, 1800–1860*, 25; Whayne et al., *Arkansas: A Narrative History*, 122–23.

11. September 1814 Writ of Venire abstract, http://144.167.100.214/arcourts/case-025/25.1t.htm (accessed January 4, 2019).

12. A jury found Morrison innocent, but the record does not indicate on what grounds. *William Morrison v. Perly Wallis* abstract, http://144.167.100.214/arcourts/case-019/19.1t.htm (accessed January 4, 2019).

13. The suit began in 1812 and the whole affair was basically dropped when new courts convened after Arkansas became a county within the new Territory of Missouri

in 1814. *Sylvanus Phillips v. Richmond Peeler* abstract, http://144.167.100.214/arcourts/case-023/23.1t.htm (January 4, 2019).

14. Henry Clay's tiebreaking vote killed Taylor's amendment. Taylor then went on to propose another amendment to the Arkansas Territory bill that would bar slavery north of the line 36°30¢ N in the future. Opponents aggressively defeated Taylor's line, but it later passed as the central feature of the Missouri Compromise. Taylor, *Negro Slavery in Arkansas*, 21–22; Forbes, *The Missouri Compromise and Its Aftermath*, 35–43 (quotation on 42–43), 45–47.

15. Burke, *On Slavery's Border*, 27–28, 48; Hilliard, *Hog Meat and Hoe Cake*, 30, 33.

16. Walz, "Migration into Arkansas," 315; Brown, "River Transportation in Arkansas, 1819–1890"; Bolton, *Territorial Ambition*, 29.

17. McNeilly, *Old South Frontier*, 35, 53–56; Taylor, *Negro Slavery in Arkansas*, 48; Hanson and Moneyhon, *Historical Atlas of Arkansas*, 37. Enslaved populations grew faster in and made up greater proportions of the states surrounding Arkansas in these years. Between 1820 and 1830, Missouri's enslaved population increased from 10,222 (15% of the total population) to 25,096 (18%). In that decade, bondspeople in Louisiana increased from 69,064 (45% of the total population) to 109,588 (51%). In those same years, Mississippi's enslaved population grew from 32,814 (43% of the population) to 65,659 (48%). U.S. Bureau of the Census, Fourth Census of the United States, 1820, AR, MO, LA, MS; U.S. Bureau of the Census, Fifth Census of the United States, 1830, AR, MO, LA, MS.

18. McNeilly, *Old South Frontier*, 13–15, 17–21, 138; Bolton, *Territorial Ambition*, 29, 39–40, 46; Hanson and Moneyhon, *Historical Atlas of Arkansas*, 32; Campbell, *Empire for Slavery*, 22–26; Torget, *Seeds of Empire*.

19. Kaye, "The Second Slavery," 627, 632; *Arkansas Gazette*, September 30, 1829; U.S. Bureau of the Census, Fourth Census of the United States, 1820, AR, MS; U.S. Bureau of the Census, Fifth Census of the United States, 1830, AR; Kaye, *Joining Places*, 97; McNeilly, *Old South Frontier*, 13–15, 25; *Biographical and Historical Memoirs of Western Arkansas*, 117.

20. Whayne et al., *Arkansas: A Narrative History*, 113–17; Kitty Sloan, "Indian Removal," in *Encyclopedia of Arkansas History and Culture*, ed. Lancaster (accessed January 15, 2019).

21. DuVal, "Debating Identity, Sovereignty, and Civilization," 39, 25–27, 36, 37–38, 40–41, 43–44, 47–49; *Arkansas Gazette*, October 14, 1823, October 17, 1826.

22. Conditions in their new home in the Red River Valley in Louisiana proved so horrible that many Quapaw returned, only to be removed again to Indian Territory in 1833. DuVal, "Debating Identity, Sovereignty, and Civilization," 50–53.

23. Whayne et al., *Arkansas: A Narrative History*, 115; Sloan, "Indian Removal"; *History of Benton, Washington*, 142–43; Beckert, *Empire of Cotton*, 105, 107.

24. *History of Benton, Washington*, 153; *Arkansas Gazette*, November 18, 1820.

25. *Arkansas Gazette*, July 10, 1833; Bolton, *Territorial Ambition*, 62–67; *Arkansas Gazette*, November 28, 1832, August 15, 1826.

26. Davidsonville declined after Jackson became the county seat in 1829. *William Drope v. John Miller*, John Miller plea, http://144.167.100.214/arcourts/case-066/66.4t.htm (accessed January 4, 2019); Cande, "Rediscovering Davidsonville," 342, 344, 348–49, 352–54, 356–57.

27. Kwas, *Digging for History at Old Washington*, 84.

28. R. Blanton to Col. James S. Deas, November 30, 1859, folder 2, James Sutherland Deas Papers. Several documents related to Deas's early transactions are found in folder 1.

29. Valencius, *Health of the Country*, 15.

30. *Laws of Arkansas Territory*, 268, 329, 521–30.

31. In these years, the law did not reserve whipping as a punishment strictly for enslaved and free blacks; it also provided for the whipping of whites who neglected to pay fines. *Laws of Arkansas Territory*, 521–25.

32. *Laws of Arkansas Territory*, 523 (quotation), 524.

33. *Marie Celeste Lanusse (nee Macarty) v. William Flanakin*, Declaration, J. B. Lanusse deposition, verdict, http://144.167.100.214/arcourts/case-061/61.2t.htm (accessed January 4, 2018).

34. *Arkansas Gazette*, November 11, 1823.

35. *Andrew Latting v. Benjamin Miles*, depositions by Henry Robinson, Nicholas Merriwhether, Abram DeHart, and Thomas Marney, http://144.167.100.214/arcourts/case-059/59.1.htm (accessed January 4, 2019).

36. *Latting v. Benjamin Miles*, depositions.

37. Latting also served as the *Gazette*'s agent in Chicot County, and when he died in 1828, the *Gazette* printed a glowing obituary. *Latting v. Miles* (1825) abstract, depositions; *Arkansas Gazette*, August 26, 1828.

38. Despite the scathing testimony against him, Latting seems to have retained many supporters. For example, a rival eventually unseated him from the "council" of the territorial assembly in 1825, but narrowly. *Arkansas Gazette*, August 15, 1825.

39. The record does not include a bond that would have replaced Murray's presence as security. *Wright Daniel v. Alexander W. Mitchell* (1827), Declaration and Writ of Attachment, http://144.167.100.214/arcourts/case-067/67.2t.htm (accessed January 4, 2019).

40. *Miller, Montgomery & Crittenden v. Bentley* (1827), http://144.167.100.214/arcourts/case-069A/69a.3.htm (accessed January 4, 2019).

41. *George Bentley v. William E. Woodruff* (1830), http://144.167.100.214/arcourts/case-129/129.2.htm (accessed January 4, 2019).

42. E. Beanland to James K. Polk, December 1, 22, 1833, April 1, October 4, 10, 1834; James Walker to James K. Polk, December 14, 1833; Adlai O. Harris to James K. Polk, January 8, 1834, all in Weaver and Bergeron, *Correspondence of James K. Polk*, vol. 2.

43. Featherstonhaugh, *Excursion through the Slave States*, 81–86; *Arkansas Gazette*, November 18, 1828, November 4, 1834, June 15, 1831, July 14, 1835; *Randolph Recorder* (TN) reprinted in *Arkansas Gazette*, August 19, 1834; Bolton, *Fugitives from Injustice*.

44. Rothman, *Flush Times and Fever Dreams*, 34, 39, 78, 269, 284.

45. Ledbetter, "The Constitution of 1836," 221.

46. Malone, *Dictionary of American Biography*; Cash, "Arkansas Achieves Statehood"; Whayne et al., *Arkansas: A Narrative History*, 127–28.

47. Ledbetter, "The Constitution of 1836," 221–22; Cash, "Arkansas Achieves Statehood," 294, 300; Whayne et al., *Arkansas: A Narrative History*, 129.

48. Hanson and Moneyhon, *Historical Atlas of Arkansas*, 39; Ledbetter, "The Constitution of 1836," 224; McNeilly, *Old South Frontier*, 4–5.

49. Whayne et al., *Arkansas: A Narrative History*, 128–30; Ledbetter, "The Constitution of 1836," 224, 233.

50. Ledbetter, "The Constitution of 1836," 233, 244; Taylor, *Negro Slavery in Arkansas*, 44, 46.

51. Cash, "Arkansas Achieves Statehood," 308; Schermerhorn, *Business of Slavery*, 119, 122.

52. Campbell, *Empire for Slavery*, 35–49; Torget, *Seeds of Empire*.

53. Territorial governor Miller's letter published in the *Religious Intelligencer*, February 10, 1821; *Arkansas Times and Advocate*, July 10, 1833; *Arkansas Gazette*, July 10, 1833, January 14, 1823; *United States v. Osage* (1824), abstract, arcourts.ualr.edu (accessed January 4, 2019); Steven Teske, "Antoine Barraque," in *Encyclopedia of Arkansas History and Culture*, ed. Lancaster (accessed January 4, 2019).

54. For examples, see ads placed by William Woodruff, Noah Badgett, and Chester Ashley in the *Arkansas Gazette*, October 20, 1835, September 23, 1840, November 10, 1841.

55. Valencius, *Health of the Country*, 15; Casey, *Getting Back into Place*, xxvii; Pred, "Place as Historically Contingent Process."

2 / Domains

1. In the record, the names "Parmelia" and "Amelia" are used interchangeably for the same person. *Menifee's Administrators v. Menifee et al.* (1847), 8 Ark. 9.

2. Stewart, *"What Nature Suffers to Groe,"* 90, 147; Smith, *African American Environmental Thought*, 25; McCurry, *Masters of Small Worlds*, 7; Lefebvre, *The Production of Space*, 26, 62.

3. Hilliard, *Hog Meat and Hoe Cake*, 38; Valencius, *Health of the Country*, 20; Lefebvre, *The Production of Space*, 73, 85; Pelham to Ballard, March 8, 1857, folder 254, Ballard Papers (hereafter BP).

4. Bragg and Webb, "'As False as the Black Prince of Hades'"; Rohrbough, *The Land Office Business*; Colten, *Southern Waters*, 41; Hughes, *Life and Wars of Gideon Pillow*, 142.

5. Stewart, *"What Nature Suffers to Groe,"* 185; Beckert, *Empire of Cotton*, 91, 103, 116–17; Baptist, *The Half Has Never Been Told*, 352–53, 358–59; Pargas, *Slavery and Forced Migration in the Antebellum South*. The classic study of the agricultural problem in the tobacco regions remains Craven, *Soil Exhaustion as a Factor in the Agricultural History of Virginia and Maryland*.

6. Berlin, *Generations of Captivity*, 161–244; Deyle, *Carry Me Back*, 43; Kennedy, *Agriculture of the United States in 1860*, 12–13, 503–4; Tadman, *Speculators and Slaves*, 12; BW, 36, 66, 104, 126, 134, 45, 53, 104; Baptist, "'Stol' and Fetched Here,'" in *New Studies in the History of American Slavery*, ed. Baptist and Camp, 243–44, 252–54.

7. Malloy, "'The Health of Our Family,'" 1–2, 22; *Trammel v. Thurmond* (1856), 17 Ark. 203.

8. Shugart Plantation Journal, May 1, 1839, March 28, 1840, box 1, folder 1.

9. Deyle, *Carry Me Back*, 3–4, 44; BW, 23–24; Malloy, "'The Health of Our Family,'" 86; see also Johnson, *Soul by Soul*.

10. Molly Finley interview, BW, 24; Beckert, *Empire of Cotton*, 103–4, 109.

11. *Sessions v. Hartsook* (1861), 23 Ark. 519; Solomon Lambert interview, BW, 249.

12. Scarborough, *Masters of the Big House*, 125, 176.

13. *Anderson v. Dunn* (1858), 19 Ark. 651–66; *Whitfield v. Browder* (1852), 13 Ark. 143–50; *Pond v. Obaugh* (1855), 16 Ark. 95.

14. While Joan Cashin interpreted family correspondence to suggest sympathy on the part of lonely white women on the frontier for their bondspeople, court records reveal white women to be more than willing to separate black families. Cashin, *A Family Venture*; Moren et al. v. McCown et al. (1861), 23 Ark. 99; See also Jones-Rogers, *They Were Her Property*.

15. Maulding et al. v. Scott et al. (1852), 13 Ark. 89.

16. Valencius, *Health of the Country*, 51; Cora Scroggins interview, *BW*, 173; Adeline Blakeley, WPA Early Settlers' Personal History Interviews, Early Settlers' Personal History Questionnaire.

17. John Mebane Allen Papers (1 volume); U.S. Bureau of the Census, Seventh Census of the United States, 1850, Slave Inhabitants, Alamance County, NC. Jenny's journey is told more completely in Jones, "Bondwomen on Arkansas's Cotton Frontier," 30–32.

18. Harve Osborne interview, *BW*, 172.

19. T. W. Cotton interview, *BW*, 244; Molly Hudgen interview, *BW*, 246–47.

20. Bolsterli, *Remembrance of Eden*, 33–34, 41.

21. This entry in the WPA ex-slave interviews is particularly racist and problematic, including the writer's description of Waddell as a "faithful old black mammy." It is used here only for the description of 1850s Lonoke County. Emmeline Waddell interview, *BW*, 236–37; Vlach, *Back of the Big House*, 137, 8, 10.

22. Daniel C. Littlefield, "Colonial and Revolutionary United States," in *Oxford Handbook of Slavery in the Americas*, ed. Paquette and Smith, 210.

23. Ellen Briggs Thompson interview, *BW*, 170; Molly Finley interview, *BW*, 24; James Gill interview, *BW*, 271; Dock Wilborn interview, *BW*, 294–95; McNeilly, *Old South Frontier*, 127.

24. Bolsterli, *Remembrance of Eden*, 31–32; McConnell, "The Colony at Union Valley," 7–8; U.S. Bureau of the Census, Eighth Census of the United States,1860), Slave Inhabitants, Washington County, AR.

25. McNeilly, *Old South Frontier*; McCurry, *Masters of Small Worlds*, 6.

26. Lefebvre, *The Production of Space*, 62; Vlach, *Back of the Big House*, 1, 5, 43; Leslie C. Stewart-Abernathy, "Separate Kitchens and Intimate Archaeology: Constructing Urban Slavery on the Antebellum Cotton Frontier in Washington, Arkansas," in *Household Chores and Household Choices*, ed. Barile and Brandon, 53; McCurry, *Masters of Small Worlds*, 7.

27. Mauldin, *Unredeemed Land*, 19; Ford Diary, January 24, 1849 (quotation); March 13, 20, 1839, Shugart Plantation Papers; Rich. T. Nicholson to Col. Ballard, February 5, 1857, folder 252, BP; H. L. Berry to Col. Ballard, January 18, 1858, folder 268, BP.

28. Brown Diary, January 14, 19, 25, 27, 29, February 4, 1853; Jack Sanders to [R. C. Ballard], January 18, 1857, folder 252, BP; Rich. T. Nicholson to Dear Sir, February 5, 1857, folder 252, BP. Nineteenth-century methods of deadening timber and grubbing are outlined in Periam, *Home and Farm Manual*, 285 and Hazard, *The Register of Pennsylvania*, 37.

29. Stanley, *The Autobiography of Henry Morton Stanley*, quoted in DeBlack, "A Garden in the Wilderness," 113; Bolton, *Arkansas, 1800–1860*, 131.

30. Belle Williams interview, *BW*, 55; Pelham to Ballard, March 4, 1857, folder 254, BP; Swanson, *Remaking Wormsloe Plantation*, 89; Smith, *African American Environmental Thought*, 25.

31. Pelham to Ballard, March 4, 1857; Valencius, *Health of the Country*, 88.
32. R. C. Smith interview, *BW*, 390.
33. Sarah Winston interview, *BW*, 113; Katie Rowe interview, *BW*, 145.
34. Kaye, *Joining Places*, 55–61; Bolsterli, *Remembrance of Eden*, 95–96; Pelham to Ballard, April 14, 1857, folder 256, BP.
35. Vlach, *Back of the Big House*, 35, 84, 64; Solomon Lambert interview, *BW*, 249; Lucretia Alexander interview, *BW*, 412; Harriet McFarlin Payne interview, *BW*, 31; Plomer Harshaw interview, *BW*, 6.
36. Stewart-Abernathy, "Separate Kitchens and Intimate Archaeology," 61–64, 66–67, 69, 71–72; Vlach, *Back of the Big House*, 44; Kwas, *Digging for History at Old Washington*, 89; Dock Wilborn interview, *BW*, 294; Sharpless, *Cooking in Other Women's Kitchens*, 4.
37. Molly Finley interview, *BW*, 24.
38. Glymph, *Out of the House of Bondage*, 74; the slaveholding yeoman household as a political unit in the antebellum South is analyzed in McCurry, *Masters of Small Worlds*; Peggy Sloan interview, *BW*, 107; Fox-Genovese, *Within the Plantation Household*, 35.
39. Stewart-Abernathy, "Separate Kitchens and Intimate Archaeology," 71–72; Kwas, *Digging for History at Old Washington*, 89.
40. Senia Rassberry interview, *BW*, 211; Eva Strayhorn interview, *BW*, 223; Ellen Briggs Thompson interview, *BW*, 170; Mary Jane Hardridge interview, *BW*, 196.
41. Kaye, *Joining Places*, 85, 87, 89; Bolsterli, *Remembrance of Eden*, 33–35; Harriet McFarlin Payne interview, *BW*, 31; Brown Diary, February 7, 1854.
42. Jones, *Labor of Love, Labor of Sorrow*, 27; Zenia Culp interview, *BW*, 366; Harriet McFarlin Payne interview, *BW*, 30; Mandy Tucker interview, *BW*, 215; Hannah Jameson interview, *BW*, 165.
43. Bolsterli, *Remembrance of Eden*, 41, 49.
44. Hilliard Diary, undated entry, page 2 of typed transcription.
45. At times these women included criticism of whites' family members. Bolsterli, *Remembrance of Eden*, 39–40.
46. Ford Diary, March 24, 1849; Annie Page interview, *BW*, 370.
47. Bolsterli, *Remembrance of Eden*, 43–44.
48. Hilliard Diary, March 29, April 3, 4, 12, 1850; Glymph, *Out of the House of Bondage*, 63–96.
49. *Rose v. Rose* (1849), 9 Ark. 508, transcript and record, 3, 11, 16, 43–45, 48, 56, 63, 69.
50. Griffith, "Slavery in Independence County," appendix 3, "Slave Transactions," 64, 53; Phillips County Probate Book E, 157, 192, Phillips County courthouse, Helena, AR; *Gaines v. Briggs* (1848), 9 Ark. 46–47; for white women as shrewd slaveholders, see Jones-Rogers, *They Were Her Property*.
51. Louis Davis interview, *BW*, 434; Katie Arbery interview, *BW*, 359; Bolsterli, *Remembrance of Eden*.
52. Dock Wilborn interview, *BW*, 296.
53. John Bates interview, *BW*, 318; Dock Wilborn interview, *BW*, 296.
54. Relph, *Place and Placelessness*; David Seamon and Jacob Sowers, "Place and Placelessness (1976): Edward Relph," in *Key Texts in Human Geography*, ed. Hubbard, Kitchin, and Valentine, 45; Schermerhorn, *Unrequited Toil*, 111; Taylor, *Embattled Freedom*, 86.

55. DeBlack, "A Garden in the Wilderness," 135–36; Nancy Snell Griffith, "James W. Mason," in *Encyclopedia of Arkansas History and Culture*, ed. Lancaster (accessed May 27, 2020); Blake Wintory, "Biography of Marie Louise (Slade) Mason, 1844–1919," in *Online Biographical Dictionary of the Woman Suffrage Movement in the United States: WASM Edition: Black Women Suffragists*, ed. Dublin and Sklar.

56. Augustus Robinson interview, *BW*, 50; Joseph Samuel Badgett interview, *BW*, 92; Minnie Johnson Stewart interview, *BW*, 167.

57. Stewart, *"What Nature Suffers to Groe,"* 90.

58. U.S. Bureau of the Census, Seventh Census of the United States, 1850, Productions of Agriculture, AR, MS; Eighth Census of the United States, 1860, Productions of Agriculture, AR, MS.

59. W. G. Sargent to Col. John Eaton, Jr., July 1, 1864, Records of United States Army Continental Commands (Record Group 393), Part I, Geographical Divisions, Departments, and Military (Reconstruction) Districts, file G-103, series "Letters Received, 1864–67" (entry 269), National Archives and Records Administration, Washington, DC. Cockrill had come to Jefferson County from Tennessee in the 1850s. In 1860, he held 160 enslaved people, living in 34 cabins, in Vaugine Township. He may have been a seasonally absentee planter, as he also held a plantation in Alabama and was living in Nashville (with his family and eight enslaved people) at the time of the 1860 census. U.S. Bureau of the Census, Eighth Census of the United States, 1860, Free Inhabitants and Slave Inhabitants, Jefferson County, AR, and Davidson County, TN.

60. Minnie Johnson Stewart interview, *BW*, 167; John Pelham to R. C. Ballard, November 15, 1857, folder 263, BP.

61. "Atrocious Murder," *Arkansas Gazette*, February 1, 1849, p. 2; *Austin, a Slave v. the State* (1854), series 1, gray box 37A, folder 2454, pp. 13–15, 21–22, Arkansas Supreme Court Briefs and Records.

62. Hahn, *Nation under Our Feet*, 20.

63. Rosetta Davis interview, *BW*, 269; William Brown interview, *BW*, 86; Lucindy Allison interview, *BW*, 71, 72; Adrianna Kerns interview, *BW*, 102; Sallie Crane interview, *BW*, 136.

64. Shugart Plantation Journal, January 10, March 16, 22, 28, 29, April 2, October 19, 24, 1839.

65. Most letters from John Pelham and H. L. Berry to R. C. Ballard mention the status of the carpenters' projects.

66. McNeilly, *Old South Frontier*, 146.

67. Brown Diary, May 5, 9, 1854.

68. Jones, *Labor of Love, Labor of Sorrow*, 22; Jno. B. Pelham to Col. Ballard, December 5, 1857, subseries 1.3, folder 264, BP; Brown Diary, February 5–7, 26, March 1, 1853.

69. Jno. B. Pelham to Col. Ballard, March 22, 1857, folder 255, BP.

70. Jno. B. Pelham to Col. Ballard, April 20, 1857, folder 257, BP.

71. Hilliard Diary, May 2, 1850; Charlie McClendon interview, *BW*, 207; T. W. Cotton interview, *BW*, 244; Dock Wilborn interview, *BW*, 296; Stewart, "If John Muir Had Been an Agrarian," 146.

72. Griffith, "Slavery in Independence County," appendix 3, "Slave Transactions"; *Arkansas Gazette*, August 5, 1847.

73. Eventually Leeper seems to have given up on his Washington County venture, selling out and moving to Texas. Matthew Leeper to David Walker, August 28, 1853,

in "Letters of Matthew Leeper," 26; Shugart Plantation Papers, January 16–18, April 7, September 10, 1839.

74. Johnson, *River of Dark Dreams*, 232–33.
75. Bolsterli, *Remembrance of Eden*, 75–76, 35.
76. Peter Brown interview, *BW*, 262.
77. *Arkansian*, July 2, 1859, in "Files from the Arkansian," *Flashback* 39 (November 1989).
78. Zorn, "An Arkansas Fugitive Slave Incident and Its International Repercussions"; Bolton, *Fugitives from Injustice*.
79. Nelson Denson interview, *BW*, 38; Molly Finley interview, *BW*, 23; Stewart, "If John Muir Had Been an Agrarian," 144–46.
80. Cornwall, "Historical Sketch," 38; Stewart-Abernathy, "Separate Kitchens and Intimate Archaeology," 57.
81. John Wesley interview, in *Born in Slavery*; Scott Bond interview, *BW*, 74; Horatio Williams interview, *BW*, 217.
82. Stewart, "If John Muir Had Been an Agrarian," 143–53; Mart A. Stewart, "Slavery and African American Environmentalism," in *"To Love the Wind and the Rain,"* ed. Glave and Stoll, 11; Stewart, *"What Nature Suffers to Groe,"* 178; Johnson, *River of Dark Dreams*, 228–29; Vlach, *Back of the Big House*, 13; Anthony Taylor interview, *BW*, 61; Kaye, *Joining Places*, 1–5, 32.
83. Mandy Tucker interview, *BW*, 214–15; Henry H. Buttler interview, *BW*, 190.
84. James Milo Alexander Testimony, Heirs of Joseph Deputy Claim, Approved Claims, Southern Claims Commission.
85. Testimony of Hon. James Speed before the American Freedmen's Inquiry Commission, p. 35, November 1863, Letters Received, ser. 12; Kaye, *Joining Places*, 38, 153; Hahn, *Nation under Our Feet*, 17–18.
86. George Kye interview, *BW*, 67; Laura Hart interview, *BW*, 355; Molly Finley interview, *BW*, 24; Ellen Briggs Thompson interview, *BW*, 170; Newberry, "Clark County Plantation Journal," 408. Enslaved Christians may have been members of Cane Hill's early Presbyterian congregation. An entry of "Lucy Cox, colored" is found in the minutes for July 23, 1833, Cumberland Presbyterian Church Presbytery Records, Cane Hill, University of Arkansas Libraries Special Collections.
87. Charley Ross interview, *BW*, 60; Sweetie Ivery Wagoner interview, *BW*, 23.
88. Bolsterli, *Remembrance of Eden*, 43; Eva Strayhorn interview, *BW*, 221–22.
89. Bolsterli, *Remembrance of Eden*, 62–64.
90. Pate Newton interview, WPA Early Settlers' Personal History Interviews.
91. *Hervy v. Armstrong*, 15 Ark. 162–69.
92. *Hervy v. Armstrong*, 15 Ark. 166.
93. Gal. 3:28, King James Version.
94. Ellen Briggs Thompson interview, *BW*, 169; O. W. Green interview, *BW*, 48.
95. Valencius, *Health of the Country*, 52; George Newton interview, *BW*, 16.
96. Bolsterli, *Remembrance of Eden*, 64–65.
97. Forret, *Race Relations at the Margins*, 41–43; *Collins v. Woodruff*, 9 Ark. 463.
98. Forret, *Race Relations at the Margins*, 53, 56–63.
99. *Reed v. the State* (1855), 16 Ark. 505.
100. *Dennis (a slave) v. State* (1843), 5 Ark. 230.

101. Cornwall, "Historical Sketch," 30; Jno. B. Pelham to Col. Ballard, March 8, 1857, folder 254, BP.

102. U.S. Bureau of the Census, Eighth Census of the United States, 1860, Free Inhabitants and Slave Inhabitants, Clark County, AR; Charles Green Dortch interview, *BW*, 94; Adrianna Kerns interview, *BW*, 101 (quotation).

103. H. L. Berry to Col. Ballard, February 18, 1859, folder 302, BP; K. Rayner to Rice Ballard, January 31, 1859, folder 300, BP.

104. Gould, *Digest of the Statutes of Arkansas*, 964–65; Kaye, *Joining Places*, 164–65.

105. Brown Diary, July 31, 1852, August 4, 10, 1853.

106. Lucindy Allison interview, *BW*, 71.

107. Gould, *Digest of the Statutes of Arkansas*, 741–42.

108. For a more in-depth discussion of slave mobility within and beyond Arkansas, see Jones, "Chattels, Pioneers, and Pilgrims for Freedom"; Solomon Lambert interview, *BW*, 248; James Bertrand interview, *BW*, 186; Charley Ross interview, *BW*, 60; Columbus Williams interview, *BW*, 375.

109. Mary Ann Brooks interview, *BW*, 421; James Bertrand interview, *BW*, 186.

110. Ellen Briggs Thompson interview, *BW*, 168; Charlie Norris interview, *BW*, 368; John Holt interview, *BW*, 384; Adrianna Kerns interview, *BW*, 101; Charley Ross interview, *BW*, 59; Judia Fortenberry interview, *BW*, 409.

111. Taylor, *Embattled Freedom*, 104; Lack, "Urban Slave Community," 273–74. In 1850, Matilda Fulton held seven enslaved people, including a fifty-year-old man and a twenty-year-old man. U.S. Bureau of the Census, Seventh Census of the United States, 1850, Slave Inhabitants, Pulaski County, AR.

112. Bolsterli, *Remembrance of Eden*, 34.

113. Blassingame, *The Slave Community*, 164–65.

114. Newberry, "Clark County Plantation Journal," 402; Bolsterli, *Remembrance of Eden*, 45.

115. Hahn, *Nation under Our Feet*, 41; H. L. Berry to Col. Ballard, February 3, 1859, folder 301, BP.

116. John Bates interview, *BW*, 319.

117. Lefebvre, *The Production of Space*, 77; Louis Davis interview, *BW*, 433; Charles Green Dortch interview, *BW*, 95–96; Hahn, *Nation under our Feet*, 40–42.

118. Paulette, *Empire of Small Places*, 2; Johnson, *River of Dark Dreams*, 229.

119. Affidavit of Aaron Williams, Eliza Frazier Pension Application no. 220802, for service of Simon Frazier (54th USCT), Civil War and Later Pension Files.

120. Affidavit of Adolph McGee, Eliza Frazier Pension Application no. 220802, for service of Simon Frazier (54th USCT), Civil War and Later Pension Files.

121. Affidavit of Wright Allen, Eliza Frazier Pension Application no. 220802, for service of Simon Frazier (54th USCT), Civil War and Later Pension Files.

122. Hilliard Diary, May 2, 4, 1850; *Arkansas Gazette*, May 6, 1853. For a full exploration of violence between bondspeople, see Forret, *Slave against Slave*.

123. H. L. Berry to Col. Ballard, January 15, 1859, folder 299, BP. After promising not to tell anyone and pleading with Ballard to come to the plantation, Berry's letters become increasingly vague and then fall silent on the matter, possibly at the urging of his employer.

124. Forret, *Race Relations at the Margins*, 17, 28, 33–34, 39, 52.

125. *Sarah v. The State*, series 1, box 66, docket no. 4686, pp. 19–20, Arkansas Supreme Court Briefs and Records.

126. *Bone v. The State*, series 1, box 13, folder 228, pp. 21–22, Arkansas Supreme Court Briefs and Records. In the attempt to try to get Sarah out of the 175-lash punishment, and Bone from his 300-lash sentence, the defense attorneys supplied by their enslaver did not deny that the incidents took place but argued that the responsibility for them lay not with the bondspeople but with Sims as their owner.

127. Sarah Ridge held thirteen bondspeople in Benton County, a large holding for that area. *Ridge v. Featherston* (1854), 15 Ark. 160; U.S. Bureau of the Census, Seventh Census of the United States, 1850, Slave Inhabitants, Benton County, AR.

128. *Ridge v. Featherston* (1854), 15 Ark. 160.

129. *Smith v. Jones* (1847), 8 Ark. 109; *Lindsay v. Harrison* (1848), 8 Ark. 302; *Maulding v. Scott* (1852), 13 Ark. 88; *Roane v. Rives* (1854), 15 Ark. 328; *Trammell v. Thurmond* (1856), 17 Ark. 203; William Brown interview, *BW*, 89; Katie Rowe interview, *BW*, 147; Mollie Barber interview, *BW*, 261.

130. *Humphries v. McCraw* (1848), 9 Ark. 92–98; Griffith, "Slavery in Independence County," appendix 3, "Slave Transactions," 39, 41, 53, 61. Damian Alan Pargas examines local movement in *Slavery and Forced Migration in the Antebellum South*.

131. Hempstead County Tax Rolls, 1847; U.S. Bureau of the Census, Seventh Census of the United States, 1850, Free Inhabitants and Slave Inhabitants, Sevier County, AR; U.S. Bureau of the Census, Eighth Census of the United States, 1860, Free Inhabitants and Slave Inhabitants, Sevier County, AR.

132. Hempstead County Tax Rolls, 1847; U.S. Bureau of the Census, Seventh Census of the United States, 1850, Free Inhabitants and Slave Inhabitants, Clark County, AR; U.S. Bureau of the Census, Eighth Census of the United States, 1860, Free Inhabitants and Slave Inhabitants, Clark County, AR.

133. Pulaski County Tax Rolls, 1838; Hempstead County Tax Rolls, 1847; U.S. Bureau of the Census, Seventh Census of the United States, 1850, Free Inhabitants and Slave Inhabitants, Hempstead County, AR; U.S. Bureau of the Census, Eighth Census of the United States, 1860, Free Inhabitants and Slave Inhabitants, Pulaski County, AR.

134. Hempstead County Tax Rolls, 1847; U.S. Bureau of the Census, Seventh Census of the United States, 1850, Free Inhabitants and Slave Inhabitants, Ouachita County, AR; U.S. Bureau of the Census, Eighth Census of the United States, 1860, Free Inhabitants and Slave Inhabitants, Shelby County, TN.

135. Gould, *Digest of the Statutes of Arkansas*, 257–58, 272 (second quotation); Chris M. Branam, "Slave Codes," in *Encyclopedia of Arkansas History and Culture*, ed. Lancaster (accessed January 4, 2019).

136. *Austin, a Slave v. the State* (1854), 14 Ark. 555; Lankford, "Austin's Secret."

137. Johnson, *River of Dark Dreams*, 218–19, 222, 225.

138. Griffith, "Slavery in Independence County," 14.

139. Gould, *Digest of the Statutes of Arkansas*, 822–23. While the law gave counties the power to establish area patrols, it did not require them.

140. *Hervy v. Armstrong* (1854), 15 Ark. 164.

141. For a more complete discussion of slave lynching in Arkansas, see Kelly Houston Jones, "'Doubtless Guilty': Lynching and Slaves in Antebellum Arkansas,"

in *Bullets and Fire*, ed. Lancaster, 17–34; Lack, "Urban Slave Community," 280; Smallwood, "Slave Insurrection."

142. English, *Digest of the Statutes of Arkansas*, 945.

143. Gould, *Digest of the Statutes of Arkansas*, 1027–29; Blackett, *The Captive's Quest for Freedom*, 52–53.

144. Conviction for "stealing" any enslaved person, whether the culprit was "black, white, or yellow," meant imprisonment for five to twenty-one years, a bit more than the five to fifteen possible for horse-stealing. Gould, *Digest of the Statutes of Arkansas*, 338, 342, 344–45.

145. Valencius, *Health of the Country*, 257; Gould, *Digest of the Statutes of Arkansas*, 483, 553–54, 556–57; Billy D. Higgins, "Act 151 of 1859," in *Encyclopedia of Arkansas History and Culture*, ed. Lancaster (accessed January 4, 2019).

146. Washington County wills transcribed in *Flashback* 10, no. 4 (October 1960): 29–30; Griffith, "Slavery in Independence County," 16.

147. Gould, *Digest of the Statutes of Arkansas*, 483, 550–52; Nathan Miller interview, *BW*, 357.

148. *Campbell et al. v. Campbell et al.* (1853), 13 Ark. 514.

149. *Wilson v. Dean* (1850), 10 Ark. 308–9.

150. Woodruff had filed to dismiss this petition but the probate court decreed in favor of Aramynta and her children. The circuit court found that this dispute was not the jurisdiction of the probate court; the Arkansas Supreme Court agreed. *Aramynta v. Woodruff* (1847), 7 Ark. 422–24.

151. *Jackson v. Bob* (1857), 18 Ark. 399–413.

152. *Harriet and others v. Swan & Dixon* (1857), 18 Ark. 496. The will to free Harriet and her children was supported by Albert Pike, who authenticated the signatures of the attorney and witness on the will; Kennington, *In the Shadow of Dred Scott*, 5–7.

153. Smith, *African American Environmental Thought*, 28; Casey, *Getting Back into Place*, 30, xxxiii; Valencius, *Health of the Country*, 96; "Savage and Mortal Combat," *Arkansas Gazette*, February 2, 1842.

3 / Alluvial Empires

1. Colten, *Southern Waters*, 11, 27; McNeilly, *Old South Frontier*, 4–5; Valencius, *Health of the Country*, 133.

2. Taylor, *Negro Slavery in Arkansas*, 27.

3. McNeilly, *Old South Frontier*, 4–5; Berlin, *Many Thousands Gone*, 7–13.

4. Taylor, *Negro Slavery in Arkansas*, 26.

5. U.S. Bureau of the Census, Seventh Census of the United States, 1850, Schedule 2 (Slave Inhabitants), Schedule 4 (Productions of Agriculture), Hempstead County, AR; Eighth Census of the United States, 1860, Schedule 2 (Slave Inhabitants), Schedule 4 (Productions of Agriculture), Hempstead County, AR.

6. U.S. Bureau of the Census, Seventh Census of the United States, 1850, Slave Inhabitants, Hempstead County, AR; Eighth Census of the United States, 1860, Slave Inhabitants, Hempstead County, AR.

7. U.S. Bureau of the Census, Seventh Census of the United States, 1850, Productions of Agriculture and Slave Inhabitants, Hempstead County, AR; Eighth Census of the United States, 1860, Productions of Agriculture and Slave Inhabitants, Hempstead

County, AR. Hempstead County cotton production increased from 2,552 bales to 16,548 bales between the harvest of 1849 and the harvest of 1859 (a 548% increase).

8. U.S. Bureau of the Census, Seventh Census of the United States, 1850, Productions of Agriculture and Slave Inhabitants, Conway County, AR; Eighth Census of the United States, 1860, Productions of Agriculture and Slave Inhabitants, Conway County, AR.

9. Kennedy, *Agriculture of the United States in 1860*, 224.

10. Battershell, "The Socioeconomic Role of Slavery in the Upcountry."

11. Because of the condition of the agricultural manuscript census for Pope County, there are whole sections that are illegible, and it is not possible to determine exactly how much of the county's cotton was grown by enslaved people on the river. Only about 560 bales, or 15%, originated there for certain. The actual percentage must be higher, but probably not as high as in Conway County. U.S. Bureau of the Census, Eighth Census of the United States, 1850, Productions of Agriculture and Slave Inhabitants, Pope County, AR; Kennedy, *Agriculture of the United States in 1860*, 224.

12. Georgena Duncan used Pope County and Conway County to represent "river valley slavery" in "'One negro, Sarah.'"

13. U.S. Bureau of the Census, Eighth Census of the United States, 1860, Productions of Agriculture and Slave Inhabitants, Independence County, AR.

14. Moneyhon, *The Impact of the Civil War and Reconstruction on Arkansas*, 18–21; Kennedy, *Agriculture of the United States in 1860*, 224.

15. McNeilly, *Old South Frontier*, 4. McNeilly, Taylor, and Battershell acknowledge the importance of rivers but generally adhere to the "imaginary line."

16. Hanson and Moneyhon, *Historical Atlas of Arkansas*, "4. Surface Water Bodies"; Woodruff, *American Congo*, 8. See also Buchanan, *Black Life on the Mississippi*.

17. U.S. Bureau of the Census, Eighth Census of the United States, 1860, Free Inhabitants and Slave Inhabitants, Chicot County and Phillips County, AR. For rumors of rebellion reaching Arkansas, see Jones, "White Fear of Black Rebellion," in *The Elaine Massacre and Arkansas*, ed. Lancaster.

18. Baptist, *The Half Has Never Been Told*; Schermerhorn, *Unrequited Toil*.

19. Moneyhon, *The Impact of the Civil War and Reconstruction on Arkansas*, 51, 21, 19; Kaye, *Joining Places*.

20. McNeilly, *Old South Frontier*; U.S. Bureau of the Census, Seventh Census of the United States, 1860, Schedule 2 (Slave Inhabitants); testimony of Hon. James Speed before the American Freedmen's Inquiry Commission, pp. 32–33, November 1863, Letters Received, ser. 12.

21. Extensive information on the management of absentee operations can be found in R. C. Ballard Papers, subseries 1.3; U.S. Bureau of the Census, Seventh Census of the United States, 1860, Slave Inhabitants, Chicot County, AR.

22. Together, Chicot, Crittenden, Desha, Phillips, and Mississippi Counties, Arkansas, held 82,706 acres in improved farmland and 9,410 enslaved people in 1850. Tipton, Shelby, and Lauderdale Counties, Tennessee, and De Soto, Tunica, Coahoma, Bolivar, and Washington Counties, Mississippi, together held 397,672 acres in improved farmland and 42,195 enslaved people. Chicot, Crittenden, Desha, Phillips, and Mississippi Counties, Arkansas, together held 229,905 acres in improved farmland and 24,018 bondspeople in 1860. Shelby and Lauderdale Counties, Tennessee, and De Soto, Tunica, Coahoma, and Bolivar Counties, Mississippi, held a total of 501,589 acres in

improved farmland and 56,728 enslaved people in 1860. Data for Washington County, Mississippi, are missing from that census enumeration. If the enslaved population of Washington County held steady at the 1850 total, the difference would be 63%. Like the surrounding counties, however, Washington County's enslaved population would have grown. Thus, the percentage difference was probably much greater than 63. U.S. Bureau of the Census, Eighth Census of the United States, 1860, Productions of Agriculture, Slave Inhabitants, AR, MS.

23. James Milo Alexander Testimony, Heirs of Joseph Deputy Claim; *Southern Shield* (Helena), November 11, 1854, January 6, 1855, June 27, 1857; Johnson, *River of Dark Dreams*, 243. In 1870, Alexander and his son were in the same area holding the offices of justice of the peace and constable. U.S. Bureau of the Census, Ninth Census of the United States, 1870, Population, Phillips County, AR.

24. *Southern Shield* (Helena), March 19, July 9, 1853. See also Bolton, *Fugitivism*.

25. *Biographical and Historical Memoirs of Southern Arkansas*, 11; Christ, *Civil War Arkansas*, 8.

26. Kolchin, *American Slavery*, 177–78; Morris, *Becoming Southern*, 115; Lack, "Urban Slave Community," 258; Hanson and Moneyhon, *Historical Atlas of Arkansas*, "3. Soil Patterns," "4. Surface Water Bodies."

27. Moneyhon, *The Impact of the Civil War and Reconstruction on Arkansas*, 19, 20; U.S. Bureau of the Census, Seventh Census of the United States, 1850, Free and Slave Inhabitants, Pulaski and Chicot Counties, AR.

28. *Arkansas Gazette*, February 7, 1826, March 30, 1830, February 1, 1832.

29. *Arkansas Gazette*, April 6, 1830, January 12, 1836.

30. *Arkansas Gazette*, January 12, 1836.

31. *Arkansas Gazette*, April 14, 1841.

32. Lack, "Urban Slave Community."

33. *Arkansas Gazette*, February 1, 1849.

34. James Jackson, Southern Claims Commission, Claim #20344; U.S. Bureau of the Census, Eighth Census of the United States, 1860, Free Inhabitants, Pulaski County, AR.

35. *Arkansas Gazette*, February 2, 1842

36. *Arkansas Gazette*, June 4, 1852; *State v. Cadle* (1858), 19 Ark. 613.

37. Pulaski County Indictment Records, Books B–C, Arkansas State Archives.

38. *Arkansas Gazette*, October 20, 1854.

39. Lack, "Urban Slave Community," 273.

40. U.S. Bureau of the Census, Seventh Census of the United States, 1850, Manufactures, Pulaski County, AR; U.S. Bureau of the Census, Eighth Census of the United States, 1860, Manufacturing Schedule Manufactures, Pulaski County, AR.

41. "Our History," Wesley Chapel United Methodist Church, https://wesleychapelumclr.org/our-history/ (accessed July 1, 2020).

42. Lack, "Urban Slave Community," 269–70.

43. Lack, "Urban Slave Community," 272.

44. "Fugitive Negroes," *Arkansas Gazette*, November 18, 1828, p. 3; Lack, "Urban Slave Community," 277; *Arkansas Gazette*, May 29, October 30, 1839, March 23, 1842.

45. Lee, "How Titsworth Springs on Mount Magazine Got Its Name." Sweetie Ivery Wagoner, who was interviewed by the WPA in the 1930s, was unable to recall where her parents were enslaved. It may be that they were held on one of these places,

although she remembered the first name of the owner of the plantation as Newt. Near the Titsworth plantations complex lived a small slaveholder listed as C. B. Ivey. Sweetie Ivery Wagoner interview, *BW*, 21–22; U.S. Bureau of the Census, Eighth Census of the United States, 1860, Free Inhabitants and Slave Inhabitants, Franklin County, AR.

46. Colten, *Southern Waters*, 41; *Arkansas Gazette*, April 14, 1841; Griffith, "Slavery in Independence County," appendix 3, "Slave Transactions," 55.

47. *History of Benton, Washington*, 1332, 1378; *Confederate Women of Arkansas in the Civil War*.

48. Drennan served in Arkansas's state constitutional convention and House of Representatives, and he was a trustee of the Arkansas Real Estate Bank. Carolyn Yancey Kent, "John Drennen," in *Encyclopedia of Arkansas History and Culture*, ed. Lancaster (accessed July 1, 2020); Dunn, "Wealth, Slaves, and John Drennen."

49. U.S. Bureau of the Census, Seventh Census of the United States, 1850, Free Inhabitants and Slave Inhabitants, Crawford County, AR; U.S. Bureau of the Census, Eighth Census of the United States, 1860, Free Inhabitants and Slave Inhabitants, Crawford County, AR.

50. Purdue, *Slavery and the Evolution of Cherokee Society*; Barbara Krauthamer, "Slavery," in *Encyclopedia of Oklahoma History and Culture*, digital.library.okstate.edu/encyclopedia (accessed January 4, 2019); Naylor, *African Cherokees in Indian Territory*, 1–2, 15–16; Porter, *The Black Seminoles*, 133, 121–23.

51. Littlefield, *Africans and Seminoles*, 162.

52. Littlefield, *Africans and Seminoles*, 163–65.

53. Littlefield, *Africans and Seminoles*, 173–75.

54. *Goodspeed History of Washington*, 515, 560; *Powell v. The State* (1860), 21 Ark. 509–11.

55. *Omey v. The State* (1861), 23 Ark. 281; U.S. Bureau of the Census, Eighth Census of the United States, 1860, Free Inhabitants, Crawford County, AR.

56. Moneyhon and Hanson, *Historical Atlas of Arkansas*, "3. Soil Patterns," "4. Surface Water Bodies"; Goodspeed, *History of Washington*, 424, 432.

57. U.S. Bureau of the Census, Eighth Census of the United States, 1860, Free Inhabitants and Slave Inhabitants, Benton County, AR; Van Winkle's Mill Site National Register Nomination Form, 10-900 (2002), http://www.arkansaspreservation.com/National-Register-Listings/PDF/BE3502.nr.pdf (accessed October 30, 2020); Brandon, "Van Winkle's Mill."

58. U.S. Bureau of the Census, Eighth Census of the United States, 1860, Free Inhabitants and Slave Inhabitants, Benton County, AR.

59. Smith, "Slavery in Washington County," 18–23, 50–53; Poorman, "Experience of the Kidd Family"; U.S. Bureau of the Census, Eighth Census of the United States, 1860, Free Inhabitants and Slave Inhabitants, Washington County, AR; Michael A. Hughes, "Wartime Gristmill Destruction in Northwest Arkansas," in *Civil War Arkansas*, ed. Bailey and Sutherland.

60. Rothrock, "Thomas Andrew Henson"; Hilliard, "A Frontier Town: Fayetteville," 22; U.S. Bureau of the Census, Eighth Census of the United States, 1860, Free Inhabitants and Slave Inhabitants, Washington County, AR.

61. *History of Benton, Washington*, 159–60.

62. *History of Benton, Washington*, 191–92.

63. *History of Benton, Washington*, 786; Vernon, "The Story of Anthony Bewley."

64. "Historic Old Landmark Ninety-Nine Years Old," *Baxter Bulletin* (Mountain Home, AR), January 8, 1909; "Historic Old Home Attracting Visitors," *Courier News* (Blytheville, AR), August 21, 1973; "List of Col. Ashely's Appointments" and "Gen Byrd's Appointments," *Arkansas Intelligencer* (Van Buren), September 14, 1844; "Southern Meeting in Izard County," *Arkansas Gazette*, April 19, 1850; Hahn, *Nation under Our Feet*.

65. Izard County Tax Assessments, 1830–1833, 1839, 1841, 1843, 1853, Arkansas State Archives, Little Rock; see also Taylor, "Slavery in Izard County in the Final Decade."

66. George Lankford, "Batesville," in *Encyclopedia of Arkansas History and Culture*, ed. Lancaster (accessed January 4, 2019); Griffith, "Slavery in Independence County," 6.

67. Martin, "Slavery's Invisible Engine."

68. Griffith, "Slavery in Independence County," appendix 3, "Slave Transactions," 39, 55, 47, 61, 41, 54.

69. Griffith, "Slavery in Independence County," appendix 3, "Slave Transactions," 49, 51, 55, 45–46, 66, 67, 29; U.S. Bureau of the Census, Eighth Census of the United States, 1860, Free Inhabitants and Slave Inhabitants, Independence County, AR.

70. Cornwall, "Historical Sketch," 23–39; Griffith, "Slavery in Independence County," appendix 3, "Slave Transactions," 44, 50.

71. Betty Brown interview, *BW*, 129; Randolph County Tax Records, 1855, 1861; U.S. Bureau of the Census, Seventh Census of the United States, 1850, Free Inhabitants and Slave Inhabitants, Randolph County, AR; U.S. Bureau of the Census, Eighth Census of the United States, 1860, Free Inhabitants and Slave Inhabitants, Randolph County, AR.

72. Betty Brown interview, *BW*, 128–29; U.S. Bureau of the Census, Eighth Census of the United States, 1860, Free Inhabitants and Productions of Agriculture, Randolph County, AR.

73. Hanson and Moneyhon, *Historical Atlas of Arkansas*, "3. Soil Patterns," "4. Surface Water Bodies"; *Biographical and Historical Memoirs of Western Arkansas*, 469; Rebecca DeArmond-Huskey, "Bayou Bartholomew," in *Encyclopedia of Arkansas History and Culture*, ed. Lancaster (accessed January 4, 2019).

74. U.S. Bureau of the Census, Seventh Census of the United States, 1850, Free Inhabitants, Ashley County, AR.

75. *Daniel v. Guy* (1857), 19 Ark. 121–38 and (1861), 23 Ark. 50; Shafer, "White Persons Held to Racial Slavery," 134–43; Kevin D. Butler, "Guy v. Daniel," in *Encyclopedia of Arkansas History and Culture*, ed. Lancaster (accessed January 4, 2019).

76. Kennington, *In the Shadow of Dred Scott*, 7.

77. Union, Lafayette, Columbia, Ashley, and Chicot Counties, Arkansas (346,908), as compared to Carroll, Moorehouse, Union, Claiborne, Bossier, and Caddo Parishes, Louisiana (559,105). U.S. Bureau of the Census, Eighth Census of the United States, 1860, Productions of Agriculture and Slave Inhabitants, AR, LA.

Counties on either side of the Arkansas-Texas line looked fairly similar in improved acreage in 1860. Sevier and Lafayette had a higher enslaved population and more improved acres but are also larger in area than Bowie and Cass. Bondspeople in Sevier and Lafayette Counties, Arkansas, numbered 7,677, and 6,126 in Bowie and Cass Counties, Texas. In those counties, 97,300 acres were improved in Arkansas and

228 / NOTES TO CHAPTER 4

80,535 in Texas. U.S. Bureau of the Census, Eighth Census of the United States, 1860, Productions of Agriculture and Slave Inhabitants, AR, TX.

Northern Arkansas counties had more improved acres and a higher enslaved population than southern Missouri. Benton, Madison, Carroll, Fulton, Lawrence, Randolph, Greene, and Mississippi Counties, Arkansas, boasted 230,352 acres of improved farmland and 3,601 enslaved people in 1860, while McDonald, Barry, Stone, Taney, Ozark, Howell, Oregon, Ripley, Butler, Dunklin, and Pemiscot Counties, Missouri, had 137,185 improved acres and 1,091 bondspeople that year. U.S. Bureau of the Census, Eighth Census of the United States, 1860, Productions of Agriculture and Slave Inhabitants, AR, MO.

78. Nelson Densen interview, *BW*, 36; Hanson and Moneyhon, *Historical Atlas of Arkansas*, "3. Soil Patterns," "4. Surface Water Bodies"; Guy Lancaster, "Red River," in *Encyclopedia of Arkansas History and Culture*, ed. Lancaster (January 4, 2019); Houston, "Slaveholders and Slaves of Hempstead County, Arkansas," 8, 15–19; *Arkansas Gazette*, February 2, 1842, February 11, 1850.

79. *Washington Telegraph*, April 18, 1849.

4 / Flesh and Fiber

1. Stewart, *"What Nature Suffers to Groe,"* 147; Valencius, *Health of the Country*, 85, 192, 195–96, 205; Johnson, *River of Dark Dreams*, 228.

2. Lefebvre, *The Production of Space*, 85.

3. Hannah Allen interview, *BW*, 353; Kaye, *Joining Places*, 85; Mauldin, *Unredeemed Land*, 11.

4. Bolton, *Territorial Ambition*, 44, 46, 40, 55; *Humphries v. McCraw* (1848), 9 Ark. 92–98.

5. Bolton, *Territorial Ambition*, 43, 44, 49; Shugart Plantation Journal, August 11, 15, 1839; Brown Diary, August 13, 15, 1853.

6. Beckert, *Empire of Cotton*, 103; Olmstead and Rhode, "Biological Innovation and Productivity Growth," 1142; Swanson, *Remaking Wormsloe*, 68–69; McNeilly, *Old South Frontier*, 135–37; Pargas, "In the Fields of a 'Strange Land,'" 564; Gray, *Agriculture in the Southern United States*, 540, 550, 554; Stewart, "What Nature Suffers to Groe," 129; Pargas, *The Quarters and the Fields*, 87.

7. Valencius, *Health of the Country*, 15, 81; Cornwall, "Historical Sketch," 26.

8. Malloy, "'The Health of Our Family,'" 77–78, 98; Valencius, *Health of the Country*, 15, 22–24.

9. DeBow, *The Seventh Census of the United States*, 554–57; Kennedy, *Agriculture of the United States in 1860*, 6–9.

10. McNeilly, *Old South Frontier*, 97–100.

11. Newberry, "Clark County Plantation Journal," 405, 408; Ford Diary, March 22, 1849; Kaye, *Joining Places*, 92, 96–99; Cyntha Jones interview, *BW*, 118; Stewart, "What Nature Suffers to Groe," 135.

12. Jno. B. Pelham to Dear Sir, December 17, 1857, folder 265, BP; Wagram Plantation Journal, January 17, 1857, BP; DeBlack, "A Garden in the Wilderness," 114.

13. H. L. Berry to Col. Ballard, January 6, 1859, folder 298, BP; H. L. Berry to Col. Ballard, January 8, 1859, folder 298, BP; H. L. Berry to Col. Ballard, February 1, 1859, folder 301, BP; Brown Diary, February 26, March 2, 1853; Shugart Plantation Journal,

January 15–22, 1839; Rich. T. Nicholson to Dear Sir, February 22, 1857, folder 253, BP; H. L. Berry to Dear Col., January 18, 1858, folder 268, BP; Newberry, "Clark County Plantation Journal," 403; Hahn, *Nation under Our Feet*, 20.

14. Brown Diary, January 4, 9, 11–14, 16, 21, 23, 1854; Ford Diary, February 26, 1849; Wagram Plantation Journal, January 23, 1857; H. L. Berry to Col. Ballard, January 8, 24, 1859, folder 322, BP. Lucille's brother Andy (and perhaps her father, Caney) was probably also at Wagram to welcome the newest family member. Jacqueline Jones explores women's labor under slavery in her chapter "Working for Whites," in *Labor of Love, Labor of Sorrow*.

15. Brown Diary, January 25, 1853.

16. Brown Diary, January 25, February 4, 5, 6, 15, 1853; *BW*, 48, 140, 102, 25; Wagram Plantation Journal, January 23–24, 1857, BP; Jack Sanders to R. C. Ballard, January 18 or 19, 1857, folder 251, BP; Rich. T. Nicholson to R. C. Ballard, February 5, 1857, folder 252, BP; H. L. Berry to Col. Ballard, January 18, 1858, folder 268, BP; H. L. Berry to Col. Ballard, January 24, 1859, folder 300, BP; Ford Diary, January 12, 17, 20, 1849.

17. Valencius, *Health of the Country*, 239; Solomon Lambert interview, *BW*, 247.

18. Lucretia Alexander interview, *BW*, 411.

19. Brown Diary, January 26, July 20, 1854.

20. *Brunson v. Martin* (1856), series 1, box 19, folder 307, p. 14, Arkansas Supreme Court Briefs and Records.

21. Wagram Plantation Journal, January 27, 1857.

22. H. L. Berry to Col. Ballard, October 1, 1858, folder 291, BP; H. L. Berry to Col. Ballard, November 23, 1858, folder 293, BP; H. L. Berry to Col. Ballard, December 19, 1857, folder 265, BP (quotation); Newberry, "Clark County Plantation Journal," 403, 407.

23. Kolchin, *American Slavery*, 108; Emma Moore interview, *BW*, 15; Louis Lucas interview, *BW*, 203. Louis Lucas mentioned that the farm where he was held employed a black overseer for a time. Van Deburg, "The Slave Drivers of Arkansas," 239–40.

24. Bolsterli, *Remembrance of Eden*, 34.

25. Charles Green Dortch interview, *BW*, 95.

26. Deposition of James Pine, Heirs of Joseph Deputy (Phillips County, AR), Claim No. 18147, Southern Claims Commission.

27. Malloy, "'The Health of Our Family,'" 78, 94–95, 102–3; Leslie, "The Reuben and Orrin Letters."

28. Jno. B. Pelham to Col. Ballard, February 28, 1857, folder 251, BP.

29. Henry C. Buckner to Col. Ballard, January 4, 1860, folder 322, BP.

30. Henry C. Buckner to Col. R. C. Ballard, February 7, 1860, folder 324, BP; Henry C. Buckner to Col. R. C. Ballard, March 20, 1860, folder 327, BP.

31. Ford Diary, January 5, 6, 27, February 9, 19, 22, 1849. Levi had taken a much milder route than Wilborn, who had stabbed Walworth's overseer to death a few years earlier and was hanged by an angry mob for it. "Mob Violence," *Arkansas Gazette*, July 13, 1846, pp. 3–5.

32. H. L. Berry to Col. Ballard, January 18, 1858, subseries 1.3, folder 299, BP.

33. Griffith, "Slavery in Independence County," appendix 3, "Slave Transactions," 7; Phillips County Probate Book E, 148–49.

34. Griffith, "Slavery in Independence County," 7–8, appendix 3, "Slave Transactions," 38; *Washington Telegraph*, January 5, 1853, July 12, 1854; Martin, *Divided Mastery*, 2–3; *Berry v. Diamond* (1857), 19 Ark. 263.

35. Rich. T. Nicholson to R. C. Ballard, February 5, 1857, folder 252, BP; Newberry, "Clark County Plantation Journal," 403–4; DeBlack, "A Garden in the Wilderness," 114–15; Kaye, *Joining Places*, 96, 100; Ford Diary, January 30, 1849.

36. Brown Diary, July 13, 17, 1852, February 12, March 25, 28, May 30, June 21–22, 1853.

37. Jno. B. Pelham, March 22, 1857, folder 257, BP; Newberry, "Clark County Plantation Journal," 406.

38. John Jones interview, *BW*, 13; Emma Moore interview, *BW*, 15; Adrianna Kerns interview, *BW*, 102; Sallie Crane interview, *BW*, 136.

39. Katie Rowe interview, *BW*, 144.

40. King, *Stolen Childhood*, xxi–xxii, 71–106; Schwartz, *Born in Bondage*.

41. George Kye interview, *BW*, 67; Lewis Chase interview, *BW*, 309.

42. Jno. B. Pelham to Col. Ballard, March 4, 1857, folder 254, BP.

43. Ford Diary, January 7, 1849; H. L. Berry to Col. Ballard, December 30, 1858, folder 296, BP.

44. Speed testimony, p. 32, American Freedmen's Inquiry Commission; Jones, *Labor of Love, Labor of Sorrow*, 10.

45. Jno. B. Pelham to Col. Ballard, February 26, 28, 1857, folder 253, BP.

46. Molly Finley interview, *BW*, 24.

47. H. L. Berry to Col. Ballard, June 15, 1859, folder 309, BP; Hilliard Diary, March 17, 1850; Valencius, *Health of the Country*, 79–80.

48. John Wells interview, *BW*, 70; DeBlack, "A Garden in the Wilderness," 85; Ford Diary, February 2, 1849.

49. Jno. B. Pelham to Col. Ballard, March 14, 1857, folder 255, BP.

50. Jno. B. Pelham to Dear Col., February 28, 1857, folder 253, BP.

51. Brown Diary, April 7, May 14, 16, June 2, 1853.

52. H. L. Berry to Col. Ballard, July 1, 1859, folder 309, BP.

53. Jno. B. Pelham to Dear Sir, December 17, 1857, folder 265, BP; H. L. Berry to Dear Col., December 18, 1857, folder 265, BP; H. L. Berry to Col. Ballard, [January] 30, 1858, folder 269, BP; H. L. Berry to Col. Ballard, February 2, 1858, folder 270, BP; H. L. Berry to Col. Ballard, February 13, 16, 27, 1858, folder 271, BP; H. L. Berry to Col. Ballard, March 4, 1858, folder 272, BP.

54. Rich. T. Nicholson to Dear Sir, February 22, 1857, folder 253, BP; H. L. Berry to Col. Ballard, March 4, 1858, folder 272, BP; H. L. Berry to Col. Ballard, July 1, 1859, folder 310, BP; H. L. Berry to Col. Ballard, February 26, 1859, folder 302, BP; DeBlack, "A Garden in the Wilderness," 89–90, 114, 161.

55. Jno. B. Pelham to Dear Col., February 28, 1857, folder 253, BP; Ford Diary, February 5, 1849.

56. Jno. B. Pelham to Col. Ballard, March 4, 1857, folder 254, BP; Jno. B. Pelham to Col. Ballard, March 14, 1857, folder 255, BP; H. L. Berry to Col. Ballard, March 14, 29, 1859, folder 304, BP; H. L. Berry to Col. Ballard, April 2, 1859, folder 305, BP.

57. S. Max Edelson, "Clearing Swamps, Harvesting Forests," in *Environmental History and the American South*, ed. Sutter and Manganiello, 107, 115, 118–19, 122–24; Jno. B. Pelham to Col. Ballard, March 14, 1857, folder 255, BP.

58. Shugart Plantation Journal, February 2, 13, March 30, 1839; Pelham to Ballard, March 14, 1857; Newberry, "Clark County Plantation Journal," 402; Mauldin, *Unredeemed Land*, 12.

59. Shugart Plantation Journal, February 22–24, April 2, 6, August 15, 1839; Brown Diary, July 17, 1852, August 8, 16, 25, 1853; Newberry, "Clark County Plantation Journal," 403; Ford Diary, January 1, February 12–16, 1849; H. L. Berry to Col. Ballard, February 18, 1859, folder 302, BP.

60. Shugart Plantation Journal, January 1, 9, 15, February 1, 16, March 28–19, 1839; H. L. Berry to Col. Ballard, May, 14, 1859, folder 307, BP; DeBlack, "A Garden in the Wilderness," 113; "Outrageous Murder," *Arkansas Gazette*, April 4, 1851, p. 3; *Abraham v. Gray* (1853), 14 Ark. 303–4.

61. H. L. Berry to Col. Ballard, April 17, 1859, folder 306, BP; Gray, *Agriculture in the Southern United States*, 549.

62. H. L. Berry to Col. Ballard, March 11, 1859, folder 304, BP; DeBlack, "A Garden in the Wilderness," 114; Ford Diary, March 16, 1849.

63. Bolton, *Territorial Ambition*, 46.

64. Moneyhon, *The Impact of the Civil War and Reconstruction on Arkansas*, 21–24; DeBlack, "A Garden in the Wilderness," 119, 167.

65. Rich. T. Nicholson to Dear Sir, February 22, 1857, folder 253, BP; Kaye, *Joining Places*, 99.

66. Jno. B. Pelham to Col. Ballard, February 28, 1857, folder 253, BP.

67. Brown Diary, February 18, 28, April 9, 1853; DeBlack, "A Garden in the Wilderness," 119.

68. Newberry, "Clark County Plantation Journal," 404–5.

69. Elmira Hill interview, *BW*, 199, Hannah Jameson interview, *BW*, 165; R. C. Smith interview, *BW*, 390; Hilliard, *Hog Meat and Hoe Cake*, 176–77.

70. Jno. B. Pelham to Col. Ballard, April 4, 1857, folder 256, BP; Jno. B. Pelham to Col. Ballard, February 28, 1857, folder 253, BP; Kaye, *Joining Places*, 99.

71. H. L. Berry to Col. Ballard, April 23, 1859, folder 306, BP; Brown Diary, May 10, 13–14, 1853; Newberry, "Clark County Plantation Journal," 405; Gray, *Agriculture in the Southern United States*, 702.

72. Frank Briles interview, *BW*, 1.

73. Shugart Plantation Journal, May 7, 1839.

74. Jno. B. Pelham to Col. Ballard, February 28, 1857, folder 253, BP.

75. Jno. B. Pelham to Col. Ballard, March 4, 8, 1857, folder 254, BP; Henry C. Buckner to Col. R. C. Ballard, March 20, 1860, folder 327, BP.

76. H. L. Berry to Col. Ballard, May 8, 14, 1859, subseries 1.3, folder 307, BP; H. L. Berry to Col. Ballard, June 1, 1859, folder 308, BP; H. L. Berry to Col. Ballard, July 25, 1859, folder 311, BP; H. L. Berry to Col. Ballard, June 20, 1859, folder 309, folder 311, BP; H. L. Berry to Col. Ballard, July 9, 1859, folder 310, BP; DeBlack, "A Garden in the Wilderness," 118.

77. Jno. B. Pelham to Col. Ballard, April 4, 1857, folder 256, BP.

78. Hauser, "'Scarce fit for anything but Slaves and Brutes,'" 114, 118–21.

79. Brown Diary, June 30, July 1, 1853; H. L. Berry to Col. Ballard, July 25, 1859, folder 311, BP; H. L. Berry to Col. Ballard, August 16, 1859, folder 306, BP; DeBlack, "A Garden in the Wilderness," 157–58.

80. Brown Diary, July 14, 17, 27, 31, August 2, 4, 5, 11, 1852, August 8, 15–16, 1853; Jno. B. Pelham to Dear Sir, December 11, 1857, folder 264, BP; H. L. Berry to Col. Ballard, July 25, 1859, folder 311, BP; Newberry, "Clark County Plantation Journal," 407, 408.

232 / NOTES TO CHAPTER 4

81. Newberry, "Clark County Plantation Journal," 406–8; Berry, *Swing the Sickle for the Harvest Is Ripe*, 3.
82. Brown Diary, July 4, 1853.
83. H. L. Berry to Col. Ballard, July 15, 1859, folder 308, BP.
84. Stewart, *"What Nature Suffers to Groe,"* 121.
85. Olmstead and Rhode, "Biological Innovation and Productivity Growth," 1142; Newberry, "Clark County Plantation Journal," 408; Jno. B. Pelham to Col. Ballard, September 16, 1857, folder 259, BP; *BW*, 371, 4, 102, 305, 244, 124, 216.
86. Hahn, *Nation under Our Feet*, 21–22.
87. Shugart Plantation Journal, August 2, 3, 1839; Jno. B. Pelham to Dear Col., September 16, 1857, folder 259, BP.
88. Brown Diary, September 10, 24, 1853.
89. Jno. B. Pelham to Dear Col., September 16, 1857, folder 259, BP.
90. H. L. Berry to Col. Ballard, July 25, 1859, folder 311, BP; H. L. Berry to Col. Ballard, August 22, 1859, folder 313, BP.
91. Brown Diary, October 13, November 9, 1852.
92. Jno. B. Pelham to Dear Col., October 26, 1857, folder 261, BP; H. L. Berry to Col. Ballard, August 22, 1859, folder 313, BP.
93. Brown Diary, October 13, November 6, 1852, January 14, 25, August 30, 1853; Jno. B. Pelham to Col. Ballard, December 5, 1857, folder 264, BP.
94. Walker Diary, Stebbins Supplement, folder 6.
95. Brown Diary, September 3, 12, 1853.
96. Newberry, "Clark County Plantation Journal," 408; Jno. B. Pelham to Ballard, October 23, 1857, folder 261, BP.
97. Baptist, *The Half Has Never Been Told*, 134–36, 361, 363; Beckert, *Empire of Cotton*, 104–5, 114–15; Olmstead and Rhode, "Biological Innovation and Productivity Growth."
98. Brown Diary, August 20, October 14, 1852.
99. Brown Diary, January 10, 1853.
100. Brown Diary, January 12, February 24, March 12, 1853.
101. Shugart Plantation Journal, August 25, September 2, 17, October 1, 1839.
102. Hilliard Diary, October 11, 1849.
103. Jno. B. Pelham to Col. Ballard, September 16, 1857, folder 259, BP; Jno. B. Pelham to Dear Col., October 26, 1857, folder 261, BP; Jno. B. Pelham to Dear Col., November 25, 1857, folder 263, BP.
104. Jno. B. Pelham to Col. Ballard, October 13, 1857, folder 260, BP.
105. Pelham to Ballard, September 16, October 13, 1857.
106. Jno. B. Pelham to Dear Col., December 13, 1857, folder 265, BP.
107. Jno. B. Pelham to Col. Ballard, October 23, 1857, folder 261, BP; Jno. B. Pelham to Col. Ballard, October 26, 1857 and October 30, 1857, folder 261, BP; Jno. B. Pelham to Col. Ballard, November 25, 1857, folder 263, BP.
108. Jno. B. Pelham to Col. Ballard, November 2, 13, 1857, folder 262, BP; Jno. B. Pelham to Col. Ballard, December 18, 1857, folder 265, BP.
109. Peter Brown interview, *BW*, 262. Daniel blamed these violent escalations on Scott's intemperance with whiskey. Bolsterli, *Remembrance of Eden*, 36.
110. *Brunson v. Martin* (1856), series 1, box 19, folder 307, pp. 13–19, Arkansas Supreme Court Briefs and Records.

111. Newberry, "Clark County Plantation Journal," 402, 409; DeBlack, "A Garden in the Wilderness," 96.

112. Brown Diary, November 12, 18, 1852, October 3, 6, 7, 17, November 4, 1853; Newberry, "Clark County Plantation Journal," 403.

113. Brown Diary, September 1–2, 1853; H. L. Berry to Col. Ballard, October 25, 31, 1859, folder 317, BP; Newberry, "Clark County Plantation Journal," 408; Jno. B. Pelham to Col. Ballard, October 16, 1857, folder 260, BP; Jno. B. Pelham to Col. Ballard, November 13, 1857, folder 262, BP; Jno. B. Pelham to Col. Ballard, November 27, 1857, folder 263, BP; John Bates interview, *BW*, 318; Hilliard, *Hog Meat and Hoe Cake*, 137.

114. Hannah Jameson interview, *BW*, 165.

115. Columbus Williams interview, *BW*, 376; Louis Davis interview, *BW*, 434; Pate Newton interview, WPA Early Settlers' Personal History Interviews.

116. Moneyhon, *The Impact of the Civil War and Reconstruction on Arkansas*, 21–24; U.S. Bureau of the Census, Seventh Census of the U.S., 1850, Productions of Agriculture and Slave Inhabitants, Phillips County, AR.

117. Ford Diary, December 25, 1848; Brown Diary, December 25, 1853; O. W. Green interview, *BW*, 48; H. L. Berry to Col. Ballard, December 30, 1858, folder 296, BP.

118. Cindy Kinsey interview, *BW*, 330; Molly Finley interview, *BW*, 24; Louis Davis interview, *BW*, 434; Sargent report.

119. Charlie McClendon interview, *BW*, 206; Bolsterli, *Remembrance of Eden*, 34.

120. Brown Diary, December 25–30, 1853.

121. DeBlack, "A Garden in the Wilderness," 114; Ford Diary, December 23–24, 1848; Newberry, "Clark County Plantation Journal," 409.

122. Bolsterli, *Remembrance of Eden*, 69 (quotations); Pate Newton interview, WPA Early Settlers' Personal History Interviews.

123. Ford Diary, December 24, 1848, January 14, February 11, March 18, 1849.

124. Shugart Plantation Journal, December 21, 23, 1839; Kaye, *Joining Places*, 99; Newberry, "Clark County Plantation Journal," 403.

125. Hilliard, *Hog Meat and Hoe Cake*, 98, 93–94, 107–9, 132–34.

126. U.S. Bureau of the Census, Eighth Census of the United States, 1860, Free Inhabitants, Slave Inhabitants and Productions of Agriculture, Phillips County, AR.

127. U.S. Bureau of the Census, Eighth Census of the United States, 1860, Slave Inhabitants and Productions of Agriculture, Ouachita and Izard Counties, AR.

128. DeBlack, "A Garden in the Wilderness," 105; Stewart, "From King Cane to King Cotton," 68; Brown Diary, November 27, 29, 1852; Ford Diary, February 11, 1849; Newberry, "Clark County Plantation Journal," 405; Nelson Densen interview, *BW*, 38; Hilliard, *Hog Meat and Hoe Cake*, 117–18.

129. Hilliard Diary, May 3–4, 1850; Ford Diary, January 28, March 10, 1849.

130. Shugart Plantation Journal, January 1, 1839; Newberry, "Clark County Plantation Journal," 407; Doc Quinn interview, *BW*, 242; John Bates interview, *BW*, 318.

131. Cornelius was found guilty and sentenced to a year in prison. By then, Clift was dead and at least one of Cornelius's accusers was himself imprisoned for theft. U.S. Bureau of the Census, Eighth Census of the United States, Free Inhabitants and Slave Inhabitants, 1860, Saline County, AR; transcript, *Elihu Cornelius v. the State* (1850).

132. Bolsterli, *Remembrance of Eden*, 59–60.

133. Shugart Plantation Journal, February 16, 1839.

234 / NOTES TO CHAPTER 5

134. Charley Ross interview, *BW*, 60; Hannah Jameson interview, *BW*, 165; Louis Davis interview, *BW*, 433; Louis Young interview, *BW*, 298.
135. Bolsterli, *Remembrance of Eden*, 34.
136. Hannah Allen interview, *BW*, 353; John Bates interview, *BW*, 318; Columbus Williams interview, *BW*, 376; Hannah Jameson interview, *BW*, 164–65.
137. Gould, *Digest of the Statutes of Arkansas*, 373–74.
138. Louis Young interview, *BW*, 297.
139. Lucretia Alexander interview, *BW*, 413; Speed testimony, p. 33, American Freedmen's Inquiry Commission.
140. George Kye interview, *BW*, 67.
141. Sweetie Ivery Wagoner interview, *BW*, 22.
142. Columbus Williams interview, *BW*, 376; Reuben [Blackwell] to Bronson Burton Beardsley, April 2, 1852, quoted in Malloy, "'The Health of Our Family,'" 98.
143. Bolsterli, *Remembrance of Eden*, 37; Minnie Johnson Stewart interview, *BW*, 167.
144. Dinah Perry interview, *BW*, 210; Mandy Tucker interview, *BW*, 214; Harriett McFarlin Payne interview, *BW*, 30; George Kye interview, *BW*, 66–67; Bolsterli, *Remembrance of Eden*, 59–60.
145. Bolsterli, *Remembrance of Eden*, 60.
146. Bolsterli, *Remembrance of Eden*, 61; Molly Finley interview, *BW*, 24.
147. James Speed testimony, p. 33.
148. Charlie Norris interview, *BW*, 368; Emma Moore interview, *BW*, 15.
149. Joe Ray interview, *BW*, 142; Molly Finley interview, *BW*, 24; Columbus Williams interview, *BW*, 376; Emma Moore interview, *BW*, 15; Adeline Blakely, Malinda Sutton, William Smith, Harry Parker, Pate Newton, Primus Moore, WPA Early Settlers' Personal History Interviews; Camp, *Closer to Freedom*, 32–33.
150. Hannah Jameson interview, *BW*, 165; Hannah Allen interview, *BW*, 353.
151. Bolsterli, *Remembrance of Eden*, 37, 41.
152. H. L. Berry to R. C. Ballard, January 15, 1859, folder 299, BP.
153. Scott Bond interview, *BW*, 73–74; Sweetie Ivery Wagoner interview, *BW*, 23; Ellen Briggs Thompson interview, *BW*, 169.
154. Camp, *Closer to Freedom*, 193–94.
155. Lucretia Alexander interview, *BW*, 413; Jno. B. Pelham to Dear Col., April 28, 1857, folder 257, BP.
156. Joe Ray interview, *BW*, 142.
157. U. S. Bureau of the Census, Seventh Census of the United States, 1850, Free Inhabitants, Slave Inhabitants, and Productions of Agriculture, AR; U.S. Bureau of the Census, Eighth Census of the United States, 1860, Free Inhabitants, Slave Inhabitants, and Productions of Agriculture, AR; Beckert, *Empire of Cotton*, 104. Georgia's, Tennessee's, and South Carolina's share decreased.

5 / The Material of Survival

1. Smith, *African American Environmental Thought*, 28; Casey, *Getting Back into Place*, 23.
2. Penningroth, *The Claims of Kinfolk*; Camp, *Closer to Freedom*; Fett, *Working Cures*; Forret, *Race Relations at the Margins*; Kaye, *Joining Places*, 103–4, 112–13.

3. John Bates interview, *BW*, 316.
4. Oscar Felix Junell interview, *BW*, 257; Vlach, *Back of the Big House*, 156–57.
5. John B. Pelham to Col. Ballard, March 8, 1857, folder 254, BP.
6. Minnie Johnson Stewart interview, *BW*, 169; Plomer Harshaw interview, *BW*, 6; George Kye interview, *BW*, 66–67; William Brown interview, *BW*, 88; John Bates interview, *BW*, 316; Columbus Williams interview, *BW*, 376; Peggy Sloan interview, *BW*, 107; Betty Brown interview, *BW*, 128; Joe Ray interview, *BW*, 142; Katie Rowe interview, *BW*, 145; Louis Davis interview, *BW*, 431.
7. R. C. Smith interview, *BW*, 390; Melinda Pollard interview, *BW*, 19; T. W. Cotton interview, *BW*, 245; George Kye interview, *BW*, 66.
8. Bolsterli, *Remembrance of Eden*, 32; Vlach, *Back of the Big House*, 155–56; Mandy Tucker interview, *BW*, 215; Joe Bean interview, *BW*, 382; Lou Fergusson interview, *BW*, 142; Charles Green Dortch interview, *BW*, 96; George Washington Claridy interview, *BW*, 162; Columbus Williams interview, *BW*, 376; George Kye interview, *BW*, 66; Harriet McFarlin Payne interview, *BW*, 3.
9. Casey, *Getting Back into Place*, 117; Relph, *Place and Placelessness*; Tuan, *Space and Place*, 144–45, 138. The abundance of studies on bondspeople's social and cultural lives owes much to John Blassingame's classic *The Slave Community*; "labor camp" is used throughout Baptist, *The Half Has Never Been Told*; Camp, *Closer to Freedom*.
10. Mollie Barber interview, *BW*, 261.
11. Word's mother was purchased from Phil Ford in Kentucky and taken by Bill Word to Arkansas. Sam Word interview, *BW*, 35; Bond's father was the nephew of someone who had hired Bond's mother's labor from a previous master. Scott Bond interview, *BW*, 77.
12. Casey, *Getting Back into Place*, 31; Solomon Lambert interview, *BW*, 248; Columbus Williams interview, *BW*, 376; Benberry and Dobard, *A Piece of My Soul*, 12–13, 16–17; Alice Trammell, "Floral Applique," created before 1912, from Michigan State University Museum, Michigan Quilt Project Quilt Index, http://quiltindex.org/2018/view/?type=fullrec&kid=27-92-57163 (accessed December 18, 2018); U.S. Bureau of the Census, Eighth Census of the United States, 1860, Free Inhabitants and Slave Inhabitants, Union County, AR.
13. Louis Davis interview, *BW*, 434; Adeline Blakely interview, *BW*, 380.
14. Joe Bean interview, *BW*, 381; Bolsterli, *Remembrance of Eden*, 87–88; Rebecca Thomas interview, *BW*, 340; James Bertrand interview, *BW*, 186. Bertrand was probably enslaved by partners C. P. Bertrand and J. Scull, of Jefferson County. U.S. Bureau of the Census, Eighth Census of the United States, 1860, Slave Inhabitants, Jefferson County, AR; John B. Pelham to Col. Ballard, March 22, 1857, folder 255, BP.
15. *Washington Telegraph*, April 18, 1849; Glymph, *Out of the House of Bondage*, 87.
16. Louis Davis interview, *BW*, 432; Peggy Sloan interview, *BW*, 107; Charley Ross interview, *BW*, 60; Charles Green Dortch interview, *BW*, 96; George Kye interview, *BW*, 66–67; Ellen Briggs Thompson interview, *BW*, 170; Scott Bond interview, *BW*, 73–74.
17. Charley Ross interview, *BW*, 60; George Kye interview, *BW*, 67; Joe Ray interview, *BW*, 143; Hannah Allen interview, *BW*, 353.
18. Evelyn Jones interview, *BW*, 235; Callie Washington interview, *BW*, 416; Bolsterli, *Remembrance of Eden*, 62–64; Camp, *Closer to Freedom*, 60.
19. Cindy Kinsey interview, *BW*, 328; George Kye interview, *BW*, 67.

20. Evelyn Jones interview, *BW*, 235.

21. Bolsterli, *Remembrance of Eden*, 62.

22. Kennard then gave Mary Overton to his daughter, who married a doctor named James Cox. The Coxes moved Mary Overton to Hill County, Texas. Mary Overton interview, *BW*, 53.

23. Callie Washington interview, *BW*, 418; Fannie Sime interview, *BW*, 370; Hannah Jameson interview, *BW*, 165; Solomon Lambert interview, *BW*, 250.

24. W. G. Sargent to Col. John Eaton Jr., July 1, 1864, Records of United States Army Continental Commands (Record Group 393), Part I, Geographical Divisions, Departments, and Military (Reconstruction) Districts, file G-103, series "Letters Received, 1864–67" (entry 269).

25. Zenia Culp interview, *BW*, 366; Solomon Lambert interview, *BW*, 248.

26. Ellen Briggs Thompson interview, *BW*, 169.

27. Cora Scroggins interview, *BW*, 173; White and White, *Stylin'*, 32–33.

28. Harriett McFarlin Payne interview, *BW*, 31; O'Neil, "Bosses and Broomsticks."

29. Kaye, *Joining Places*, 73–74; West, *Chains of Love*, 31–32; see also Hunter, *Bound in Wedlock*.

30. Casey, *Getting Back into Place*, 175; Dock Wilborn interview, *BW*, 296; Harriett McFarlin Payne interview, *BW*, 31; Lou Fergusson interview, *BW*, 141; Columbus Williams interview, *BW*, 377; Kaye, *Joining Places*, 55–61.

31. W. G. Sargent to Col. John Eaton Jr., July 1, 1864, Records of United States Army Continental Commands (Record Group 393), Part I, Geographical Divisions, Departments, and Military (Reconstruction) Districts, file G-103, series "Letters Received, 1864–67" (entry 269), National Archives and Records Administration, Washington, DC.

32. Affidavit of Hueston Blackburn, Eliza Frazier Pension Application no. 220802, for service of Simon Frazier (54th USCT), Civil War and Later Pension Files.

33. Affidavit of Walker Frazier, Eliza Frazier Pension Application, Civil War and Later Pension Files.

34. John Holt interview, *BW*, 384.

35. For a treatment of marriage and separation, see Williams, *Help Me to Find My People*.

36. Peggy Sloan interview, *BW*, 107; Laura Shelton interview, *BW*, 124; Swanson, *Remaking Wormsloe Plantation*, 76.

37. Hilliard, *Hog Meat and Hoe Cake*, 64; George Kye interview, *BW*, 67; Charles Green Dortch interview, *BW*, 96; Fannie Parker interview, *BW*, 121; Senia Rassberry interview, *BW*, 211; Callie Washington interview, *BW*, 416; T. W. Cotton interview, *BW*, 246.

38. T. W. Cotton interview, *BW*, 246.

39. Joe Bean interview, *BW*, 382; Laura Shelton interview, *BW*, 125; Sweetie Ivery Wagoner interview, *BW*, 22; Cyntha Jones interview, *BW*, 119; U.S. Bureau of the Census, Eighth Census of the United States, 1860, Slave Inhabitants, Drew County, AR; U.S. Bureau of the Census, Seventh Census of the United States, 1850, Slave Inhabitants, Drew County, AR; Bolsterli, *Remembrance of Eden*, 73; Jno B. Pelham to Col. Ballard, February 26, 28, 1857, folder 253, BP; Jno B. Pelham to Col. Ballard, March 4, 1857, folder 254, BP; Adrianna Kerns interview, *BW*, 101.

40. Steckel, "A Dreadful Childhood"; T. W. Cotton interview, *BW*, 245. Charlie Norris said his mother told him that sometimes she would breastfeed the white babies,

and sometimes Susan Murphy, her enslaver, would breastfeed him while she was out working. Charlie Norris interview, *BW*, 368.

41. Sallie Crane interview, *BW*, 137; Emma Moore interview, *BW*, 15.

42. Adrianna Kerns interview, *BW*, 101; Tom Haynes interview, *BW*, 117.

43. George Kye interview, *BW*, 67; J. F. Boone interview, *BW*, 397; Peggy Sloan interview, *BW*, 107; John Young interview, *BW*, 127.

44. Jane Osbrook interview, *BW*, 259.

45. Mary Myhand interview, *BW*, 45.

46. Joe Bean interview, *BW*, 382; Louis Lucas interview, *BW*, 203.

47. Solomon Lambert interview, *BW*, 250; Molly Finley interview, *BW*, 24; Joe Ray interview, *BW*, 142; Hannah Jameson interview, *BW*, 164; Callie Washington interview, *BW*, 418; Joe Bean interview, *BW*, 382.

48. Joe Ray interview, *BW*, 143; Norman Burkes interview, *BW*, 364; Louis Young interview, *BW*, 297; Sweetie Ivery Wagoner interview, *BW*, 22; Zenia Culp interview, *BW*, 366; Columbus Williams interview, *BW*, 376; note dated March 15, appended to John B. Pelham to Col. Ballard, March 14, 1857, folder 255, BP; Louis Davis interview, *BW*, 432; Adeline Blakely interview, *BW*, 380; Hannah Jameson interview, *BW*, 164.

49. Augustus Robinson interview, *BW*, 50.

50. Dock Wilborn interview, *BW*, 296; Jesse Meeks interview, *BW*, 120; George Kye interview, *BW*, 67; Charlie Hinton interview, *BW*, 201; Mandy Tucker interview, *BW*, 214; T. W. Cotton interview, *BW*, 245–46.

51. Sallie Crane interview, *BW*, 137; Columbus Williams interview, *BW*, 376; Parrish Washington interview, *BW*, 216; Bolsterli, *Remembrance of Eden*, 60, 74.

52. Callie Washington interview, *BW*, 418; Molly Finley interview, *BW*, 24; Ellen Briggs Thompson interview, *BW*, 169; Bob Benford interview, *BW*, 362; John Bates interview, *BW*, 318; Cindy Kinsey interview, *BW*, 330.

53. Curry, "Belger Cauthron"; Zenia Culp interview, *BW*, 366.

54. Callie Washington interview, *BW*, 416; John Bates interview, *BW*, 316. See also Scott Giltner, "Slave Hunting and Fishing in the Antebellum South," in *"To Love the Wind and the Rain,"* ed. Glave and Stoll, 21–36.

55. Hilliard Diary, April 12, 1850.

56. Pate Newton interview, WPA Early Settlers' Personal History Interviews; Bolsterli, *Remembrance of Eden*, 33; McNeilly, *Old South Frontier*, 127.

57. Hilliard, *Hog Meat and Hoe Cake*, 72, 76; Giltner, "Slave Hunting and Fishing in the Antebellum South," 25–26.

58. Johnson, *River of Dark Dreams*, 231; *BW*, 382, 428; *Ridge v. Featherston* (1854), 15 Ark. 160; Proctor, *Bathed in Blood*, 144; Giltner, "Slave Hunting and Fishing in the Antebellum South," 27.

59. Mittie Freeman interview, *BW*, 428; Betty Brown interview, *BW*, 129; Hannah Allen interview, *BW*, 353; Callie Washington interview, 418.

60. Scott Bond interview, *BW*, 74.

61. Doc Quinn interview, *BW*, 242.

62. Shugart Plantation Journal, February 10, 1839; Bolsterli, *Remembrance of Eden*, 75, 89; Joe Bean interview, *BW*, 382.

63. Bolsterli, *Remembrance of Eden*, 58.

64. Hilliard Diary, April 3, 4, 1850.

65. Gould, *Digest of the Statutes of Arkansas*, 1086. Only pelts with both ears qualified.
66. Brown Diary, August 19, 1854.
67. Hilliard Diary, May 15 (quotation), 19, 1850.
68. Callie Washington interview, *BW*, 418; Cindy Kinsey interview, *BW*, 330.
69. Mandy Tucker interview, *BW*, 215; Solomon Lambert interview, *BW*, 248.
70. Louis Davis interview, *BW*, 434.
71. Bob Benford interview, *BW*, 362.
72. Note dated March 15, appended to John B. Pelham to Col. Ballard, March 14, 1857, folder 255, BP.
73. Shugart Plantation Papers, ledger; Molly Finley interview, *BW*, 24–25.
74. Charlie Hinton interview, *BW*, 201. Understanding of mercury's negative effects was growing. "Mercury," *Medical News-paper; or, The Doctor and the Physician*, February 5, 1822.
75. Stewart, "From King Cane to King Cotton," 61; Liza Smith interview, *BW*, 425.
76. Henry Turner interview, *BW*, 290; Liza Smith interview, *BW*, 425; Stewart, "What Nature Suffers to Groe," 142.
77. Birch, "A Comparative Analysis of Nineteenth Century Pharmacopoeias in the Southern United States," 431.
78. Moerman, *Native American Medicinal Plants*, 135; Louis Davis interview, *BW*, 435.
79. Slippery Elm remains a popular and effective herbal supplement. Moerman, *Native American Medicinal Plants*, 494–95; Moreland, "Traditional Uses of Ten Herbs in Relation to Their Current Pharmacognosy," 186–88; USDA National Plant Data Center, Plant Fact Sheet, plants.usda.gov (accessed October 19, 2019).
80. Hulda Williams interview, *BW*, 218.
81. Eda Rains interview, *BW*, 334; USDA National Plant Data Center, Plant Fact Sheet.
82. Callie Washington interview, *BW*, 419.
83. Cindy Kinsey interview, *BW*, 329; Louis Davis interview, *BW*, 434; Callie Washington interview, *BW*, 419.
84. Liza Smith interview, *BW*, 425; Joe Ray interview, *BW*, 143.
85. Mandy Tucker interview, *BW*, 214; Bolsterli, *Remembrance of Eden*, 60.
86. Fett, *Working Cures*, 118, 6.
87. Stewart, "Slavery and African American Environmentalism," 14.
88. George Kye interview, *BW*, 67; Stewart, "What Nature Suffers to Groe," 141, 144–45.
89. O. W. Green interview, *BW*, 48.
90. Wagram Plantation Journal.
91. Zenia Culp interview, *BW*, 366; Scott Bond interview, *BW*, 73–74.
92. Betty Robertson Coleman interview, *BW*, 4.
93. Katie Rowe interview, *BW*, 148.
94. Because Harmon Bishop's neighbor was slaveholder Samuel R. Jones and family, it seems likely that Sallie Crane had been whipped at his house, and Betty Jones may have been from the neighboring place. Sallie Crane interview, *BW*, 136–37; Minnie Stewart Johnson interview, *BW*, 167; J. F. Boone interview, *BW*, 397; U.S. Bureau of the Census, Eighth Census of the United States, 1860, Free Inhabitants and Slave Inhabitants, Hempstead County, AR.

95. Columbus Williams interview, *BW*, 375.
96. Nate's story is told in greater detail in Jones, "'A Rough, Saucy Set of Hands to Manage,'" 1, 16–17.
97. Bolsterli, *Remembrance of Eden*, 36.
98. Penningroth, *The Claims of Kinfolk*, 6.
99. Betty Brown interview, *BW*, 129; Stewart, "Slavery and African American Environmentalism," 14.
100. Sam Word interview, *BW*, 34–35.
101. Bolsterli, *Remembrance of Eden*, 72–73, 78.
102. R. C. Smith interview, *BW*, 390–91.
103. Hannah Allen interview, *BW*, 353.
104. Mollie Barber interview, *BW*, 260.
105. Brown Diary, October 21, 25, 26, November 7, 14–18, 29, December 2, 5–9, 14, 1853.
106. Ellen Briggs Thompson interview, *BW*, 170.
107. Smith, *African American Environmental Thought*, 19; Elmira Hill interview, *BW*, 199; Hannah Jameson interview, *BW*, 164; Hahn, *Nation under Our Feet*, 31; Pargas, *The Quarters and the Fields*, 97.
108. Penningroth, *The Claims of Kinfolk*, 6; Katie Rowe interview, *BW*, 147.
109. *Pleasant v. The State* (1853), 13 Ark. 363. A witness for the defense testified that Sophia had once served an enslaved woman at her table.
110. Katie Rowe interview, *BW*, 147.
111. R. C. Smith interview, *BW*, 391; Columbus Williams interview, *BW*, 377; Laura Shelton interview, *BW*, 124; Annie Page interview, *BW*, 369.
112. Jones, "'A Rough, Saucy Set of Hands to Manage,'" 13.
113. McNeilly, *Old South Frontier*, 127.
114. Kaye, *Joining Places*, 103–9, 114, 186, 221; Carey, *Sold Down the River*, 99–103, 43.
115. Forret, *Race Relations at the Margins*, 33.
116. Gould, *Digest of the Statutes of Arkansas*, 1032, 1035, 1051–52, 382, 1031; Ford Diary, December 15, 1848.
117. Lack, "Urban Slave Community," 263–66, 258; Matilda A. Harbison Claim, Claim #9868, Southern Claims Commission.
118. John Dodson and Wesley Dodson testimony, Wesley Dodson Approved Claim #19121, Southern Claims Commission; U.S. Bureau of the Census, Eighth Census of the United States, 1860, Slave Inhabitants, Washington County, AR.
119. Pargas, *The Quarters and the Fields*, 89, 94.
120. James, who was twenty years old at the time, had run away from James McCray of Hinds County, Mississippi. Rich. T. Nicholson to R. C. Ballard, February 5, 1857, folder 252, BP; Jno. B. Pelham to Col. Ballard, April 28, 1857, folder 257, BP.
121. Genovese, *Roll, Jordan, Roll*, 623; Johnson, *River of Dark Dreams*, 214, 215.
122. Cyntha Jones interview, *BW*, 118.
123. Lack, "Urban Slave Community," 274.
124. Ford Diary, December 17.
125. Solomon Lambert interview, *BW*, 249.
126. Hahn, *Nation under Our Feet*, 25–26.
127. Johnson, *River of Dark Dreams*, 211; Fields, "Dysplacement and Southern History," 21.

6 / Battlegrounds

1. Moneyhon, *The Impact of the Civil War and Reconstruction on Arkansas*, 97; *Journal of Both Conventions of the State of Arkansas*, 41–49 (quotation); DeBlack, *With Fire and Sword*, 24.

2. The historiography of Civil War Arkansas is rich but lacks much from the point of view of enslaved people. Moneyhon's *The Impact of the Civil War and Reconstruction on Arkansas* includes discussion of the wartime condition of bondspeople in the course of surveying the effect of the war on the state, finding that the Civil War "caused changes in slavery, appearing to be on the verge of destroying it even behind Confederate lines" (122). Surveys of the war, like DeBlack's *With Fire and Sword*, advance our understanding of wartime Arkansas but are not designed to deeply investigate the lives of bondspeople in wartime. *Civil War Arkansas, 1863*, by Mark Christ, includes the effects of the Emancipation Proclamation and the flight of black Arkansans to Union lines, but it is not in the scope of that study to dig deeply into life among enslaved people as the battles raged. Further, Moneyhon has contributed to the literature on the transition from slavery to freedom with an article that details the labor of freedpeople on federally owned and operated cotton plantations. Moneyhon, "From Slave to Free Labor"; DeBlack, *With Fire and Sword*; Christ, *Civil War Arkansas*.

3. William Smith, WPA Early Settlers' Personal History Interviews.

4. Ryan Poe demonstrates that both enslaved people's and white officials' actions influenced emancipation in southwest Arkansas in "The Contours of Emancipation." For the historiography of emancipation, see McPherson, "Who Freed the Slaves?"; Joseph P. Reidy, "Emancipation," in *A Companion to the Civil War and Reconstruction*, ed. Ford, 277–98; introduction to *Beyond Freedom*, ed. Blight and Downs, 1–7.

5. Hahn, *Nation under Our Feet*, 65–66; Adrianna Kerns interview, *BW*, 102.

6. Carl H. Moneyhon, "1861: 'The Die Is Cast,'" *Rugged and Sublime*, ed. Christ, 3.

7. For Arkansas's secession, see Gigantino, *Slavery and Secession in Arkansas*; Stephens, "Cornerstone Address."

8. Italics added. *Journal of Both Conventions of the State of Arkansas*, 382.

9. Cutrer, *Theater of a Separate War*, 14–23, 33–61; for guerilla warfare, see Sutherland, *Savage Conflict*; Stith, *Extreme Civil War*.

10. Clampitt, "The Civil War and Reconstruction in Indian Territory," 121–28; Warde, *When the Wolf Came*, 48–49. See also Krauthamer, *Black Slaves, Indian Masters*.

11. Simons, *In Their Words*, 13; Sargent report.

12. Moneyhon, "1861," 18.

13. In some sources the man's name is spelled Pendergrass. Pulaski County Indictment Book C, pp. 435–36; U.S. Bureau of the Census, Eighth Census of the United States, 1860, Free Inhabitants, Pulaski County, AR.

14. *Mary v. The State* (1862), 24 Ark. 50; Pulaski County Indictment Book C, 436–37, 441.

15. Testimony of Robert Houston and Mingo Scott, Claim of Robert Houston, #21992, Approved Claims, Southern Claims Commission; Melinda Pollard interview, *BW*, 17–18.

16. Mary Estes Peters interview, *BW*, 281.

17. Doc Quinn, *Born in Slavery*. Another version of Quinn's testimony is found in Doc Quinn interview, *BW*, 242–43.

18. In addition to hiding themselves, some bondspeople were directed to hide cotton in their homes and in the cane to avoid its capture by Union forces. Solomon Lambert interview, *BW*, 248–49.

19. Simons, *In Their Words*, 25.

20. Kenneth Rayner to Thomas Ruffin, December 25, 1862, in *Papers of Thomas Ruffin*, ed. Hamilton, 3:282; Berlin et al., *Freedom*, ser. 1, vol. 3, *The Wartime Genesis of Free Labor: The Lower South*, 660.

21. First quotation from William E. Woodruff Papers, second quotation from David H. Reynolds Papers, Special Collections, University of Arkansas, both quoted in Simons, *In Their Words*, 35, 36; Moneyhon, *The Impact of the Civil War and Reconstruction on Arkansas*, 115.

22. Simons, *In Their Words*, 33; Manning, *Troubled Refuge*, 26.

23. DeBlack, *With Fire and Sword*, 60.

24. Shea, "The Aftermath of Prairie Grove," 213; Poorman, "Experience of the Kidd Family." For the significance of the Pea Ridge and Prairie Grove campaigns, see Shea and Hess, *Pea Ridge: Civil War Campaign in the West*; Baxter, *Pea Ridge and Prairie Grove*.

25. Berlin et al., *Freedom* ser. 1, vol. 1, *The Destruction of Slavery*, 249–60; Manning, *Troubled Refuge*, 26.

26. William Shea, "A Semi-Savage State," in *Civil War Arkansas*, ed. Bailey and Sutherland, 95.

27. Christ, *Civil War Arkansas*, 104; Berlin et al., *Freedom*, series 1, vol. 2, *The Wartime Genesis of Free Labor*, 665; Taylor, *Embattled Freedom*, 96; Manning, *Troubled Refuge*.

28. Manning, *Troubled Refuge*, 190–92.

29. Mart A. Stewart, "Walking, Running, and Marching into an Environmental History of the Civil War," in *The Blue, the Gray, and the Green*, ed. Drake, 214–17; Boston Blackwell interview, *BW*, 187.

30. DeBlack, "A Garden in the Wilderness," 193–94.

31. Malloy, "'The Health of Our Family,'" 113, 115; W. G. Sargent to Col. John Eaton Jr., July 1, 1864, Records of United States Army Continental Commands (Record Group 393), Part I, Geographical Divisions, Departments, and Military (Reconstruction) Districts, "Letters Received, 1864–67"; Alfred, enslaved by Jonathan MacLean, returned in spring 1864, possibly because he felt that he was in danger. Simons, *In Their Words*, 116.

32. Affidavit of Aaron Williams, Application of Eliza Frazier, W-220802, Civil War and Later Pension Files; Taylor, *Embattled Freedom*, 61.

33. The Fraziers were owned by John Frazier; Wright Allen was owned by John Marks. Affidavits of Walker Frazier and Emanuel Frazier, Eliza Frazier Pension Application no. 220802, for service of Simon Frazier, Civil War and Later Pension Files; Christ, *Civil War Arkansas*, 104; Steven L. Warren, "Black Union Troops," in *Encyclopedia of Arkansas History and Culture*, ed. Lancaster (accessed October 30, 2020).

34. Hahn, *Nation under Our Feet*, 84.

35. Downs, *Sick from Freedom*, 6, 22; Taylor, *Embattled Freedom*, 112.

36. Christ, *Civil War Arkansas*, 104.

37. Lemke, *Mecklin Letters*, November 30, 1863, p. 28. Mecklin includes the account of a sixteen-year-old boy successfully hiding from Union recruiters on December 30, 1863, p. 31.

38. O. W. Green interview, *BW*, 48; Bureau of Refugees, Freedmen, and Abandoned Lands, Records of the Assistant Commissioner for Arkansas, Register of Rebel Property in Scott, Sebastian, and Crawford Counties Subject to Confiscation; U.S. Bureau of the Census, Eighth Census of the United States, 1860, Slave Inhabitants, Sebastian County, AR.

39. Worthington instantly became the largest slaveholder in the county, by far. There were only 850 slaves in the entire county in the 1860 count: 1864 County Tax Records, Tarrant County, TX; U.S. Bureau of the Census, Eighth Census of the United States, 1860, Slave Inhabitants, Tarrant County, TX; "163: Arkansas Black Woodyard Operator to the Arkansas Freedmen's Bureau Assistant Commissioner," in *Freedom: A Documentary History of Emancipation*, ed. Hayden et al., 530.

40. DeBlack, *With Fire and Sword*, 93, 97; Massey, *Refugee Life in the Confederacy*, 4; Brandon, "Van Winkle's Mill," 435; *Tri-Weekly Telegraph* (Houston), October 7, 1863.

41. Molly Finley interview, *BW*, 24.

42. *Arkansas True Democrat*, April 15, 1863.

43. Myhand was born in White County, Tennessee, taken to Missouri, then to Benton County, Arkansas. Zenia Culp interview, *BW*, 365; Mary Myhand interview, *BW*, 45; Moses Mitchell interview, *BW*, 28; Mandy Thomas interview, *BW*, 373.

44. John Wells interview, *BW*, 69; Senia Rassberry interview, *BW*, 211.

45. Affidavit of John Bradley, H. K. Weatherby, and John W. Miller, Thomas McGehee Application for Arrears of Pay and Bounty, Brief in the Case of Isaac Hobson, Disallowed Claims of U.S. Colored Troops, 1864–1893, 54th USCT, Records of the Pay and Bounty Division, box 60, entry 449, Records of the Accounting Officers of the Department of the Treasury.

46. Wooster, *Civil War Texas*, 33 (quotation); *Marshall Republican*, October 7, 1864; Massey, *Refugee Life in the Confederacy*, 61.

47. Massey, *Refugee Life in the Confederacy*, 64; Wooster, *Civil War Texas*, 32.

48. Massey, *Refugee Life in the Confederacy*, 27; Dougan, *Confederate Arkansas*, 108; Huff, "Guerillas, Jayhawkers and Bushwhackers," 145; Sutherland, "Guerillas," 257; Campbell, *Empire for Slavery*, 246.

49. Civil War Diary of Evan Atwood; Huff, "Guerillas, Jayhawkers and Bushwhackers," 145 (quotation).

50. DeBlack, *With Fire and Sword*, 102; Betty Brown interview, *BW*, 130.

51. B. H. Epperson to Gov. Flanagin, July 28, 1864, Item #917, Kie Oldham Collection, Arkansas History Commission, Little Rock; U.S. Bureau of the Census, Eighth Census of the United States, 1860, Slave Inhabitants, Yell County, AR.

52. Mary Ann Brooks interview, *BW*, 421.

53. Massey, *Refugee Life in the Confederacy*, 95; "A Camden Girl as a Refugee in Texas," Camden Civil War Record Book, Eno Collection, University of Arkansas Libraries, Special Collections, Fayetteville.

54. Moneyhon, *The Impact of the Civil War and Reconstruction in Arkansas*, 133–34; Dougan, *Confederate Arkansas*, 114; "Camden Refugees in Texas," Camden Civil War Record Book, Eno Collection, University of Arkansas Libraries.

55. "Camden Refugees in Texas."

56. Campbell, *Empire for Slavery*, 243–45, 248; John Wells interview, *BW*, 69; Lou Fergusson interview, *BW*, 141.

57. "A Camden Girl as a Refugee in Texas"; Moses Mitchell interview, *BW*, 28.

58. Manning, *Troubled Refuge*, 10; Josephine Howell interview, *BW*, 400.

59. Bolsterli, *Remembrance of Eden*, 70.

60. Bolsterli, *Remembrance of Eden*, 86, 101; Virginia Sims interview, *BW*, 423.

61. Brandon, "Van Winkle's Mill," 434–35; quotation in Carl H. Moneyhon, "Disloyalty and Class Consciousness in Southwestern Arkansas," in *Civil War Arkansas*, ed. Bailey and Sutherland, 124; Bolsterli, *Remembrance of Eden*, 96; Moneyhon, *The Impact of the Civil War and Reconstruction on Arkansas*, 114–15.

62. Johnston, "Bullets for Johnny Reb," in *Civil War Arkansas*, ed. Bailey and Sutherland, 57–58, 69; Bernard Reed, "Saltpeter Mining," in *Encyclopedia of Arkansas History and Culture*, ed. Lancaster (accessed January 4, 2019).

63. DeBlack, *With Fire and Sword*, 61; Shepherd Rhone interview, *BW*, 287.

64. Moneyhon, *The Impact of the Civil War and Reconstruction on Arkansas*, 114–15.

65. Testimony of Robert Houston, Claim of Robert Houston, #21992, Approved Claims, Southern Claims Commission.

66. James Pine Testimony, Heirs of Joseph Deputy Claim, Approved Claims, Southern Claims Commission.

67. Howell Cobb to James A. Seddon, January 8, 1865, transcript, *Encyclopedia of Virginia*, encyclopediavirginia.org (accessed October 30, 2020); John Brown quoted in Moneyhon, "1861," 154; for the myth of black Confederate soldiers debunked, see Levin, *Searching for Black Confederates*.

68. Scott was technically enslaved by Major William Field, the father of Mrs. Rapley. Matilda A. Harbison Claim, Approved Claims, #9868, Southern Claims Commission.

69. Virginia Sims interview, *BW*, 423; Fannie Sims interview, *BW*, 370–71.

70. Matilda Hatchett interview, *BW*, 403.

71. Taylor, *Embattled Freedom*, 132, 136, 99–100; Leslie, "Arabella Lanktree Wilson's Civil War Letter," 264; Stith, *Extreme Civil War*.

72. Lemke, *Mecklin Letters*, January 17, 1864 p. 35, September 19, 1863, p. 16.

73. Lemke, *Mecklin Letters*, pp. 5–6, August 23, 1863, p. 10.

74. Lemke, *Mecklin Letters*, August 23, 1863, p. 10, January 28, 31, 1864, pp. 38, 40, September 19, 1863, p. 16.

75. Sutherland, "Guerillas," 284; Howard, "No County for Old Men," 345–47.

76. Lemke, *Mecklin Letters*, January 24, 1864, p. 37, January 28, 1864, p. 38.

77. One of the measures of loyalty in these claims was whether the claimant risked their life as a Unionist. Thus, there was incentive not only to claim Union loyalty but to claim threats based on that loyalty. Martha Bradley Claim, Claim #315, Records of the Southern Claims Commission.

78. Lemke, *Mecklin Letters*, October 11, 1863, p. 18, November 2, 1863, p. 23, November 9, 1863, p. 24.

79. Lemke, *Mecklin Letters*, September 15, 1863, p. 15.

80. Dane, *Tattered Glory*, 240–41.

81. W. S. Jett, "A Bit of Civil War History by W. S. Jett," in Dane, *Tattered Glory*, 243.

82. Bolsterli, *Remembrance of Eden*, 85; Glymph, *Out of the House of Bondage*, 97–105.

83. Eva Strayhorn interview, *BW*, 224–27.
84. Eva Strayhorn interview, *BW*, 225–27.
85. Taylor, *Embattled Freedom*, 82.
86. James Jackson Testimony, James Jackson Claim.
87. *True Democrat* (Little Rock), July 8, 1863.
88. McKiel claimed loyalty to the union. He eventually represented Phillips County in the state convention to reconstitute Arkansas's government for readmission to the union. Taylor, *Embattled Freedom*, 106–9, 112.
89. Testimony of James Pine, Testimony of Aleck Castile, Heirs of Joseph Deputy Claim, 18147, Records of the Southern Claims Commission; Brig. Genl. Elias S. Dennis to Lt. Col. Willard Slocum, September 24, 1864, Military Commands, 13th AC (Letters Sent), Entry #1944, vol. 17/67.
90. Testimony of Peggy Deputy (first quotation) and Aleck Castile (second and third quotations), Heirs of Joseph Deputy Claim.
91. James Milo Alexander Testimony, Heirs of Joseph Deputy Claim.
92. Clark worked in "old man Alexander's" barber shop until he left again for Nashville, this time with free papers, after the arrival of General Curtis's army in Helena in 1862, when he was sixteen years old. Moses Clark testimony, Heirs of Joseph Deputy Claim.
93. Whayne et al., *Arkansas: A Narrative History*, 214; Poe, "The Contours of Emancipation," 116–19.
94. Katie Rowe interview, *BW*, 144–45.
95. Katie Rowe interview, *BW*, 145; Annie Page interview, *BW*, 369.
96. Moses Mitchell interview, *BW*, 29.
97. Henry Rector, "Speech to the House of Representatives, December 11, 1860," in Gigantino, *Slavery and Secession in Arkansas*, 64; Brig. Gen. Buford to Hon. Sec. of War, December 11, 1863, CN 299 District of Eastern Arkansas, series 4664 (Letters Sent), vol. 37/96, District of Arkansas, pp. 240–42 (#80, 1863).
98. Whayne et al., *Arkansas: A Narrative History*, 225.
99. Taylor, *Embattled Freedom*, 8.

Conclusion

1. Reuben Johnson, "My Struggles for Education," *Christian Recorder*, May 23, 1878; "Blissville, Arkansas," *Harper's Weekly*, June 2, 1866, p. 346.
2. Valencius, *Health of the Country*, 191; W. G. Sargent to Col. John Eaton Jr., July 1, 1864, Records of United States Army Continental Commands (Record Group 393), Part I, Geographical Divisions, Departments, and Military (Reconstruction) Districts, "Letters Received, 1864–67."
3. "319: Freedmen's Bureau Superintendent at Fort Smith, Arkansas, to the Arkansas Freedmen's Bureau Assistant Commissioner," in *Freedom: A Documentary History of Emancipation*, ed. Hayden et al., 935; Fields, "Dysplacement in Southern History," 22.
4. Kenneth Rayner to Thomas Ruffin, July 5, 1869, *Papers of Thomas Ruffin*, ed. Hamilton, 4:223; Cantrell, *Kenneth and John B. Rayner and the Limits of Southern Dissent*, 153–54. Rayner became disconsolate and described his friend and brother-in-law Isaac Hilliard as in a similar state, devolving into a "morbid melancholy, approaching imbecility."
5. Brandon, "Van Winkle's Mill," 443–44.

6. "Black Arkansas Woodyard Operator to the Arkansas Freedmen's Bureau Assistant Commissioner," in *Freedom: A Documentary History of Emancipation*, ed. Hayden et al., 530. The definitive history of the Freedmen's Bureau in Arkansas remains Finley, *From Slavery to Uncertain Freedom*.

7. "35A: Freedmen's Bureau Superintendent for Ashley County, Arkansas, to the Headquarters of the Arkansas Freedmen's Bureau Assistant Commissioner; and the Assistant Commissioner to the Superintendent," in *Freedom: A Documentary History of Emancipation*, ed. Hayden et al., 184–85.

8. "277: Affidavit of an Arkansas Freedman," in *Freedom: A Documentary History of Emancipation*, ed. Hayden et al., 825.

9. Matkin-Rawn, "'The Great Negro State of the Country'"; Barnes, *Journey of Hope*.

Bibliography

Primary Sources

Manuscript and Microfilm Collections

Arkansas State Archives, Little Rock
Bureau of Refugees, Freedmen, and Abandoned Lands. Records of the Assistant Commissioner for Arkansas, Register of Rebel Property in Scott, Sebastian, and Crawford Counties Subject to Confiscation. Volume 78. (Photocopy from National Archives, Washington, DC.)
Civil War Diary of Evan Atwood
Hempstead County Tax Rolls, 1847–1854
Kie Oldham Collection
Pulaski County Indictment Records, 1848–1863
Pulaski County Tax Rolls, 1838
Maggie E. Walker Diary, Stebbins Supplement

Southern Historical Collection, University of North Carolina, Chapel Hill
John Mebane Allen Papers
R. C. Ballard Papers, subseries 1.3

University of Arkansas at Little Rock/Pulaski County Law Library Archives

Arkansas Supreme Court Briefs and Records
Rose v. Rose (1849)
Austin, a Slave v. the State (1854)

Bone v. The State (1856)
Sarah v. The State (1856)

Mullins Library Microfilm Collections, University of Arkansas, Fayetteville
John Brown Diary
Miriam Hilliard Diary
Shugart Plantation Papers

Special Collections, University of Arkansas Libraries, Fayetteville
Cumberland Presbyterian Church Presbytery Records
James Sutherland Deas Papers
Clara Bertha Eno Papers
Horace J. Ford Diary

Freedmen and Southern Society Project Records, College Park Maryland

National Archives and Records Administration, Washington, DC
American Freedmen's Inquiry Commission, Letters Received, ser. 12, Adjutant General's Office, Record Group 94
Civil War and Later Pension Files, Department of Veterans Affairs, Record Group 15
Disallowed Claims of U.S. Colored Troops, 1864–1893, 54th USCT, Records of the Pay and Bounty Division, box 60, entry 449, Records of the Accounting Officers of the Department of the Treasury, Record Group 217
Records of United States Army Continental Commands (Record Group 393), Part I, Geographical Divisions, Departments, and Military (Reconstruction) Districts, "Letters Received, 1864–67"

Fort Worth Library, Fort Worth, Texas
Texas County Tax Lists, 1835–1910

Digital Collections

Territorial Briefs and Records, William H. Bowen School of Law, University of Arkansas at Little Rock, www.arcourts.ualr.edu
William Morrison v. Perly Wallis
Sylvanus Phillips v. Richmond Peeler
William Drop v. John Miller
Marie Celeste Lanusse (nee Macarty) v. William Flanakin
Andrew Latting v. Benjamin Miles
Miller, Montgomery & Crittenden v. Bentley
George Bentley v. William E. Woodruff
Israel Dodge v. Sam Roane

Wright Daniel v. Alexander W. Mitchell
United States v. Osage

WPA Early Settlers' Personal History Interviews, Special Collections, University of Arkansas Libraries libinfo.uark.edu/SpecialCollections/wpa

Fold3, Records of the Southern Claims Commission, fold3.com
Martha Bradley
Heirs of Joseph Deputy
Matilda A. Harbison
Robert Houston
James Jackson

HeritageQuest
California State Census of 1852
Fourth Census of the United States (1820)
Fifth Census of the United Stated (1830)
Sixth Census of the United States (1840)
Seventh Census of the United States (1850)
Eighth Census of the United States (1860)

Published Primary Sources

Arkansas Supreme Court Reports, Vols. 7–19.
Bolsterli, Margaret Jones, ed. *Remembrance of Eden: Harriet Bailey Bullock Daniel's Memories of a Frontier Plantation in Arkansas, 1849–1872.* Fayetteville: University of Arkansas Press, 1993.
Born in Slavery: Slave Narratives from the Federal Writers' Project, 1936–1938. Library of Congress, Folklore Subjects, Social Customs-Reminiscences of an Ex-Slave. *Arkansas Narratives*, Vol. 2. memory.loc.gov.
Confederate Women of Arkansas in the Civil War, 1861–'65: Memorial Reminiscences. Little Rock, AR: H. G. Pugh, 1907.
Dane, Nancy, comp. *Tattered Glory: A Documentary Civil War History of the Arkansas River Valley.* Published by Nancy Dane, 2005.
DeBow, J. D. B. *The Seventh Census of the United States: 1850, Embracing a Statistical View of Each of the States and Territories.* Washington, DC: Robert Armstrong, Public Printer, 1853.
English, E. H. *A Digest of the Statutes of Arkansas; embracing all laws of a general and permanent character in force at the close of the session of the General Assembly of 1846.* Little Rock: Reardon & Garritt, 1848.
Featherstonhaugh, George William. *Excursion through the Slave States: From Washington on the Potomac to the Frontier of Mexico.* J. Murray, 1844.
Gould, Josiah. *A Digest of the Statutes of Arkansas; embracing all laws of a gen-

eral and permanent character, in force at the close of the session of the General Assembly of 1856. Little Rock, AR: Johnson and Yerkes, State Printers, 1858.

Hamilton, J. G. de Roulhac, ed. *The Papers of Thomas Ruffin*. Vols. 3 and 4. Raleigh: Edwards & Beoughton Printing, 1920.

Hempstead, Samuel H. *Reports of Cases Argued and Determined in the United States Superior Court for the Territory of Arkansas . . . And in the United States District Court for the Territory of Arkansas . . . and in the United States Circuit Court for the District of Arkansas . . . 1856*. Boston: Little Brown, 1856.

Journal of Both Conventions of the State of Arkansas. Little Rock, AR: Johnson and Yerkes, State Printers, 1861.

Kennedy, Joseph C. G. *Agriculture of the United States in 1860: Compiled from the original returns of the eighth census, under the direction of the secretary of the interior*. Washington, DC: Government Printing Office, 1864.

Lankford, George E. *Bearing Witness: Memories of Arkansas Slavery, Narratives from the 1930s WPA Collections*. 2nd ed. Fayetteville: University of Arkansas Press, 2006.

Laws of Arkansas Territory, Compiled and arranged by J. Steele and J. M. Campbell, under the direction and superintendence of John Pope, Esq., Governor of the Territory of Arkansas. Little Rock: J. Steele, 1835.

Lemke, Walter J., ed. *The Mecklin Letters, written in 1863–64 at Mt. Comfort by Robert W. Mecklin, the Founder of Ozark Institute*. Fayetteville, AR: Washington County Historical Society, 1955.

"Letters of Matthew Leeper." *Flashback* 33 (May 1983): 26–31.

Newberry, Farrar. "A Clark County Plantation Journal for 1857." *Arkansas Historical Quarterly* 18 (Winter 1959): 401–9.

Weaver, Herbert, and Paul H. Bergeron, eds. *Correspondence of James K. Polk*. Vol. 2, *1833–1834*. Nashville: Vanderbilt University Press, 1972.

Secondary Sources

Arnold, Morris S. *Colonial Arkansas, 1686–1804: A Social and Cultural History*. Fayetteville: University of Arkansas Press, 1991.

Bailey Anne J., and Daniel E. Sutherland, eds. *Civil War Arkansas: Beyond Battles and Leaders*. Fayetteville: University of Arkansas Press, 2000.

Baptist, Edward E. *The Half Has Never Been Told: Slavery and the Making of American Capitalism*. New York: Basic Books, 2014.

Baptist, Edward E., and Stephanie M. H. Camp, eds. *New Studies in the History of American Slavery*. Athens: University of Georgia Press, 2006.

Barile, Kerri, and Jamie C. Brandon, eds. *Household Chores and Household Choices: Theorizing the Domestic Sphere in Historical Archaeology*. Tuscaloosa: University of Alabama Press, 2004.

Barnes, Kenneth C. *Journey of Hope: The Back-to-Africa Movement in Arkansas in the Late 1800s*. Chapel Hill: University of North Carolina Press, 2004.

Battershell, Gary. "The Socioeconomic Role of Slavery in the Upcountry." *Arkansas Historical Quarterly* 58 (Spring 1999): 45–60.
Baxter, William. *Pea Ridge and Prairie Grove, or, Scenes and Incidents of the War in Arkansas*. Fayetteville: University of Arkansas Press, 2000.
Beckert, Sven. *Empire of Cotton: A Global History*. New York: Knopf, 2015.
Beckert, Sven, and Seth Rockman, eds. *Slavery's Capitalism: A New History of American Economic Development*. Philadelphia: University of Pennsylvania Press, 2016.
Benberry, Cuesta, and Raymond Dobard. *A Piece of My Soul: Quilts by Black Arkansans*. Fayetteville: University of Arkansas Press, 2000.
Bennet, Tony, and Patrick Joyce. *Material Powers: Cultural Studies, History and the Material Turn*. London: Routledge, 2010.
Berlin, Ira. *Generations of Captivity: A History of African-American Slaves*. Cambridge, MA: Belknap Press, 2003.
———. *Many Thousands Gone: The First Two Centuries of Slavery in North America*. Cambridge, MA: Belknap Press, 2000.
Berlin, Ira, Barbara J. Fields, Thavolia Glymph, Joseph P. Reidy, and Leslie S. Rowland, eds. *Freedom: A Documentary History of Emancipation, 1861–1867*, ser. 1, vol. 1, *The Destruction of Slavery*. New York: Cambridge University Press, 1985.
Berlin, Ira, Thavolia Glymph, Steven F. Miller, Joseph P. Reidy, Leslie S. Rowland, and Julie S. Saville, eds. *Freedom: A Documentary History of Emancipation, 1861–1867*, ser. 1, vol. 3, *The Wartime Genesis of Free Labor: The Lower South*. New York: Cambridge University Press, 1990.
Berlin, Ira, Steven F. Miller, Joseph P. Reidy, and Leslie S. Rowland, eds. *Freedom: A Documentary History of Emancipation, 1861–1867*, ser. 1, vol. 2, *The Wartime Genesis of Free Labor: The Upper South*. New York: Cambridge University Press, 1993.
Berry, Daina Ramey. *Swing the Sickle for the Harvest Is Ripe: Gender and Slavery in Antebellum Georgia*. Urbana-Champaign: University of Illinois Press, 2007.
Billingsley, Carolyn Earle. *Communities of Kinship: Antebellum Families and the Settlement of the Cotton Frontier*. Athens: University of Georgia Press, 2004.
Biographical and Historical Memoirs of Southern Arkansas. Chicago: Goodspeed Publishing, 1890.
Biographical and Historical Memoirs of Western Arkansas. Chicago: Southern Publishing Company, 1891.
Birch, Joanne L. "A Comparative Analysis of Nineteenth Century Pharmacopoeias in the Southern United States: A Case Study Based on the Gideon Lincecum Herbarium." *Economic Botany* 63 (December 2009): 427–40.
Blackett, R. J. M. *The Captive's Quest for Freedom: Fugitive Slaves, the 1850 Fugi-*

tive Slave Law, and the Politics of Slavery. New York: Cambridge University Press, 2018.

Blassingame, John W. *The Slave Community: Plantation Life in the Antebellum South.* Rev. and enlarged ed. New York: Oxford University Press, 1979.

Blight, David W., and Jim Downs, eds. *Beyond Freedom: Disrupting the History of Emancipation.* Athens: University of Georgia Press, 2017.

Bolton, S. Charles. *Arkansas, 1800–1860: Remote and Restless.* Fayetteville: University of Arkansas Press, 1998.

———. *Fugitives from Injustice: Freedom-Seeking Slaves in Arkansas, 1800–1860.* Omaha, NE: National Park Service, 2006.

———. *Fugitivism: Escaping Slavery in the Lower Mississippi Valley, 1820–1860.* Fayetteville: University of Arkansas Press, 2019.

———. "Slavery and the Defining of Arkansas." *Arkansas Historical Quarterly* 58 (Spring 1999): 1–23.

———. *Territorial Ambition: Land and Society in Arkansas, 1800–1840.* Fayetteville: University of Arkansas Press, 1993.

Bragg, Don C., and Tom Webb. "'As False as the Black Prince of Hades': Resurveying in Arkansas, 1849–1859." *Arkansas Historical Quarterly* 73 (Autumn 2014): 268–92.

Brandon, Jamie. "Van Winkle's Mill: Recovering Lost Industrial and African-American Heritages in the Ozarks." *Arkansas Historical Quarterly* 67 (Winter 2008): 429–45.

Breen, T. H. "Back to Sweat and Toil: Suggestions for the Study of Agricultural Work in Early America." *Pennsylvania History* 49 (October 1982): 241–58.

Brown, Mattie. "River Transportation in Arkansas, 1819–1890." *Arkansas Historical Quarterly* 1 (December 1942): 292–308.

Buchanan, Thomas C. *Black Life on the Mississippi: Slaves, Free Blacks, and the Western Steamboat World.* Chapel Hill: University of North Carolina Press, 2004.

Burke, Diane Mutti. *On Slavery's Border: Missouri's Small-Slaveholding Households, 1815–1865.* Athens: University of Georgia Press, 2010.

Camp, Stephanie H. M. *Closer to Freedom: Enslaved Women and Everyday Resistance in the Plantation South.* Chapel Hill: University of North Carolina Press, 2004.

Campbell, Randolph B. *An Empire for Slavery: The Peculiar Institution in Texas, 1821–1865.* Baton Rouge: Louisiana State University Press, 1989.

Cande, Kathleen. "Rediscovering Davidsonville, Arkansas's First County Seat Town, 1815–1830." *Arkansas Historical Quarterly* 67 (Winter 2008): 342–58.

Cantrell, Gregg. *Kenneth and John B. Rayner and the Limits of Southern Dissent.* Urbana-Champaign: University of Illinois Press, 1993.

Carey, Anthony Gene. *Sold Down the River: Slavery in the Lower Chattahoochee Valley of Alabama and Georgia.* Tuscaloosa: University of Alabama Press, 2011.

Casey, Edward. *Getting Back into Place: Toward a Renewed Understanding of the Place-World.* 2nd ed. Bloomington: Indiana University Press, 2009.
Cash, Marie. "Arkansas Achieves Statehood." *Arkansas Historical Quarterly* 2 (December 1943): 292–308.
Cashin, Joan. *A Family Venture: Men and Women on the Southern Frontier.* New York: Oxford University Press, 1991.
Christ, Mark K. *Civil War Arkansas, 1863.* Norman: University of Oklahoma Press, 2010.
———, ed. *Rugged and Sublime: The Civil War in Arkansas.* Fayetteville: University of Arkansas Press, 1994.
Clampitt, Bradley R. "The Civil War and Reconstruction in Indian Territory: Historiography and Prospects for New Directions in Research." *Civil War History* 64, no. 2 (2018): 121–45.
Colten, Craig E. *Southern Waters: The Limits to Abundance.* Baton Rouge: Louisiana State University Press, 2014.
Cornwall, Joseph H. "Historical Sketch of the Family of Reverend J. A. Cornwall in Arkansas." *Independence County Chronicle* (April–July 1990): 23–40.
Craven, Avery O. *Soil Exhaustion as a Factor in the Agricultural History of Virginia and Maryland.* Reprint. Columbia: University of South Carolina Press, 2006.
Curry, Patricia L. "Belger Cauthron: From Slavery to Freedom and a Tragic Death." *Wagon Wheels* (Logan Co. Historical Society) 10, no. 2 (Summer 1990): 19–21.
Cutrer, Thomas W. *Theater of a Separate War: The Civil War West of the Mississippi River, 1861–1865.* Chapel Hill: University of North Carolina Press, 2017.
DeBlack, Thomas A. "A Garden in the Wilderness: The Johnsons and the Making of Lakeport Plantation, 1831–1876." PhD diss., University of Arkansas, 1995.
———. *With Fire and Sword: Arkansas, 1861–1874.* Fayetteville: University of Arkansas Press, 2003.
Deyle, Steven. *Carry Me Back: The Domestic Slave Trade in American Life.* New York: Oxford University Press, 2005.
Dougan, Michael B. *Confederate Arkansas: The People and Policies of a Frontier State in Wartime.* University: University of Alabama Press, 1976.
Downs, Jim. *Sick from Freedom: African-American Illness and Suffering during the Civil War and Reconstruction.* New York: Oxford University Press, 2012.
Drake, Brian Allen. *The Blue, the Gray, and the Green: Toward an Environmental History of the Civil War.* Athens: University of Georgia Press, 2015.
Dublin, Thomas, and Kathryn Kish Sklar. *Online Biographical Dictionary of the Woman Suffrage Movement in the United States: WASM Edition: Black Women Suffragists.* June 2020. https://documents.alexanderstreet.com/d/1007602873.

DuBois, W. E. Burghardt. *The Souls of Black Folk: Essays and Sketches*. Chicago: A. C. McClurg, 1903.
Duncan, Georgena. "Manumission in the Arkansas River Valley: Three Case Studies." *Arkansas Historical Quarterly* 66 (Winter 2007): 422–43.
———. "'One negro, Sarah . . . one horse named Collier, one cow and calf named Pink.'" *Arkansas Historical Quarterly* 69 (Winter 2010): 325–45.
Dunn, Katie. "Wealth, Slaves, and John Drennen: A Look at an Antebellum Arkansas Businessman." *Journal of the Fort Smith Historical Society* 39 (April 2015): 11–19.
DuVal, Kathleen. "Debating Identity, Sovereignty, and Civilization: The Arkansas Valley after the Louisiana Purchase." *Journal of the Early Republic* 26 (Spring 2006): 25–58.
Elkins, Stanley. *Slavery: A Problem in American Institutional and Intellectual Life*. Chicago: University of Chicago Press, 1959.
Epps, Kristen. *Slavery on the Periphery: The Kansas-Missouri Border in the Antebellum and Civil War Eras*. Athens: University of Georgia Press, 2016.
Fett, Sharla M. *Working Cures: Healing, Health, and Power on Southern Slave Plantations*. Chapel Hill: University of North Carolina Press, 2002.
Fields, Barbara J. "Dysplacement and Southern History." *Journal of Southern History* 82 (February 2016): 7–26.
Finley, Randy. *From Slavery to Uncertain Freedom: The Freedmen's Bureau in Arkansas, 1865–1869*. Fayetteville: University of Arkansas Press, 1996.
Forbes, Robert Pierce. *The Missouri Compromise and Its Aftermath: Slavery and the Meaning of America*. Chapel Hill: University of North Carolina Press, 2007.
Ford, Lacy, ed. *A Companion to the Civil War and Reconstruction*. Malden, MA: Blackwell, 2005.
Forret, Jeff. *Race Relations at the Margins: Slaves and Poor Whites in the Antebellum Southern Countryside*. Baton Rouge: Louisiana State University Press, 2006.
———. *Slave against Slave: Plantation Violence in the Old South*. Baton Rouge: Louisiana State University Press, 2015.
Fox-Genovese, Elizabeth. *Within the Plantation Household: Black and White Women of the Old South*. Chapel Hill: University of North Carolina Press, 1998.
Genovese, Eugene. *Roll, Jordan, Roll: The World the Slaves Made*. New York: Vintage, 1976.
Gigantino, James J., II. *Slavery and Secession in Arkansas: A Documentary History*. Fayetteville: University of Arkansas Press, 2015.
Glave, Dianne D., and Mark Stoll, eds. *"To Love the Wind and the Rain": African Americans and Environmental History*. Pittsburgh: University of Pittsburgh Press, 2006.

Glymph, Thavolia. *Out of the House of Bondage: The Transformation of the Plantation Household.* New York: Cambridge University Press, 2008.
Gray, Lewis C. *History of Agriculture in the Southern United States to 1860.* Vol. 2. Washington, DC: Carnegie Institution of Washington, 1933.
Griffith, Nancy Snell. "Slavery in Independence County." With Appendix 1: "Slave Biographies." Appendix 2: Slave Marriages." Appendix 3: "Slave Transactions." *Independence County Chronicle* (April–July 2000): 5–70.
Gutman, Herbert. *The Black Family in Slavery and Freedom, 1750–1925.* New York: Vintage, 1977.
Hahn, Steven. *A Nation under Our Feet: Black Political Struggles in the Rural South from Slavery to the Great Migration.* Cambridge, MA: Belknap Press of Harvard University Press, 2003.
Hahn, Steven, Steven F. Miller, Susan E. O'Donovan, John C. Rodrigue, and Leslie S. Rowland, eds. *Freedom: A Documentary History of Emancipation, 1861–1867,* ser. 3, vol. 1, *Land and Labor, 1865.* Chapel Hill: University of North Carolina Press, 2008.
Hanson, Gerald T., and Carl H. Moneyhon, eds. *Historical Atlas of Arkansas.* Norman: University of Oklahoma Press, 1989.
Hauser, Jason. "'Scarce fit for anything but Slaves and Brutes': Climate in the Old Southwest, 1798–1855." *Alabama Review* 70 (April 2017): 112–25.
Hayden, René, Anthony E. Kaye, Kate Masur, Steven F. Miller, Susan E. O'Donovan, Leslie S. Rowland, and Stephen A. West, eds. *Freedom: A Documentary History of Emancipation, 1861–1867,* ser. 3, vol. 2, *Land and Labor, 1866–1867.* Chapel Hill: University of North Carolina Press, 2013.
Hazard, Samuel. *The Register of Pennsylvania: Devoted to the Preservation of Facts and Documents, and Every Other Kind of Useful Information Regarding the State of Pennsylvania.* Philadelphia: Printed by W. F. Geddes, 1829.
Hersey, Mark. "Environmental History in the Heart of Dixie." *Alabama Review* 70 (April 2017): 99–111.
Hilliard, Jerry E. "A Frontier Town: Fayetteville." *Flashback* 33 (May 1983): 18–25.
Hilliard, Samuel Bowers. *Hog Meat and Hoe Cake: Food Supply in the Old South, 1840–1860.* Carbondale: Southern Illinois University Press, 1972.
History of Benton, Washington, Carroll, Madison, Crawford, Franklin, and Sebastian Counties . . . Besides a Valuable Fund of Notes, Original, Observations, Etc., Etc. Chicago: Goodspeed Publishing, 1889.
Houston, Kelly E. "Slaveholders and Slaves of Hempstead County, Arkansas." Master's thesis, University of North Texas, 2008.
Howard, Rebecca. "No County for Old Men: Patriarchs and the Guerilla War in Northwest Arkansas." *Arkansas Historical Quarterly* 75 (Winter 2016): 336–54.
Hubbard, Phil, Rob Kitchin, and Gill Valentine, eds. *Key Texts in Human Geography.* London: Sage, 2008.

Huff, Leo. "Guerillas, Jayhawkers and Bushwhackers in Northern Arkansas during the Civil War." *Arkansas Historical Quarterly* 24 (Summer 1965): 127–48.

Hughes, Nathaniel Cheairs. *The Life and Wars of Gideon J. Pillow*. Reprint. Knoxville: University of Tennessee Press, 2011.

Hunter, Tera. *Bound in Wedlock: Slave and Free Black Marriage in the Nineteenth Century*. Cambridge, MA: Belknap Press of Harvard University Press, 2017.

Jaffe, Alexandra. "Transcription in Practice: Nonstandard Orthography." *Journal of Applied Linguistics* 3 (March 2009). DOI: 10.1558/japl.v3i2.163.

Johnson, Walter. *River of Dark Dreams: Slavery and Empire in the Cotton Kingdom*. Cambridge, MA: Harvard University Press, 2012.

———. *Soul by Soul: Life inside the Antebellum Slave Market*. Cambridge, MA: Harvard University Press, 1999.

Jones-Branch, Cherisse, and Gary T. Edwards, eds. *Arkansas Women: Their Lives and Times*. Athens: University of Georgia Press, 2018.

Jones, Jacqueline. *Labor of Love, Labor of Sorrow: Black Women, Work, and the Family, from Slavery to the Present*. New York: Basic Books, 1985.

Jones, Kelly Houston. "Chattels, Pioneers, and Pilgrims for Freedom: Arkansas's Bonded Travelers." *Arkansas Historical Quarterly* 75 (Winter 2016): 319–35.

———. "'A Rough, Saucy Set of Hands to Manage': Slave Resistance in Arkansas." *Arkansas Historical Quarterly* 71 (Spring 2012): 1–21.

Jones-Rogers, Stephanie. *They Were Her Property: White Women as Slave Owners in the American South*. New Haven: Yale University Press, 2019.

Kaye, Anthony. *Joining Places: Slave Neighborhoods in the Old South*. Chapel Hill: University of North Carolina Press, 2007.

———. "The Second Slavery: Modernity in the Nineteenth-Century South and the Atlantic World." *Journal of Southern History* 75 (August 2009): 627–50.

Kennington, Kelly M. *In the Shadow of Dred Scott: St. Louis Freedom Suits and the Legal Culture of Slavery in Antebellum America*. Athens: University of Georgia Press, 2017.

King, Wilma. *Stolen Childhood: Slave Youth in Nineteenth-Century America*. 2nd ed. Bloomington: University of Indiana Press, 2011.

Kolchin, Peter. *American Slavery: 1619–1877*. New York: Hill and Wang, 2003.

Krauthamer, Barbara. *Black Slaves, Indian Masters: Slavery, Emancipation, and Citizenship in the Native American South*. Chapel Hill: University of North Carolina Press, 2013.

Kwas, Mary L. *Digging for History at Old Washington*. Fayetteville: University of Arkansas Press, 2009.

Lack, Paul D. "An Urban Slave Community: Little Rock, 1831–1862." *Arkansas Historical Quarterly* 41 (Autumn 1982): 258–87.

Lancaster, Guy, ed. *Bullets and Fire: Lynching and Authority in Arkansas, 1840–1950*. Fayetteville: University of Arkansas Press, 2018.

———, ed. *The Elaine Massacre and Arkansas: A Century of Atrocity and Resistance, 1819–1919*. Little Rock, AR: Butler Center Books, 2018.

———, ed. *Encyclopedia of Arkansas History and Culture*. Central Arkansas Library System. www.encyclopediaofarkansas.net.

Lankford, George. "Austin's Secret: An Arkansas Slave at the Supreme Court." *Arkansas Historical Quarterly* 74 (Spring 2015): 56–73.

Ledbetter, Cal, Jr. "The Constitution of 1836: A New Perspective." *Arkansas Historical Quarterly* 41 (Autumn 1982): 215–52.

Lee, John C. "How Titsworth Springs on Mount Magazine Got Its Name." *Wagon Wheels: The Logan County Historical Society* 13 (Winter 1993): 35–36.

Lefebvre, Henri. *The Production of Space*. Trans. Donald Nicholson-Smith. Oxford: Blackwell, 1991.

Leslie, James W. "Arabella Lanktree Wilson's Civil War Letter." *Arkansas Historical Quarterly* 47 (Autumn 1988): 257–72.

———. "The Reuben and Orrin Letters." *Jefferson County Historical Quarterly* 18 (1990): 12–30.

Levin, Kevin. *Searching for Black Confederates: The Civil War's Most Persistent Myth*. Chapel Hill: University of North Carolina Press, 2019.

Littlefield, Daniel F., Jr. *Africans and Seminoles: From Removal to Emancipation*. Westport, CT: Greenwood Press, 1977.

Malloy, Sarah Brooke. "'The Health of Our Family': The Correspondence of Amanda Beardsley Trulock, 1837–1868." Master's thesis, University of Arkansas, 2005.

Malone, Dumas, ed. *Dictionary of American Biography, Under the Auspices of the American Council of Learned Societies, Volume VVI*. New York: Charles Scribner's Sons, 1935.

Manning, Chandra. *Troubled Refuge: Struggling for Freedom in the Civil War*. New York: Vintage, 2016.

Martin, Bonnie. "Slavery's Invisible Engine: Mortgaging Human Property." *Journal of Southern History* 76 (November 2010): 817–66.

Martin, Jonathan D. *Divided Mastery: Slave Hiring in the American South*. Cambridge, MA: Harvard University Press, 2004.

Massey, Mary Elizabeth. *Refugee Life in the Confederacy*. Baton Rouge: Louisiana State University Press, 1964.

Matkin-Rawn, Story. "'The Great Negro State of the Country': Arkansas's Reconstruction and the Other Great Migration." *Arkansas Historical Quarterly* 72 (Spring 2013): 1–41.

Mauldin, Erin Stewart. *Unredeemed Land: An Environmental History of Civil War and Emancipation in the Cotton South*. New York: Oxford University Press, 2018.

McArthur, Priscilla. *Arkansas in the Gold Rush*. Little Rock, AR: August House, 1986.

McConnell, Lloyd. "The Colony at Union Valley." *Flashback* 26, no. 4 (November 1976): 7–15.

McCurry, Stephanie. *Confederate Reckoning: Power and Politics in the Civil War South*. Reprint. Cambridge, MA: Harvard University Press, 2012.

———. *Masters of Small Worlds: Yeoman Households, Gender Relations, and the Political Culture of the Antebellum South Carolina Low Country*. New York: Oxford University Press, 1995.

McNeilly, Donald P. *The Old South Frontier: Cotton Plantations and the Making of Arkansas Society, 1819–1861*. Fayetteville: University of Arkansas Press, 2000.

McPherson, James. "Who Freed the Slaves?" *Proceedings of the American Philosophical Society* 139 (March 1995): 1–10.

Meacham, Sarah Hand. "Pets, Status, and Slavery in the Late Eighteenth-Century Chesapeake." *Journal of Southern History* 97 (August 2011): 521–54.

Merritt, Keri Leigh. *Masterless Men: Poor Whites and Slavery in the Antebellum South*. New Haven: Yale University Press, 2017.

Moerman, Daniel E. *Native American Medicinal Plants: An Ethnobotanical Dictionary*. Abridged ed. Portland, OR: Timber Press, 2009.

Moneyhon, Carl H. "From Slave to Free Labor: The Federal Plantation Experiment in Arkansas." *Arkansas Historical Quarterly* 53 (Summer 1994): 137–60.

———. *The Impact of the Civil War and Reconstruction on Arkansas: Persistence in the Midst of Ruin*. Reprint. Fayetteville: University of Arkansas Press, 2002.

———. "The Slave Family in Arkansas." *Arkansas Historical Quarterly* 58 (Spring 1999): 24–44.

Moore, John Hebron. *The Emergence of the Cotton Kingdom in the Old Southwest: Mississippi, 1770–1860*. Baton Rouge: Louisiana State University Press, 1988.

Moreland, Adele. "Traditional Medicinal Uses of Ten Herbs in Relation to Their Current Pharmacognosy." *Bios* 46 (December 1975): 183–89.

Morris, Christopher. *Becoming Southern: The Evolution of a Way of Life, Warren County and Vicksburg, Mississippi, 1770–1860*. New York: Oxford University Press, 1995.

Naylor, Celia E. *African Cherokees in Indian Territory: From Chattel to Citizens*. Chapel Hill: University of North Carolina Press, 2008.

Olmstead, Alan L., and Paul W. Rhode. "Biological Innovation and Productivity Growth in the Antebellum Cotton Economy." *Journal of Economic History* 68 (December 2008): 1124–56.

O'Neil, Patrick W. "Bosses and Broomsticks: Ritual and Authority in Antebellum Slave Weddings." *Journal of Southern History* 75 (February 2009): 29–48.

Otto, John S. "Slavery in the Mountains: Yell County, Arkansas, 1840–1860." *Arkansas Historical Quarterly* 39 (Spring 1980): 35–52.

Paquette, Robert L., and Mark M. Smith. *The Oxford Handbook of Slavery in the Americas.* Oxford: Oxford University Press, 2010.

Pargas, Damian Alan. "In the Fields of a 'Strange Land': Enslaved Newcomers and the Adjustment to Cotton Cultivation in the Antebellum South." *Slavery & Abolition* 1 (December 2013): 562–78.

———. *The Quarters and the Fields: Slave Families in the Non-Cotton South.* Gainesville: University Press of Florida, 2010.

———. *Slavery and Forced Migration in the Antebellum South.* New York: Cambridge University Press, 2015.

Patton, Adell, Jr. "The Back-to-Africa Movement in Arkansas." *Arkansas Historical Quarterly* 51 (Summer 1992): 164–77.

Paulette, Robert. *An Empire of Small Places: Mapping the Southeastern Anglo-Indian Trade, 1732–1795.* Athens: University of Georgia Press, 2012.

Penningroth, Dylan C. *The Claims of Kinfolk: African American Property and Community in the Nineteenth-Century South.* Chapel Hill: University of North Carolina Press, 2003.

Periam, Jonathan. *Home and Farm Manual: A New and Complete Pictorial Cyclopedia of Farm, Garden, Household, Architectural, Legal, Medical, and Social Information.* New York: Thompson & Co., 1884.

Phillips, Ulrich Bonnell. *American Negro Slavery: A survey of the supply, employment and control of Negro labor as determined by the plantation régime.* New York: D. Appleton & Company, 1918.

Poe, Ryan M. "The Contours of Emancipation: Freedom Comes to Southwest Arkansas." *Arkansas Historical Quarterly* 70 (Summer 2011): 109–30.

Poorman, Forrest Dutton. "The Experience of the Kidd Family during the Civil War: Part One." *Flashback: The Journal of the Washington County Historical Society* 44, no. 3 (August 1994): 25–29.

Porter, Kenneth W. *The Black Seminoles: History of a Freedom-Seeking People.* Gainesville: University Press of Florida, 1996.

Pred, Allan. "Place as Historically Contingent Process: Structuration and the Time-Geography of Becoming Places." *Annals of the Association of American Geographers* 74, no. 2 (March 2010): 279–97.

Proctor, Nicholas W. *Bathed in Blood: Hunting and Mastery in the Old South.* Charlottesville: University Press of Virginia, 2002.

Purdue, Theda. *Slavery and the Evolution of Cherokee Society, 1540–1866.* Knoxville: University of Tennessee Press, 1979.

Raboteau, Albert J. *Slave Religion: The "Invisible Institution" in the Antebellum South.* Updated ed. New York: Oxford University Press, 2004.

Relph, E. *Place and Placelessness.* Los Angeles: Sage, 1976.

Rohrbough, Malcolm J. *The Land Office Business: The Settlement and Administration of American Public Lands, 1789–1837. New York: Oxford University Press, 1968.

Rosa, Jonathan, and Nelson Flores. "Unsettling Race and Language: Toward a Raciolinguistic Perspective." *Language in Society* 46 (November 2017): 621–47.

Rothman, Joshua D. *Flush Times and Fever Dreams: A Story of Capitalism and Slavery in the Age of Jackson.* Athens: University of Georgia Press, 2012.

Rothrock, Thomas. "Thomas Andrew Henson." *Flashback: The Journal of the Washington County Historical Society* 10, no. 2 (April 1960): 17–20.

Scarborough, William K. *Masters of the Big House: Elite Slaveholders of the Mid-Nineteenth-Century South.* Baton Rouge: Louisiana State University Press, 2006.

Schermerhorn, Calvin. *The Business of Slavery and the Rise of American Capitalism, 1815–1860.* New Haven: Yale University Press, 2015.

———. *Unrequited Toil: A History of United States Slavery.* Cambridge: Cambridge University Press, 2018.

Schwartz, Marie. *Born in Bondage: Growing Up Enslaved in the Antebellum South.* Cambridge, MA: Harvard University Press, 2000.

Scott, James C. *Weapons of the Weak: Everyday Forms of Peasant Resistance.* New Haven: Yale University Press, 1985.

Shafer, Robert S. "White Persons Held to Racial Slavery in Antebellum Arkansas." *Arkansas Historical Quarterly* 44 (Summer 1985): 134–55.

Sharpless, Rebecca. *Cooking in Other Women's Kitchens: Domestic Workers in the South, 1865–1960.* Chapel Hill: University of North Carolina Press, 2010.

Shea, William L. "The Aftermath of Prairie Grove: Union Letters from Fayetteville." *Arkansas Historical Quarterly* 71 (Summer 2012): 203–16.

Shea, William L., and Earl J. Hess. *Pea Ridge: Civil War Campaign in the West.* Chapel Hill: University of North Carolina Press, 1992.

Simons, Don R. *In Their Words: A Chronology of the Civil War in Chicot County, Arkansas, and Adjacent Waters of the Mississippi River.* Sulphur, LA: Wise Publications, 1999.

Smallwood, James M. "Slave Insurrection." *Handbook of Texas Online.* Texas State Historical Association. www.tshaonline.org (accessed January 4, 2019).

Smith, C. Wayne, and J. Tom Cothren, eds. *Cotton: Origin, History, Technology, and Production.* New York: Wiley, 1999.

Smith, Kimberly K. *African American Environmental Thought: Foundations.* Lawrence: University Press of Kansas, 2007.

Smith, Ted J. "Slavery in Washington County, Arkansas, 1828–1860." Master's thesis, University of Arkansas, 1995.

Stampp, Kenneth M. *The Peculiar Institution: Slavery in the Ante-Bellum South.* New York: Vintage Books, 1989.

Steckel, Richard. "A Dreadful Childhood: The Excess Mortality of American Slaves." *Social Science History* 10, no. 4 (2016): 427–65.

Stewart, Mart A. "From King Cane to King Cotton: Razing Cane in the Old South." *Environmental History* 12 (January 2007): 59–79.
———. "If John Muir Had Been an Agrarian: American Environmental History West and South." *Environment and History* 11 (May 2005): 139–62.
———. "Rice, Water, and Power: Landscapes of Domination and Resistance in the Lowcountry, 1790–1880." *Environmental History Review* 15 (Autumn 1991): 47–64.
———. *"What Nature Suffers to Groe": Life, Labor, and Landscape on the Georgia Coast, 1680–1920*. Athens: University of Georgia Press, 2002.
Stith, Matthew M. *Extreme Civil War: Guerrilla Warfare, Environment, and Race on the Trans-Mississippi Frontier*. Baton Rouge: Louisiana State University Press, 2017.
Sutherland, Daniel E. "Guerillas: The Real War in Arkansas." *Arkansas Historical Quarterly* 52 (Autumn 1993): 257–85.
———. *Savage Conflict: The Decisive Role of Guerilla Warfare in the American Civil War*. Chapel Hill: University of North Carolina Press, 2009.
Sutter, Paul S., and Christopher J. Manganiello, eds. *Environmental History and the American South: A Reader*. Athens: University of Georgia Press, 2009.
Swanson, Drew A. *Remaking Wormsloe Plantation: The Environmental History of a Lowcountry Landscape*. Athens: University of Georgia Press, 2012.
Tadman, Michael T. *Speculators and Slaves: Masters, Traders, and Slaves in the Old South*. Madison: University of Wisconsin Press, 1989.
Taylor, Amy Murrell. *Embattled Freedom: Journeys through the Civil War's Slave Refugee Camps*. Chapel Hill: University of North Carolina Press, 2018.
Taylor, Orville W. *Negro Slavery in Arkansas*. 1958. Reprint, (Original printing Duke University Press). Fayetteville: University of Arkansas Press, 2000.
———. "Slavery in Izard County in the Final Decade, 1850–1860." *Izard County Historian* 10, no. 2 (April 1979): 8–14.
Torget, Andrew. *Seeds of Empire: Cotton, Slavery, and the Transformation of the Texas Borderlands, 1800–1850*. Chapel Hill: University of North Carolina Press, 2015.
Toudji, Sonia. "Intimate Frontiers: Indians, French, and Africans in Colonial Mississippi Valley." PhD diss., University of Arkansas, 2012.
Tuan, Yi-Fu. *Space and Place: The Perspective of Experience*. Minneapolis: University of Minnesota Press, 1977.
Valencius, Conevery Bolton. *The Health of the Country: How American Settlers Understood Themselves and Their Land*. New York: Basic Books, 2002.
Van Deburg, William L. "The Slave Drivers of Arkansas: A New View from the Narratives." *Arkansas Historical Quarterly* 35 (Autumn 1976): 231–45.
Vernon, Leroy M. "The Story of Anthony Bewley, Methodist Preacher, Charged with Being an Abolitionist." *Flashback* 10, no. 4 (October 1960): 15–26.
Vlach, John Michael. *Back of the Big House: The Architecture of Plantation Slavery*. Chapel Hill: University of North Carolina Press, 1993.

Walz, Robert B. "Migration into Arkansas, 1820–1880: Incentives and Means of Travel." *Arkansas Historical Quarterly* 17 (Winter 1958): 309–24.

Warde, Mary Jane. *When the Wolf Came: The Civil War and Indian Territory*. Fayetteville: University of Arkansas Press, 2013.

West, Emily. *Chains of Love: Slave Couples in Antebellum South Carolina*. Urbana-Champaign: University of Illinois Press, 2004.

Whayne, Jeannie M., ed. *Shadows over Sunnyside: An Arkansas Plantation in Transition, 1830–1945*. Fayetteville: University of Arkansas Press, 1993.

Whayne, Jeannie M., Thomas A. DeBlack, George Sabo III, and Morris S. Arnold. *Arkansas: A Narrative History*. 2nd ed. Fayetteville: University of Arkansas Press, 2013.

White, Shane, and Graham J. White. "Slave Hair and African American Culture in the Eighteenth and Nineteenth Centuries." *Journal of Southern History* 61 (February 1995): 45–76.

———. *Stylin': African American Expressive Culture from Its Beginnings to the Zoot Suit*. Ithaca, NY: Cornell University Press, 1998.

Williams, Heather Andrea. *Help Me to Find My People: The African American Search for Family Lost in Slavery*. Chapel Hill: University of North Carolina Press, 2012.

Woodruff, Nan. *American Congo: The African American Freedom Struggle in the Delta*. Cambridge, MA: Harvard University Press, 2003.

Wooster, Ralph A. *Civil War Texas: A History and a Guide*. Texas State Historical Association, 1999.

Zorn, Roman J. "An Arkansas Fugitive Slave Incident and Its International Repercussions." *Arkansas Historical Quarterly* 16 (Summer 1957): 139–49.

Index

Italicized page numbers refer to illustrations. The letter *t* following a page number denotes a table. For full index of names and plantations visit the author's website: www.kellyhoustonjones.com.

abolitionism, 70, 95–96, 180
Adams, John Quincy, 31
agricultural settlement plan, 207
alcohol, 86–87, 92–93, 165, 171–72, 180
Alexander, James Milo, 56, 82–83, 200
Alexander, Lucretia, 111, 138, 141
Allen, Hannah, 140, 152
Allen, Wright, 64, 185
Allison, Lucindy, 51, 61
Anthony House hotel, 87
Arkansas: map of (1852), *xiv*; and animal raising, 135; Civil War, guerilla warfare, 180; climate of, 106–7, 122; and cotton production, 17, 18, 173–76; geography, upcountry versus lowcountry, 74–78; improved acreage, 49, 101, 227n77; population, 17, 31, 35, 180; postwar, 203; reputation of as morass, 34; secession of, divided whites, 179–80; settlement of, 11–14, 15, 17–18, 37–40; statehood, 29–31
Arkansas Post, 11, 13–14
Arkansas River, 83–88; and Indian Territory, 89–93
Arkansas Territory, 17, 18–22, 28–29

Ballard, Franklin, and Company, 36

Ballard, Rice C., 36, 41, 51, 81, 148. *See also* Berry, H. L.; Pelham, John; Wagram plantation
Barber, Mollie, 150, 171
Bates, John, 63, 137, 147
Bean, Joe, 151, 157, 163
Bean, Mark, 94, 151
Berry, H. L., 111–12, 114, 118–19
Berry, J. C., 115, 131
Betsey (enslaved individual), 170, 197
Billy (enslaved individual), 38, 58, 112
Bleeding Kansas, 54, 95
Bogan, Eliza, 62, 137, 199
Bond, Scott, 140, 150, 152, 163, 168
Bozeman plantation, 62, 107, 119–20, 121, 123, 135, 137
Bradley, Eliza, 22, 195–96
Brooks, Mary Ann, 61–62, 189
Brown, Betty, 162–63, 170
Brown, John (enslaver): on Arkansas heat, 125; and Christmas, 131–32; on Confederate army and enlistment of enslaved soldiers, 193; and cotton production, 52, 100, 124–25, 126, 171; and enslaved people, and wages paid, 132, 171; and enslaved people, fishing, 164; and enslave people's labor outside

of cotton, 61, 120; overseer, hiring of, 111; working in fields with enslaved people, 110, 118
Brown, Peter, 53–54, 128
Brunson, R. A., 111, 129
Bullock, Harriet. *See* Daniel, Harriet Bailey Bullock
Bullock, R. C., 45–46, 127–28. *See also* Daniel, Harriet Bailey Bullock; Sylvan Home
Bullock plantation. *See* Sylvan Home

cattle production, 105, 134, 136, 141
Cherokee Indians, 19–20
Chicot County, Arkansas, *xiv*, 76, 80, 90
Choctaw Indians, 19
Clark County Agricultural Society, 107
Cockrill, Sterling, 50, 132, 154–55, 156, 164, 180
Cockrill plantation, 56, 167
Code Noir, 13
Compagnie d'Occident, 12
Confiscation Acts, 183–84, 199
Conway County, Arkansas, *xiv*, 76–77
corn production, 107, 129–31, 134, 141–42; and cotton production, comparison, 120, 130–31, 134; by county, 108t; and hog production, 134; and slavery, ties to, 105
Cornwall, J. H., 55, 60, 98
Cotton, T. W., 38, 157
cotton production: acreage and yields, increase of, 107–10, 125–26, 142; boom of, 82; in cold weather, 110; by county, 76–78, 108t; cultivation of crop, 115–17, 120, 121, 123–29; and food crops, 120–21; gang labor system, 106; on large-scale plantations, 80; maintenance of crops, 122; overlap of years' crops, 133; prices for, 106; varieties of cotton, 125–26, 133; wartime, hiding of cotton, 190
Crane, Sallie, 51, 158, 169
Creek Indians, 91–93
Curtis, Samuel, 183–84, 199
Cynthia (enslaved individual), 49, 187

Dabney, Adeline, 107, 158
Dabney, Simpson, 107, 158
Daniel, Harriet Bailey Bullock: childhood experiences with enslaved people, 44–45, 161; on enslaved people and running away, 53; on hog killing, 132–33; on religion and church, 57–58, 59; on violence against enslaved people, 128–29, 190. *See also* Sylvan Home
Davidsonville trading post, 21–22
Davis, Louis, 130, 131, 137, 166–67
Densen, Nelson Taylor, 55, 135
Deputy, Joseph, 56, 192, 199–200
diseases and illnesses, 106–7, 117
doctors, 165
domesticity, 43–47
Dortch, Charles Green, 60, 112

Emancipation Proclamation, 181, 184, 187
enslaved people: Arkansas, running away to, 27–29; as bearers of white family's histories, 45; children, experiences of, 116, 149, 151, 158, 188; communication networks, 53, 63–64, 96; community, geography of, 55–59; as entertainment for enslavers, 48; hunting and fishing, 162–65; and land, relationship with, 206–8; leisure, 59–62, 129–33, 136–38, 141, 150, 161; on Lincoln's election, 178; literacy, 1, 113, 140–41, 172; personal gardens, 121, 171; placemaking, 147, 148–51; population, 18–19, 75–78, 79–81, 82, 94, 96, 109t, 141–42, 227n77; relationships with whites, 59–60, 65–66; and religion, 56–59, 87, 137–38, 141, 172; restrictions on, movement within public space, 61–62; sexual exploitation of, 48–49; social networks, 93–94, 99, 115, 174–75; uncultivated zones, knowledge of, 62–64, 133, 135, 161–65, 184–85; in urban areas, 86–88; violence against, 69, 94–95 (*see also* whippings); violence against other enslaved people, 64–65; well-being and illnesses, 106–7, 110, 117, 119, 127–28, 158–61, 165–70; whites' disputes with neighbors, navigation of, 136; women nursing white babies, 158
——AND CIVIL WAR: Confederate army, impressment, 191–93; Confiscation Acts, 183–84; forced migration to Texas, 187–90, 196–98; and labor, changes in nature of, 190–91, 194–96, 197; labor to support Confederate war effort, 191–93; navigation of Confederate versus Federal control, 193–94; as

refugees, 184, 199, 241n31; resistance and insubordination, 201; restrictions increased, 180; running away, reasons not to, 194–201; U.S. Army, enlistment in, 64, 185–86, 199; U.S. Army, impressment, 186–87; U.S. troops, hiding from, 181–83; U.S. troops, proximity to, 182–84, 191, 198–200; women and white women enslavers, 196–98
———AS COMMODITIES: as collateral, 26, 105; as currency, 21; and ownership, claims of, 15–16; sale of, 190; sale of to pay debts, 66, 72; slave mortgages, 97; transport of, 26–27
———FAMILIES: babies and mothers, 117–18, 123, 137, 139–40; births, 124; children and childcare, 139–40, 156; children and death, 121, 124; homemaking, 140–41, 155–56; marriages, 121, 123, 155–57; marriages, abroad, 62, 137, 157, 196, 199; separation of, 35–38, 188
———LABOR: animal husbandry, 133–36; of children, 124, 129; daily routines, 138–41; description of, 98; divorced from benefits of, 175–76; domestic, 144; as drivers or foremen, 112–13; during Civil War, 190–97; fencing and structure maintenance, 119–20, 129; food crops, 122; gendered, 50–52, 61, 64, 115–17, 122, 125, 140, 143, 144, 190; hiring out by enslaver, 38, 72, 114–15, 131, 138, 190; hiring out by self, 82–83, 85–86; knowledge of cash crop production, 107; overseers, relationships, 110–12; for own household, 140; skilled, 51–52, 127–28; task versus gang labor system, 106; wages for, 132, 152, 170–71; "working socials," 123
———MATERIAL LIFE: clothing and shoes, 151–54; contraband, 171–72; at enslavers' discretion, 173–74; food, 157–65; homemaking, 149–50, 154–55; property, 152–53, 170–74; social aspects, 154; and status, 152–54
———RESISTANCE: arson, 180; hiding in woods, 52–54; murder, 120; running away, 24, 54–55, 69–70, 87, 88, 113–14, 126–27, 146, 174; slow downs, 126–28; theft, 175; uncultivated zones, 55–59; violence against enslaver, 50

enslavers: black emancipation, fear of, 187; and children of enslaved people, property increase, 156; during Civil War, 181–83, 187–90, 192–93, 196, 197–98, 200–202; communities, kinship networks, 56; control over enslaved people, 67–70; and enslaved people's folk medicine, 168; and enslaved people's material life as reflection of own status, 154; entrance into slaveholding class, 89–90; generosity, performance of, 164–65; and hunting with enslaved people, 163; movement of, 66–67; owner-absenteeism, 41, 81, 111–12, 126; population of, 75–78; whipping, use of, 128–29; work in fields with enslaved people, 110, 118

"the Family," 28, 29
Fayetteville, Arkansas, 94–96, 194–95. See also urban centers
Fed (enslaved individual), 112, 129
Fergusson, Lou, 110, 155–56, 190
Finley, Molly: on Christmas celebration, 131; on enslaved people's well-being, 165; on enslavers' fleeing to Texas during Civil War, 187; on father, selling of, 36; on labor in freezing weather, 110; on plantation, building of, 38–39; on religion, 43, 57; on uncultivated zones, 55
flooding, 117–19
food-stealing, 157, 158–59
Ford, Horace, 114, 131
Fort Gibson, 89, 90
Fort Smith, 89–90, 207
Franklin and Armfield, 36
Frazier, Simon, 64, 185
Frazier, Walker, 156, 185
free blacks, 22–23, 31, 70–72, 85
Freedmen's Bureau, 208–9
freedom suits, 71–73, 101
freedpeople, 203–4, 206–10
Fugitive Slave Law, 70, 90, 178; and Indian Territory, 92
Fulton, Matilda, 62, 87

Ginnis (enslaved individual), 51, 127
Green, O. W., 58–59, 168
guerillas, 183, 188–89, 193–94, 198–200

Haitian Revolution, 14–15, 24
Heard, Ben, 130, 169
Helena, Arkansas, 82–83, *144, 145,* 184, 198–200. *See also* urban centers
Hempstead County, Arkansas, *xiv,* 75–76, 200–201
Hilliard, Isaac, 182, 244n4
Hilliard, Miriam, 45, 46, 64–65, 127, 163, 164
Hilliard family, 135, 162
hog production, 105, 132–36, 141
Holt, John, 62, 156
horse-stealing, 86
Hunts family, 53–54, 128

Illinois River, 94
improved acreage, 49, 101, 105, 109t, 119, 227n77
indentured servants, 12
Independence County, Arkansas, *xiv,* 78, 97, 105
Indian Removal Act (1830), 20
Indian removals, 19–20, 89
Indian Territory, 90–93, 179–80. *See also* Native Americans
insurrections, whites' fear of, 23, 25, 69–70, 79–80, 85, 180
interracial socialization, 59–60, 84, 102–3, 180
Izard County, Arkansas, *xiv,* 134, 135t

Jackson, James, 86, 198
Jameson, Hannah, 129–30, 154, 171
Jefferson County, Arkansas, *xiv*
Johnson, Lycurgus, 120, 121, 185
Johnson, Reuben, 1, 203
Jones, Cynthia, 158, 175
Jones, Isaac, 172, 201
Jones family, 38–39, 55. *See also* Finley, Molly

Kerns, Adrianna, 51, 60, 62, 178
Kidd, Tandy, 94, 183
Kinsey, Cindy, 131, 153, 161, 164, 166, 167
Kye, George, 138, 139, 160–61, 168

Lambert, Solomon, 36, 111, 150, 155, 175, 181
land grants, 13–14, 34–35
landscape, 34, 39–43
land speculation, 21, 33, 90
Latting, Andrew, 24–26, 28–29

Lincoln, Abraham: election of, 178. *See also* Emancipation Proclamation
Little Rock, Arkansas, 3, 21, 84–88, 198, 203–4. *See also* urban centers
Louisiana Purchase, 14–15
Lucas, Louis, 112, 159

Magness, Morgan, 97, 105
Manchester revival, 153
manhood, 116
Manuel (enslaved individual), 62, 175
manumissions, 71–73, 174
maroon communities, 88
Mart (enslaved individual), 62–63, 135
Martin, James, 129, 169
Mason, James, 49, 167, 187, 208
Mason, Martha, 49, 187
McClendon, Charlie, 52, 132
McKiel plantation, 137, 199
Mecklin, Robert, 186, 194–95, 196
Mecklin, Wesley, 194–95, 196
Menifee, Nimrod, 33, 73
Merinda (Rindy) (enslaved individual), 194–95, 196
Merrick, Ephraim, 22, 102
Milam, Betty, 99–100
Milam, John, 99–100
Miles (enslaved individual), 65, 113–14
miscegenation, 13, 99–100
Mississippi River, 79–83, 118–19, 182–83
Missouri Compromise, 16–17, 29
Mitchell, Moses, 188, 190, 201
Moore, Emma, 112, 129, 158–59
Moriah (enslaved individual), 38, 45, 162, 190–91
Myhand, Mary, 159, 188

Nashville Convention, 96
Nat (enslaved individual), 35, 127
Native Americans: and African slavery, 89, 90–93; and Civil War, 179–80; herbal remedies of, 166; Quapaw Indians, 11–13, 19–20, 32; whites' views of, 89
Newton, Pate, 58, 130
North Fork River, 96
Northwest Ordinance, 12

Osage Indians, 13, 19, 32
Osotouy, 12
Ouachita County, Arkansas, *xiv,* 134, 135t
Ouachita River, 100–101

INDEX / 267

overseers, 110–14, 128–29, 138–41. *See also* Berry, H. L.; Pelham, John
Ozarks, 94–96, 183

Page, Annie, 45, 172, 201
Panic of 1837, 31
Parmelia (enslaved individual), 33, 73
passing, 100–101
Patrick Benjamin & Co., 206
patrols, 58, 68–69, 79, 102–3
Payne, Harriett McFarlin, 139, 149–50, 155
Pea Ridge, Battle of, 183
Pelham, John: arrival at Wagram plantation, 113; on beauty of Wagram plantation, 34, 41; on cotton-picking numbers, 125; enslaved people's curfew, 141; firing of, 127; and flooding, 118; on food distribution, 158, 160; on free labor, hiring of, 60; on manhood, 116; on tobacco privileges, 165
Phillips County, Arkansas, 80, 130–31
Pike, Albert, 179, 223n152
Pine, James, 112, 192, 199
plantations: term, use of, 80; along Red River, 102; enslaved population numbers, 80–81; layout of, 40–43, 49–51, 89, 93–94, *145*; and owner absentee-ism, 41, 81, 111–12, 126; compared to smaller farm operations, 107, 121, 157–58
Polk, James K.: as enslaver, 27–28
Pope County, Arkansas, 77
posses, 69, 95–96
Prairie Grove campaign, 183
Pulaski County, Arkansas, 84

Quapaw Indians, 11–13, 19–20, 32
quilts, *143*, 150–51, 164
Quinn, Doc, 135, 163, 181

Ranza (enslaved individual), 55, 98
Rassberry, Senia, 44, 188
Ray, Joe, 148, 167
Rayner, Kenneth, 182, 207
Real Estate Bank, 31
Rector, Henry M., 177, 201–2
Red River, 102–3
religion: power dynamics of space, 56–59; and religion of enslaved people, 87, 137–38, 141, 172
Reuben (enslaved individual), 113, 138–39, 185, 206

Rob (enslaved individual), 45–46, 163
Rose (enslaved individual), 59, 137, 154, 167; as cook and keeper of children, 41, 139, 161, 163. *See also* Daniel, Harriet Bailey Bullock; Sylvan Home
Ross, Charley, 137, 152
Rowe, Katie, 41, 66, 116, 168–69

St. Domingue, 14–15, 24
Saline River, 100–101
Scroggins, Cora, 37, 155
secession, 177–79
"second Middle Passage," 35–38
second slavery, 18–20, 80–81
Seminole Indians, 89, 90–93
Sevier, Ambrose H., 28, 29
Shawnee Village, Arkansas, 28
Shelton, Laura, 44, 157–58, 172
Shugart, Henry: doctors, cost of, 165; and domestic slave trade, participation in, 35; enslaved people, and cotton production, 121, 124, 133; enslaved people, labor outside of cotton production, 119–20; enslaved people, leisure of, 137; enslaved people and child's death, 124; enslaved people and running away, 53, 127; and hunting with enslaved people, 163
Sims, Virginia, 191, 193
slave codes, 13, 22–24, 30–31
slave-stealing, 24–26, 28–29
slave trade, domestic, 35–38, 66–67
Small, Silas, 62, 137, 199
Smith, Liza, 165, 167
Smith, R. C., 41, 42, 149, 170
Speed, James, 81, 138, 139–40
Stewart, Minnie Johnson, 49, 50, 139
Stover, Abraham, 57, 139, 153
Strayhorn, Eva, 44, 197–98
Susan (enslaved individual), 35, 127
Swamp Land Acts (1849 and 1850), 34–35
Sylvan Home: construction and layout of, 39, 41, 56; enslaved children, meals, 161; and enslaved labor, gendered, 45–46; enslaved mothers and babies, 137, 139; enslaved people, knowledge of land around plantation, 56, 63; enslaved people, material life of, 151, 154, 170; enslaved people, running away, 53; and enslaved people in supervisory roles, 112; enslaved people's abroad marriages,

62, 137; food distribution, 158, 161; healing and remedies, 167; hunting and fishing on, 162, 163; labor to support Confederate war effort, 191; overseer of, 111; religion as controlled by enslavers, 48, 59, 139, 140; wartime scarcity, 190–91

Tallmadge amendment, 16–17
Tappan house, *145*
Templeton and Richardson, 36
Texas: annexation of as slave state, 31; enslavers' flight to during Civil War, 187–90, 196, 197–98
Thompson, Ellen Briggs, 38, 44, 56–57, 155, 171
Three-Fifths Compromise, 30
tobacco, 165
Trulock, Amanda, 113, 138–39, 185, 206
Trulock, James, 35, 36, 106–7
Tucker, Mandy, 139, 167
Turner, George, 118, 121, 127–28
Turner, Nat, 23, 85

Union army: enlistment of enslaved people, 64, *146*; and harassment of enslavers, 196–97; occupation of urban centers of Arkansas, 198; proximity to and running away, 191; and United States Colored Troops, *146*, 185–87, 203–4, 208
Union County, Arkansas, *xiv*, 78
Unionists, 195–96, 199, 244n88
urban centers, 102–3, 198; and economic opportunities for enslaved people, 170, 172, 173. *See also* Fayetteville, Arkansas; Helena, Arkansas; Little Rock, Arkansas

vagrancy laws (postwar), 208
Van Buren County, Arkansas, 78
Van Winkle, Aaron Anderson, 93, 207–8
Van Winkle, Peter, 93–94, 187, 191

Wagoner, Sweetie Ivery, 57, 140–41, 160, 225n45
Wagoola (enslaved individual), 66, 162
Wagram plantation: and cotton production, 110, 115, 124–25; and enslaved people, 107, 121, 124, 140, 174; flooding at, 117–19; and food crops, 120; and gendered labor, 52, 117, 122; and intra-racial violence, 65; medical practices at, 168; overseers of, 111, 113–14; and owner-absentee-ism, 41, 111. *See also* Ballard, Rice C.; Berry, H. L.; Pelham, John
Walker, David, 53, 94
Walworth, John P. and plantation, 45, 110, 114, 133, 135, 173, 175
Washington, Callie, 153, 159, 166–67
Washington County, Arkansas, *xiv*, 20
Wells, John, 188, 190
wheat production, 122
whippings, 128–29, 157, 168–70, 175
White River, 93–100
whites, nonslaveholding, 59–61, 93, 115, 119
Williams, Aaron, 64, 185
Williams, Columbus, 130, 138, 149, 150–51, 156, 169
womanhood, 116–17
women, white enslavers: and enslaved people, protection of as property, 47–48, 114–15; and enslaved women, relationship during Civil War, 196–98
Woodlawn plantation, 53–54, 128
Woodruff, William E., 27, 72, 87, 182–83
Word, Sam, 150, 170
Worthington, Elisha, 49, 187

Young, Louis, 137–38, 160

Early American Places

On Slavery's Border: Missouri's Small Slaveholding Households, 1815–1865
by Diane Mutti Burke

Sounds American: National Identity and the Music Cultures of the Lower Mississippi River Valley, 1800–1860
by Ann Ostendorf

The Year of the Lash: Free People of Color in Cuba and the Nineteenth-Century Atlantic World
by Michele Reid-Vazquez

Ordinary Lives in the Early Caribbean: Religion, Colonial Competition, and the Politics of Profit
by Kirsten Block

Creolization and Contraband: Curaçao in the Early Modern Atlantic World
by Linda M. Rupert

An Empire of Small Places: Mapping the Southeastern Anglo-Indian Trade, 1732–1795
by Robert Paulett

Everyday Life in the Early English Caribbean: Irish, Africas, and the Construction of Difference
by Jenny Shaw

Natchez Country: Indians, Colonists, and the Landscapes of Race in French Louisiana
by George Edward Milne

Slavery, Childhood, and Abolition in Jamaica, 1788–1838
by Colleen A. Vasconcellos

Privateers of the Americas: Spanish American Privateering from the United States in the Early Republic
by David Head

Charleston and the Emergence of Middle-Class Culture in the Revolutionary Era
by Jennifer L. Goloboy

Anglo-Native Virginia: Trade, Conversion, and Indian Slavery in the Old Dominion, 1646–1722
by Kristalyn Marie Shefveland

Slavery on the Periphery: The Kansas-Missouri Border in the Antebellum and Civil War Eras
by Kristen Epps

In the Shadow of Dred Scott: St. Louis Freedom Suits and the Legal Culture of Slavery in Antebellum America
by Kelly M. Kennington

Brothers and Friends: Kinship in Early America
by Natalie R. Inman

George Washington's Washington: Visions for the National Capital in the Early American Republic
by Adam Costanzo

Borderless Empire: Dutch Guiana in the Atlantic World, 1750–1800
by Brian Hoonhout

Complexion of Empire in Natchez: Race and Slavery in the Mississippi Borderlands
by Christian Pinnen

Toward Cherokee Removal: Land, Violence, and the White Man's Chance
by Adam J. Pratt

A Weary Land: Slavery on the Ground in Arkansas
by Kelly Houston Jones

Generations of Freedom: Gender, Movement, and Violence in Natchez, 1779–1865
by Nik Ribianszky

Lightning Source UK Ltd.
Milton Keynes UK
UKHW011341120822
407223UK00003B/791